SOFTWARE ENGINEERING

Concepts and Techniques

Proceedings of the NATO Conferences

Edited by

Peter Naur, Brian Randell, J. N. Buxton

PETROCELLI/CHARTER

NEW YORK 1976

Library of Congress Cataloging in Publication Data

Main entry under title:

Software engineering.

    Conferences sponsored by the NATO Science Committee;
held at Garmisch, Ger., Oct. 7-11, 1968 and Rome, Italy,
Oct. 27-31, 1969.
    Includes index.
    1. Electronic digital computers--Programming--Con-
gresses. I. Naur, Peter. II. Randell, Brian,
1936-   III. Buxton, J. N. IV. North Atlantic
Treaty Organization. Science Committee.
QA76.6.S618   001.6'425   75-44008
ISBN 0-88405-334-2

The conferences on Software Engineering were held under the auspices of the NATO Science Committee as part of its continuing effort to promote the useful progress of science through international cooperation.

The Science Committee conferences are deliberately designed and structured to focus expert attention on what is *not* known rather than on what is known. The participants are carefully selected to bring together a variety of complementary viewpoints. Through intensive group discussion, they seek to reach agreement on conclusions and recommendations for future research which will be of value to the scientific community.

CONTENTS

CONTENTS

STATEMENT FROM THE SERIES EDITOR

This book points the way to the future of software. It examines our shortcomings ir software practice and technique and suggests alternatives that could overcome many of the problems. But most important, it lays out, by implication, the frame of mind that we take to produce dependable software.

The few software professionals who have had access to an earlier version of this boo. have found it a gold mine. It is a source to which they return frequently for renewed inspiration and the stimulation of positions thoughtfully taken and briefly but well presente The current publication of this book in its new format will make its guidance more widely available and give it the larger audience its worth deserves.

The contributors to this book offer a rich background of diverse experience. The editors have blended the contributions by topic area and have included "working papers" expanding on some of the topics in a more specialized manner. Some of these papers are classics.

Dr. Dijkstra's two landmark papers on structured programming are here, and the contributions of others included here help place those two papers in perspective. It is significant that Dr. Dijkstra's first one does not even mention the term "structured programming" but instead concentrates on the software need and a possible solution in terms of approach and technique.

The paper by J. D. Aron on estimating and the one by Jules I. Schwartz on system development should be required reading for all managers of large projects. Yet how many projects suffer today from a failure to heed the experience reported? The testing of software receives its due attention. The excellent paper by Llewelyn and Wickens adds to the coverage and relates well to other contributions on software evaluation and reliability.

Some of the best thinking available on these and other topics can be found in this book.

Ned Chapin

PART I

Report on a Conference Sponsored by the

NATO SCIENCE COMMITTEE

Garmisch, Germany, October 7-11, 1968

Chairman: Professor F. L. Bauer

Co-chairmen: Professor L. Bolliet and Dr. H. J. Helms

Editors: Peter Naur and Brian Randell

HIGHLIGHTS

The present report is concerned with a problem crucial to the use of computers, viz. the so-called software, or programs, developed to control their action. The report summarises the discussions at a Working Conference on Software Engineering, sponsored by the NATO Science Committee. The Conference was attended by more than fifty people, from eleven different countries, all concerned professionally with software, either as users, manufacturers, or teachers at universities. The discussions cover all aspects of software including

- relation of software to the hardware of computers
- design of software
- production, or implementation of software
- distribution of software
- service on software.

By including many direct quotations and exchanges of opinion, the report reflects the lively controversies of the original discussion.

Although much of the discussions were of a detailed technical nature, the report also contains sections reporting on discussions which will be of interest to a much wider audience. This holds for subjects like

- the problems of achieving sufficient reliability in the data systems which are becoming increasingly integrated into the central activities of modern society
- the difficulties of meeting schedules and specifications on large software projects
- the education of software (or data systems) engineers
- the highly controversial question of whether software should be priced separately from hardware.

Thus, while the report is of particular concern to the immediate users of computers and to computer manufacturers, many points may serve to enlighten and warn policy makers at all levels. Readers from the wider audience should note, however, that the conference was concentrating on the basic issues and key problems in the critical areas of software engineering. It therefore did not attempt to provide a balanced review of the total state of software, and tends to understress the achievements of the field.

PREFACE

In working out the present report on the Conference on Software Engineering organised by the NATO Science Committee, every attempt was made to make it useful to a wide circle of readers. Thus parts of it are written for those who have no special interest in computers and their software as such, but who are concerned with the impact of these tools on other parts of society. This class includes, for example:

- civil servants
- politicians
- policy makers of public and private enterprises.

These readers should find material of interest in Section 1 (Background of Conference) and Section 2 (Software Engineering and Society).

A somewhat narrower readership for the report includes those who need an understanding of the nature of software engineering, although they are not themselves working in the field. These readers are typically:

- managers of business enterprises using computers
- researchers in fields other than software engineering and computer science
- university officials
- computer marketing personnel.

These readers should find points of interest in Section 3 (Software Engineering), Section 7.1 (Software: the State of the Art), Section 7.2 (Education), and Section 7.3 (Software Pricing) as well as in Sections 1 and 2.

Finally, a large part of the report addresses itself to those directly engaged in the design, production (implementation), and service of software. These technical areas are first given an approximately uniform coverage in Sections 4 (Design), 5 (Production), and 6 (Service). The succeeding chapters 7 (Special Topics), 8 (Invited Addresses) and 9 (Working Papers), present more detailed treatment of a selected set of topics.

The main problem in deciding on a structure for the report was to decide between one of two different basic classifications, the one following from the normal sequence of steps in the development of a software product, from project start, through design, production or development, to distribution and maintenance, the other related to aspects like communication, documentation, management, programming techniques, data structures, hardware considerations, and the like. The final structure is based on the first of these two classifications. However, in many places an unavoidable influence from the second type of classification has crept in. The editors are only too aware of this problem and have attempted to mitigate its effects by provision of a detailed index.

The text of the report derives mainly from two sources, viz. the working papers contributed by the participants before or during the conference (mostly in June 1968), and the discussions during the conference. The discussions were recorded by several reporters and most were also recorded on magnetic tape. The reporters' notes were then collated, correlated with footage numbers on the magnetic tape, and typed. Owing to the high quality of the reporters' notes it was then, in general, possible to avoid extensive amounts of tape transcription, except where the accuracy of quotations required verification. However, to give an impression of the editors' task, here is an example, albeit extreme, of the typed notes:

```
536  DIJKSTRA
F    –
H    ––
P    ––?––
```

(here "536" is the tape footage number, and the letters F,H and P identify the reporters). This section of tape was transcribed to reveal that what was actually said was:

> *There is tremendous difference if maintenance means adaptation to a changing problem, or just correcting blunders. It was the first kind of maintenance I was talking about.*
>
> *You may be right in blaming users for asking for blue-sky equipment, but if the manufacturing community offers this with a serious face, then I can only say that the whole business is based on one big fraud. [Laughter and applause]*

For use in the report the source texts, and some additional transcribed material, have been sorted out according to the subject classification developed during the conference. Whenever possible the material in the working papers has been integrated into Sections 3 to 7 of the report. However, in some cases it has been found more convenient to place the working material in Section 9, and merely to make the appropriate references in the main sections of the report.

To avoid misinterpretations of the report it must be kept in mind that the participants at the conference were acting as individuals, and in no sense as representatives of the organizations with which they are affiliated.

In order to retain the spirit and liveliness of the conference, every attempt has been made to reproduce the points made during the discussion by using the original wording. This means that points of major disagreement have been left wide open, and that no attempt has been made to arrive at a consensus or majority view. This is also the reason why the names of participants have been given throughout the report.

The actual work on the report was a joint undertaking by several people. The large amounts of typing and other office chores, both during the conference and for a period thereafter, were done by Miss Doris Angermeyer, Miss Enid Austin, Miss Petra Dandler, Mrs Dagmar Hanisch, and Miss Erika Steif. During the conference notes were taken by Larry Flanigan, Ian Hugo and Manfred Paul. Ian Hugo also operated the tape recorder. The reviewing and sorting of the passages from the written contributions and the discussions was done by Larry Flanigan, Bernard Galler, David Gries, Ian Hugo, Peter Naur, Brian Randell and Gerd Sapper. The final write-up was done by Peter Naur and Brian Randell, assisted by Ian Hugo. The preparation of the final typed copy of the report was done by Miss Kirsten Andersen at Ragnecentralen, Copenhagen, under the direction of Peter Naur.

Peter Naur
Brian Randell

1. BACKGROUND OF CONFERENCE

Discussions were held in early 1967 by the NATO Science Committee, comprised of scientists representing the various member nations, on possible international actions in the field of computer science. Among the possible actions considered were the organising of a conference, and perhaps, at a later date, the setting up of an International Institute of Computer Science.

In the Autumn of 1967 the Science Committee established a Study Group on Computer Science. The Study Group was given the task of assessing the entire field of computer science, and in particular, elaborating the suggestions of the Science Committee.

The Study Group concentrated on possible actions which would merit an international, rather than a national effort. In particular it focussed its attentions on the problems of software. In late 1967 the Study Group recommended the holding of a working conference on Software Engineering. The phrase "software engineering" was deliberately chosen as being provocative, in implying the need for software manufacture to be used on the types of theoretical foundations and practical disciplines, that are traditional in the established branches of engineering.

It was suggested that about 50 experts from all areas concerned with software problems — computer manufacturers, universities, software houses, computer users, etc. — be invited to attend the conference. It was further suggested that every effort should be made to make the conference truly a working conference, whose discussions should be organised under the three main headings: Design of Software, Production of Software, and Service of Software.

Prominent leaders in the field were appointed as group leaders to direct the work within each of the three working groups. Dr. Arnth-Jensen, of the Scientific Affairs Division of NATO, was put in charge of conference arrangements. At a meeting held in Brussels in March 1968 the group leaders and the Study Group met and agreed on the final details of the conference.

The Conference was to shed further light on the many current problems in software engineering, and also to discuss possible techniques, methods and developments which might lead to their solution. It was hoped that the Conference would be able to identify present necessities, shortcomings and trends and that the findings could serve as a signpost to manufacturers of computers as well as their users.

With this hope in mind the present report is made widely available.

2. SOFTWARE ENGINEERING AND SOCIETY

One of the major motivations for the organizing of the conference was an awareness of the rapidly increasing importance of computer software systems in many activities of society. Thus, although much of the conference was concerned with detailed technical questions, many of the discussions were of a more general nature, and should be of interest to a wide spectrum of readers. It is for the benefit of this wider audience that representative discussions of various points relating to the impact of software engineering on society have been abstracted from later sections of this Report, and collected in this introductory section.

First three quotations which indicate the rate of growth of software:

Helms: In Europe alone there are about 10,000 installed computers — this number is increasing at a rate of anywhere from 25 per cent to 50 per cent per year. The quality of software provided for these computers will soon affect more than a quarter of a million analysts and programmers.

David: No less a person than T.J. Watson said that OS/360 cost IBM over $50 million a year during its preparation, and at least 5,000 man-years' investment. TSS/360 is said to be in the 1,000 man-year category. It has been said, too, that development costs for software equal the development costs for hardware in establishing a new machine line.

d'Agapeyeff: In 1958 a European general purpose computer manufacturer often had less than 50 software programmers, now they probably number 1,000-2,000 people; what will be needed in 1978?

Yet this growth rate was viewed with more alarm than pride.

David: In computing, the research, development, and production phases are often telescoped into one process. In the competitive rush to make available the latest techniques, such as on-line consoles served by time-shared computers, we strive to take great forward leaps across gulfs of unknown width and depth. In the cold light of day, we know that a step-by-step approach separating research and development from production is less risky and more likely to be successful. Experience indeed indicates that for software tasks similar to previous ones, estimates are accurate to within 10—30 percent in many cases. This situation is familiar in all fields lacking a firm theoretical base. Thus, there are good reasons why software tasks that include novel concepts involve not only uncalculated but also uncalculable risks.

This is not meant to indicate that the software field does not have its successes.

Hastings: I work in an environment of some fourteen large installations using OS/360. These are complex systems, being used for many very sophisticated applications.

People are doing what they need to do, at a much lower cost than ever before, and they seem to be reasonably satisfied.

Buxton: Ninety-nine percent of computers work tolerably satisfactorily. There are thousands of respectable Fortran-oriented installations using many different machines, and lots of good data processing applications running steadily.

> *However, there are areas of the field which were viewed by many participants with great concern.*

Kolence: The basic problem is that certain classes of systems are placing demands on us which are beyond our capabilities and our theories and methods of design and production at this time. There are many areas where there is no such thing as a crisis — sort routines, payroll applications, for example. It is large systems that are encountering great difficulties. We should not expect the production of such systems to be easy.

David and Fraser: Particularly alarming is the seemingly unavoidable fallibility of large software, since a malfunction in an advanced hardware-software system can be a matter of life and death.

Dijkstra: The dissemination of knowledge is of obvious value — the massive dissemination of error-loaded software is frightening.

> *There was general agreement that "software engineering" is in a very rudimentary stage of development as compared with the established branches of engineering.*

McIlroy: We undoubtedly produce software by backward techniques. We undoubtedly get the short end of the stick in confrontations with hardware people because they are industrialists and we are the crofters. Software production today appears in the scale of industrialization somewhere below the more backward construction industries.

Kolence: Programming management will continue to deserve its current poor reputation for cost and schedule effectiveness until such time as a more complete understanding of the program design process is achieved.

Fraser: One of the problems that is central to the software production process is to identify the nature of progress and to find some way of measuring it. Only one thing seems to be clear just now. It is that program construction is not always a simple progression in which each act of assembly represents a distinct forward step and that the final product can be described simply as the sum of many sub-assemblies.

Graham: Today we tend to go on for years, with tremendous investments to find that the system, which was not well understood to start with, does not work as anticipated. We build systems like the Wright brothers built airplanes — build the whole thing, push it off the cliff, let it crash, and start over again.

> *Of course any new field has its growing pains:*

Gillette: We are in many ways in an analogous position to the aircraft industry, which also has problems producing systems on schedule and to specification. We perhaps have more examples of bad large systems than good, but we are a young industry and are learning how to do better.

Many people agreed that one of the main problems was the pressure to produce even bigger and more sophisticated systems.

Opler: I am concerned about the current growth of systems, and what I expect is probably an exponential growth of errors. Should we have systems of this size and complexity? Is it the manufacturer's fault for producing them or the user's for demanding them? One shouldn't ask for large systems and then complain about their largeness.

Buxton: There are extremely strong economic pressures on manufacturers, both from users and from other manufacturers. Some of these pressures, which are a major contributory cause of our problems, are quite understandable. For example, the rate of increase of air traffic in Europe is such that there is a pressing need for an automated system of control.

This being the case, perhaps the best quotation to use to end this short section of the report is the following:

Gill: It is of the utmost importance that all those responsible for large projects involving computers should take care to avoid making demands on software that go far beyond the present state of technology, unless the very considerable risks involved can be tolerated.

3. SOFTWARE ENGINEERING

3.1 THE NATURE OF SOFTWARE ENGINEERING

The content of software engineering was explained in several ways during the conference. Nash and Selig provided figures 1 and 2 indicating the various activities of a software project. These diagrams also indicate some of the terminology used in the field.

The need for feedback was stressed many times.

Perlis: Selig's picture requires a feedback loop, for monitoring of the system. One must collect data on system performance, for use in future improvements.

The project activity was described in more detail by Fraser.

Fraser: (from "The nature of progress in software production") Design and implementation proceeded in a number of stages. Each stage was typified by a period of intellectual activity followed by a period of program reconstruction. Each stage produced a useable product and the period between the end of one stage and the start of the next provided the operational experience upon which the next design was based. In general the products of successive stages approached the final design requirement; each stage included more facilities than the last. On three occasions major design changes were made but for the most part the changes were localised and could be described as "tuning".

The first stage did not terminate with a useable object program but the process of implementation yielded the information that a major design change would result in a superior and less expensive final product. During the second stage the entire system was reconstructed; an act that was fully justified by subsequent experience. The second major design change had its origin in the more usual combination of an inelegant system and a demanding environment. Over a period of time we discovered the failure characteristics of the hardware that was being used and assembled a list of techniques designed to overcome these. The final major design change arose out of observing the slow but steady escalation of complexity in one area of the system. As is often the case, this escalation had its origins in the conceptual inadequacy of the basic design. By replacing the appropriate section of the system kernel we simultaneously removed an apparent need for a growing number of specialised additions to the superstructure and considerably enhanced the quality of the final product.

The disadvantages of not allowing feedback were commented on by Galler.

Galler: Let me mention some bad experiences with IBM. One example concerns a request to allow user extensions of the PL/1 language. After a week of internal discussion at IBM it was decided that this could not be done because the language designers were not to tell the implementers how to implement the desired extensions. Another example: the OS/360

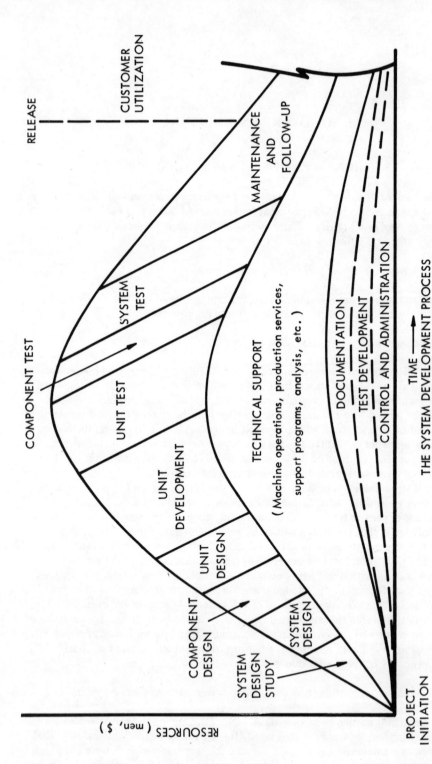

Figure 1. From Nash: Some problems in the production of large-scale
software systems.

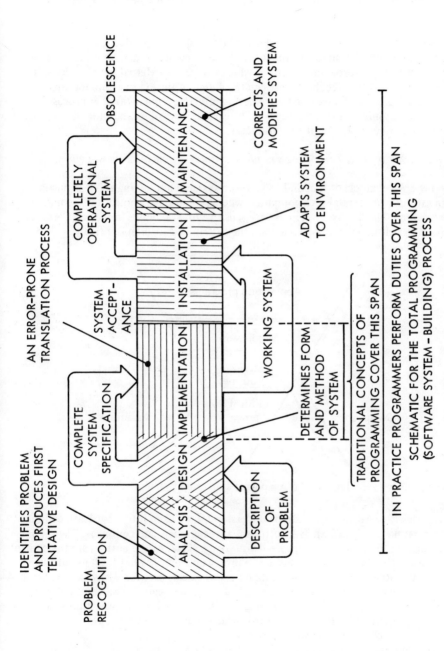

Figure 2. From Selig: Documentation for service and users. Originally due to Constantine.

job control language was developed without any users having the chance to see the options beforehand, at the design stage. Why do these things happen?

External and internal design and their mutual feedback were described by Selig.

Selig: External specifications at any level describe the software product in terms of the items controlled by and available to the user. The internal design describes the software product in terms of the program structures which realize the external specifications. It has to be understood that feedback between the design of the external and internal specifications is an essential part of a realistic and effective implementation process. Furthermore, this interaction must begin at the earliest stage of establishing the objectives, and continue until completion of the product.

Another over-all view of the substance of software engineering was given.

d'Agapeyeff: An example of the kind of software system I am talking about is putting all the applications in a hospital on a computer, whereby you get a whole set of people to use the machine. This kind of system is very sensitive to weaknesses in the software, particularly as regards the inability to maintain the system and to extend it freely.

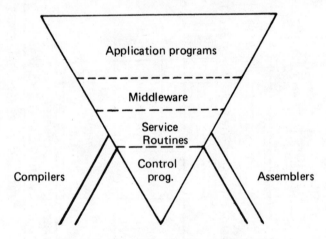

Figure 3. d'Agapeyeff's Inverted Pyramid.

This sensitivity of software can be understood if we liken it to what I will call the inverted pyramid (see figure 3). The buttresses are assemblers and compilers. They don't help to maintain the thing, but if they fail you have a skew. At the bottom are the control programs, then the various service routines. Further up we have what I call middleware. This is because no matter how good the manufacturer's software for items like file handling processes, the initial message analysis and above all the real-time schedules, because in this type of situation the application programs interact and the manufacturers' software tends to throw them off at the drop of a hat, which is somewhat embarrassing. On the top you have a whole chain of application programs.

The point about this pyramid is that it is terribly sensitive to change in the underlying software such that the new version does not contain the old as a subset. It becomes very expensive to maintain these systems and to extend them while keeping them live.

3.2 SOFTWARE ENGINEERING MANAGEMENT AND METHODOLOGY

Several participants were concerned with software engineering management and methodology, as exemplified by the following remarks.

Kolence: (from "On the interaction between software design techniques and software management problems") A software design methodology is composed of the knowledge and understanding of what a program is, and the set of methods, procedures, and techniques by which it is developed. With this understanding it becomes obvious that the techniques and problems of software management are interrelated with the existing methodologies of software design.

D'Agapeyeff: (from "Reducing the cost of software") Programming is still too much of an artistic endeavour. We need a more substantial basis to be taught and monitored in practice on the:
(i)   structure of programs and the flow of their execution;
(ii)   shaping of modules and an environment for their testing;
(iii) simulation of run time conditions.

Kinslow: There are two classes of system designers. The first, if given five problems will solve them one at a time. The second will come back and announce that these aren't the real problems, and will eventually propose a solution to the single problem which underlies the original five. This is the "system type" who is great during the initial stages of a design project. However, you had better get rid of him after the first six months if you want to get a working system.

Berghuis: (from "The establishment of standard programming and management techniques throughout the development and production of software and their enforcement") Independent software packages don't exist; they run on an equipment (hardware), they need procedures by which to be operated and that indicates that we have to define what a system, project, phase of a project, releases, versions, etc., mean. Also we have to consider the organisation from the point of view of developing systems and in fact we are faced with the differences between functional and project organisation. We are also faced with the difficulties of system-engineering.

Detailed information related to one particular, large project is given below.

Harr: (from "The design and production of real-time software for Electronic Switching Systems") In order to set the stage for a discussion on techniques for management of program design and production, I would like to first review with you the program design process. By program design process I mean all of the activities required to produce a documented, tested and working program. Regardless of how large or small a programming task is, it requires essentially the following sequence of steps:
1. The design process
    a. Specification of the complete hardware-software system.
    b. Definition of the functions to be performed by the program.
    c. Design and documentation of the master (overall) program plan.
    d. Subdivision of the large system program into manageable program blocks.
    e. At this point, the interfaces between the program blocks must be precisely defined and documented. Since the usual means of passing data between program jobs is via the use of data in the memory of the system, the memory should be formulated and defined for the interfaces between each program block.
    f. Basic program subroutines defined and documented.

g. Detail design, coding and documentation of each program block.
h. Design and documentation of test methods for each program block in parallel with step (g).
i. Compilation and hand check of each program block.
j. Simulation of each program block using test methods planned during the design of the program.
k. Test and evaluation of the program blocks in the system.
l. Integration of complete program in the system.
m. Final load testing of the complete software-hardware package to see that the program meets all of its design requirements.
2. Organization used in the program design process
   a. Structure of the programming groups as below.

ORGANIZATION OF PROGRAM GROUPS (1961)

	NO. OF PROGRAM DESIGNERS	
SYSTEM PLANNING AND REQUIREMENTS DEPT		36
OPERATION	13	
MAINTENANCE	13	
ADMINISTRATION	9	
SYSTEM PROGRAM DESIGN DEPT		34
OPERATION AND ORDER STRUCTURE	12	
COMPILER	11	
SIMULATION	10	
	TOTAL	70

ORGANIZATION OF PROGRAM GROUPS (1963)

	NO. OF PROGRAM DESIGNERS	
ESS REQUIREMENTS		38
SUBURBAN OFFICES	19	
METROPOLITAN OFFICES	11	
PROCESSOR AND ADMINISTRATION	17	
ESS PROGRAM DESIGN		45
SYSTEM	18	
NETWORK	14	
COMPILER	12	
ESS MAINTENANCE PROGRAM		47
PROCESSOR	10	
MEMORY	21	
PERIPHERAL	15	
	TOTAL	130

b. Types of personnel used as program designers include two-year trade school graduates, B.S., M.S., and Ph.D's in Electrical Engineering and Mathematics.
c. Communications within and between programming groups as below.

COMMUNICATIONS WITHIN AND BETWEEN PROGRAMMING GROUPS

GROUP MEETINGS ON DESIGN SPECIFICATIONS

FORMAL PROGRAM DESIGN SPECIFICATIONS

INFORMAL ENGINEERING AND PROGRAMMING MEMORANDA

PROGRAM CHARACTERIZATION DATA

FORMAL PROGRAM DOCUMENTATION

d. Control and measurement of a programmer's output. See curves (figures 4 and 5)
and summary below.

SUMMARY OF FOUR NO. 1 ESS PROGRAM JOBS

The data covers design through check out of an operational program.

	Prog Units	No. of Programmers	Years	Man Years	Prog Words	Words Man Yr
OPERATIONAL	50	83	4	101	52,000	515
MAINTENANCE	36	60	4	81	51,000	630
COMPILER	13	9	2¼	17	38,000	2230
TRANSLATION DATA ASSEMBLER	15	13	2½	11	25,000	2270

3. Program Documentation
   a. Methods and standards used in preparation and editing of: Program descriptions,
   flowcharts, listings and program change notices.
   b. Preparation and updating of program user's manuals covering operational and
   maintenance procedures.
4. Development of general purpose computer tools, i.e.:
   a. A macro-compiler, assembler and loader.
   b. Parameter compiler.
   c. Translation data assembler.
   d. Simulators for:
      (i).   Studying traffic and real-time capabilities
      (ii). Testing hardware design
   e. Summary of general purpose computer support programs.
5. Program test and evaluation support programs.
   a. By simulation on a general purpose machine.
   b. On the system itself:
      (i)   First by program blocks
      (ii)   Second by program functions
      (iii) Finally under many load tests as a complete hardware-software system.

*Inspired by a proposal by Fraser in "Classification of software production
methods", a working party was formed to work on the classification of the subject matter of software production methods. This working party, with the members Bemer, Fraser, Glennie, Opler, and Wiehle, submitted the report titled
"Classification of subject matter", reproduced in section 9.*

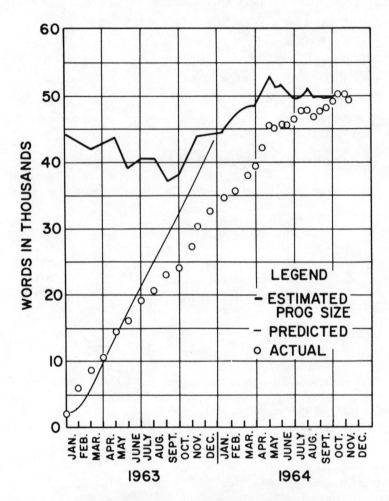

SCHEDULE OF WRITING SUCCASUNNA
CALL PROGRAM
(WRITTEN-NOT DEBUGGED)

Figure 4. From Harr: The design and production of real-time software for Electronic Switching Systems.

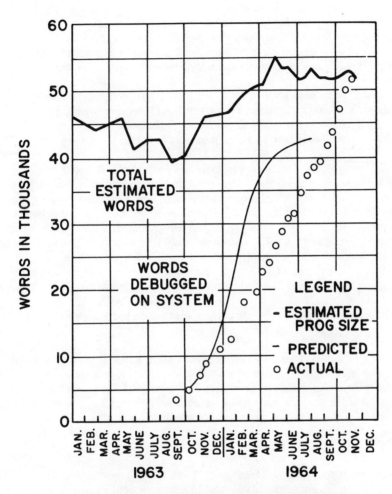

SCHEDULE OF DEBUGGING SUCCASUNNA
CALL PROGRAMS

Figure 5. From Harr: The design and production of real-time software for
Electronic Switching Systems.

3.3. DESIGN AND PRODUCTION IN SOFTWARE ENGINEERING

The difficulties associated with the distinction between design and produc-tion (or implementation) in software engineering was brought out many times during the conference. To clarify this matter it must first be stressed that the difficulty is partly one of terminology. Indeed, what is meant here by produc-tion in software engineering is not just the making of more copies of the same software package (replication), but the initial production of coded and checked programs. However, as evidenced by quotations below, the appropriateness of the distinction between design and production was contested by several par-ticipants.

Added to these basic difficulties is that the conference was organized around the three concepts, design, production, and service. In organizing the report this distinction was retained, mostly for expediency.

First we quote an attempt to clarify the distinction.

Naur: (from "The profiles of software designers and producers") Software production takes us from the result of the design to the program to be executed in the computer. The distinction between design and production is essentially a practical one, imposed by the need for a division of the labor. In fact, there is no essential difference between design and production, since even the production will include decisions which will in-fluence the performance of the software system, and thus properly belong in the design phase. For the distinction to be useful, the design work is charged with the specific responsibility that it is pursued to a level of detail where the decisions remaining to be made during production are known to be insignificant to the performance of the system.

The practical dangers of the distinction are stressed in the two following remarks.

Dijkstra: Honestly, I cannot see how these activities allow a rigid separation if we are going to do a decent job. If you have your production group, it must produce something, but the thing to be produced has to be correct, has to be good. However, I am convinced that the quality of the product can never be established afterwards. Whether the correct-ness of a piece of software can be guaranteed or not depends greatly on the structure of the thing made. This means that the ability to convince users, or yourself, that the product is good, is closely intertwined with the design process itself.

Kinslow: The design process is an iterative one. I will tell you one thing which can go wrong with it if you are not in the laboratory. In my terms design consists of:
1. Flowchart until you think you understand the problem.
2. Write code until you realize that you don't.
3. Go back and re-do the flowchart.
4. Write some more code
   and iterate to what you feel is the correct solution.

If you are in a large production project, trying to build a big system, you have a deadline to write the specifications and for someone else to write the code. Unless you have been through this before you unconsciously skip over some specifications, saying to yourself: I will fill that in later. You know you are going to iterate, so you don't do a complete job the first time. Unfortunately, what happens is that 200 people start writing code. Now you start through the second iteration, with a better understanding of the problem, and it is too late. This is why there is version 0, version 1, ... version N. If you are building a big system and you are writing specifications, you don't have the chance to iterate, the iteration is cut short by an arbitrary deadline. This is a fact that must be changed.

Ross: The most deadly thing in software is the concept, which almost universally seems to be followed, that you are going to specify what you are going to do, and then do it. And that is where most of our troubles come from. The projects that are called successful, have met their specifications. But those specifications were based upon the designers' ignorance before they started the job.

3.4 MISCELLANEOUS NOTES ON THE SUBJECT OF THE CONFERENCE

A few remarks reflect on the subject of the conference as a whole.

Barton: The scope of this conference is not large enough. In design we should start by designing hardware and software together. This will require a kind of general-purpose person, "a computer engineer".

Babcock: (from "Variations on software available to the user") The future of new operating system developments in the future may depend more and more on new hardware just on the horizon. The advent of slow-write, read-only stores makes it possible for the *software* designer to depend on a viable machine that has flexible characteristics as opposed to rigid operation structures found in most of today's machines. If the software designer had access to a microprogramming high-level language compiler, then systems could be designed to the specific problem area without severe hardware constraints. Major U.S. manufacturers including IBM, UNIVAC, Standard Computer, RCA are building or seriously considering such enhancements.

4. DESIGN

4.1. INTRODUCTION

4.1.1. Sources of Techniques

Part of the discussion was concerned with the sources of the right attitude to design. The suggestion that designers should record their wrong decisions, to avoid having them repeated, met the following response:

McClure: Confession is good for the soul -

d'Agapeyeff: - but bad for your career.

A more general suggestion was made:

Naur: (from "The profiles of software designers and producers") . . . software designers are in a similar position to architects and civil engineers, particularly those concerned with the design of large heterogeneous constructions, such as towns and industrial plants. It therefore seems natural that we should turn to these subjects for ideas about how to attack the design problem. As one single example of such a source of ideas I would like to mention: Christopher Alexander: Notes on the Synthesis of Form (Harvard Univ. Press, 1964).

4.1.2. Need for Hardware Based on Program Structure

This point was elaborated in two contributions.

d'Agapeyeff: (from "Reducing the cost of software") Instead of crude execution of absolute code, allow the machine to use a higher level intermediate code (perhaps through interpretation via a fast read-only store) in order to:
1. increase run time checks and therefore program reliability;
2. provide more facilities for program development;
3. reduce the problem of conversion to new machines;
4. allow all communication with the programmer to be in source language.
Another point is that programming would be simplified if certain processes could be declarative rather than procedural. This is an extension of the idea of channel command words. It appears this could be applied to much of I/O, file processing and checking. The functions must, however, operate in a uniform manner, indicate their progress (e.g. by separate clocks) and allow for dynamic alteration of the declarations.

Finally we need more redundant information, available in the machine, safely recording what has just happened (e.g. last operand addresses and contents, etc.) so that there can be greater automatic retrieval after an error. The current tendency for programs to be arbitrarily thrown off must be reversed.

Barton: In design you have to start at the level of organization of programs and machines, with the design of hardware and software together. This must be in the hands of one or a few individuals and will require a kind of general purpose person. What do these persons know? As far as programming is concerned they can only know what the state of the art is, what can be learned from existing systems, the extrapolations that people have made on these, and what happens in languages, in operating systems, in control programs. They are not expert programmers or experts in things like syntax directed compilers. They must be people who are interested in synthesizing, extracting essentials out of what has been learned. On the hardware side they are not hardware designers either, but they are concerned about putting together the gross logic of machines. These are the only parts of the design that can be done by just a few people. These people have to rely on two other groups. Their decision making stops on the programming side with the choice of a basic language to use, just as in conventional design practice you start with the engineers handing over a machine language. In this approach the designers can hand over a language at a higher level, but it need not pay any attention to the standards that exist in the field at the given time, it should just embody their best understanding of the tools, concepts and ideas of programming. If ultimate users use that language they would use it in the same way they would use an assembly language furnished by the manufacturer. At any rate, the systems designers can then hand over to compiler implementors something which is more complete and takes account of more problems before the languages demanded by the market place are implemented. The systems designers, on the other hand, hand over to the engineers a gross logical organization. Then logical detailing and circuit development takes place. Circuit development and logic nowadays are getting closely intertwined. With the programmers and engineers, there will be feedback going on for a considerable time, for months or even a year. But this is feedback into one place, the place where there is some central, authoritative, decision making. That is not at the time the machine has been designed; it is before you have anything at all.

There is one more source of feedback, besides the logic designers and compiler implementors, namely from the world of application. Whenever an application acquires a uniqueness, enormous size perhaps, or extraordinary complexity, that does not seem to fit into the existing languages, there are three paths of feedback. One is into the area of language design, which will take care of the question of expression. The other is into the area of logic design, because completely new logic devices may be required. Third, into the one point which is right at the top, the area of system design, where people are concerned with the organization of hardware and programs together.

In all this, we don't have to wait for theory; in fact, unless you look at the problem in this way we will never get a theory.

4.1.3. Relation to Mathematics

A few statements were made on the importance of mathematics in software design.

Perlis: Software systems are mathematical in nature. A mathematical background is not necessary for a designer, but can only add to the elegance of the design.

Bauer: What is needed is not *classical* mathematics, but *mathematics.* Systems should be built in levels and modules, which form a mathematical structure.

Kolence: (from "On the interaction between software design techniques and software management problems") At the abstract level, a concise mathematical notation is required by which to express the essential structures and relationships irrespective of the particular software product being implemented. For example, in the area of computer central processor design, the notation that satisfies this requirement is Boolean Algebra. The notation of Ken Iverson is an attempt to provide an equivalent notation for software.

4.2 DESIGN CRITERIA

4.2.1. General Design Criteria

> *Several general design criteria were stressed.*

Perils: I adopt as a basic principle of design that the user should be able, in principle, though perhaps not shown how by the manufacturer, to reach every variable which actually appears in the implementation. For example, in formatting, if the system uses a variable that sets margins, then that should be available. You may perhaps not find it in the first volume of system description, but you should come across it later on.

Letellier: (from "The adequate testing and design of software packages") . . . it will always be found that extensions are to be made after some time of use and a software package must be thought of as *open-ended,* which means enough syntactic flexibility in the input and modularity in the implementation.

Smith: There is a tendency that designers use fuzzy terms, like "elegant" or "powerful" or "flexible". Designers do not describe how the design works, or the way it may be used, or the way it should operate. What is lacking is discipline, which is caused by people falling back on fuzzy concepts, instead of on some razors of Occam, which they can really use to make design decisions. Also designers don't seem to realize what mental processes they go through when they design. Later they can neither explain, nor justify, nor even rationalize, the processes they used to build a particular system. I think that a few Occam's razors floating around can lead to great simplifications in building software. Just the simple: how something will be used, can often really sharpen and simplify the design process. Similarly, if we use the criterion: it should be easy to explain, it is remarkable how simple the design process becomes. As soon as one tries to put into the system something that takes more than a paragraph or a line to explain, throw it out — it is not worth it. We have applied this to at least one system and it worked beautifully. As a result we had documentation at the same time as we had the system. Another beautiful razor is: the user should have no feeling that he is dealing with an inanimate object, rather he should feel that he is dealing with some responsive personality, who always responds in some reasonable way. Criteria like these have nothing to do with "powerful linguistic features" or "flexibility" and right at the beginning I think we should throw the fuzzy terms out of the window.

David: (in "Some thoughts about production of large software systems") . . . experience . . . has led some people to have the opinion that any software systems that cannot be completed by some four or five people within a year can never be completed; that is, reach a satisfactory steady-state. While no one has stated this opinion as an immutable "law", the question of what techniques can lead to a counter-example arises ... .

Define a subset of the system which is small enough to bring to an operational state within the "law" mentioned above, then build on that subsystem. This strategy requires that the system be designed in modules which can be realized, tested, and modified independently, apart from conventions for intermodule communication.

Gillette: (from "Aids in the production of maintainable software") Three fundamental design concepts are essential to a maintainable system: *modularity, specification,* and *generality.* Modularity helps to isolate functional elements of the system. One module may be debugged, improved, or extended with minimal personnel interaction or system discontinuity. As important as modularity is specification. The key to production success of any modular construct is a rigid specification of the interfaces; the specification, as a side benefit, aids in the maintenance task by supplying the documentation necessary to train, understand, and provide maintenance. From this viewpoint, specification should encompass from the innermost primitive functions outward to the generalized functions such as a general file management system. Generality is essential to satisfy the requirement for extensibility.

4.2.2 User Requirements

Several remarks were concerned with the influence of users upon the design.

Hume: One must be careful to avoid over-reacting to individual users. It is impossible to keep all of the users happy. You must identify and then concentrate on the requirements common to a majority of users, even if this means driving a few users with special requirements away. Particularly in a university environment you take certain liberties with people's freedom in order to have the majority happy.

Babcock: In our experience the users are very brilliant people, especially if they are your customers and depend on you for their livelihood. We find that every design phase we go through we base strictly on the users' reactions to the previous system. The users are the people who do our design, once we get started.

Berghuis: Users are interested in systems requirements and buy systems in that way. But that implies that they are able to say what they want. Most of the users aren't able to. One of the greatest difficulties will be out of our field as soon as the users realize what kind of problems they have.

Smith: Many of the people who design software refer to users as "they", "them". They are some odd breed of cats living there in the outer world, knowing nothing, to whom nothing is owed. Most of the designers of manufacturers' software are designing, I think, for their own benefit — they are literally playing games. They have no conception of validating their design before sending it out, or even evaluating the design in the light of potential use. The real problem is training the people to do the design. Most designers of software are damn well incompetent, one way or another.

Paul: The customer often does not know what he needs, and is sometimes cut off from knowing what is or what might be available.

Perlis: Almost all users require much less from a large operating system than is provided.

The handling of user requests within a design group caused some discussion.

Goos: A main question: Who has to filter the recommendations coming from outside? The man or group who filters user requests to see what fits together is the most important aspect of design guided by user requirements.

Hume: Experience is the best filter.

Randell: Experience can be misused as a filter. It is very easy to claim that one's own experience denies the validity of some of the needs expressed by users. For example, this was one of the causes for IBM's slowness in responding to users' expressed needs for time sharing facilities.

Galler: We should have feedback from users early in the design process.

Randell: Be careful that the design team will not have to spend all its time fending off users.

Goos: One must have the "filter" inside, not outside, the design group.

Letellier: (from "The adequate testing and design of software packages") . . . any limitations, such as a number of variables or a maximum dimension, must be discussed with the user; new concepts have to be understood by the designer who must refrain from sticking to his own programmer's concepts; this is not as simple as it looks.
    As soon as a draft of the external specifications is drawn up, the designer must go to the users and ask them to describe typical uses of the product to make sure that operational flexibility will be convenient.

The effect a software system can have on the users also gave rise to comment.

Hume: (from "Design as controlled by external function") It must be noted that the software can control or alter the way that users behave and this in turn generates demands for equipment. For example, software that offers a variety of languages in an interactive mode requires a different hierarchical arrangement of storage than that required if only one language is to be available.

Ross: On this point of the system affecting the user, one little example is that recently a new command was put into the MAC CTSS system called BUY TIME, by which the individual user is able to purchase time within his own allotment from his supervisor, instead of having to go and ask the supervisor for more time or tracks. When this system was put into effect, our own group began to use significantly more resources and my group leaders assure me that there is more work being done at the same time. It is interesting that just taking out of their loop the finding of the man who could assign them more time really had an impact on their work.

Perlis: I think everybody who works with a big computer system becomes aware that the system influences the way people react to it. In a study we made we observed, what should have been obvious, but had not been, that if one depends on a system over which one has no control, the one thing you wish from it is that the system match your expectations of it. So anyone who runs a system and gives the service he promises, however bad that may be, is giving something much better than someone who promises a great deal and then does not deliver it, except perhaps on a random basis.

Quite specific user wishes were also discussed. The views are summarized below.

Hume: (from "Design as controlled by external function") . . . Library programs should be designed to take as little as possible of the user's time and offer him the greatest confidence in the results. When this requirement is satisfied the methods employed should be as economical of machine time as possible. . . .
    Because the various modes of operating (interactively and with fast or regular compilers) all have their special advantages, it is most useful to have the same language processed by all three methods. . . .

Operating systems should have scheduling algorithms that maintain the quality of service under changing user demands. In many instances as a system gets more heavily loaded, service to users deteriorates. The control of users' demands by bad service is to be deplored.

Operating systems should be simple for the user. The default options, when leaving information unspecified in a control card, for instance, should always be the most commonly wanted ones. In time-sharing or multiprogrammed environments each user's information should be assiduously protected. Nothing is more disconcerting than the possibility of interference from some other user. This is perhaps a greater concern than privacy of files.

An important part of any operating system is the accounting scheme. Assignment of charges to various parts of the computer resource—memory, processor time, disk space, etc., can influence the use made of these facilities. Any rationing schemes or assessing of prices should ensure that good user practice is encouraged. Since this costing is internal to the system it should aim to produce external minimal costs for the user-equipment system as a whole.

d'Agapeyeff: (from "Reducing the cost of software") Is one operating system per machine enough? Can one operating system within a single framework (although with many options) satisfactorily meet the needs of all classes of users (e.g. bureaus, universities, business batch processing, commercial online installations) or if not, how many different systems are likely to be necessary?

Only a few remarks were directly concerned with the problems of quite specific designs, possibly because these problems are so numerous.

Kolence: (from "On the interaction between software design techniques and software management problems") The definition of certain types of external charcteristics may effectively dictate a basic internal design structure which results in unsatisfactory operational characteristics. Two opposing examples are useful to illustrate this point. In commercial data processing, the functions associated with a given run in a batch processing system may be so numerous that extremely tight coding is necessary to fit the program into core. In this instance, the evolutionary power of the program, (that is, the ability to modify the system,) will be severely limited. On the other hand, requirements to permit additional features or use of various input/output formats may be so extensive that a table driven design is dictated. This design type usually has slow operational speeds.

4.2.3. Reliability and Design

Reliability is one of the several issues that goes across the design-production distinction. Reference should therefore also be made to section 5.1.2. One remark specially mentioning design is given below.

Fraser: I just want to make the point that reliability really is a design issue, in the sense that unless you are conscious of the need for reliability throughout the design, you might as well give up.

4.2.4. Logical Completeness

Logical completeness was put forward as an important design criterion. This gave rise to the following remarks.

Perils: Logical completeness means that the system must be capable of performing at least a "basic" set of operations before it can be classified as a system of certain kind. We are not interested in modest systems which do only half the job that one would ordinarily expect; that is too modest. I think that all of us agree that we could list a set of processes that we feel must be included in any language translator, without which we would not call it such. Designing perfect, but incomplete, systems is probably worse than designing somewhat unreliable, but complete, systems.

Genuys: I would like to know what exactly you mean by logical completeness.

Randell: We certainly don't have a complete answer. It is just that you will sometimes see a system that is obviously not logically complete; that can, for instance, produce tapes that it cannot read back.

Ross: The idea is the mathematicians' concept of *closure,* of a group for example, where for every operation you have an inverse operation. It is that idea iterated many times in all parts of the system.

Perlis: Another example: building an assembly system in which the routines that are assembled cannot be entered into the library, except by a totally separate set of actions and tasks, and possibly recoding and so forth.

Genuys: I think I would just prefer another term because this one has a certain logical flavor, and I am not certain that . . .

Perlis: (Interrupting) The word "logical" has a meaning outside the realm of logic, just as the word "complete" does. I refuse to abrogate to the specialist in mathematics the word "completeness" and in logic, the word "logical".

Bauer: The concept seems to be clear by now. It has been defined several times by examples of what it is not.

4.3. DESIGN STRATEGIES AND TECHNIQUES

4.3.1. Sequencing the Design Process

> *The problem of the proper order in which to do things during design is currently a subject for research in software engineering. This was reflected in the extensive discussions during the conference.*

Naur: In the design of automobiles, the knowledge that you can design the motor more or less independently of the wheels is an important insight, an important part of an automobile designer's trade. In our field, if there are a few specific things to be produced, such as compilers, assemblers, monitors, and a few more, than it would be very important to decide what are their parts and what is the proper sequence of deciding on their parts. That is really the essential thing, what should you decide first. The approach suggested by Christopher Alexander in his book: "Notes on the Synthesis of Form", is to make a tree structure of the decisions, so that you start by considering together those decisions that hang most closely together, and develop components that are sub-systems of your final design. Then you move up one step and combine them into larger units, always based on insight, of some kind, as to which design decisions are related to one another and which ones are not strongly related. I would consider this a very promising approach.

David: (from "Some thoughts about the production of large software systems (2)")
Begin with skeletal coding: Rather than aiming at finished code, the first coding steps
should be aimed at exploring interfaces, sizes of critical modules, complexity, and adequacy of the modules [. . .] . Some critical items should be checked out, preferably on
the hardware if it is available. If it is not, simulation is an alternative. The contributions
of this step should be insight and experience, with the aim of exploring feasibility.

Kolence: (from "On the interaction between software design techniques and management
problems") Consider how the understanding of the types of structures and relationships
that exist in a software product affect the manager's decision on how to begin the development of a design, by establishing the initial design specifications. The most important concepts which must be available to him are those of external product characteristics and
internal program design. A set of specifications must be developed on the external features of a product but at the same time these features must be properly related to the
internal design structure of the program to be produced. Unless this relationship is understood, and made explicit, the manager runs the risk of becoming committed to the development of minor external features which may be disproportionately expensive to implement
by the desired internal design.

. . . . .

The last element of a design methodology to which we will relate the problems of software management is that of defining an overall standard process. The existence of a standard set of steps through which any given software design proceeds to implementation is
something which exists in an installation whether or not it has been formally observed
and described. Many sets of standard steps may exist, one set for each programmer in the
installation. The program manager must determine for each design process what requirements for interfacing exist within his group and with other groups in the installation. If a
formalized description of the general process does not exist, then the programming
manager is required to re-establish it with each job assignment he makes.

*The specific sequencing principles "top-down" and "bottom-up" were in-
troduced as follows.*

Randell: (from "Towards a methodology of computer systems design") There is probably
no single "correct" order in which to take a series of design decisions, though some orderings can usually be agreed to be better than others. Almost invariably some early
decisions, thought at the time to have been clearly correct, will turn out to have been
premature.
    There are two distinct approaches to the problem of deciding in what order to make
design decisions. The "top-down" approach involves starting at the outside limits of the
proposed system, and gradually working down, at each stage attempting to define what a
given component should do, before getting involved in decisions as to how the component
should provide this function. Conversely the "bottom-up" approach proceeds by a gradually increasing complexity of combinations of building-blocks. The top-down approach
is for the designer who has faith in his ability to estimate the feasibility of constructing a
component to match a set of specifications. The opposite approach is for the designer
who prefers to estimate the utility of the component that he has decided he can construct.
    Clearly the blind application of just one of these approaches would be quite foolish.
This is shown all too frequently in the case of designers who perhaps without realizing it
are using an extreme "bottom-up" approach, and are surprised when their collection of
individually optimized components result in a far from optimum system. The "top-down"
philosophy can be viewed mainly as an attempt to redress the balance. In fact a designer
claiming to follow the top-down approach, and specifying what a particular component

is to do before he designs the component, can hardly avoid using his previous experience and intuition as to what is feasible.

In the following passage the "top-down" approach seems to be taken for granted.

Kolence: (from "On the interaction between software design techniques and software management problems") However, perhaps a more important notational need is for one which permits an initial description of the internal design of software to be broken apart into successively more detailed levels of design, ultimately ending up with the level of code to be used. Current flowcharting practices do not exhibit this property, and so each time a portion of the design is detailed, it no longer fits naturally into the initial design description. In particular, it may be that the entire flow sequence of an area of the design is radically altered when it is re-expressed in more detailed terms.

The "top-down" and "bottom-up" approaches were discussed in a working paper by Gill, reproduced as a whole in section 9. Two remarks are particularly pertinent.

Gill: (from "Thoughts on the Sequence of Writing Software") The obvious danger in either approach is that certain features will be propagated through the layers and will finally cause trouble by proving undesirable and difficult to remove, when they should have been eliminated in the middle layers. ... In practice neither approach is ever adopted completely; design proceeds from top and bottom, to meet somewhere in between, though the height of the meeting point varies with circumstances.

The whole question caused considerable discussion.

Barton: I think at this point in the field we are almost forced to start in the middle, if we are concerned with the problem of general software construction and the organization of the machines to go with these programs. To give an example of how to determine where the middle is: we have seen an enormous variety of programming languages develop, but if you want to get all the ideas in programming you could probably select somewhere between six and twelve languages and see all the ideas fairly well represented in this composite language. Now if one starts with a middle language, which sort of extracts the ideas of programming, and ruthlessly discards all questions of detail in style, such as precedence of operator conventions, then you can do two kinds of things with it. First, this forms the specification of a machine, though at this point we don't know how much of that machine is going to be soft and how much is going to be hard. But some people can go away and work on it. But you can also say to people who are concerned with producing particular processors, where human preferences will get into the language: this is the target language you will work into; go away and implement in this language. Now if you are successful at this in between point you may have achieved the specification of a machine language that would be widely acceptable. If you haven't been quite that successful, you will at least give the software designers who work with the initial machine a kind of minimum task to perform. They can consider this language as a tool they would use in the development of further languages. If you are successful in picking an in between point you will avoid the disadvantages of the propagation of undesirable features up or down.

Gill: I would like to add to my paper by pointing out that one of the problems is that many designers are aware of the danger of propagating features too far through their work and they overcorrect for this by deliberately suppressing hardware features which they think the user ought not to have to worry about. The user then finds that he has absolutely no way of controlling these aspects of the hardware.

Fraser: In the designs I have been involved in, and which have not involved too many people, I have not been able to identify whether these have been "top-down" or "bottom-up". They seem to me to be more like frame stressing, where one is trying to stress a structure with welded joints. You fix all the joints but one, and see what happens to the one, then fix that joint and free another and see what happens to that. It's a sort of iterative process which follows an arbitrary pattern through the structure. Perhaps this only holds for small designs, with few people and good communications. About large designs, I don't know.

Perlis: Fundamentally, the procedure you mention, which is "fit-and-try", will work very well with three or four people. If you have a hundred people the "fit-and-try" process diverges because of lack of control.

McIlroy: Talking about where one starts is, I think, perhaps a slight lie. One starts in fact with the grand conception, including the top and the bottom. One can see this in a conception like that of Algol 68. This starts with the top, which is the program, and the bottom, which is the word, the machine word. These are the two fundamental premises, everything else is fitted somehow in between. This is the way a designer starts on Day One. However, he has to do a very large job, and therefore he must structure it in some way. So now we come on the day after Day One to the issues of how to put on a structure.

Barton: In the beginning was the word, all right — [general laughter] — but it wasn't a fixed number of bits!

4.3.2. Structuring the Design

> *The structure of the software resulting from the design process was discussed extensively. The background ideas are reported on partly in working papers reproduced in section 9: E.W. Dijkstra: "Complexity controlled by hierarchical ordering of function and variability" and B. Randell: "Towards a methodology of computing systems design". Other background passages are given below.*

Kolence: (from "On the interaction between software design techniques and software management problems") A design methodology, above all, should be coherent. A design expressed in one notation should permit the various functions required to realize a design to be defined efficiently in terms of that notational description of the design. Software design notation, for example, should decompose naturally from the highest level of design description down to design documents which suffice for maintenance of the final software.

. . . . .

Other types of relationships should also be considered in making the choice of how to break a design apart and what potential problem areas are implied by any given design decomposition. Currently a software manager is greatly hampered by the use of fuzzy concepts about such things as data structures (particularly files and records) and the properties of the operators over such data structures. In fact, the central concept in all software is that of a program, and a generally satisfactory definition of program is still needed. The most frequently used definition — that a program is a sequence of instructions — forces one to ignore the role of data in the program. A better definition is that a program is a set of transformations and other relationships over sets of data and container structures. At least this definition guides the designer to break up a program design problem into the problems of establishing the various data and container structures required, and defining the operators over them. The definition requires that attention be paid to the properties of the data regardless of the containers (records, words, sectors, etc.), the properties of the containers themselves, and the properties of the data when combined with containers. It also forces the designer to consider how the operators relate to these structures.

> *Dijkstra's paper: "Complexity controlled by hierarchical ordering of function and variability" gave rise to several remarks.*

Van der Poel: I agree with the systematics behind the ideas of Dijkstra and his layered structure. In fact when you develop a program systematically in his fashion you have given the proof of its correctness and can dispense with testing altogether. There are, however, a few points to make.

Dijkstra requires that you should be able to verify the correctness of that proof. However, if you insist on having seen every piece of programming yourself, of course you can never step up to a high level of programming. At some stage you will have to believe the correctness of a piece of software which has not been seen or proved by yourself, but by some other party.

Another point is that I think the picture a bit unrealistic on the kind of errors. Errors cut right across the layers, because these are just abstractions. The machine does not know anything about sub-routines, and an error can cut across all these layers in such a way that very illogical results can ensue.

My next point is that I miss an important point in Dijkstra's deductions, and that is he doesn't include the solution of the problem. When he constructs a program then in fact the solution of the problem has been made already. I would like to ask how do we solve the problem. At least I do not know it. When you can visualize a flow diagram or a program in an abstract way, somehow you have solved the problem first; and there is some missing link, some invention, some intuition, some creation process involved which is not easily or not at all symbolised or mechanised. When it's mechanised it is no problem anymore, it's just a mechanical solution of the problem.

Then about errors and error propagation and testing: a program is a piece of information only when it is executed. Before it's really executed as a program in the machine it is handled, carried to the machine in the form of a stack of punch cards, or it is transcribed, whatever is the case, and in all these stages, it is handled not as a program but just as a bunch of data. What happens to errors which occur at that stage, and how can you prove the correctness of all these transmission steps?

Then, as a last question I would like to put the following. The specifications of a problem, when they are formulated precisely enough, are in fact equivalent to the solution of the problem. So when a problem is specified in all detail the formulation can be mapped into the solution; but most problems are incompletely specified. Where do you get the additional information to arrive at the solution which includes more than there was in the first specification of the problem?

Dijkstra: I see in the remarks you made three main elements, one of them the error propagation at a rather mechanical, clerical level. The problem of clerical errors is very serious if it is neglected in practice. On the other hand there are very effective and cheap methods to deal with it by using suitable redundancy.

Next you said that you missed in my description something which you described as, how does one solve a problem. Well, as you, I am engaged in the education business. If I look for someone with a position analogous to the way in which I experience my own position, I can think of the teacher of composition at a school of music. When you have got a class of 30 pupils at a school of music, you cannot turn the crank and produce 30 gifted composers after one year. The best thing you can do is to make them, well, say, sensitive to the pleasing aspects of harmony. What I can do as a teacher is to try to make them sensitive to, well, say, useful aspects of structure as a thinking aid, and the rest they have to do themselves.

With respect to the tackling of an incompletely specified problem, even if your problem is completely specified, the first thing you do is forget about some of the specifications and bring them in later on. It does not in fact make very much difference whether the problem you have to solve is completely specified or not, provided the specifications are not conflicting when the task to be done is subject to alteration. It only means that the things left open will be readily answered in the case of the completely specified one. In a sense, treating the completely specified problem is more difficult because then you have to decide for yourselves which of the aspects of the problem statement you can allow yourselves to forget for the time being. If you have a completely specified problem it means that in the earlier stages of analysis you have to find yourself the useful generalisation of the problem statements. Whereas, if you have an incompletely specified problem you have to solve a class of problems and you start with given class and that's easier.

Randell: Though I have a very great liking for what Dijkstra has done, as usual part of this is because of how he has explained it and part of it is in spite of how he has explained it. There's one particular example I would like to give of this. The word "proof" causes me to have a sort of mental hiccough each time he uses it. Whenever I try to explain his work to somebody else I say "satisfy oneself as to the logical correctness of".

Paul: What is a proof about an algorithm?

McIlroy: A proof is something that convinces other mathematicians.

Perlis: I think that we have gotten switched off the main track, in that Dijkstra's paper has another point besides the idyllic one of proof, and that is that there is also a design process described in the paper. He may have designed that process to make proof easy but I regard that as putting the cart, as it were, before the horse. The design process was organised as a view of constructing a complex system, which is that of building a layering of virtual machines, the organisation being that at one layer something is a variable which at another layer becomes a constant, one layer or many layers below it, and this is the way he chose to design the system. Now that design process is, I think, independently valuable whether you prove anything or not.

4.3.3. Feedback Through Monitoring and Simulation

The use of feedback from a partly designed system to help in design, was discussed at length. The center of interest was the use of simulation during design. This subject was introduced in the working paper: B. Randell: "Towards a methodology of computer systems design", reproduced in section 9. This paper gave rise to an extended discussion.

Barton: What Randell is doing is also being done by a small organization in a production environment that can't afford research, and the approach seems to work.

Perlis: The critical point is that the simulation *becomes* the system.

McIlroy: I would have much more faith in a manager's statement: "The system is two weeks from completion" if he had used this technique.

Bauer: But one should be careful not to use wrong parameters during the simulation.

Graham: The important point in Randell's paper is the use of simulation. To-day we tend to go on for years, with tremendous investments, to find that the system, which was not well understood to start with, does not work as anticipated. We work like the Wright brothers built airplanes: build the whole thing, push it off the cliff, let it crash, and start over again. Simulation is a way to do trial and error experiments. If the system is simulated at each level of design, errors can be found and the performance checked at an early stage. To do simulation we should use a high level language and the standard simulation techniques, with the steps:
1) describe functions
2) describe data structures
3) describe as much of the model as you know, guess at the rest; the language will need primitives for description of high-level elements;
4) describe input/output patterns
5) describe variables and functional relations for on-line display.

Galler: Question to Graham: The Multics system of Project MAC was very carefully designed. Was it simulated?

Graham: No, the designers did not believe they could find adequate mathematical models. The decision was not really made consciously.

Haller: There is a special problem in simulating highly parallel processes on a sequential machine.

Wodon: A general point: the amount of simulation is a reflection of the amount of ignorance.

McIlroy: I feel attracted to the simulation approach. But is it not as hard to write the simulation model as the system itself? What about writing the actual system, but starting with dummy modules?

Randell: You have to go pretty far down the design process to be able to use dummy modules. Simulation should come earlier, even at the gross level.

Perlis: I'd like to read three sentences to close this issue.
1. A software system can best be designed if the testing is interlaced with the designing instead of being used after the design.
2. A simulation which matches the requirements contains the control which organizes the design of the system.
3. Through successive repetitions of this process of interlaced testing and design the model ultimately becomes the software system itself. I think that it is the key of the approach that has been suggested, that there is no such question as testing things after the fact with simulation models, but that in effect the testing and the replacement of simulations with modules that are deeper and more detailed goes on with the simulation model controlling, as it were, the place and order in which these things are done.

4.3.4. High-Level Languages

The use of high-level languages in writing software systems was the subject of a debate.

d'Agapeyeff: (from "Reducing the cost of software") In aiming at too many objectives the higher-level languages have, perhaps, proved to be useless to the layman, too complex for the novice and too restricted for the expert. ... I maintain that high-level programming languages have, to this extent, failed.

Fraser: Software is generally written in a low-level language. Has anyone written low-level software in a high-level language? Would you do it again?

David: (from "Some thoughts about the production of large software systems" (2)) Few large systems have been written in high-level languages. This is not surprising since there are inevitable penalties in size and performance of compiled code, and these factors have been paramount in people's minds. In my opinion, this view is no longer appropriate in many instances since techniques are available to overcome these penalties. Secondary memories can take the squeeze out of the size issue, and performance can be brought to a high level with the aid of a traffic analysis of flow of control in the system. Thus, those modules crucial to performance can become the subject of special attention. Indeed, the vast range of programmer performance indicated earlier may mean that it is difficult to obtain better size-performance software using machine code written by an army of programmers of lesser average calibre.

The advantages of coding in a high-level language lie in increased programmer productivity, fewer bugs in the code, fewer programmers required, increased flexibility in the product, "readability" of the source code ("self-documentation") and some degree (unspecified) of machine independence (better called "portability"). Many of these advantages have a face validity which is fortunate since they are difficult to support with hard evidence. There is evidence, however, on the flexibility issue drawn from the Multics experience. Multics is coded almost entirely in a subset of PL/1 known as EPL. The early versions of Multics were large and slow. Major improvements were made by imploring the EPL compiler (3 times), by capitalizing on experienced programmers' ability to produce EPL code which compiles for fast execution (3-10 times), and by changing strategies in the system to optimize its performance (3-10 times). Important in this process was metering of the system performance. Some idea of the magnitude of the improvements achieved can be obtained from the following: the overall system was at one time well over 1 million words; this was reduced to 300,000 by the combination of measures mentioned above. Further reduction of as much as 100,000 more is thought possible. In certain modules of the system, the improvements to date can be documented by the following approximate figures:

Module	Size Improvement	Performance Improvement	Effort
Page Fault Mechanism	26/1	50/1	3 man-months
Interprocess Communication	20/1	40/1	2 man-months
Segment Management	10/1	20/1	1/2 man-month
Editor	16/1	25/1	1/2 man-month
I/O	4/1	8/1	3 man-months

These figures indicate that major changes can be made in the software without a massive effort. To me, this flexibility is an absolute necessity for software incorporating new concepts, since initial versions must undergo evaluation to reach a satisfactory state. In my opinion, this is true of *any* large software package – it must be coded so as to make evaluation easy.

Barton: Processors for higher-level languages are written in higher-level languages now. Soon we will have conversational languages for this sort of thing. The thing is that people don't program well. They need the best tools. All questions of efficiency can be handled by improving hardware and generalizing language. — At Burroughs we found Algol very successful. Later, influenced by Simula, we thought you have to provide programmers with a still more convenient tool.

Haller: It's not sensible to make software better by making hardware better. (d'Agapeyeff: Agreed).

Graham: Multics is written essentially in a subset of PL/1 except for a very few basic programs. Whether we would do it again: yes. The advantages show up particularly in big projects, with complex tasks. We get increased productivity of programmers. The programs are more easily understood, hence we can move people around easier, or replace them easier. One cannot predict the best techniques in advance, hence there is a need to re-write parts of the system on the fly, which is easier with a high-level language. The machine code produced is not as good as that of good bit twiddlers, but probably as good as that of the average programmer.

Ross: The AED system is written in itself. I am for using higher-level languages. In this way we really capture what the system is all about and carry it over to the machine. We can build into a higher-level language and related packages a higher level of knowledge than the average programmer possesses, hence the possibility of giving the programmer better programs than he would write in assembly code himself.

Perlis: We tried a formula manipulator based on Algol, using the compiler, but found debugging easier with low-level language. Compilers often do not interface well with machines. It's unfair to say that you wrote a system in a high-level language when in fact you are using only very few features, whereas many things that you need are not there at all.

Randell: In debates like this most people agree on the benefits of high-level languages, but back in the field very few large projects use such languages. I believe the reason is that project managers, if left to make the decision, will decide on the basis of their own small world. They will seek to optimise the easily measurable figures on which they expect to be judged, and will aim to minimise core store used and maximise speed. They will ignore advantages such as portability, ease of re-coding, etc., even though in the long term these factors may well be of paramount importance. If such decisions were made at a higher level of the organisation, the outcome would be very different.

> *This point was also made by Barton, in stating that part of system design is the design of a style which will permeate down through the organisation, quoted in section 4.4.*

McClure: I want to defend the Fortran H compiler. It is perhaps the most complex Fortran compiler that has ever been written. It is unfair to compare it with compilers written in machine language, that do not do the same functions. It is indeed doubtful whether it could have been written in anything but a high-level language. I know of other successful uses of high-level languages for writing assemblers and compilers. The point of using high-level languages is to suppress unnecessary detail, which is vital in complex problems.

David: The answer is: use high-level for research production, low-level for commercial production.

Barton: Efficiency depends on the integrated design of the original system, including both its hardware and software.

Kjeldaas: We have made software products using high-level as well as low-level languages, and our experience is that the high-level language projects were the most successful ones.

Bauer: People are praising or condemning specific products — what was the cause of the success or failure in these cases?

Kinslow: TSS/360 was done in assembly language, and I would do it again that way, at least at monitor level. Reason: need for efficiency; I am afraid a high-level language wouldn't provide the bit manipulation needed. I don't believe in the suggestion to start designing in, say PL/1, and then shift to assembly code, because PL/1 will affect the design approach. In a monitor one cannot accept any control level between designer and machine.

Smith: There are critical matters, such as basic software for a new machine. Here the software designer must be fully aware of the checked features of the machine, he must discuss all facets of the new machine with the hardware designers and must know and avoid the problematic areas of the machine.

Galler: Let us not forget that macro languages are really high-level languages and are used widely.

Kolence: (from "On the interaction between software design techniques and software management problems") An understanding of the relationships between the types of languages used, and the types of internal designs provided, would be of great value to the software manager. It is simply not true that all internal program designs can be implemented in a higher level language. Many installations settle on a given higher level language by which to implement all systems, and in so doing restrict themselves to implementing a limited structural class of programs. Unknowingly they may be eliminating certain classes of internal designs which can perform their system requirements in a much more effective manner than otherwise possible.

4.4. COMMUNICATION AND MANAGEMENT IN DESIGN

Several remarks were made on the need for special notations or languages for communication during the design process.

Kolence: (from "On the interactions between software design techniques and software management problems") Another area of difficulty which faces the designer of a program is how to relate the descriptions of the external and internal designs. The notation of external characteristics tends to be narrative and tabular, whereas internal design notation normally consists of flow charts and statements about key internal containers and tables. An external set of characteristics which is appropriately cross-referenced to the internal design, and which clearly illustrates the impact of features or sets of features on the internal design would be of great value to both the designer and the manager.

The general difficulties are further compounded by the lack of a notation by which the internal design explicitly shows the data interfacing requirements between flowcharts at a detailed level. Thus the manager cannot easily determine if various portions of a design mesh properly.

Still a third type of notational need exists. It is well understood that many portions of any given internal design are common to a great number of different programs. An attempt has been made to capitalize on this knowledge by providing system macros at a relatively high level of language statement. However, these macros are not common across machine lines, and indeed are not even common across languages in general. A notation by which to describe these general relationships in a concise, machine and language independent form would be of great value to the software industry by reducing design costs.

Lastly a requirement on notational form exists to permit the design description of a program to be used to define the checkout requirements of a system. Actually, this requirement is on both the external characteristic and the internal structure design notational forms. The problems of programming management, once the system is in the checkout states, are well known. A standard joke in the industry is that a program typically remains 90 % debugged for about 25 % of the total implementation time. A notational form, in conjunction with a greater understanding of the properties and structures of a program, is required to permit the program manager to properly monitor the progress of checkout.

David: (from "Some thoughts about the production of large software systems (2)")
Design Before Coding: The basic structure of the software, including modular divisions and interfaces, should be determined and documented before a coding begins. Specifications for modules and interfaces can be described in English, carefully phrased to avoid ambiguities.

Gillette: One type of error we have to contend with is inconsistency of specifications. I think it is probably impossible to specify a system completely free of ambiguities, certainly so if we use a natural language, such as English. If we had decent specification languages, which were non-ambiguous, perhaps this source of error could be avoided.

Barton: Putting the integration of programming in machine organizations into the hands of one, or at most a few, people, gives an interesting opportunity to impose styles upon the workers under them. The old question of how do you implement programming systems, is it wise to use higher-level languages and so on, is often debated. I like to note that you can eliminate any need for debate in a working organization by imposing such a style through the initial system design. I have observed that people who have such a style imposed on them spend very little time objecting — it's too late to object. Part of system design is the design of a style which will permeate down through the organization, however large. You can't have anarchy down there, at least you have to restrict the area of anarchy.

Dijkstra: I have a point with respect to the fact that people are willing to write programs and fail to make the documentation afterwards. I had a student who was orally examined to show that he could program. He had to program a loop, and programmed the body of it and had to fill in the Boolean condition used to stop the repetition. I did not say a thing, and actually saw him, reading, following line by line with his finger, five times the whole interior part of his coding. Only then did he decide to fill in the Boolean condition — and made it wrong. Apparently the poor boy spent ten minutes to discover what was meant by what he had written down. I then covered up the whole thing and asked him, what was it supposed to do, and forced out of him a sentence describing what it had to do, regardless of how it had been worked out. When this formulation had been given, then one line of reasoning was sufficient to fill in the condition. The conclusion is that making the predocumentation at the proper moment, and using it, will improve the efficiency with which you construct your whole thing incredibly. One may wonder, if this is so obvious, why doesn't it happen? I would suggest that the reason why many programmers experience the making of predocumentation as an additional burden, instead of a tool, is that whatever predocumentation he produces can never be used mechanically. Only if we provide him with more profitable means, preferably mechanical, for using predocumentation, only then will the spiritual barrier be crossed.

Perlis: The point that Dijkstra just made is an extremely important one, and will probably be one of the major advantages of conversational languages over non-conversational ones. However, there is another reason why people don't do predocumentation: They don't have a good language for it since we have no way of writing predicates describing the state of a computation.

The use of the computer itself to help in the documentation of the design was suggested many times, see particularly section 4.3.3 and 5.3.1. One other remark is given below.

Gillette: In the large, automation has not been exploited very well to aid in the communication process. Some experiments have been made, however. In developing the documentation for OS/360 the programmers had consoles in their offices and they could edit the texts with the aid of the computer. I have read some of the OS/360 documents, and I am not sure the experiment was successful. At Control Data we have used text editors, but there is a great bottleneck, and that is getting the original text into an editable form.

Many problems of software engineering were recognized to be of a general managerial nature, as in the following remark.

David: We must distinguish two kinds of competence, or incompetence, one is in the substance of the subject matter, the other comes in when a person is promoted to coordinate activities. There is a principle, a kind of corollary to Parkinson's Law, called the Peter Principle, named after a high school principal in Long Island. It goes like this: "In the real world people are eventually promoted to their final level of incompetence". That is, if a person is extremely competent at the particular level he happens to be working at, he is immediately promoted. This brings upon him additional responsibility. If he does well at that job he is eventually promoted again, and again, until he reaches the level where he no longer performs satisfactorily, and he is never promoted again. So people are left in a state of incompetence. This, in part, is the problem of any big project area.

Samelson: By far the majority of problems raised here are quite unspecific to software engineering, but are simply management problems. I wonder whether all other branches of large scale engineering have the same problems, or whether our troubles simply indicate that programmers are unfit to direct large efforts. Perhaps programmers should learn management before undertaking large scale jobs.

Randell: I have a question on the huge range of variability of programmer performance. Are similar ranges found in other engineering areas?

David: The variation range in programming is in fact greater than in other fields.

Certain remarks reflected on the relation between the group structure and the structure of the systems produced.

Endres: It is important that the structure of the system and the structure of the organization are parallel. This helps very much in communication. Communication should follow the same lines along which decisions are made.

Pinkerton: The reason that small groups have succeeded in the past, and that large groups have failed, is that there is a need for a certain structure of communication, and a structure of decision making in the development of software. This succeeds with small groups, because it can all be done intuitively by one person serving as most of the network, but it has failed with the large groups. For large groups to succeed, (and we do need large groups), we just have to face organizational structure for communications and decisions. Second, this does induce a structure on the system. We ought to consider how a system designed with a group with a certain structure might have a reflecting structure.

Randell: As was pointed out by Conway ("How do committees invent?" — Datamation, April 1968) the system being produced will tend to have a structure which mirrors the structure of the group that is producing it, whether or not this was intended. One should take advantage of this fact and then deliberately design the group structure so as to achieve the desired system structure.

5. PRODUCTION

5.1. INTRODUCTION

Section 3 of this report contains much material on the place of Production in the total task of designing, implementing, delivering, maintaining, etc., a software system. During the conference a working party produced a report, "Classification of subject matter", which attempted to list and classify the procedures that constitute the production process and the technical components involved in the production task. This report is reproduced in its entirety in Section 9. The conference covered only a small part of the subject matter listed by the working party, so the organization of this section of the conference report does not exactly follow the classification proposed by the working party.

5.5.1. The Problems of Scale

The rate of growth of the size of software systems is dramatically represented by figure 6 (prepared by McClure). This shows, on a logarithmic scale, the amount of code (compiled instructions) provided as standard programming support (Type 1 programs in IBM terminology) for a variety of computers. The reader is invited to use this chart in order to make his own predictions as to the amount of programming support that will be provided with systems delivered in 1975, and to speculate on the number of systems programmers that might then be required.

Additional data regarding the size of some current systems was given by Nash, in his paper "Some problems in the production of large scale software systems". The data, which concerns the number and size of modules in an early version of OS/360 (released in the first quarter of 1966) is reproduced below.

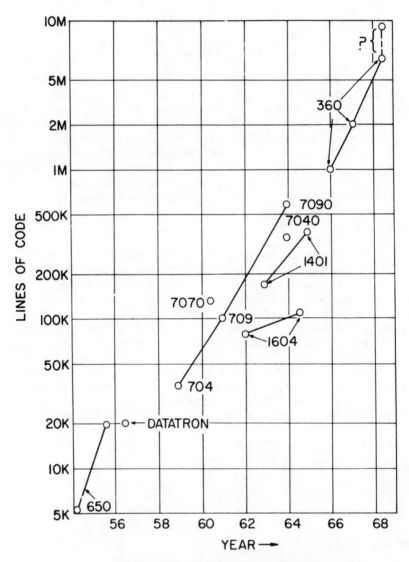

GROWTH IN SOFTWARE REQUIREMENTS

Figure 6. Provided by McClure.

Component	Number of Modules	Number of Statements
Data Management	195	58.6 K
Scheduler	222	45.0
Supervisor	76	26.0
Utilities	86	53.0
Linkage Editor	24	12.3
Testran	74	20.4
Sys. Gen.	32	4.4
	(709)	(219.7)
Assembly E	32	43.0
Cobol E	77	50.6
Fortran E	50	28.7
Sort	175	56.5
	(334)	(178.8)
TOTAL	1043	398.5 K

The situation that has been brought about by even the present level of programming support was described by one conference member as follows.

David: (from "Some thoughts about the production of large software systems (2)") Production of large software has become a scare item for management. By reputation it is often an unprofitable morass, costly and unending. This reputation is perhaps deserved. No less a person than T. J. Watson said that OS/360 cost IBM over 50 million dollars a year during its preparation, and at least 5000 man-years' investment. TSS/360 is said to be in the 1000 man-year category. It has been said, too, that development costs for software equal the development costs for hardware in establishing a new machine line. The commitment to many software projects has been withdrawn. This is indeed a frightening picture.

As was pointed out by d'Agapeyeff, Europe is not lagging far behind:

d'Agapeyeff: (from "Reducing the cost of software") In 1958 a European general purpose computer manufacturer often had less than 50 software programmers, now they probably number 1,000–2,000 people; what will be needed in 1978?

The question arose as to whether it was necessary to have large teams on a single project.

Buxton: The good systems that are presently working were written by small groups. More than twenty programmers working on a project is usually disastrous.

Perlis: We kid ourselves if we believe that software systems can only be designed and built by a small number of people. If we adopt that view this subject will remain precisely as it is today, and will ultimately die. We must learn how to build software systems with hundreds, possibly thousands of people. It is not going to be easy, but it is quite clear that when one deals with a system beyond a certain level of complexity, e.g. IBM's TSS/360, regardless of whether well designed or poorly designed, its size grows, and the sequence of changes that one wishes to make on it can be implemented in any reasonable way only by a large body of people, each of whom does a mole's job.

> *The term "the problems of scale" was used to describe the problems of large software systems.*

David: (from "Some thoughts about the production of large software systems (2)") Regardless of how brave or cowardly the system planners happen to be, they do face difficulties in undertaking large software projects. These have been called "problems of scale", and the uninitiated sometimes assume that the word "scale" refers entirely to the size of code; for example, any project of more than 50,000 source statements. This dimension is indeed a contributory factor to the magnitude of the problems, but there are others. One of increasing importance is the number of different, non-identical situations which the software must fit. Such demands complicate the tasks of software design and implementation, since an individually programmed system for each case is impractical.

A related dimension involves the number of different hardware configurations which the software must accommodate, and another is the range of input error conditions which it must handle gracefully. I'm sure you can think of many more. So, the problems of scale grow with many factors in addition to sheer code size.

Opler: A logarithmic scale in units of man-years is a useful means of characterizing the scale of a software project. People discussing techniques and possible solutions to the various problems associated with the production of software systems should make clear what scale of system they are considering — 1, 10, 100, 1000 . . . man-years.

> *The reasons that scale brought problems in its train were discussed by David and Harr.*

David: (from "Some thoughts about the production of large software systems (2)") The problems of scale would not be so frightening if we could at least place limits beforehand on the effort and cost required to complete a software task. Experience indicates, however, that in the past (and probably in the foreseeable future) estimates of the effort (man-years) to complete tasks involving new software concepts are likely to be low by factors of 2.5 to 4. Similar factors, perhaps not as great, are common for code size and performance. When one considers that a change of 20 — 50 % in any one of these items can mean the difference between economic and deficit operation, one can indeed sympathize with the person who must commit his company or himself to such a task.

Many factors contribute to this situation. There is no theory which enables us to calculate limits on the size, performance, or complexity of software. There is, in many instances, no way even to specify in a logically tight way what the software product is supposed to do or how it is supposed to do it. We can wish that we had the equivalent of Shannon's information theorems, which tell how much information can be transmitted over a channel of given bandwidth and given signal-to-noise ratio, or Winograd's theorem specifying the minimum addition time, given the switching and delay times in the basic circuitry, but we don't have such existence limits for software.

Harr: (from "The design and production of real-time software for Electronic Switching Systems") Now why do we often fail to complete systems with large programs on schedule? Most likely some or all of the following events occur during the design process which cause the schedules to be missed.
1. Inability to make realistic program design schedules and meet them. For the following reasons:
   a. Understimation of time to gather requirements and define system functions.

b. Underestimation of time to produce a workable (cost and time-wise) program design.
c. Underestimation of time to test individual programs.
d. Underestimation of time to integrate complete program into the system and complete acceptance tests.
e. Underestimation of time and effort needed to correct and retest program changes.
f. Failure to provide time for restructuring program due to changes in requirements.
g. Failure to keep documentation up-to-date.

2. Underestimation of system time required to perform complex functions.
3. Underestimation of program and data memory requirements.
4. Tendency to set end date for job completion and then to try to meet the schedule by attempting to bring manpower to the job by splitting job into program design blocks in advance of having defined the overall system plan well enough to define the individual program blocks and their appropriate interfaces.

5.1.2. The Problems of Reliability

Users are making ever more heavy demands on system reliability, as was indicated by Harr, for example.

Harr: A design requirement for our Electronic Switching System was that it should not have more than two hours system downtime (both software and hardware) in 40 years.

The subject of the consequences of producing systems which are inadequate with respect to the demands for reliability that certain users place on them was debated at length. This debate is reported in Section 7.1. However, as Smith pointed out, it is possible to over-estimate the user's needs for total reliability.

Smith: I will tell you about an experiment, which was triggered by an observation that most people seem to work under remarkably adverse conditions: even when everything is falling apart they work. It was a little trick on the JOSS system. I had noticed that the consoles we had provided, beautiful things, were hard to maintain, and that people used them even when they were at an apparently sub-useful level. So I wandered down into the computer center at peak time and began to interject, at my discretion, bits into the system, by pressing a button. I did this periodically, once or twice an hour over several hours. Sometimes they caused the system to go down, leading to automatic recoveries, and messages being sent out to the users. But the interesting thing was that, though there are channels for complaints, nobody complained. This was not because this was the normal state of things. What you may conclude seems to be that, in a remote terminal system, if the users are convinced that if catastrophes occur the system will come up again shortly, and if the responses of the system are quick enough to allow them to recover from random errors quickly, then they are fairly comfortable with what is essentially an unreliable system.

Other quotations on the subject of total system reliability included:

d'Agapeyeff: (from "Reducing the cost of software") Engineering advances and back-up facilities through duplex equipment have reduced the danger of hardware faults and increased user expectancy of reliability (especially in on-line real time installations) but programming has grown more complex and unreliable while software has not provided analogous back-up facilities.

Harr: Time-shared systems need a level of reliability far beyond that which we have been getting from our batch-processing systems. This can be achieved only by a careful matching of hardware and software. The essence of the approach that we used to achieve high reliability in our Electronic Switching System was to plan on the basis that even when the system went live it would still have errors in it. Sure enough, it did.

d'Agapeyeff: I agree with this approach. You must design and implement your system so that it will continue to give service in the presence of both hardware and software errors.

Harr: It requires a very careful program design to ensure that your crucial system tables will not be mutilated except in the very rarest of types of error situation.

Bemer: One interesting question is how much the software people are prepared to pay for extra hardware to assist in maintaining data integrity. My guess would be perhaps 15-20 % of the normal hardware cost.

Harr: We definitely need better techniques for changing a program in the field while continuing to provide service.

d'Agapeyeff: In large on-line systems the cost of testing a change is almost 100 times as much as the cost of producing the change. We cannot afford to go through this process too often.

> *One final pair of quotations are given below, to indicate the need for quantifying our notions of reliability.*

Opler: How many errors should we be prepared to accept in a system containing one million instructions?

Perlis: Seven!

[Laughter].

5.2. PRODUCTION — MANAGEMENT ASPECTS

5.2.1. Production Planning

> *There was much discussion on the difficulties of planning the production of a system that involved a high research content.*

Genuys: If the job has been done before, estimates are fairly easy. If the research content is high, estimates are difficult. The trouble is that it is not always possible to tell beforehand which jobs are which.

McClure: It's research if it's different. Even if it is just higher performance, it is still research.

> *An illustration of how the original estimate of the work involved in producing a particular piece of software gets more reliable as the group of people doing the work gains experience with that particular problem was provided by McClure (figure 7). This shows, for three Fortran compilers produced by the same group, both the original estimate of the work required and the work actually needed.*

David: (from "Some thoughts about production of large software systems (2)") Computing has one property, unique I think, that seriously aggravates the uncertainties associated with software efforts. In computing, the research, development, and production phases are often telescoped into one process. In the competitive rush to make available the latest techniques, such as on-line consoles served by time-shared computers, we strive to take great forward leaps across gulfs of unknown width and depth. In the cold light of day, we know that a step-by-step approach separating research and development from production is less risky and more likely to be successful. Experience indeed indicates that for software tasks similar to previous ones, estimates are accurate to within $10 - 30\%$ in many cases. This situation is familiar in all fields lacking a firm theoretical base.

Thus, there are good reasons why software tasks that include novel concepts involve not only uncalculated but also uncalculable risks.

It was however pointed out by McClure that research content was not the only problem in preparing estimates:

McClure: (from "Projection versus performance in software production") Before undertaking a project to produce a new software system or component, read the following statements, checking all that apply:
  1. The new system will be substantially superior to its predecessor and to competitive systems.
  2. The new system corrects a basic philosophical defect in the previous system.
  3. The specification is not yet complete, but it will be finished before any important programming decisions are made.
  4. The specification is absolutely firm, unless, of course, the Acme Company signs a big order and requests some slight changes.
  5. The programming team will be made up by selecting only the best programmers from other projects.
  6. Because of expansion, a fresh team of programmers with applicable experience will be hired.
  7. The new computer is a great machine; the programmers will love it as soon as they can get their manuals.
  8. The programmers will, of course, have to share the machine with the hardware team checking out the new peripherals and the diagnostic package.
  9. Interfacing this system to the rest of the software is trivial and can be easily worked out later.
  10. Although the assembler (compiler, loader, file system, etc.) is not completely checked out, it will be ready long before coding is complete.
  11. The debug package isn't done but this system can easily be checked out at the console.
  12. The budget is only preliminary but it's obviously conservative.
  13. The project manager may have missed his budget on his last project, but he has learned his lesson and won't miss this time.
For each statement checked on the preceding list add ten percent to the estimated cost and one month to the estimated time. If statement six is checked, add thirty per cent and six months. The result should come much closer to the final result than the original estimate under the assumption that the original estimate was honestly made.

The major contribution on techniques for estimating the amount of time it will take to complete a system was by Nash.

Nash: (from "Some problems of management in the production of large-scale software systems") Consider one of the most difficult problems facing producers of large software

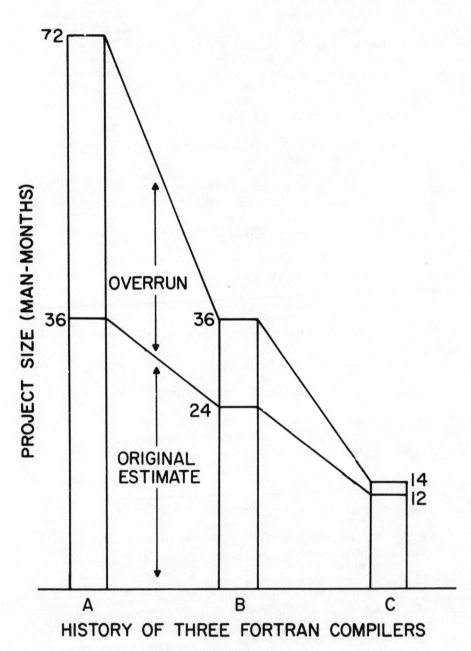

Figure 7. Provided by McClure.

systems, namely, estimating the time required for completion. Suppose we could establish 100 equal teams to implement the same system, in as nearly equal conditions as could be achieved. Then the times actually required by the various teams would follow some distribution, which might be similar to that in figure 8. Even if we had such data to draw on, it is still no simple task to estimate a completion date for the same project thereafter. A sound approach would be to use the most likely time at the outset, but to take a progressively more conservative view as the development proceeded. The spread of the distribution curve would reduce as the end-point was approached as in figure 9, and at the point where a commitment should be made, a 90 % probability would be more reasonable.

However in practice no such data exists and we have to rely on experience and judgement to assess the likely nature of such distributions. How, then, can commitments be made with any degree of certainty? There is one valuable tool available in the later parts of a development cycle, namely Test Status. In any large-scale software production extensive testing is necessary, which normally takes the form of a large number of carefully designed test-cases to run successfully before the system can be released. The test progress consists of a number of discrete events, i.e. test-case successes, which tend to occur in some pattern, and which pattern can be predicted before-hand. If the pattern of successes followed a normal distribution, the test history curve would follow the Cumulative Normal Distribution curve, figure 10. Other distributions produce other cumulative curves, of which a selection is shown in figure 11. From studying test histories of previous developments, a judgement can be made about the nature of the curve applicable to a particular project. For most new projects curves around the 2.5 value are found to be applicable. For improvements to an existing product, successes tend to occur early on, and curve 1.0 can be used. In the case of an existing product being adopted for new environment, for example converting a language processor to run under a different operating system, successes are slow to start but rise quickly once under way, as typified by the higher valued curves.

As an example of the use of this technique, figure 12 shows the actual case history of a project, which was a major extension of a large component of OS/360.

The original test prediction, curve A, was made at the beginning of August. By mid-September it was clear that actual progress, shown by the irregular line, was lagging about 2 weeks behind the plan. The end-date was therefore postponed by four weeks, to allow for the cumulative effect of the lag, and a new prediction made, curve B. In October, it was again evident that the plan was not being met, but by working a substantial amount of overtime, this was corrected to reach the required objective.

There are several important conditions that must be observed if this technique is to be of any value. First, the system build plan must be such that simple test-cases can be run as early as possible, so that testing stretches over a maximum period. This allows the measurement of progress against prediction to give warnings of trouble at an early stage. Second, the set of test-cases must be constructed so that simple tests can be used in the early stages, building up progressively to more complex cases. Third, for the method to work smoothly, careful measures must be taken to avoid changes to the build system causing serious regression, i.e. the familiar event where a correction introduces further errors. With these provisos, test planning and status control can be a valuable tool in managing the later part of a development cycle.

There was some discussion of the problems of estimating the costs of software projects:

Ercoli: I maintain that if proper management and accounting methods are used so that a software job can be considered as composed by well defined and normalized arts then the cost per instruction in implementing each part is roughly $5 per debugged instructions. This is also the average cost of software for known applications and for efforts

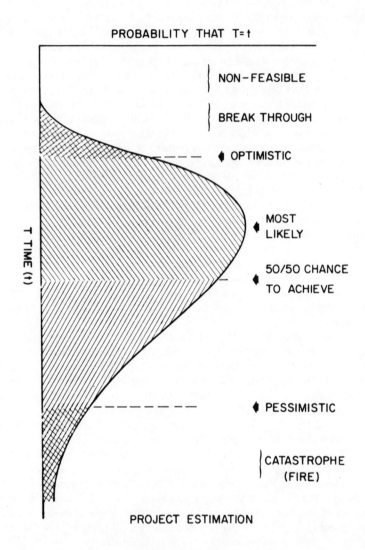

Figure 8. From Nash: Some problems of management in the production
of large-scale software systems.

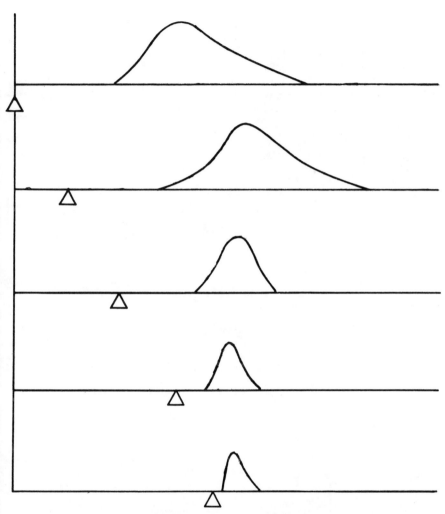

NOTE △ ≡ TIME OF ESTIMATE

THE PROBABILITY DISTRIBUTION AS
A FUNCTION OF TIME OF ESTIMATE

Figure 9. From Nash: Some problems of management in the production
of large-scale software systems.

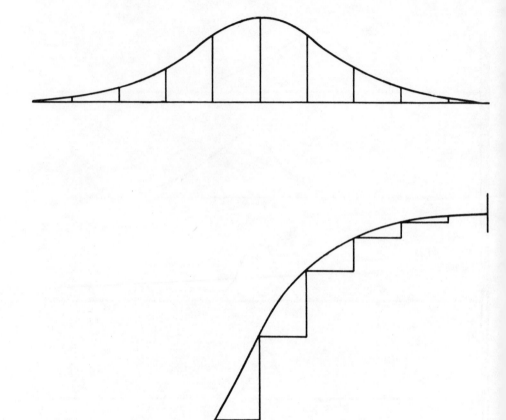

CUMULATIVE NORMAL DISTRIBUTION

Figure 10. From Nash: Some problems of management in the production
of large-scale software systems.

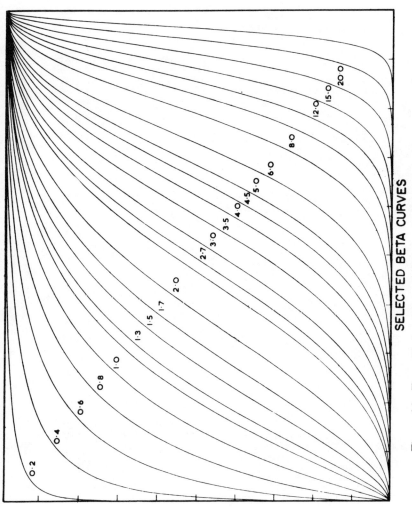

Figure 11. From Nash: Some problems of management in the production of large-scale software systems.

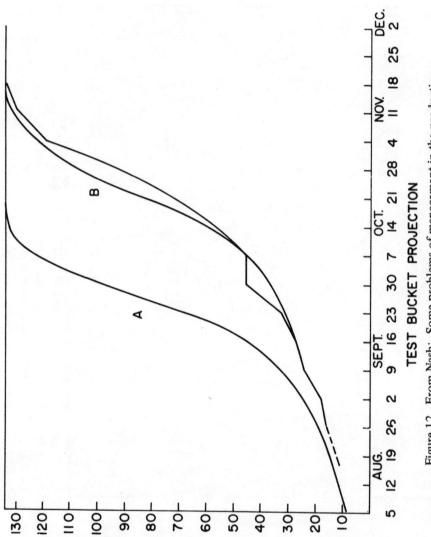

Figure 12. From Nash: Some problems of management in the production of large-scale software systems.

below the limit of about 15 man-years. If the general cost of software production is considered then there are wide variations: as low as $1 per instructions when using semiautomatic means of software production (such as compiler generators) or as high as $20 per instruction in cases of very large operating systems. I would have liked to have replaced these figures by a rough graph on semilogarithmic paper indicating cost per instruction against size of project but it was lost with my luggage.

Endres: I believe that cost/instruction can vary by a factor of 50.

Sallé: It is very difficult to use cost per instruction in estimate because there is no general agreement on what the average cost per instruction is, and also because the ratio varies according to which phase of the production process you are in. The number of tables, number of interfaces, etc., are at least as important for costing as the number of instructions. If these figures are to be used for planning they should be correlated with a number of other important parameters such as range of hardware configurations, number of customers, research content, etc. In fact I think cost/instruction should be the last thing one uses for planning purposes.

Barton: I've just realized that the cost/instruction measure has to be meaningless. Now I don't know the right measure but I suggest as a first approximation to one a weighting which would take into account the number of times the instruction had been used.

5.2.2. Personnel Factors

> *Many of the problems of producing large software systems involve personnel factors:*

David: (from "Some thoughts about production of large computer systems (2)") Also, system programmers vary widely in their productivity. Figures from an experiment by SDC indicate the following range of performance by 12 programmers with 2 to 11 years' experience in completing the solution to a specific logic proglem (Comm. ACM 11 (1968), 6):

Performance on	*Worst/Best*
Debug Time Used	26/1
Computer Time Used	11/1
Coding Time	25/1
Code Size	5/1
Running Time	13/1

These figures confirm my own informal observations. Of course the importance of individual talent to projects generally is widely appreciated and is traditionally reflected in promotions and dismissals. Yet, in software projects, talent is often so scarce that marginal people are welcomed. More to the point, the range of productivity indicated above seems quite large compared to what one might expect or tolerate on a hardware project, increasing the difficulty of accurate estimation.

Fraser: I would never dare to quote on a project unless I knew the people who were to be involved.

Opler: In managing software projects the real problem is "spot the lemon – and spot the lemon early".

This started a somewhat surprising line of conversation.

David: I have heard rumours that the Japanese are extremely good at producing software.

Perlis: There is apparently some truth in it. I believe it to be due to three factors.
1. A man stays at one job for his entire working life – there is no concept of mobility.
2. They have a tremendous amount of self-discipline.
3. The complexities of their language give them good preparation for the complexities of software systems.

Opler: I agree – yet by American standards they work long hours for low pay.

There were several comments on the personnel factors involved in very large projects:

David: (from "Some thoughts about production of large computer systems") Among the many possible strategies for producing large software systems, only one has been widely used. It might be labeled "the human wave" approach, for typically hundreds of people become involved over a several year period. This technique is less than satisfactory. It is expensive, slow, inefficient, and the product is often larger in size and slower in execution than need be. The experience with this technique has led some people to opine that any software system that cannot be completed by some four or five people within a year can never be completed; that is, reach a satisfactory steady-state.

d'Agapeyeff: There is the problem of morale. For example I have no idea how you keep your people when you try the "human wave" approach to the production of large systems. In my experience programmers are rather difficult to shove around like platoons in the army.

The benefits of the small team, in those situations which it is sufficient for, were discussed by Babcock and by Cress and Graham.

Babcock: (from "Variations on software available to the user") Before I leave the software area, let me discuss briefly the staff. We selected a few very highly talented, creative people who 1. designed the system, 2. implemented the system, 3. continually developed and researched new capabilities for the system.

The staff comprised over a century of programming experience and I feel this tight control over the entire production is one of the major factors in the success of Rush. No minor programmer ever wrote a bug fix, no minor programmer ever maintained the system. From the beginning, it has been a group of experts who followed every development to the finish.

Cress and Graham: (from "Production of software in a university environment") Much of the design and programming is done by students. They are eager to learn, full of energy and add a vitality to the project which keeps it alive. But they must be supervised!

We have never experienced personnel turn-over during the development of software. This is probably because of the desire to be successful, coupled with the relatively short duration of the projects. We try not to hire people who want a job; instead we try to hire people who want to do *the* job under consideration.

A common property of all our project groups has been that they have been small, and faced with a relatively well-defined task. We find that, with the objective always in sight, the spirit of the group can be maintained.

Finally, we include comments by Perlis on how the realities of personnel factors might be faced in structuring a large group of people:

Perlis: A man can communicate with about five colleagues on a software project without too much difficulty. Likewise he can supervise about five people and know pretty well what they are doing. One would structure 120 people in three levels, in which no man is talking to more than about eight people, both across his level and up and down – which is well within our capabilities I think, since most of the communication will go across rather than down. We have confused the simplicities of administration with the aims of production. When someone comes into a structure we naturally assume that he starts at the bottom and works his way up, whereas the bottom is the place where the information is most difficult to get at in order to find out what you should be doing. So a new person should start perhaps one level down from the top. Another interesting concept we might apply is that used in the Air Force, to fly a number of hours each month, in order to retain one's "wings". So, in a system which will take a long time to complete, for example a year, nobody should be allowed to function permanently at one level, but should percolate. In a situation where code actually has to be produced, nobody should be allowed in the system who doesn't write some given number of lines of code per month.

I think that one of the major problems with the very large programming projects has been the lack of competence in programming which one observes as soon as one goes above the very bottom level. People begin to talk in vague general terms using words like "module", and very rarely ever get down to the detail of what a module actually is. They use phrases like "communicate across modules by going up and then down" – all of the vague administratese which in a sense must cover up a native and total incompetence.

5.2.3. Production Control

One of the big problems of controlling the production of a large system is obtaining information which will reveal how much progress has been made.

Fraser: (from "The nature of progress in software production") One of the problems that is central to the software production process is to identify the nature of progress and to find some way of measuring it. Only one thing seems to be clear just now. It is that program construction is not always a simple progression in which each act of assembly represents a distinct forward step and that the final product can be described simply as the sum of many sub-assemblies.

. . . . .

Various attempts were made at measuring progress without much success. As the work advanced we evolved a simple method of accounting for the components that went to form or support the final product. But this approach was no better than the various "seat of the pants" methods which are still much in evidence. We experienced one of the classic problems of metering; that of interference between the measuring device and the process that is being measured. At one time we kept totals of the number of subroutines that were classed as "tested" and compared this number with the total number of subroutines in the final product. But, once a programmer's performance is formalised in this way it changes his attitude to his work. The effect was to produce an apparent increase in productivity but this was accompanied by a drop in quality. Of course, the latter did not come to light until very much later.

Towards the end of the production task, when most of the required techniques had been developed, it became very much easier to measure performance. At this stage we were better able to assess the performance of the programmers individually and the methodology had become quite standard throughout the group. The only confidence that I can gather from this experience is that of estimating the production rate for known men performing a known task that relies only on a known technology.

Kolence: The main interest of management is in knowing what progress has been made towards reaching the final goal of the project. The difficulty is to identify observable events which mark this progress.

David: Psychology is a central point in the problem of measuring progress. Instead of looking for nice quantifiable measures, why not just ask people to give their own estimate of the amount of progress that has been made. In a controlled environment you will soon have enough evidence on which to calculate how the various individuals' estimates should be weighted.

Fraser: (from "The nature of progress in software production") Perhaps the most effective way of assessing the progress of a team project is to study the interface documentation. In the early stages particularly, a programming task resembles frame stressing by relaxation. The progress of the relaxation process can be assessed by studying the magnitude and pattern of successive adjustments to the structure. Similarly, the adequacy and stability of interface details provide one good measure of project status. One might even suggest, a little dangerously perhaps, that rapid change to interface descriptions is a sign of good progress and that the work content of a development project could be measured by the number of changes that must occur during the process of design development.

Harr: (from "The design and production of real-time software for Electronic Switching System") Each program designer's work should be scheduled and bench marks established along the way so that the progress of both of his documentation and programs can be monitored. (Here we need a yardstick for measuring a programmer's progress other than just program words written.) The yardstick should measure both what has been designed and how, from the standpoint of meeting the design requirements. Programmers should be required to flowchart and describe their programs as they are developed, in a standard way. The bench marks for gauging the progress of the work should be a measure of both the documents and program produced in a given amount of time.

A standard for program documentation when programs are written in symbolic machine language should be set and each program should include this standard documentation in the "remarks field" of the symbolic program.

This documentation should include sufficient information and in such a way that a computer program can flow trace any program according to specified conditions.

Then a computer program can be used to assist in evaluating and checking the progress of the program design. Computer studies of the real-time used under varying conditions can be made and studies to see that memory interfaces are satisfied can be made.

McClure: I know of one organisation that attempts to apply time and motion standards to the output of programmers. They judge a programmer by the amount of code he produces. This is guaranteed to produce insipid code — code which does the right thing but which is twice as long as necessary.

> *The difficulties of measuring real as opposed to apparent progress were made clear by Smith:*

Smith: I've only been seven months with a manufacturer and I'm still bemused by the way they attempt to build software. SDS imposes rigid standards on the production of software. All documents associated with software are classified as engineering drawings.

They begin with planning specification, go through functional specifications, implementation specifications, etc., etc. This activity is represented by a PERT-chart with many nodes. If you look down the PERT-chart you discover that all the nodes on it up until the last one produce nothing but paper. It is unfortunately true that in my organisation people confuse the menu with the meal.

The analogy with engineering drawings, however, raised the question of measuring the quality of work produced, as well as progress towards the project goal.

McIlroy: I think we should consider patterning our management methods after those used in the preparation of engineering drawings. A drawing in a large organisation is usually signed by the draughtsman, and then after that by a draughting supervisor when he agrees that it looks nice. In programming efforts you generally do not see that second signature— nor even the first, for that matter. Clarity and style seem to count for nothing — the only thing that counts is whether the program works when put in place. It seems to me that it is important that we should impose these types of aesthetic standards.

McClure: I know of very few programming establishments where supervisors actually bother to read the code produced by their staff and make some effort to understand it. I believe that this is absolutely essential.

Buxton: I know of very few programming establishments in which the supervisor is capable of reading code — some present company excepted!

5.2.4. Internal Communication

There was considerable discussion on the means by which programmers working on a project might communicate with each other.

Buxton: We could use more and better and faster communication in a software group as a partial substitute for a science of software production. We can't define the interfaces, we don't really know what we're doing, so we must get in a position where we can talk across the interfaces.

Dijkstra: I believe that both the total density of information flow necessary between groups, and the percentage of irrelevant information that a given group gets, can be greatly reduced by effectively structuring the object to be constructed and ensuring that this structure is reflected in the structure of the organisation making the product.

Gillette: An attack on the problem of communication is crucial for successful production. We are not using automation (remote consoles, text-editing, etc.) as much as we should.

Buxton: I know myself that if I'm setting up a software group to carry out a project I'm extremely careful that all the people working on it are close personal friends, because then they will talk together frequently, and there will be strong lines of communication in all directions. One in fact uses personal relationships to support technical communication.

Nash: There are dangers in uncontrolled mass-communication. You can get into trouble if people start taking advantage of information that they gain by chatting that they should not know (and which may well lose its validity in a day or so).

*A detailed discussion of the importance of careful documentation was given
by Naur:*

Naur: (from "The profiles of software designers and producers") In order to characterise
the work of the production programmer I would first of all stress the importance of
documentation during production. Both the need for documentation of software systems,
and the difficulties in filling these needs, are well known items in software work. It is my
experience that the most constructive way to solve this problem is to insist that the
production of essential parts of the documentation is a natural part of the production of
the software program, and that the two proceed in parallel.

In discussing documentation one should keep in mind that this is aimed at the
human reader, and should be developed along the principles of report writing set forth
in several different texts on the subject. Of particular significance is the insistence, among
competent report writers, that reports be structured hierarchically and written from the
top of the hierarchy, i.e. starting with a brief synopsis. I feel strongly that in software
production this principle should be followed carefully, at all levels of work. If this is done,
the first thing to be done by the software producer about to start writing a piece of software, is the writing of a synopsis of what his piece of program is supposed to be doing.
The next level may consist of a description of a few pages describing the essential data
structures and the major processes to which they will be subjected. This description
should include carefully selected examples, to illustrate the functions and their most
important variations (these will be useful later as test cases). The lowest level of the
hierarchy is the program text itself.

This way of work not only has the advantage that important parts of the documentation are actually produced. It also leads to better programs. In fact, when working out
the higher level descriptions in written form, the software producer inevitably will be
forced to think out his data and program structures more carefully than otherwise. This
regularly leads to programs with clearer structure, higher efficiency, and fewer bugs.

This way of developing the software and its documentation also allows for mutual
review, check, and criticism within small groups of software programmers. This should
take place frequently while the work is in progress and can very well be done within
groups of two people who look into another's work. In my experience this is a highly
effective way of organizing the software work.

David: One has to avoid flooding people with so much information that they ignore it all.
Selective dissemination of information, by means of a system such as Mercury (see W.S.
Brown, J.R. Pierce, J.F. Traub: The Future of Scientific Journals, Science, December
1967) at Bell Laboratories should be tried in a large software project.

Randell: It is relatively easy to set up a communication system, manual or automatic,
which will let me find information that I already realise I need to know. It is more difficult
to make sure I also get information which I need, but of whose very existence I am ignorant.

*Finally, several people gave interesting case histories of the methods used
for internal communication within a production team.*

Opler: I think I know how to organise reasonably successful communication for projects
of between 10 and 50 people. I am quite sure I don't know how to do it with projects
of much greater size. The method we used was as follows. From the moment the project
is created every member of the staff receives a three-ring binder and perhaps half-a-dozen
pages stating the very first decisions and ground rules for the project, including an index.
As the project proceeds everybody contributes sheets, which must be countersigned by

their management. As the project grows so does the notebook. Hopefully the document classification system remains adequate. We had at most a one-day delay between origination of a document and distribution to all members of the group. This had interesting side-effects. I noticed that one part of the book was not filling in very fast − this led to early discovery of a worker who was lagging behind, and who eventually had to be dismissed.

Fraser: The question of what methods should be used for organising information flow between members of a production team depends largely on the size of the team. I was associated with a 30-man project, producing a commercial compiler (NEBULA) for the I.C.T. ORION Computer. We had three, or rather four, forms of information flow.
The first was based on the fact that the compiler was written in a high-level language and hence provided, in part, its own documentation.
The second form of information flow was based on documentation kept in a random access device which was regularly accessed by every member of the team. This was a steel filing cabinet kept in my office. It contained files consisting of scruffy bits of paper with various notes and messages from one member of the team to another. This was probably the most important form of communication we had. Its merits were that there was only one set of authoritative information, and that the indexing scheme, albeit crude, was sufficient to allow one to find, in most cases, the relevant information when you needed to make a decision. I don't see any advantage in automating such a system for a group of 30 men. A filing cabinet is easy to use, and there were not many occasions when there were long queues outside my office.
The other filing system we had was an automated text-handling system, in which we kept the official project documentation. This was not much use for day-to-day communication, but invaluable for program maintenance and also program revision in the light of further developments.
There was a fourth communications mechanism which every project has, and which perhaps doesn't get encouraged as much as it should be. There are certain people in any organisation who are remarkably effective at passing gossip. Many of the potential troubles in a system can be brought into the open, or even solved, by encouraging a bit of gossip.

Nash: I would like to report on documentation of the F-level PL/1 compiler, where we had a team of about two dozen people on the actual development. We did not have any private memos, or notes, although we had a considerable amount of verbal communication. What we did establish was a book which described in complete detail every part of the compiler. All members of the team were obliged to describe their parts of the compiler ny means of flow-diagrams and English prose in complete detail at design time. The book grew very large − eventually to about 4000 pages. It was a lot of work to maintain it − perhaps 10-20 % of our total effort − but it was worth it.

d'Agapeyeff: We make great use of seminars as an aid in preventing disasters, and in determining what to do when a disaster occurs. To participate in such seminars it is necessary to communicate fully and to a greater degree than has been possible here. For example, if I were suddenly to recruit you lot and form a rather good software house it would be excellent publicity, but it would not actually work. It certainly wouldn't work at first, because you do not have a sufficient level of communication. One way to obtain this is by a commonality of experience. This is a major difficulty because it leads exactly to the point made by Buxton. It encourages you to work with your friends. But you have to remember that those who are incompetent find each other's company congenial.

5.3. PRODUCTION—TECHNICAL ASPECTS

5.3.1. Tools

As a partial solution to the problems of making a success of the "human-wave" approach to producing large systems, David suggested:

David: (from "Some thoughts about production of large software systems (1)") A reliable, working system incorporating advanced programming and debugging tools must be available from the beginning. One requirement is an accessible file system for storing system modules and prototypes. An adequate file system should act as a common work space for system programmers and should have back-up facilities to insure against loss of valuable records.

The most ambitious plans for a set of tools to aid in the production of large systems that were presented at the conference were those contained in a working paper by Bemer.

Bemer: (from "Machine-controlled production environment")
Tools for Technical Control of Production
1. Goals
   a. Maximizing programmer effectiveness and personnel resources.
   b. Minimizing time and costs for original production, changes and checkout.
   c. Maintaining the best-conditioned system from a quality viewpoint.
2. Attainment
   By utilizing the machine-controlled production environment, or software factory.
   Program construction, checkout and usage are done entirely within this environment using the tools it contains. Ideally it should be impossible to produce programs exterior to this environment. This environment should reside on the computing system intended for use, or in the case of manufacture of a new system, on the most powerful previous system available.
3. Functions Provided
   a. Service
      (i)   Computing power and environment
      (ii)   A file system
      (iii) Compilation
      (iv) Building test systems
      (v)   Building final systems and distribution
      (vi) Information during the process

          • Listings/automatically produced flowcharts/indexing
          • Index and bibliography of software units
          • Direct graph of system linkages
          • Current specifications
          • User documentation, text editing
          • Classification of mistake types
          • Production records to predict future production

      (vii) Diagnostic aids
      (viii) Source language program convertors
      (ix)   File convertors

b. Control
   (i)   Access by programmer
   (ii)   Code volume
   (iii)   Documentation matching to program
   (iv)   Software and hardware configurations, and matching
   (v)   Customizing
   (vi)   Replication and distribution
   (vii)   Quality Control
   (viii) Instrumentation
   (ix)   Labor distribution
   (x)   Scheduling and costing

Buxton: I would be interested to know how much of the system described by Bemer is actually working.

Bemer: We have about a quarter of it presently built and working. It is a very large project. Many improvements are already seen to be necessary – such as in terminal equipment.

Opler: IBM is also developing such a system. The cost is enormous, and a vast amount of hardware is needed.

Fraser: I welcome Bemer's system as a long term project, but I think pieces should be implemented first to see how they work. There is one point that worries me: human monitoring of production is very adaptive – the automated system may disguise some of what is happening.

Bemer: We are starting gradually, and building up. My motto is "do something small, useful, now!".

McIlroy: It would be immoral for programmers to automate everybody but themselves. The equivalent to what Bemer is discussing is done by all big manufacturers to assist the process of hardware design. However, in addition to the storage of information provided voluntarily by the programmer, one should take advantage in such a system of the change to accumulate additional information without bothering the programmer.

Harr: One has to be very careful in designing such a system to ensure that one does not end up slowing down the progress of software production, and/or adding significantly to the programmer's burden by increasing the amount of information that he has to provide.

Ross: If you don't know what you're doing in producing software, then automating the system can be dangerous. However, I am in principle in favour of such program production tools.

David: We have had some experience of using an on-line system for program development, in fact to aid in the production of a large military system. The on-line system, called TSS/635, was developed specifically for this task, and provided means of accessing a large data base, and facilities for on-line program development. It worked reasonably well, but as the project has evolved, people have used the on-line system less and less, and are now starting to switch to a batch system running on the machine for which the military system is being developed. There could be many reasons for this – unreliability of the on-line system was certainly one. However, I believe that another was that people preferred to spend their money developing software which would be useful for development, for the computer for which they were developing the military system.

Cress and Graham: (from "Production of software in the university environment") The danger of writing a special piece of software to expedite production is that we have a project within a project. Often the inner project is more interesting and it is certainly more volatile in design. Thus it is never really complete, as its effectiveness is not known until it is used. This makes it extremely difficult to make deadlines and stick to them.

5.3.2. Concepts

> *The above title has been chosen, perhaps somewhat arbitrarily, for a report on a discussion about the basic techniques or ways of thinking, that software engineers should be trained in.*
> *It is perhaps indicative of the present state of software production that this topic was one of the most difficult to report on.*

Ross: I would like to present some ideas of mine merely as a starting point for this discussion. The hope is that we will trade ideas on the actual techniques whereby we might work toward the evolution of a true software engineering discipline and technology. The three main features of my view of what software engineering and technology are all about are:
1. The underlying theory or philosophy, about what I call the "plex" concept.
2. How this translates into the ideas put forward by McIlroy on software components — for which I use the term "integrated package of routines".
3. How you systematically compose large constructs out of these smaller constructs — for which I use the term "automated software technology".

A "plex" has three parts: Data, Structure, and Algorithm (i.e. behaviour). You need all three aspects if you are going to have a complete model of something — it is not sufficient to just talk about data structures, though this is often what people do. The structure shows the inter-relationships of pieces of data, and the algorithm shows how this structured data is to be interpreted. (For example a data structure could stand for two different things if you didn't know how to interpret it.) The key thing about the plex concept is that you are trying to capture the totality of meaning, or understanding, of some problem of concern. We want to do this in some way that will map into different mechanical forms, not only on different hardware, but also using different software implementations. An "idealised plex" is one in which the mechanical representation has been thrown away. This is done by degenerating the data and structure aspects of a plex — not throwing them away — but, putting the entire discussion into the algorithm domain. Thus for example one avoids talking about data, by using *read* and *store* procedures which do whatever handling of the data is necessary. Such a pair of procedures is called an "idealised component", which represents a data item (and the "box" which contains it) that is accessed by the procedures. An "idealised element" is composed of idealised components glued together, so that they can't be taken apart, and is represented by a *create-destroy* procedure pair. Finally an "idealised plex" is a set of "idealised elements" which have been hooked together into a whole structure, with many inter-relationships. So one needs further procedures for adding elements to the plex (a *growth* function) and what we call a *"mouse"* function, which is one which can be used to trace relationships, and to apply a procedure to the elements visited during the tracing. These idealised facilities allow me to talk abstractly about any object I wish to model. To actually use these ideas one needs mechanizations of the facilities. For example, a read-store procedure pair could be handled as subroutine calls, or could be compiled, if the compiler had been given declarations of the data structures being used.

van der Poel: You are using, without real definition, many terms which I just don't understand.

Perlis: The entire description could be phrased entirely in LISP, in which the "plex" is a "function", the "data" is a "function", the "structure" is a "function", and the "algorithm" is another "function". A "component" is another pair of functions, which operates on complexes of list structures which are built up out of primitives. My interpretation is that when Ross uses terms like "ideal" and "model" and so forth, he is really talking about a specific mechanisation of the process of representing complex storages in terms of elementary ones, complex algorithms in terms of elementary ones, and so forth.
In van der Poel's paper there is a five or six line program describing an assembler. Now the question that we, as people interested in software engineering, should ask ourselves is this: Is that five-line program the guts of our business or is it not? I personally feel that it is not — it is just part of it. The issue of building an assembly program goes far beyond that line description. The description is an essential beginning, and is in a certain sense no different from what Ross has talked about so far.

> Ross then went on to give a detailed description of a data structuring package built using his concepts illustrating techniques for selecting alternate mechanisations of ordered relationship in an automatic fashion.

Fraser: There is a practical problem here. It seems to me that in order to realise anything like this you have to do all your binding at run time. Is this true or have I missed a neat dodge somewhere in your AED system?

Ross: The neat dodge is some four to five more years of work on the compiler. Many things that now involve run-time action can be resolved beforehand with a more fully developed system.

Ross: Let me turn to software technology, and take the problems of banking as an example, In such a situation you would make a set of integrated packages, or as I call them "semantic packages" each covering a major area of your business, and in terms of which you could describe, albeit abstractly, the entire process of banking.
Each integrated package is a sublanguage — the question is how to process it in a systematic way.
My model of the communication process consists of:
1. Perform lexical processing of the input string (for example, recognising items from character strings)
2. Perform syntactic and semantic parsing of the input string
3. Build a model of the implications of the information transmitted by the input string, i.e. understand the information
4. Act on the information (for example, reply to the message).
One therefore makes an idealised plex for each of these four phases for each semantic package, and then provides a mechanisation of the plexes, interlocked to provide one cohesive and comprehensive language and system for banking problems.

Perlis: I wouldn't build a banking system this way. The model that you are using is too sequential. I would start with Simula and build a simulation model of an abstract "banking machine", simulate information flow on it, and gradually make it more detailed. I would choose Simula because it has facilities which enable me to construct and meter processes all at the same time.

Ross: Fine. But the only thing that is sequential is the communication process itself for each of the sublanguages. Simula would be just a different example to use instead of banking for my discussion. I think Simula's success stems largely from the fact that it already incorporates many of these ideas.

5.3.3. Performance Monitoring

The provision and the use of facilities for monitoring system performance is of importance in all stages of system manufacture. In fact both Section 4 (Design) and 6 (Service) also deal with the subject.

A concise description of performance monitoring in production was provided by Opler, and is reproduced here in its entirety.

Opler: (from "Measurement and analysis of software in production")
1. Who, When, Why?
   a. Guidance Measurement by Production Group, starting at the earliest existence of code in measurable form, for purposes of analyzing: 1) Conformity to design requirements; 2) conformity to internal conventions; 3) identifications of erroneous or deficient areas; 4) Identification of areas subject to optimizing by tuning. As separate modules are combined, measurements are repeated.
   b. Completion measurement by Production Group, immediately prior to delivery, for quality assurance of the final product.
   c. Formal measurement by control group to determine if quality of final product is acceptable.
2. What is measured?
   a. Performance: space, speed, throughput, turn around.
   b. Language: compliance with requirements, accuracy of object system.
   c. External Function: error isolation, configuration modularity, clear documentation, availability, installation ease, modification ease.
   d. Internals: serviceability, reliability (freedom from mistakes), conformity to standards.
3. How are measurements made?
   a. Gross (external) measurements: typical programs, mixes, streams; data files; special test programs for language conformity; for mathematical accuracy; for standards conformity.
   b. Fine (internal) measurements: by special hardware monitors; by special software packages; by built-in measurement schemes.
   c. By use of product operation: serviceability; configuration modularity; installation ease.

Opler: It is important to emphasize the necessity for providing sufficient resources during production of a software system to design and conduct performance measurements, and to feed the results back to those concerned, in both the design and the production groups. One warning is in order. It is fatally easy to concern oneself with only those quantities which are easy to measure, and to ignore other, possibly more important, quantities whose measurement is more difficult. Monitoring aids must be an integral part of the system, so that every attempt to use the system is potentially a source of useful data.

Kinslow: There is a whole class of what production management tends to think of as "auxiliary" functions, such as system generation, system start-up, system shut-down, and monitoring. If the budget gets tight, monitoring is the first to go, because of a lack of appreciation for its importance.

Fraser: We found it useful to monitor a system, feed the results into a simulator and then experiment with the simulator, as being much easier to fiddle with than the actual system.

> *Pinkerton provided a survey of the various techniques that have been used for monitoring systems. Because of its length this survey is reproduced in Section 9, rather than here.*
> *Finally, a description was given by Gillette of a method of automating both the testing and performance monitoring of a system.*

Gillette: (from "Aids in the production of maintainable software") System testing should be produced and maintained to exercise all parts of the system. The set should be open ended and maintenance utilities should be included. A result (i.e. output) from a system source text update should be a set of necessary control statements to enable a selective test of all modules modified and referenced entities. A control sequencer utility should exist which would selectively execute all programs to exercise specified modules. Test codes should exercise modules separately and in combination. A total system stability and performance test should be included in such a scheme. Driving the system from this source should be recoverable in event of an error so that a thorough test can be made in one pass through the test collection. Errors should be diagnosed and reported, tracing the chain of events which resulted in the error, and should attempt to isolate the causal factor to a module or referenced element. The test set should be maintained in source text language by the same facility discussed with reference to system source text. Clearly there is a need to be able to include the system module and change directories as a part of the test source environment and to be able to cross reference to these entries from within non-generative code in the source text of the test programs. Tests should be dated to permit exclusion of their usage when they become obsolete. As an output of a test validation run, each test should list the modules it has exercised, and as well, should list the interfaces and tables it has tested. It is important to document success, as well as failure.

6. SERVICE

6.1 INTRODUCTION

6.1.1. The Virtue of Realistic Goals

Much discussion centered on the conditions necessary for acceptable service to be obtained from a software system. The first point covered was the virtue of realistic design and production goals.

Opler: I am concerned about the current growth of systems, and what I expect is probably an exponential growth of errors. Should we have systems of this size and complexity? Is it the manufacturer's fault for producing them or the user's for demanding them? One shouldn't ask for large systems and then complain about their largeness.

Dijkstra: It is not clear that the people who manufacture software are to blame. I think manufacturers deserve better, more understanding users.

Llewelyn: Lots of time and money are lost in planning on what turns out to be false data provided by manufacturers. We need more realistic delivery estimates from manufacturers.

Randell: The users should demand contractual safeguards.

6.1.2. Initial System Release

The second point was concerned with the quality of initial releases of software systems.

Babcock: The initial release of a software system should *work well* (albeit with limited facilities) and must contain the basic system philosophies that ensure orderly growth.

Genuys: We need pre-release versions of systems, whether they work well or not, for training our staff.

Galler: Manufacturers should not deliver a system unless it is working well, although it need not be entirely free of bugs.

David: Define a subset of the system which is small enough to be manageable, then build on that system. This strategy requires that the system be designed in modules which can be realised, tested and modified independently, apart from conventions for intermodule communication. It also implies that the system can be a tool vital in its own development.

Kolence: Large systems must evolve, and cannot be produced all at one time. You must have an initial small core system that works really well.

Randell: The users are as much to blame for premature acceptance of systems as the manufacturers for premature release.

Samelson: The real problem is the user, since he needs software and takes it whether or not it is correct.

Glennie: Software manufacturers should desist from using customers as their means of testing systems.

6.1.3. Frequency of Releases

> *The subject of frequency of system releases, and its effect on the level of service that could be expected from a system gave rise to the following comments.*

Babcock: Fewer releases, containing major functional improvements (other than corrections) that *work well* are more desirable than frequent releases of versions containing only minor improvements.

Gillette: CDC recently undertook an extensive update of one of its software systems in order to increase its performance. Users were given the chance to wait for development to be complete or to receive incremental updates that would not have been fully integrated and tested. All users elected to receive monthly system updates. Our field analysts explained that they could cope more easily with small incremental changes.

Opler: The latest release of OS/360 was intended to introduce 16 changes (many complex), and to correct 1074 errors. The current policy is to have releases at 90 day intervals. This indicates a rate of over 11 corrections per day between versions. It is obviously better to batch improvements to a system together. On the other hand, because customers need errors to be corrected the release frequency cannot be too low. Once a year would be much too infrequent.

Hastings: Many of these 1000 errors are of course quite trivial, perhaps being just documentation errors.

d'Agapeyeff: (from "Reducing the cost of software") The growth of complexity in software has led, understandably enough, to many issues and versions of the same system. But no way has been found of making past issues sub-sets of new issues. This is causing great disturbance to users and is also causing incompatibilities (e.g. on machine A, operating system level X is unlikely to be compatible with level Y to either programmers or operators).

Babcock: One way to have a successful system is to *never* make a change in it. However, this is obviously impractical. Systems such as our Rush system never remain static, and are never 100 percent checked out. So system managers should go easy on installing new versions of on-line systems, and check them out in a dynamic environment.

Pinkerton: With less frequent releases there would be increased stability, and more opportunity for users to generate responsible feedback on system performance to the manufacturers.

Galler: OS/360 has had 16 releases in two and a half years. We should have frequent updates for corrections, but decrease the frequency of traumatic upheavals.

Gillette: (from "Comments on service group statements") [Babcock's use of the phrase "works well"] bothers me as it is largely qualitative. For an engineering group I think a metric description would be more palatable and more meaningful.

To be specific, below I have written a copy of one of the paragraphs which has been put into a Product Objectives document. We struggled a great deal to define measurable objectives in the document and this is an example. The numbers used to have relevance, historically, and that is all that need be said about them. Finally our objectives may not have been high enough in this particular area — we tried to push our luck while at the same time being realistic.

The total number of unique bugs reported for all releases in one year on ECS SCOPE will not be greater than the number given by the following formula:

Number of bugs $\leqslant 500 - 45/(I + 10)$

where I is the number of installations using ECS SCOPE. 85 percent of the reported PSRs (see Notes below) will be corrected within 30 days and 50 percent of these will be corrected within 15 days. All PSRs will be corrected within 60 days.

Notes: 1. A PSR is the reporting form which a customer uses to report a bug.

2. A bug is effectively equivalent to a PSR — it may be a mistake in the code or a misunderstnding on the part of the customer.

3. Correcting the bug may result in modified code or clarifying a definition with correction to the reference manual.

4. The limiting function is bounded and increases with the number of users.

6.1.4. Responsibility for Modified Systems

This discussion led to the subject of assigning responsibility for user-modified systems.

Babcock: In those areas that have not been affected by user modifications, software manufacturers should be responsible for all maintenance and improvements.

Paul: One cannot easily define the borderline between affected and unaffected parts.

Galler: I am concerned that manufacturers use this difficulty as an excuse for absolving themselves of any responsibility for the system after any change the user makes.

Naur: If you want to modify a system, you had better choose a manufacturer and a system that allow this. With most products the standard case is that a warranty is voided if the customer fools about with the product.

Babcock: Often there is no choice for such a system open to the user.

Bemer: This shows the need to improve the means of specifying program interfaces.

Berghuis: A paper in the Communications of the ACM in 1963 or 1964 gives the manufacturer's viewpoint. This paper, written by the ECMA, the Eurpoean Computer Manufacturer Association, states that no manufacturer will take responsibility for any user modifications.

6.2. REPLICATION, DISTRIBUTION AND MAINTENANCE

6.2.1. Replication

As discussed in Section 3.3, the replication of multiple copies of a software system is the phase of software manufacture which corresponds to the production phase in other areas of engineering. It is accomplished by simple copying operations, and constitutes only a minute fraction of the cost of software manufacture.

Randell: If software replication costs were commensurate with hardware raplication costs, there would be a great incentive for manufacturers to improve the quality of initial software releases.

The main contribution on the subject of software replication dealt with the problems associated with mass production of copies of software.

Enlart: (from "Program distribution and maintenance") We do not consider in this paper the sophisticated headache of generalized operating system testing. We assume that the development programmers did a good job and tested their product carefully by means of sample problems, selected potential users' cooperation, bench mark application, etc. ...

The development programmers will issue an information medium loaded with the programming system, together with its literature. The literature can be mass produced and stored to meet the forecasted requirements of the potential users. Unfortunately, mass production of information media is not feasible to date, for lack of standardization in machine configurations and input devices.

Another reason is the very low efficiency of the available DP material to mass produce information media. The performances of the fastest input-output devices available now are limited to technologial and physical considerations, and, in spite of their high efficiency in terms of data processing, they are definitely not mass-production tools.

The last point is the number of interfaces between program authors and users which results in the number of times a master should be duplicated to supply the Program Distribution Centers with their own master copies, enabling them to disseminate copies of the program.

Basically, every bit of information is vital, hence the requirement for the 100 percent checking of every copy. As performance checks cannot be resumed after every copy operation, it is necessary to provide the successive functions which should duplicate a program with tools and means of control, to achieve the highest ratio of reliability.

This quality control problem is worsened by the sensitivity of information media to a variety of mishandling, in or outside of the machine-room: there is no "acceptable percentage of variations" or "plus or minus acceptable tolerance" in software: a bit of information recorded on a tape is true information or false information.

If a bit is false, it will spoil the whole product, and if reported as a bug to the authors, it will cause bewilderment and useless attempts at a corrective solution. In any case, it will ruin confidence (if any) in relations between both parties.

. . . . .

In a normal data processing operation, a deficient card reader, for example, will sooner or later be discovered because it introduces inconsistencies in results.

The case is different in a program library: the deficient card reader may introduce an undetected error in hundreds of copies of a program, even if a control run to match the resulting tape with the card deck has been made.

The error will be discovered occasionally in a remote location and perhaps months later. The case is worsened if one of the faulty tapes becomes the master of a sublibrary.

. . . . .

Program distribution and maintenance requires quite a few skills in a great variety of specialized fields: programming and machine operation, file organization, wrapping and packing, shipping procedures, customs and postage regulations, reproducing and printing, together with cost evaluation and financial foresight.

Among the conditions required to smooth this thorny road, standardization (media) and formalization (documentation) are the keys to success.

Unfortunately, programmers are intellectually not prepared to recognize the problem.

Awareness of their responsibilities in the field of distribution should be a part of their basic educational training.

Software distribution is a challenge for the data processing community, and its response to it will result in either loss of energy or continuous growth.

Galler: One simple means of checking the correct functioning of the replication and distribution process would be "echo-checking". In other words, the group that produces the system that is handed to the Program Library for replication and distribution should itself be a customer of the library.

6.2.2. Distribution

Software distribution per se was only touched on briefly in the conference.

Kohler: (from "Maintenance and distribution of programs") Program distribution as a whole is a problem of organization only. In a well organized and efficiently working distribution center each request should be handled within 5 to 8 hours after it has been received. However, it is a recognized fact that a distribution center, besides receiving requests for programs, also has to deal with queries. In order to answer such enquiries properly the availability of qualified personnel must be guaranteed. Unfortunately documentation is not always perfect, even if there are the best of intentions. The user will appreciate it if he can always get his advice over the telephone.

Such service, however, can generally be rendered only by computer manufacturers, big software groups and perhaps some larger user groups.

As mentioned above, the distribution center is well advised to ask for the preparation of special forms or punched cards when clients wish to request programs, etc. In doing so it educates the user to make his request complete and, furthermore, creates the basis for automation in the distribution system.

When preparing order facilities for the user by way of special forms and prepunched cards, provision should also be made for a user's request on the method of delivery. Upon such delivery requests may depend whether a card-pack will arrive at its destination within hours of within days.

Nash: The delay between the release of a system and its arrival at a user's installation is a serious problem. Replication and shipping cause part of the delay, but the time taken to perform system integration is also a problem. We are shipping systems, not components, and the time to perform system integration depends on the number of interactions among components, which multiplies very fast as the number of components increases.

Randell: I wonder how the problems of software distribution are divided up among the three categories "initial release", "corrections to errors", and "extensions". I would suspect that the second category has the most, and that efforts to reduce the problems of program distribution should concentrate on this area.

Dijkstra: The dissemination of knowledge is of obvious value — the massive dissemination of error-loaded software is frightening.

6.2.3. Maintenance

The main contributions that were concerned directly with software maintenance were those of Gillette and Kohler.

Kohler: (from "Maintenance and distribution of programs") Maintenance and distribution are strongly interdependent: upon being written each program requires a certain amount of testing, the so-called field test. The field test is considered to be successful when the programs that are being tested have been allowed a reasonable number of fault-free machine runs and when it is thus indicated that they will effect the full spectrum of their intended applications. The duration of the field test depends upon quite a number of different factors, such as the amount of machine time allocated to a given program, the frequency of machine runs required, the complexity of the program, etc. Consequently the actual times for the duration of field tests should always be determined by the people actually responsible for the maintenance of a respective program; and great care should be taken to make sure than a given number of runs has been achieved during the test and that any faults recognized by the user have been properly recorded and reported to the interested parties. No one should hesitate to prolong the field test period if — during its course — it should become apparent that the number of existing program faults shows no, or only small, diminishing tendencies. On the other hand, it should not be expected that a complex program, after being given an appropriate field test, is completely free of errors. Owing to the complexity of certain programs, each user of electronic data processing equipment has at times to be prepared to deal with program failures, especially when handling more sophisticated applications.

Thus each maintenance depends upon the proper recording of programming errors by the user and upon the quality of such records. In those cases where the maintenance-center and the distribution-center constitute a single organisational unit, maintenance can operate with great effectiveness and, when distributing their programs to users, can influence all users as regards proper error reporting.

Gillette: (from "Aids in the production of maintainable software") The economics of software development are such that the cost of maintenance frequently exceeds that of the original development. Consider, for example, the standard software that many manufacturers provide and deliver with their hardware. This product can include a basic operating system, a machine language macro assembler, an Algol, Fortran, and Cobol compiler, a sort/merge package, a file management facility, and so on. In scope this represents something in the order of more than 250 thousand lines of generated code that must be released to customers whose configurations and requirements vary a good deal, encompassing the spectrum from batch oriented data processing shops, to hybrid time-critical, time sharing and scientific shops. Producing such systems currently requires about a two- to three-year effort involving perhaps as many as 50 personnel. Maintenance of such systems is an unending process which lasts for the life of the machine; as much perhaps as eight years.

. . . . .

Maintenance of a system is required in order to satisfy three basic problems. First, in an effort of the magnitude of that described there will be bugs in the system. These can originate from ambiguous specification and reference documentation, because of design error, or because of programmer and system checkout error. Second, design decisions and code generation cannot always result in "good" performance. In a basic operating system, for example, a code module may get executed on the average of once per 10 milliseconds while the system is operational; it is desirable to make the code as fast as possible. In the hurry to deliver an operable system it is seldom that code can be truly optimized; the emphasis is on correct execution rather than speed. Much effort is expended to improve system performance in order to remain competitive. Third, and finally, in a span of several years, new hardware is developed which must be supported and new customer needs develop which must be met. To support this a system must be extended to include capabilities beyond those that the original designer conceived. In summary, then, the maintenance process involves corrective code, improvement code, and extensi.e code.

Babcock: I am concerned about the division of responsibility for maintenance between user and manufacturer. As a user, I think it a manufacturer's responsibility to generate systems to fit a particular user's need, but I haven't been able to convince my account representative of that fact.

On the subject of pre-release checking, there is the question of how a manufacturer can ensure that a system he distributes will have been adequately checked for use in my environment. It seems to me that the only way to solve such problems is to have the manufacturer simulate my environment, or even use my environment directly, via communication lines.

Kolence: Users should expect to have to test software that is supplied to them, to ensure that it works in their environment. A large manufacturer cannot test out his software on all the environments in which it will operate. It is for this reason that manufacturers typically provide an on-site representative to help the user adapt a general system to his particular environment.

6.3. SYSTEM EVALUATION

The problem of system evaluation runs through all three areas of Design, Production and Service. This section is based on discussion of those aspects of the subject directly related to the system when in a user's environment.

6.3.1. Acceptance Testing

By far the most extensive discussion of the acceptance testing of software systems was that given by Llewelyn and Wickens in the paper "The Testing of Computer Software". For convenience this is reproduced in its entirety in Section 9, and just the conclusions are paraphrased below.

Llewelyn and Wickens: We are attempting to design a method by which a large organization could test the software supplied by computer manufacturers to its installations. In particular we wish to ensure that new installations can rapidly take on the work for which they were purchased by ensuring that their planning can be based on the best available information with regard to what software exists, and how well it performs. The present situation is that a customer has to purchase his software almost as an act of faith in the supplier — this surely cannot be allowed to continue.

Kolence: The manufacturers are always under pressure from the users to give them something that works even if it is not complete. The classic trade-off in software production is between features and schedule — not between working well and not working well. It is important therefore for users to receive an accurate set of specifications, ahead of time, of what is currently being produced, rather than of what is ultimately intended (as was the case, I believe, with published specifications for OS/360).

Opler: (from "Acceptance testing of large programming systems") The proper testing of large programming systems is virtually impossible; but with sufficient resources, enough testing can be performed to allow a good evaluation to be made. Most current systems operate under a wide variety of hardware configurations and with highly varied software component selection. A test plan must be developed considering all elements of the written specification (hardware, programming language, system facilities, documentation, performance, reliability, etc.) and describing steps to validate compliance of the final programming system. For large systems, enormous resources of computing equipment which can configure all available components are required. Many months of computer testing are often required. A significant, sometimes neglected, area of testing is in checking external documentation (user and operator manuals) for accuracy and clarity and checking internal documentation (flow charts and listings) against the final distributed program.

Dijkstra: Testing is a very inefficient way of convincing oneself of the correctness of a program.

Llewelyn: Testing is one of the foundations of all scientific enterprise. In fact it would be good to have independent tests of system function and performance published.

Galler: When the hardware doesn't work, the user doesn't pay — why should he have to pay for non-working software?

Babcock: We need software meters analogous to the present hardware meters, so that our rental costs can be adjusted to allow for time lost through software errors as well as hardware errors.

Kolence: If the users expect a supplier's software to work exactly as and when predicted, they should in all fairness apply the same standards to the software that they develop themselves.

6.3.2. Performance Monitoring

The major discussions on performance monitoring are reported in the sections of this report dealing with Design and with Production. The comments given below are of most immediate relevance to the question of monitoring the performance of an installed system.

Gillette: We have used performance monitoring principally as a maintenance tool to find bottlenecks and deficiencies.

Perlis: Delivered systems should have facilities for accumulating files or run time performance information, which could be shipped back to the manufacturer for analysis, as well as being of value to the user installation. I do not know of anywhere this is being done as a standard operating procedure.

Kolence: We have experience of performance monitoring in a user environment. In such environments extra care must be taken to avoid interference with the running of the system, and in overloading the system. Information can be monitored in relation to the overall system performance or to particular user programs. Typical data that we produce concern core storage usage and I/O channel and device activity. Information on disk cylinder usage can be very useful in learning how to reorganise data on the disk for improved transfer rates. We have found that almost all programs can be substantially improved (between 10 and 20 percent, say), without design changes in one or two man-days.

Smith: Performance monitoring when first applied can certainly lead to spectacular improvements. However, this can lead one onto the treadmill of incremental improvements to a system which is basically unsound.

Gries: Optional performance monitors should be built into compilers, so as to be available to users.

Galler: Performance monitors should be part of the system, and not in individual compilers.

6.4. FEEDBACK TO MANUFACTURERS FROM USERS

Comments relevant to this topic occurred in entirely separate contexts,
and included attempts to classify the various types of information that a user
would want to feedback to a manufacturer and the possible means of so doing.
See also Section 4.2.2.

Haller: There is feedback of different entities, on different paths, leading to three separate control loops with different time-lag:
   1. On the correctness, or otherwise, of a system. This would go to the maintenance group; time to get a reply might be up to a week.
   2. On system performance, to the production group, who might be expected to reply within, say, a month.
   3. Requests for extra facilities would go to the design group and, if accepted, a year might be the expected delay before an appropriately modified system was released.

Hastings: A user needs a fast means of obtaining corrections to program bugs. We have used a terminal-oriented on-line system for our field engineers to obtain up-to-date information from the maintenance group. Some such system as this is the only substitute for the common means of unofficial feedback, possible when one knows the right person.

Babcock: (from "Variations on software available to the user") Even with a company such as IBM — which incidentally, I am convinced, is the very best — the best was certainly none too good.
                                     . . . . .
   Time to me was money. Time-sharing is a revenue of the moment. once lost, it will not, nor cannot be captured. It took us approximately six months to learn the then current IBM service was archaic, and something must be done. We started at the bottom but found we had to work all the way to the top to be heard. There I learned there was only one concept that was really meaningful to IBM: BACK YOUR TRUCK UP.
   The fact of the matter was, IBM was in a new area too, which may be considered a plus factor in our case because, being innovators of the highest order themselves, they recognized that here was a new service problem. There were multitudes of users out of service, rather than just one.

Buxton: The best method of feedback about unsatisfactory systems is *money.* If software had a clear monetary value a user could express his belief that the software was bad in clear monetary terms by rejecting it.

Galler: The typical user is not in a position to reject a major system produced by a large manufacturer.

6.5. DOCUMENTATION

*There was much discussion of Design and Production aspects of documen-
tation, but very little from the user's point of view. The one working paper by
Selig was concerned directly with this area. This paper is quoted below, and is
the source of the set of document standards that are reprinted in section 9.
That section also contains the paper by Llewelyn and Wickens, which touches
on the reviewing of system documentation as part of acceptance testing.*

Selig: (from "Document for service and users") With the rapid proliferation of computer
languages, subroutines and programs, and the tremendous effort they represent, meticu-
lous documentation is becoming essential, not just to save money but to prevent chaos.

. . . . .

Reference manuals for the user, the operator and the programmer can be based on
the external and internal specifications [of the system] . Such documentation... must be
reader oriented and not subject oriented and good manuals are difficult to write. One
common mistake is that authors try to reach too many different groups: managers, experienced technologists and beginners. It is recommended to develop different educational
documentation with clearly defined prerequisites for the prospective readers.

Letellier: (from "The adequate testing and design of software packages") Manuals must
be of two types: a general introduction to the solution of the problem by means of the
package and a technical manual giving the exact available facilities and operation rules;
these should be as attractive as possible.

Gillette: The maintenance of documentation should be automated.

Selig: (from "Documentation for service and users") It is appropriate to mention techniques where the computer itself is producing the required documentation with considerable sophistication. Especially flow-charting and block-diagramming are readily
available. Examples of such programs are: Flow-chart plotting routine (CalComp), Auto-
flow (Applied Data Research), Com Chart (Compress), etc. A more efficient method of
automated program documentation became available in the conversational mode of computer usage. A few software systems are not self-documented, and detailed information
and instructions can be displayed at the operator's request. The design of such programs
is very similar to self-teaching manuals and this technique has become particularly well
accepted in the area of computer graphics.

Gries: The maintenance and distribution of the OS/360 documentation is automated
through the use of a text-editing system. I don't think the maintenance of this documentation would be possible without it.

6.6. REPROGRAMMING

*The only material on the subject of reprogramming was the short working
paper prepared during the conference by Babcock, which is reprinted below in
its entirety. There was no direct discussion on the subject of the users' problems
in reprogramming for changed hardware or operating systems, but the sections
of the Design area concerned with modularity and interfaces are of relevance.*

Babcock: (from "Reprogramming") We see this problem divided into three areas of
discussion

1. Conversion
2. Re-writing of systems and programs
3. Future trends

Most users have faced the conversion problems before. The cost is usually a function of the severity of the conversion, that is, from one machine to another (usually highest cost), from one operating system to another and from one language to another. The most *effective* means *today* (but not the most desired) is by rise of hardware techniques, that is, emulation.

New systems usually exhibit features that are desirable and that handle a broader range of application in a more efficient manner. To utilize these new tools, re-writing is sometimes dictated. This is perhaps the most costly of the three areas but is mandatory in many areas. We see the need for higher levels of languages, such as compiler languages of compilers, in order to make this decision less critical.

In the future, we see the need for both hardware and software facilities specially designed for the overall problem of transporting. The stress will be as great on hardware design as on software engineering because the key to portability can be exhibited in the *near* future whereas software engineering has not yet produced nor announced a true language of languages for hardware independence. Hardware portability functions can be economic in present day "Assembler-oriented" applications, but we hope for integrated hardware/software facilities to reduce substantially the costs of the reprogramming problem.

7. SPECIAL TOPICS

7.1. SOFTWARE: THE STATE OF THE ART

7.1.1. Introduction

Quite early in the conference statements of concern were made by several members about the tendency for there to be a gap, sometimes a rather large gap, between what was hoped for from a complex software system, and what was typically achieved. This topic was therefore discussed both at a special session and during the final plenary session of the conference. The essence of these discussions is given below, for the large part, as usual, in the form of more-or-less verbatim quotations.

One statement made by Buxton, given in reply to the worries of several members that the debate was unbalanced because too much attention was being paid to past and possible future software failures, is worth bringing out of context as an introduction for the reader.

Buxton: In a conference of this kind, when those present are technically competent, one has a tendency to speed up the communication by failing to state the obvious. Of course 99 percent of computers work tolerably satisfactorily; that is the obvious. There are thousands of respectable Fortran-oriented installations using many different machines and lots of good data processing applications running quite steadily; we all know that! The matter that concerns us is the sensitive edge, which is socially desperately significant.

7.1.2. Problem Areas

There was a considerable amount of debate on what some members chose to call the "software crisis" or the "software gap". As will be seen from the quotations below, the conference members had widely differing views on the seriousness, or otherwise, of the situation, and on the extent of the problem areas.

David and Fraser: (from their "Position paper") There is a widening gap between ambitions and achievements in software engineering. This gap appears in several dimensions: between promises to users and performance achieved by software, between what seems to be ultimately possible and what is achieveable now and between estimates of software costs and expenditures. The gap is arising at a time when the consequences of software failure in all its aspects are becoming increasingly serious. Particularly alarming is the seemingly unavoidable fallibility of large software, since a malfunction in an advanced hardware-software system can be a matter of life and death, not only for individuals, but also for vehicles carrying hundreds of people and ultimately for nations as well.

Hastings: I am very disturbed that an aura of gloom has fallen over this assembly. I work in an environment of many large installations using OS/360. These are complex systems, being used for many very sophisticated applications. People are doing what they need to do, at a much lower cost than ever before; and they seem to be reasonably satisfied. Perhaps their systems do not meet everybody's need, they don't meet the time sharing people's demands for example, but I don't think software engineering should be confused with time sharing system engineering. Areas like traffic control, hospital patient monitoring, etc., are very explosive, but are very distinct from general purpose computing.

Gillette: We are in many ways in an analogous position to the aircraft industry, which also has problems producing systems on schedule and to specification. We perhaps have more examples of bad large systems than good, but we are a young industry and are learning how to do better.

Randell: There are of course many good systems, but are any of these good enough to have human life tied on-line to them, in the sense that if they fail for more than a few seconds, there is a fair chance of one or more people being killed?

Graham: I do not believe that the problems are related solely to on-line systems. It is my understanding that an uncritical belief in the validity of computer-produced results (from a batch-processing computer) was at least a contributory cause of a faulty aircraft design that lead to several serious air crashes.

Perlis: Many of us would agree that Multics and TSS/360 have taken a lot longer to develop than we would have wished, and that OS/360 is disappointing. However, perhaps we are exaggerating the importance of these facts. Is bad software that important to society? Are we too worried that society will lose its confidence in us?

Randell: Most of my concern stems from a perhaps over-pessimistic view of what might happen directly as a result of failure in an automated air traffic control system, for example. I am worried that our abilities as software designers and producers have been oversold.

Opler: As someone who flies in airplanes and banks in a bank I'm concerned personally about the possibility of a calamity, but I'm more concerned about the effects of software fiascos on the overall health of the industry.

Kolence: I do not like the use of the word "crisis". It's a very emotional word. The basic problem is that certain classes of systems are placing demands on us which are beyond our capabilities and our theories and methods of design and production at this time. There are many areas where there is no such thing as a crisis — sort routines, payroll applications, for example. It is large systems that are encountering great difficulties. We should not expect the production of such systems to be easy.

Ross: It makes no difference if my legs, arms, brain and digestive tract are in fine working condition if I am at the moment suffering from a heart attack. I am still very much in a crisis.

Fraser: We are making great progress, but nevertheless the demands in the industry as a whole seem to be going ahead a good deal faster than our progress. We must admit this, even though such an admission is difficult.

Dijkstra: The general admission of the existence of the software failure in this group of responsible people is the most refreshing experience I have had in a number of years, because the admission of shortcomings is the primary condition for improvement.

7.1.3. The Underlying Causes

> *Several basic causes for what many believed were serious problem areas were suggested.*

Kinslow: In my view both OS/360 and TSS/360 were straight-through, start-to-finish, no-test-development, *revolutions.* I have never seen an engineer build a bridge of unprecedented span, with brand new materials, for a kind of traffic never seen before — but that's exactly what has happened on OS/360 and TSS/360. At the time TSS/360 was committed for delivery within eighteen months it was drawn from two things:
1. Some hardware proposed, but not yet operational, at M.I.T.
2. Some hardware, not quite operational, at the IBM Research Center.

Buxton: A possibly fairly fundamental cause of the gap between the specifications of a large software system and what one gets in practice is a deep confusion between producing a software system for research and producing one for practical use. Instead of trying to write a system which is just like last year's, only better implemented, one invariably tries to write an entirely new and more sophisticated system. Therefore you are in fact continually embarking on research, yet your salesmen disguise this to the customer as being just a production job.

David and Fraser: (from their "Position paper") The causes of this "software gap" are many, but a basic one lies in the unfortunate telescoping of research, development and production of an operational version within a single project effort. This practice leads to slipped schedules, extensive rewriting, much lost effort, large numbers of bugs, and an inflexible and unwieldy product. It is unlikely that such a product can ever be brought to a satisfactory state of reliability or that it can be maintained and modified. Though this mixing of research, development, and production is a root cause of the "software gap", there are many other contributory factors, from the lack of management talents to the employment of unqualified programmers and sheer incompetence in software design.

McClure: (from "Projection versus performance in software production") It seems almost automatic that software is never produced on time, never meets specification, and always exceeds its estimated cost. This conference is in fact predicated on this alarming situation. However, on closer inspection the situation does not appear quite so alarming, nor unexplainable, nor incorrigible. The situation is quite analogous to that pertaining in any research and development shop in any line of business whatsoever. The ability to estimate time and cost of production comes only with product maturity and stability, with the directly applicable experience of the people involved and with a business-like approach to project control. The problem with software stems specifically from the refusal of industry to re-engineer last year's model, from the inability of industry to allow personnel to accumulate applicable experience, and from emotional management.

. . . . .

One recent situation is worthy of note. The users of the IBM 7090 used a system called the Fortran Monitor System (FMS) quite satisfactorily for a number of years. Although its facilities were limited, it generally performed as it was supposed to. Very recently, the SDS Sigma 7 was delivered to the accompaniment of howls of anguish because it initially came equipped with only a basic operating system substantially superior to the old FMS. The root problem was that the manufacturer had promised far more and could not deliver on his promises. Did this failure lie in the inability of the software people to produce or in the ability of the sales office to over-promise?

Gill: (from his "Position paper") Software is as vital as hardware, and in many cases much more complex, but it is much less well understood. It is a new branch of engineering, in which research, development and production are not clearly distinguished, and its vital role is often overlooked. There have been many notable successes, but recent advances in hardware, together with economic pressures to meet urgent demands, have sometimes resulted in this young and immature technology of software being stretched beyond its present limit.

Kolence: (from "On the interaction between software design techniques and software management problems") Programming management will continue to deserve its current poor reputation for cost and schedule effectiveness until such time as a more complete understanding of the program design process is achieved.

Hastings: Some of the problems are caused by users who like to buy "futures" in software systems, and then ignore the problems inherent in this.

Buxton: There are extremely strong economic pressures on manufacturers, both from users and from other manufacturers. Some of these pressures, which are a major contributory cause of our problems, are quite understandable. For example, the rate of increase of air traffic in Europe is such that there is a pressing need for an automated system of control.

7.1.4. Possible Solutions

There were several comments on possible partial solutions, and on the difficulty of finding a simple overall solution to the problems of producing large systems.

Opler: Either of the following two courses of action would be preferable to the present method of announcing a system:
   1. Do all development without revealing it, and do not announce the product until it is working, and working well.
   2. Announce what you are trying to do at the start of the development, specify which areas are particularly uncertain, and promise first delivery for four or five years hence.

Buxton: As long as one has good reason to believe that the research content of a system is low, one can avoid either of these extremes.

Kinslow: Personally, after 18 years in the business I would like just once, just once, to be able to do the same thing again. Just once to try an evolutionary step instead of a confounded revolutionary one.

David and Fraser: (from their "Position paper") The "software gap" may not be immutable, but closing it will require metamorphosis in the practice of software production and its handmaiden, software design.

Gill: (from his "Position paper") We can see no swift and sure way to improve the technology, and would view any claims to achieve this with extreme caution. We believe that the only way ahead lies through the steady development of the best existing techniques.

Ross: My main worry is in fact that somebody in a position of power will recognize this crisis — it is a crisis right now, and has been for some years, and it's good that we are getting around to recognising the fact — and believe someone who claims to have a breakthrough, an easy solution. The problem will take a lot of hard work to solve. There is no worse word than "breakthrough" in discussing possible solutions.

Perlis: There are many good, albeit somewhat limited systems in the field now. I believe the best hope for a solution to our problems is evolution from these systems. Solutions are not likely to come out of designing a new SABRE system from scratch; that system should have been a warning to us five year ago.

7.1.5. Summary

Rather than attempt a direct summary of the set of sometimes conflicting points of view given above, it is perhaps better to finish with just one last quotation.

Gill: (from his "Position paper") It is of the utmost importance that all those responsible for large projects involving computers should take care to avoid making demands on software that go far beyond the present state of the technology, unless the very considerable risks involved can be tolerated.

7.2. EDUCATION

Most of the remarks quoted below were made during a special discussion devoted to software engineering education.

Perlis: It is a fact that there are software engineers around today who are quite competent. There are systems in many places which are quite stable and which provide magnificent service. It is also the case that there are large numbers of efforts, containing large numbers of programs and programmers, which have no software engineers on them, that is that people function as though they did not know how to build software. I have a number of questions:

1. Is it possible to have software engineers in the numbers in which we need them, without formal software engineering education?
2. Is software engineering the same as Computer Science?
3. Is software engineering best provided by baccalaureate programs in universities? Or by adult education courses? Or by two year courses following the standard grade school education?
4. Do the people educated in these programs have a growing and future role in our society?
5. Will they be useful enough in a firm or government or university, and is their value such that they can distribute their talents in other activities, or must they always remain programmers?
6. What curriculum do we have in mind for software engineers, regardless of what level we choose to educate them?
7. Is software engineering really different from what we now call systems engineering?

We should answer these questions before we start giving recommendations, e.g., in the US to the National Science Foundation, that large sums be spend on such education programs.

David. May I add another question:

8. What does software engineering and computing engineering have in common with engineering education as it is defined in the United States today, or in Western Europe?

It does seem that computing engineering and software engineering, as they exist, are outside of the classical engineering education area.

Perlis: There is in the United States a committee called COSINE, Computer Science in Engineering Education. Their view of education of engineers in computers is primarily the view of users of computers, but not that there should be a branch of engineering having as its goal the training of a new class ef engineers.

David: However, there is nothing in what they have said that would preclude a branch of engineering education concerned particularly with computing as such. We should ask ourselves seriously whether that would not be a good thing. Certainly Richard Hamming has stated that the essence of computing today is an engineering viewpoint. It certainly is not mathematics in the classical sense. In order to find colleagues who have a philosophy which may contribute to our own enterprises, engineering is a much more fruitful area than would be one of the sciences or mathematics, at least in my opinion. Incidentally I think that a lot of engineering education in the United States is stuck in the mud.

Software engineering and computing engineering have an extremely important and nice aspect to them, namely that people want to work on things that meet other people's needs. They are not interested in working on abstractions entirely, they want to have an impact on the world. This is the real strength of computing today, and it is the essence of engineering.

Ross: I agree very strongly that our field is in the engineering domain, for the reason that our main purpose is to do something for somebody. To Perlis: my answers to your questions are: no; no, BA; yes; yes; question mark; yes.

Randell: I am worried about the term "software engineering". I would prefer a name indicating a wider scope, for instance "data systems engineering".

Dijkstra: We, in the Netherlands, have the title Mathematical Engineer. Software engineering seems to be the activity for the Mathematical Engineer par excellence. This seems to fit perfectly. On the one hand, we have all the aspects of an engineering activity, in that you are making something and want to see that it really works. On the other hand, our basic tools are mathematical in nature.

I want to add another question or remark to your list. You are right in saying that lots of systems really work, these are our glimmer of hope. But there is a profound difference between observing that apparently some people are able to do something, and being able to teach that ability.

Wodon: There are many places in Europe where there is no education either in hardware or in software. This conference should drive home the point that this is ridiculous.

Hume: In University of Toronto we have a graduate department of Computer Science. We also have some bachelor degrees in Computer Science, one of which is the engineering stream in a course called Engineering Science, presumably something like mathematical engineering. In this stream there is the opportunity to choose graduate work, even in the department of electrical engineering, which has set itself up as a specialist in software. The people in this department have written compilers themselves. What really worries me about software engineering is, do universities have to engage in large software projects in order to remain experts in the field of software engineering? Do they have to hire people who have had such experience with large projects or do they have to have their professors go out and as consultants experience large software engineering projects? Then, when they come to exercise the students, do they have to have laboratories of some considerable consequence in software engineering exercises? Otherwise, who is to formulate principles of software engineering that can be used to train software engineers?

Dijkstra: To the question of how one can get experience when working in a university I have two answers: (1) If you undertake something at a university it has to be one of your main concerns to organize your activity in such a way that you get exactly the experience you need. This again must be the main concern in the choice of projects. (2) We have a Dutch proverb: "One learns from experience," suggesting that it happens automatically. Well, this is a lie. Otherwise everyone would be very, very wise. Consequently in a university with limited resources, from the experience one has got one should try, consciously, to learn as much as possible.

David: The problem of how the software engineers will get their practice is precisely the same as in other fields of engineering, and is insoluble. This is recognized in industry, where one makes sure that the young engineers coming in will get the proper kind of experience in time. Really it seems that the problem is less serious in software engineering than in other fields.

Berghuis: We need students better trained in standards, standards of communication, of documentation, of set-up, and of use of software.

Fraser: I was impressed by Douglas Ross's session [section 5.3.2] and I am convinced that there is a future in software science or technology. Nevertheless, I am convinced that much of the game in which we are involved is one of making the best of the world around us, understanding what the world wants and matching what science can offer. This, to my mind, is truly engineering. What worries me about the courses I have been associated with, is that they have been courses in mathematics, rather than courses in engineering. What is lacking is an awareness of the requirements of the world. One indication of this is the complaint that the graduates know nothing about standards and discipline.

McIlroy: With Fraser I am concerned about the connection between software engineering and the real world. There *is* a difference between writing programs and designing bridges. A program may be written with the sole purpose to help write better programs, and many of us here have spent our life writing programs from this pure software attitude. More than any other engineering field, software engineering in universities must *consciously* strive to give its students contact beyond its boundaries.

Galler: I would like to include under education the continuing education of professional people in the field, stressing an awareness of what others have done. I am appalled at the lack of attempts to educate people in what others are doing that we see throughout this industry.

Perlis: Most of the Computer Science programs in the United States, at least at the graduate level, are producing faculty for other Computer Science departments. This is appropriate, because we must first staff these departments. But it is also the case that almost all Computer Science departments are turning out PhD's who do not do computer software engineering under any stretch of that term's meaning. You have to look hard to find anything that is dedicated to utility as a goal. Under no stretch of the imagination can one say that Computer Science, at least in the United States, is fostering software engineering. In the United States National Academy of Sciences Research Board one education committee being formed is precisely to study software engineering as a possible engineering education activity. NATO would probably not be making a mistake in holding another conference within the near future concerning software engineering education.

7.3. SOFTWARE PRICING

7.3.1. Introduction

A special session on the issue of software pricing was arranged in response to the generally expressed feeling of the importance of this topic in relation to the whole future of software engineering. During the session it became clear that one of the major causes of divergent views on whether software should be priced separately from hardware was the fact that people had differing aims, and also differing estimates of the possible effects of separate pricing. The session is reported below by summarising the arguments put forward by various people for and against separate pricing, and about the desirability of preventing hardware manufacturers from providing software.

The discussion lasted over three hours, ending after midnight, yet was well-attended throughout. At the end of the discussion the opinion of those present was tested. It was clear that a large majority were personally in favour of separate pricing of software.

7.3.2. Arguments in Favour of Separate Pricing

1. Software is of obvious importance and yet is treated as though it were of no financial value. If software had a value defined in terms of money, users could express their opinion of the worth of a system by deciding to accept or reject it at a given price.

2. Systems organisations, which buy hardware, and either buy or produce software in order to sell complete systems, would flourish.

3. We are presently in a transition stage – when it ends, by far the largest proportion of people influenced by or using computers will be application oriented. Application software will become independent, in a sound practical way, of the underlying hardware and operating systems, and will be separately priced. However, the knowledge built into application programs will have to be protected by some means such as patenting.

4. From the viewpoint of the hardware manufacturer software is currently a sales aid. Most manufacturers are really in the business of selling computer time, not computers, and hence have no primary interest in making its computers run faster than the minimum speed required to sell them.

5. What the user needs is better software – he does not care too much where it comes from. The increased competition ensuing from separate pricing would cause an increase in quality of software produced by hardware manufacturers as well as increasing the number of sources of software available to the user.

6. Until software is separately priced it is difficult for the software talents of the smaller hardware manufacturers, the software houses and the universities to be effectively utilised. It is these sources and not IBM which have produced the majority of good systems and languages, such as BASIC, JOSS, SNOBOL, LISP, MTS.

7. Separate pricing would benefit hardware manufacturers, and particularly IBM, in controlling the production of software, and enabling cost/performance

*figures to be calculated, by making normal cost accounting practices imme-
diately applicable.*

*8. Even if hardware prices decrease only slightly as a result of separate
pricing, this is a small gain to the user and anyway is not the main point at issue,
which is the improved quality and service that would result.*

*9. Manufacturers will have a considerable lead over other software pro-
ducers in designing software for new machines prior to their announcement;
but this is unimportant. Most computers have two or three different software
systems associated with them during their lifetime, and not just the one that
the manufacturer devised before announcing the hardware. Furthermore, the
lead time is not always used — IBM had barely started to plan OS/360 at the
time System 360 was announced.*

7.3.3. Arguments Against Separate Pricing

*1. There will not be enough decrease in hardware prices to have any notice-
able financial effect.*

*2. Users are worried about the service they get from the total system. Se-
parate pricing would widen the gap between hardware and software design.*

*3. Purchase of software from multiple vendors will create a tower of Babel.
At the time of the IBM 704, even two competing assemblers caused much dissen-
sion.*

*4. Separate pricing would enable the software produced by manufacturers
to find its true price in a free economy, It would very likely be priced at a level
such that the total system price would be significantly increased, despite the
decrease in hardware prices.*

*5. Hardware manufacturers have such an advantage in the knowledge of
future systems and devices, and in the availability of hardware prototypes, that
independent software producers could not compete.*

*6. The lack of separate pricing of software has not prevented the growth of
independent service companies such as UCC.*

*7. Separate pricing may bring IBM, which currently owns the largest soft-
ware house in the world (namely their Federal Systems Division) in more direct
competition with the independent software houses. Thus, contrary to prevalent
opinion, the independents may have more to lose than to gain by separate
pricing.*

*8. Some people undoubtedly argue in favour of separate pricing because of
their worries about the concentration of power in the hands of a single manufacturer. However, separate pricing may well be of most benefit to IBM.*

*9. Software belongs to the world of ideas, like music and mathematics, and
should be treated accordingly.*

7.3.4. Splitting Software and Hardware Production

7.3.4.1. The Argument in Favour

*A user's dependence on his computing system is such that he should not
have to rely on a single manufacturer for all aspects of it. The dangers inherent
in an organisation with sufficient capital resources producing comprehensive
software for any industry, educational activity, research organisation or government agency are considerable and far outweigh, for instance, those of a national
or international data bank. A hardware manufacturer who also produces the
software on which business and industry depend has the reins to almost un-
limited power. Preventing hardware manufacturers from producing any software*

for sale or gift would be a great encouragement to competition essential in an area which is so broad that it knows no boundaries at all.

7.3 4 2. The Argument Against

The above argument is persuasive in only a superficial way. It is the "there oughta be a law" type of reaction to a worrying situation. The computing industry is still embryonic, and a law such as this would cause an inflexibility that we would later regret. We should build on strength and not on weakness — when we begin to fear competence, if it happens to be correlated with bigness, we are trying to build on weakness and not on strength.

8. INVITED ADDRESSES

8.1. KEYNOTE SPEECH, BY A. J. PERLIS

Why has this meeting been scheduled?

Why have we agreed to participate?

I believe it is because we recognize that a practical problem of considerable difficulty and importance has arisen: The successful design, production and maintenance of useful software systems. The importance is obvious and the more so since we see only greater growth in demands and requirements in the future. The consequences of poor performance, poor design, instability and mismatching of promise and performance are not going to be limited to the computing fraternity, or even their nearest neighbors, but will affect considerable sections of our society whose ability to forgive is inversely proportional to their ignorance of the difficulties we face. The source of difficulty is distributed through the whole problem, easy to identify, and yet its cure is hard to pinpoint so that systematic improvement can be gotten.

Our problem has arisen from a change of scale which we do not yet know how to reduce to alphabetic proportions. Furthermore we must assume that additional magnification of goal will take place without necessarily being preceded by the emergence of a satisfactory theory or an organized production of tools that will permit work and costs to fall on growth curves which lie significantly below those which now exist. For example, we can see coming the need for systems which permit cooperation, e.g., between engineering and management information. Not only must we know how to build special purpose systems but how to combine them into larger ones.

We work with software knowing that the design of a software system always seems to make some complex functions available with ease and others, seemingly little different, available only in a cock-eyed way. Such shortcomings in design are probably inevitable even in the very best systems and are simply consequences of the inevitable disparity between the degree of connectivity of human thought processes and those of a programmed system. It is also true that every system creates, through the very pattern of its usage, a set of anticipated bottlenecks. To avoid these bottlenecks users of systems learn to accommodate. Every software system thus imposes an etiquette on users, as every system which is created is itself a recognition of an existing etiquette.

Software is intimately tied to language even though it obviously involves more. Computer languages are processed by software and language is used to command the processing. This causes a problem and suggests a cure. The problem arises out of the relative ease with which out of our involvement with language we propose innovation. The cure is that the same ease of innovation can be focused on improvements which will help in the creation of systems. Programming tools are created—or innovated—to harness the power of an already existing hardware system. The specialization of these tools is of major importance in making the computer available to a wide range of genius for application to a wide range of purpose. A major function of these tools is the utilization of equivalences, i.e., a program which is easily written is shown equivalent to one which is easily executed by the computer. Another major function of the tools is the management of data with their appropriate operations and language inventions. Here the essential innovations are those which force sequencing to be handled implicitly and selectively by explicit command, e.g., as in the use of patterns, keys, generators, etc. The establishment of equivalences and the management of data are often accomplished by the invention of virtual computers which themselves are tools existing only as expressions in language.

To my mind the natural way to explore and manage the software problem is through the design of virtual machines—and all that the concept of machines implies—the establishment of relevant states, their transformations, the design of communication channels, the nature of and magnitude of storages, the natural sets of operations, the I/O problem, etc. We have before us many examples which have, in more restricted areas of programming, worked amazingly well. The symbol manipulating languages—IPL and LISP to name two—have been so organized that the problems coded in them have yielded codes organized as complexes of machines, each one of which is much like those from which it was constructed. Indeed certain operations in the primitive machine carry over to all levels in these machine cascades because they are regarded as indigenous to the class of tasks handled.

Consider the case of operating systems, these are certainly hierarchical. Are there not primitive operations in these systems which are indigenous to all levels? Can we not design a background machine—and hence a set of such machines—for this hierarchy of systems? If one were so designing, would not a point of departure be a set of primitives for handling interprocess communication and, in particular, for handling interrupts? For example, is it not so that the attempt to interrupt invokes in the interruptor an interrupt which will surely be processed? Is it not the case that interrupts plant ultimate interrupts for restoring the status which held prior to the given ones?

We are going to concern ourselves here with the design, production, and servicing of objects which are complex and automatic, mechanical and symbolic, whose performance and decay, breakdown and efficiency depend in only very weak ways on the laws of physics. Their structure and rigidity depend as much on the social laws governing their usage as on their internal constraints. It should be clear that when we speak of production we do not speak so much of mass production as of specialty production and mass distribution. The problems of mass producing software are clearly less important than that of producing software at all.

This is the first conference ever held on software engineering and it behooves us to take this conference quite seriously since it will likely set the tone of future work in this field in much the same way that Algol did. We should take quite seriously both the scientific and engineering components of software, but our concentration must be on the latter.

Our problems arise from demands, appetites, and our exuberant optimism. They are magnified by the unevenly trained personnel with which we work. In our deliberations we will not, I believe, be able to avoid the education problem—software engineering does not exist without software engineers. Stability in our goals, products and performances can only be achieved when accompanied by a sufficient supply of workers who are properly trained, motivated, and interchangeable. Their production should be the subject of another meeting. Our goal this week is the conversion of mushyware to firmware, to transmute our products from jello to crystals.

8.2. MASS PRODUCED SOFTWARE COMPONENTS, BY M. D. MCILROY

Abstract

Software components (routines), to be widely applicable to different machines and users, should be available in families arranged according to precision, robustness, generality and time-space performance. Existing sources of components — manufacturers, software houses, users' groups and algorithm collections — lack the breadth of interest or coherence of purpose to assemble more than one or two members of such families, yet software production in the large would be enormously helped by the availability of spectra of high quality routines, quite as mechanical design is abetted by the existence of families of structural shapes, screws or resistors. The talk will examine the kinds of variability necessary in software components, ways of producing useful inventories, types of components that are ripe for such standardization, and methods of instituting pilot production.

The Software Industry is Not Industrialized

We undoubtedly produce software by backward techniques. We undoubtedly get the short end of the stick in confrontations with hardware people because they are the industrialists and we are the crofters. Software production today appears in the scale of industrialization somewhere below the more backward construction industries. I think its proper place is considerably higher, and would like to investigate the prospects for mass-production techniques in software.

In the phrase "mass production techniques," my emphasis is on "techniques" and not on mass production plain. Of course mass production, in the sense of limitless replication of prototype, is trivial for software. But certain ideas from industrial technique I claim are relevant. The idea of subassemblies carries over directly and is well exploited. The idea of interchangeable parts corresponds roughly to our term "modularity," and is fitfully respected. The idea of machine tools has an analogue in assembly programs and compilers. Yet this fragile analogy is belied when we seek for analogues of other tangible symbols of mass production. There do not exist manufacturers of standard parts, much less catalogues of standard parts. One may not order parts to individual specifications of size, ruggedness, speed, capacity, precision or character set.

The pinnacle of software is systems — systems to the exclusion of almost all other considerations. Components, dignified as a hardware field, is unknown as a legitimate branch of software. When we undertake to write a compiler, we begin by saying "What table mechanism shall we build." Not, "What mechanism shall we *use?*" but "What mechanism shall we *build?*" I claim we have done enough of this to start taking such things off the shelf.

Software Components

My thesis is that the software industry is weakly founded, and that one aspect of this weakness is the absence of a software components subindustry. We have enough experience to perceive the outline of such a subindustry. I intend to elaborate this outline a little, but I suspect that the very name "software components" has probably already conjured up for you an idea of how the industry could operate. I shall also argue that a components industry could be immensely useful, and suggest why it hasn't materialized. Finally I shall raise the question of starting up a "pilot plant" for software components.

The most important characteristic of a software components industry is that it will offer families of routines for any given job. No user of a particular member of a family should pay a penalty, in unwanted generality, for the fact that he is employing a standard model routine. In other words, the purchaser of a component from a family will choose one tailored to his exact needs. He will consult a catalogue, offering routines in varying degrees of precision, robustness, time-space performance, and generality. He will be confident that each routine in the family is of high quality — reliable and efficient. He will expect the routine to be intelligible, doubtless expressed in a higher level language appropriate to the purpose of the component, though not necessarily instantly compilable

in any processor he has for his machine. He will expect families of routines to be constructed on rational principles so that families fit together as building blocks. In short, he
should be able safely to regard components as black boxes.

Thus the builder of an assembler will be able to say "I *will use* a String Associates
A4 symbol table, in size 500x8," and therewith consider it done. As a bonus he may later
experiment with alternatives to this choice, without incurring extreme costs.

A Familiar Example

Consider the lowly sine routine. How many should a standard catalogue offer?
Off hand one thinks of several dimensions along which we wish to have variability:

Precision, for which perhaps ten different approximating functions might suffice

Floating-vs-fixed computation

Argument ranges $0\text{-}\pi/2, 0\text{-}2\pi$, also $-\pi/2$ to $\pi/2$, $-\pi$ to π, -big to +big.

Robustness — ranging from no argument validation through signaling of complete
loss of significance, to signaling of specified range violations.

We have here 10 precisions, 2 scalings, 5 ranges and 3 robustnesses. The last range option
and the last robustness option are actually arbitrary parameters specifiable by the user.
This gives us a basic inventory of 300 sine routines. In addition one might expect a complete catalogue to include a measurement-standard sine routine, which would deliver (at
a price) a result of any accuracy specified at run time. Another dimension of variability,
which is perhaps difficult to implement, as it caters for very detailed needs is

Time-space tradeoff by table lookup, adjustable in several "subdimensions":

(a) Table size

(b) Quantization of inputs (e.g., the inputs are known to be integral
numbers of degrees)

Another possibility is

(c) Taking advantage of known properties of expected input sequences,
for example profiting from the occurrence of successive calls for sine
and cosine of the same argument.

A company setting out to write 300 sine routines one at a time and hoping to
recoup on volume sales would certainly go broke. I can't imagine some of their catalogue
items ever being ordered. Fortunately the cost of offering such an "inventory" need not be
nearly 300 times the cost of keeping one routine. Automated techniques exist for generating approximations of different degrees of precision. Various editing and binding techniques are possible for inserting or deleting code pertinent to each degree of robustness.
Perhaps only the floating-vs-fixed dichotomy would actually necessitate fundamentally
different routines. Thus it seems that the basic inventory would not be hard to create.

The example of the sine routine re-emphasizes an interesting fact about this
business. It is safe to assert that almost all sines are computed in floating point these days,
yet that would not justify discarding the fixed point option, for that could well throw
away a large part of the business in distinct tailor-made routines for myriads of small
process-control and other real-time applications on all sorts of different hardware. "Mass
production" of software means multiplicity of what manufacturing industry would call
"models," or "sizes" rather than multiplicity of replicates of each.

Parameterized Families of Components

One phrase contains much of the secret of making families of software components: "binding time." This is an "in" phrase this year, but it is more popular in theory than
in the field. Just about the only applications of multiple binding times I can think of are
sort generators and the so-called "Sysgen" types of application: filling in parameters at the
time routines are compiled to control table sizes, and to some extent to control choice

among several bodies of code. The best known of these, IBM's OS/360 Sysgen is indeed elaborate — software houses have set themselves up as experts on this job. Sysgen differs, though, in a couple of ways from what I have in mind as the way a software components industry might operate.

First, Sysgen creates systems not by construction, but rather by excision, from an intentionally fat model. The types of adjustment in Sysgen are fairly limited. For example it can allocate differing amounts of space to a compiler, but it can't adjust the width of list link fields in proportion to the size of the list space. A components industry on the other hand, not producing components for application to one specific system, would have to be flexible in more dimensions, and would have to provide routines whose niches in a system were less clearly delineated.

Second, Sysgen is not intended to reduce object code or running time. Typically Sysgen provides for the presetting of defaults, such as whether object code listings are or are not standard output from a compiler. The entire run-time apparatus for interrogating and executing options is still there, even though a customer might guarantee he'd never use it were it indeed profitable to refrain. Going back to the sine routine, this is somewhat like building a low precision routine by computing in high precision and then carefully throwing away the less significant bits.

Having shown that Sysgen isn't the exact pattern for a components industry, I hasten to add that in spirit it is almost the only way a successful components industry could operate. To purvey a rational spectrum of high quality components a fabricator would have to systemize his production. One could not stock 300 sine routines unless they were all in some sense instances of just a few models, highly parameterized, in which all but a few parameters were intended to be permanently bound before run time. One might call these early-bound parameters "sale time" parameters.

Many of the parameters of a basic software component will be qualitatively different from the parameters of routines we know today. There will be at least

Choice of Precision. Taken in a generalized sense precision includes things like width of characters, and size of address or pointer fields.

Choice of Robustness. The exact tradeoff between reliability and compactness in space and time can strongly affect the performance of a system. This aspect of parameterization and the next will probably rank first in importance to customers.

Choice of Time-space behavior.

Choice of Algorithm. In numerical routines, as exemplified by those in the CACM, this choice is quite well catered for already. For nonnumerical routines, however, this must usually be decided on the basis of folklore. As some nonnumerical algorithms are often spectacularly unsuitable for particular hardware, a wide choice is perhaps even more imperative for them.

Choice of Interfaces. Routines that use several inputs and yield several outputs should come in a variety of interface styles. For example, these different styles of communicating error outputs should be available:

a. Alternate returns
b. Error code return
c. Call an error handler
d. Signal (in the sense of PL/1)

Another example of interface variability is that the dimensions of matrix parameters should be receivable in ways characteristic of several major programming languages.

Choice of Accessing method. Different storage accessing disciplines should be supported, so that a customer could choose that best fitting his requirements in speed and space, the addressing capabilities of his hardware, or his taste in programming style.

Choice of Data structures. Already touched upon under the topic of interfaces, this delicate matter requires careful planning so that algorithms be as insensitive to changes of data structure as possible. When radically different structures are useful for similar problems (e.g., incidence matrix and list representations for graphs), several algorithms may be required.

Application Areas

We have to begin thinking small. Despite advertisements to the effect that whole compilers are available on a "virtually off-the-shelf" basis, I don't think we are ready to make software sub-assemblies of that size on a production basis. More promising components to begin with are these:

Numerical approximation routines. These are very well understood, and the dimensions of variability for these routines are also quite clear. Certain other numerical processes aren't such good candidates; root finders and differential equation routines, for instance are still matters for research, not mass production. Still other "numerical" processes, such as matrix inversion routines, are simply logical patterns for sequencing that are almost devoid of variability. These might be sold by a components industry for completeness' sake, but they can be just as well taken from the CACM.

Input-output conversion. The basic pieces here are radix conversion routines, some trivial scanning routines, and format crackers. From a well-designed collection of families it should be possible to fabricate anything from a simple on-line octal package for a small laboratory computer to a Fortran IV conversion package. The variability here, especially in the matter of accuracy and robustness is substantial. Considerable planning will evidently be needed to get sufficient flexibility without having too many basically different routines.

Two and three dimensional geometry. Applications of this sort are going on a very wide class of machines, and today are usually kept proprietary. One can easily list a few dozen fundamental routines for geometry. The sticky dimension of variability here is in data structures. Depending on which aspect of geometrical figures is considered fundamental – points, surfaces, topology, etc. – quite different routines will be required. A complete line ought to cater for different abstract structures, and also be insensitive to concrete structures.

Text processing. Nobody uses anybody else's general parsers or scanners today, partly because a routine general enough to fulfill any particular individual needs probably has so much generality as to be inefficient. The principle of variable binding times could be very fruitfully exploited here. Among the corpus of routines in this area would be dictionary builders and lookup routines, scanners, and output synthesizers, all capable of working on continuous streams, on unit records, and various linked list formats, and under access modes suitable to various hardware.

Storage management. Dynamic storage allocation is a popular topic for publication, about which not enough real knowledge yet exists. Before constructing a product line for this application, one ought to do considerable comparison of known schemes working in practical environments. Nevertheless storage management is so important, especially for text manipulation, that it should be an early candidate.

The Market

Coming from one of the larger sophisticated users of machines, I have ample opportunity to see the tragic waste of current software writing techniques. At Bell Telephone Laboratories we have about 100 general purpose machines from a dozen manufacturers. Even though many are dedicated to special applications, a tremendous amount of similar software must be written for each. All need input-output conversion, sometimes only single alphabetic characters and octal numbers, some full-blown Fortran style I/O. All need assemblers and could use macroprocessors, though not necessarily compiling on the same hardware. Many need basic numerical routines or sequence generators. Most want speed at all costs, a few want considerable robustness.

Needless to say much of this support programming is done sub-optimally, and at a severe scientific penalty of diverting the machine's owners from their central investigations. To construct these systems of high-class componentry we would have to surround each of some 50 machines with a permanent coterie of software specialists. Were it possible quickly and confidently to avail ourselves of the best there is in support algorithms, a team of software consultants would be able to guide scientists towards rapid and improved solutions to the more mundane support problems of their personal systems.

In describing the way Bell Laboratories might use software components, I have intended to described the market in microcosm. Bell Laboratories is not typical of computer users. As a research and development establishment, it must perforce spend more of its time sharpening its tools, and less using them than does a production computing shop. But it is exactly such a systems-oriented market toward which a components industry would be directed.

The market would consist of specialists in system building, who would be able to use tried parts for all the more commonplace parts of their systems. The biggest customers of all would be the manufacturers. (Were they not it would be a sure sign that the offered products weren't good enough.) The ultimate consumer of systems based on components ought to see considerably improved reliability and performance, as it would become possible to expend proportionally more effort on critical parts of systems, and also to avoid the now prevalent failings of the more mundane parts of systems, which have been specified by experts, and have then been written by hacks.

Present Day Suppliers

You may ask, well don't we have exactly what I've been calling for already in several places? What about the CACM collected algorithms? What about users groups? What about software houses? And what about manufacturers' enormous software packages?

None of these sources caters exactly for the purpose I have in mind, nor do I think it likely that any of them will actually evolve to fill the need.

The CACM algorithms, in a limited field, perhaps come closer to being a generally available off-the-shelf product than do the commercial products, but they suffer some strong deficiencies. First they are an ingathering of personal contributions, often stylistically varied. They fit into no plan, for the editor can only publish that which the authors volunteer. Second, by being effectively bound to a single compilable language, they achieve refereeability but must perforce completely avoid algorithms for which Algol is unsuited or else use circumlocutions so abominable that the product can only be regarded as a toy. Third, as an adjunct of a learned society, the CACM algorithms section can not deal in large numbers of variants of the same algorithm; variability can only be provided by expensive run time parameters.

User's groups I think can be dismissed summarily, and I will spare you a harangue on their deficiencies.

Software houses generally do not have the resources to develop their own product lines; their work must be financed, and large financing can usually only be obtained for large products. So we see the software houses purveying systems, or very big programs, such as Fortran compilers, linear programming packages or flowcharters. I do not expect to see any software house advertising a family of Bessel functions or symbol tabling routines in the predictable future.

The manufacturers produce unbelievable amounts of software. Generally, as this is the stuff that gets used most heavily it is all pretty reliable, a good conservative grey, that doesn't include the best routine for anything, but that is better than the average programmer is likely to make. As we heard yesterday manufacturers tend to be rather pragmatic in their choice of methods. They strike largely reasonable balances between generality and specificity and seldom use absolutely inappropriate approaches in any individual software component. But the profit motive wherefrom springs these virtues also begets their prime hangup — systems now. The system comes first; components are merely annoying incidentals. Out of these treadmills I don't expect to see high class components of general utility appear.

A Components Factory

Having shown that it is unlikely to be born among the traditional suppliers of software I turn now to the question of just how a components industry might get started.

There is some critical size to which the industry must attain before it becomes useful. Our purveyor of 300 sine routines would probably go broke waiting for customers if that's all he offered, just as an electronics firm selling circuit modules for only one purpose would have trouble in the market.

It will take some time to develop a useful inventory, and during that time money and talent will be needed. The first source of support that comes to mind is governmental, perhaps channeled through semi-independent research corporations. It seems that the fact that government is the biggest user and owner of machines should provide sufficient incentive for such an undertaking that has promise for making an across-the-board improvement in systems development.

Even before founding a pilot plant, one would be wise to have demonstrated techniques for creating a parameterized family of routines for a couple of familiar purposes, say a sine routine and a Fortran I/O module. These routines should be shown to be useable as replacements in a number of radically different environments. This demonstration could be undertaken by a governmental agency, a research contractor, or by a big user, but certainly without expectation of immediate payoff.

The industrial orientation of a pilot plant must be constantly borne in mind. I think that the whole project is an improbable one for university research. Research-calibre talent will be needed to do the job with satisfactory economy and reliability, but the guiding spirit of the undertaking must be production oriented. The ability to produce members of a family is not enough. Distribution, cataloguing, and rational planning of the mix of product families will in the long run be more important to the success of the venture than will be the purely technical achievement.

The personnel of a pilot plant should look like the personnel on many big software projects, with the masses of coders removed. Very good planning, and strongly product-minded supervision will be needed. There will be perhaps more research flavor included than might be on an ordinary software project, because the level of programming here will be more abstract: Much of the work will be in creating generators of routines rather than in making the routines themselves.

Testing will have to be done in several ways. Each member of a family will doubtless be tested against some very general model to assure that sale-time binding causes no degradation over run-time binding. Product test will involve transliterating the routines to fit in representative hardware. By monitoring the ease with which fairly junior people do product test, managers could estimate the clarity of the product, which is important in predicting customer acceptance.

Distribution will be a ticklish problem. Quick delivery may well be a components purveyor's most valuable sales stimulant. One instantly thinks of distribution by communi cation link. Then even very small components might be profitably marketed. The catalogue will be equally important. A comprehensive and physically condensed document like the Sears-Roebuck catalogue is what I would like to have for my own were I purchasing components.

Once a corpus of product lines became established and profit potential demonstrated, I would expect software houses to take over the industry. Indeed, were outside support long needed, I would say the venture had failed (and try to forget I had ever proposed it).

Touching on Standards

I don't think a components industry can be standardized into existence. As is usual with standards, it would be rash to standardize before we have the models. Language standards, provided they are loose enough not to prevent useful modes of computation, will of course be helpful. Quite soon one would expect a components industry to converge on a few standard types of interface. Experience will doubtless reveal other standards to be helpful, for example popular word sizes and character sets, but again unless the standards encompass the bulk of software systems (as distinguished from users), the components industry will die for lack of market.

Summary

I would like to see components become a dignified branch of software engineering. I would like to see standard catalogues of routines, classified by precision, robustness, time-space performance, size limits, and binding time of parameters. I would like to apply routines in the catalogue to any one of a large class of often quite different machines, without too much pain. I do not insist that I be able to compile a particular routine directly, but I do insist that transliteration be essentially direct. I do not want the routine to be inherently inefficient due to being expressed in machine independent terms. I want to have confidence in the quality of the routines. I want the different types of routine in the catalogue that are similar in purpose to be engineered uniformly, so that two similar routines should be available with similar options and two options of the same routine should be interchangeable in situations indifferent to that option.

What I have just asked for is simply industrialism, with programming terms substituted for some of the more mechanically oriented terms appropriate to mass production. I think there are considerable areas of software ready, if not overdue, for this approach.

8.2.1. Discussion

Ross: What McIlroy has been talking about are things we have been playing with. For example, in the AED system we have the so-called feature-feature. This enables us to get round the problem of loaders. We can always embed our system in whatever loader system is available. The problem of binding is very much interlocked there, so we are at the mercy of the environment. An example is a generalized alarm reporting system in which you can either report things on the fly, or put out all kinds of dynamic information. The same system gives 14 different versions of the alarm handling. Macro-expansion seems to me to be the starting place for some of the technical problems that have to be solved in order to put these very important ideas into practice.

McIlroy: It seems that you have automated some of types variability that I thought were more speculative.

Opler: The TOOL system produced six years ago for Honeywell was complementary to the one McIlroy described. It has facilities for putting things together, but it did not provide the components. The difficulty we had was that we produced rudimentary components to see how the system would work, but the people for whom we developed the system did not understand that they were to provide their own components, so they just complained that the system was not good. But I am very enthusiastic about what you suggest.

Perlis: The GP system of the first Univac was a system for developing personalized software as long as you stayed on that machine. The authors of this system asked me: how would one generalize this to other computers? They did not know how to do it at the time, and I suppose it has not been done. I have a question for McIlroy. I did not hear you mention what to me is the most obvious parametrization, namely to build generalized business data file handling systems. I understand that Informatics has one out which everybody says is ok, but —. This seems to be a typical attitude to parameterized systems.

McIlroy: My reason for leaving that out is that this is an area that I don't know about.

Perlis: Probably it would be one of the easiest areas, and one with the most customers. Before d'Agapeyeff talks I have another comment.[Laughter]. Specialists in every part of software have a curious vision of the world: All parts of software but his are simple and easily parameterized; his is totally variable.

d'Agapeyeff: There is no package which has received more attention from manufacturers than file handling. Yet there is hardly a major system that I know of that is relying solely on the standard system produced by the manufacturer. It is extremely difficult to construct this software in a way that is efficient, reliable, and convenient for all systems and where the nature of the package does not impose itself upon the user. The reason is that you cannot atomize it. Where work has been successful it tends to be concerned with packages that have some structure. When you get down to small units it is not economic to make them applicable to a large set of users, using different machines with different languages, and to do all the binding work, such that it doesn't take twice as long to find out how to load it. The problems with Sysgen are not to be dispensed with, they are inherent. But why do we need to take atoms down from the shelf? What you want is a description which you can understand, because the time taken to code it into your own system is really very small. In that way you can insert your own nuances. The first step in your direction should be better descriptions.

Endres: Two notes of caution: You discarded the algorithms in the Comm. ACM in part because they are written in high-level language, so I understand that you refer to routines written in a more machine oriented language. I think you oversimplify the problem of transliteration. Or do you assume a de facto machine standard? Second question: You refer to the problems of Sysgen, where you cut out pieces from a large collection. If instead you want to put together systems, I think the problems of Sysgen become a dimen sion larger. Who will bear this cost, and maintain the system?

McIlroy: The algorithms in the Comm. ACM effectively use one language, which is suitabl for a particular class of applications. This may not be the right one for things like input/ output packages. On the second question: I am convinced, with you, that at first it will be harder to build systems by accretion, rather than by excision. The people who build components will have to be skilled systems builders, not run of the mill users.

Kjeldaas: I strongly favor this idea. I think the examples mentioned are within the state o the art. However, later we will want macros needing parameters having more intricate relations, for instance if you want some functional relationship between the parameters. We will need some language for describing the parameters. Another point: documentation can also be included in this. When you have given the parameters to the program, you can give the same parameters to the documentation, and the documentation for the particular use can be produced automatically. Catering for different machines will raise big problems, needing research.

Kolence: May I stress one point: McIlroy stated that the industrialization is concerned with the design, not the replication process. We are concerned with a mass design problem. In talking about the implementation of software components, the whole concept of how one designs software is ignored. Yet this is a key thing.

Naur: What I like about this is the stress on basic building principles, and on the fact that big systems are made from smaller components. This has a strong bearing on education. What we want in education, particularly at the more elementary level, is to start indoctrinating the knowledge of the components of our systems. A comparison with our hardware colleagues is relevant. Why are they so much more successful than we are? I believe that one strong reason is that there is a well established field of electronic engineering, that the young people start learning about Ohm's Law at the age of fourteen or thereabouts, and that resistors and the like are known components with characteristics which have been expounded at length at the early level of education. The component principles of our systems must be sorted out in such a form that they can be put into elementary education.

Gill: Two points: first on the catalogue question. I hope we can do better than the Sears-Roebuck catalogue. Surely what we want is a computerized conversational catalogue. Second point: what is it that you actually sell when you sell a piece of software, what exactly does a software contract look like?

Barton: McIlroy's talk was so well done that it took me about three minutes to realize what is wrong with this idea. Another compliment: If I were running Intergalactic Software, I would hire McIlroy for a manager. Now the serious point: Over the last few years I have taught the ACM Course "Information Structures" and used the game not to let anyone code or write anything in any programming language at all. We have just thought about data representations. If in this way you get people over the habit of writing code right away, of thinking procedurally, then some very different views on information representations come to view. In McIlroy's talk about standard components having to do with data structures I have the feeling that this is not a problem to take out of the universities yet. Now a heretical view: I don't think we have softened up enough things in machines yet. I don't think we will get anywhere trying to quantify the space-time trade-off unless we discard fixed word sizes, fixed character sizes, fixed numerical representations, altogether in machines. Without these, the thing proposed by McIlroy will prove to be just not quite practical.

Fraser: I wish to take issue with d'Agapeyeff. I think it will be possible to parameterize data representation and file management. From a particular file system experience I learned two lessons: first, there are a large number of parameters, to be selected in a non-mutually-exclusive manner. The selection of the parameters is so complicated that it is appropriate to put a compiler on the front end of the software distribution mechanism. Perhaps we are talking more about compilers than we realize. Concerning catalogues: in England a catalogue of building materials is a very ad hoc catalogue, you have left hand flanges to go with left hand gates, etc. I think the catalogue is likely to be ad hoc in that nature, rather than like an electronics catalogue where the components are more inter-changeable.

The second issue is the question of writing this compiler. Our file management generator effectively would generate a large number of different file management systems, very considerably in excess of the 300 that McIlroy mentioned. There was no question of testing all of these. We produced an ad hoc solution to this problem, but until more research is done on this problem I don't think McIlroy's suggestion is realistic.

Graham: I will speak of an adjunct to this idea. In Multics we used a subset of PL/1, although PL/1 is quite inadequate, in that the primitive operations of the language are not really suited for system design. In Multics you do a lot of directory management, simple operations like adding and deleting entries, but in a complicated directory. With a higher-level language with these operations as primitives one could easily write a new system. By simulating the primitives one could test the performance of the system before actually building it. If one had McIlroy's catalogue stored in the system, with the timings of a lot of routines, then the simulation backing up this higher-level language could in fact refer to the catalogue and use the actual timings for a new machine that this company offered and get realistic timings. Another point, I wish to rebut McIlroy's suggestion that this is not for universities; I think it is. There are very difficult problems in this area, such as parameterizing more sophisticated routines, in particular those in the compiler area. These are fit for universities.

Bemer: I agree that the catalogue method is not a suitable one. We don't have the descriptors to go searching. There is nothing so poorly described as data formats, there are no standards, and no sign that they are being developed. Before we have these we won't have the components.

McIlroy: It is for that reason that I suggest the Sears-Roebuck type now. On-line searching may not be the right answer yet.

9. WORKING PAPERS

Below we give first the list of working papers of the conference. Quotations from most of these papers are given throughout the report. The list is followed by a few papers which it was found desirable, for one reason or another, to reproduce in full. In the list these papers are marked with the page number where they appear in the report.

d'Agapeyeff: Reducing the cost of software.
Babcock: Variations on software available to the user.
Babcock: Reprogramming.
Bemer, Fraser, Glennie, Opler, and Wiehle: Classification of subject matter [pages 100-103].
Bemer: Checklist for planning software system production [pages 103-114].
Bemer: Machine-controlled production environment — tools for technical control of production.
Berghuis: The establishment of standard programming and management techniques throughout the development and production of software and their enforcement.
Berghuis: Systems Management
Cress and J.W. Graham: Production of software in the university environment.
Dadda: Designing a program library for electronic engineering computer-aided design.
Dahl, Myhrhaug and Nygaard: Some uses of the external class concept in SIMULA 67.
David: Some thoughts about production of large software systems (1).
David: Some thoughts about production of large software systems (2).
David and Fraser: Position Paper.
Dijkstra: On useful structuring.
Dijkstra: Complexity controlled by hierarchical ordering of function and variability [pages 114-116].
Donner: Modification of existing software.
Enlart: Program distribution and maintenance.
Enlart: Service level evaluation in software.
Enlart: Services provided to EPL users.
Ercoli: On the economics of software production.
Fraser: I. Classification of software production methods.
Fraser: II. The nature of progress in software production.
Gill: Thoughts on the sequence of writing software [pages 116-118].
Gill: Position paper.
Gillette: Aids in the production of maintainable software.
Gillette: Comments on service group statements.
Harr: The design and production of real time software for electronic switching system.
Hastings: Software usage and modifications for the industrial user.
Hume: Design as controlled by external function.
Kjeldaas: The use of large computers to reduce the cost of software production for small computers.
Kohler: Maintenance and distribution of programs.

Kolence: On the interactions between software design techniques and software management problems.
Letellier: The adequate testing and design of software packages.
Llewelyn and Wickens: Software testing [pages 118-124].
McClure: Projection versus performance in software production.
Nash: Some problems of management in production of large-scale software systems.
Naur: The profiles of software designers and producers.
Opler: Acceptance testing of large programming systems — abstract.
Opler: Measurement and analysis of software in production.
Pinkerton: Performance monitoring and systems evaluation [pages 125-126].
van der Poel: A simple macro compiler for educational purposes in LISP.
Randell: Towards a methodology of computer systems design [pages 127-129].
Reenskaug: Adapting to object machines.
Ross: Example of discovering the essence of a problem.
Ross: Example of mechanical transformation from beads to arrays.
Ross: Problem modeling.
Selig: Documentation standards [pages 129-131].
Selig: On external and internal design.
Wodon: Influence of data structures on system design.

CLASSIFICATION OF SUBJECT MATTER
by
R.W. Bemer, A.G. Fraser, A.E. Glennie, A. Opler, and H.R. Wiehle

Introduction

At this early stage in the discussion on software production methods it is desirable to find an appropriate way of classifying the subject matter. A working party was given the task of finding an appropriate classification method and its conclusions are given here.
As a by-product of its deliberations, the working party produced a list of production cost elements and this is appended.

Classification Method

It is convenient to identify two major divisions of the management function. These are identified here as *Production Management* and *Technical Direction.* The former is subdivided into the procedures that constitute the production process whereas the latter is conveniently identified by the technical components involved in the production task.
In the lists which follow, aspects of the subject which working group P consider to be especially important are marked with an asterisk.

Production Management

1.   PREPARING A PRODUCTION CAPABILITY — HUMAN
        1.1   Training — technology and methods
        1.2   Indoctrination in conventions for coding, testing, documentation
        1.3   Organization structure
                  Quality, types and background of programmers used
                  Project or product oriented
                  Group size
               x Internal communications

1.4 Productivity
Evaluation
Methods of output increase
1.5 Support Services — Documentors, clerical, operators, etc.

2. PREPARING A PRODUCTION CAPABILITY — NONHUMAN
2.1 Support equipment and availability (real or paper)
Local/remote access
2.2 Physical facilities — offices, file storage, data preparation
x 2.3 Machine-controlled production environment
Software tools — job specific (simulators, etc.)
Software tools — general (high level languages, flow charters, text editors, indexers, etc.)
Software tools — management (accounting, control, progress)

3. PRODUCTION PLANNING
3.1 Requirements and specifications
3.2 Choice of standards and conventions for the project
3.3 Estimating
Magnitude of code and documentation
Costs (standards of comparison)
3.4 Budget
3.5 Workforce allocation, phase-in
3.6 Structural breakdown of system, interfaces
3.7 Configuration management (relative to hardware configurations)
3.8 Identification of software units, and their maintenance categories
3.9 Work schedules
3.10 Negotiation of changes, inquiries
3.11 Implementation plan for user documentation
x 3.12 Reliability, maintainability plans
3.13 Test plan
3.14 Special problems of complex, large systems (over 100 manyears, new varieties such as interactive, control and deadline)

4. ADMINISTRATION AND METERING OF THE PRODUCTION PROCESS (SOFTWARE AND TEST SOFTWARE)
4.1 Cost accounting
4.2 Size control (elimination of duplication through multiple usage)
x 4.3 Progress reporting and supervision
x 4.4 Measuring production performance
4.5 Schedule adjustment
4.6 Change control
4.7 Control of innovation and reinvention
4.8 Standards control
4.9 Technical reviews
x 4.10 Instrumentation and analysis of software
4.11 Feedback to design
x 4.12 Internal communication and documentation
4.13 User documentation
4.14 Quality control and component tests
4.15 System assembly

       4.16 Final project report (Innovations, pitfalls, recording major decisions and justification, etc.)

5.   **FINAL PROCESSING**
        5.1   System generation
x 5.2   Quality assurance and measurement of performance
x 5.3   Quality assurance of documentation
        5.4   Release approval
        5.5   Delivery methods – shipping and installation
        5.6   Customizing and subsetting
        5.7   Maintenance and installation tools
        5.8   Transfer to service for maintenance, enhancement and replacement versions

Technical Direction

1.   TERMINOLOGY AND TECHNOLOGY OF SOURCE TASK
2.   PRODUCTION MACHINE AND ITS SOFTWARE
        2.1   Hardware configuration to be used in production
x 2.2   Operating system (on-line or batch)
        2.3   Software for information handling
x 2.4   Programming languages
        2.5   Aids to documentation
        2.6   Debugging aids
        2.7   Environment construction for testing
        2.8   Simulator for parts of object machine (or bootstrap)
x 2.9   Tools for technical control of production
        2.10 Aids to assembly and coordination of testing

3.   OBJECT MACHINE AND ITS SOFTWARE
        3.1   Hardware configuration to be used
x 3.2   Method of adapting to object machine
        3.3   Static structure of object program (binding, linking, etc.)
        3.4   Dynamic structure of object program (re-entrance, relocation, etc.)
        3.5   Run-time interface with machine and operating system
        3.6   Run-time interface with other software
        3.7   Facilities available at assembly or compile time
        3.8   Tools for performance measurement

4.   THE PRODUCT
        4.1   Object program
        4.2   Matching documentation (various audiences)
        4.3   Set of test cases and results
x 4.4   Procedure for generating, maintaining and modifying the system
        4.5   Specification of installation procedure

5.   STANDARDS AND CONVENTIONS
        5.1   Applicable industry and international standards
        5.2   Standards and conventions to be used in house

ADDENDUM – SOFTWARE COST ELEMENTS

NORMAL   *SEMINORMAL*

Training   Duplication
Personnel turnover   Waiting for Test time
Design   Waiting for return
Functional description   Programmer fatigue (irregular schedules,
Review – Conceptual   lack of direction)
Coding   Communications misunderstanding
Testing – Quality control   Deterioration
Review – Implementation   Design inflexibility for change
Machine time – Test
Technical documentation
User documentation
Supplies – Paper, cards, tapes
Input Data Preparation
Rework and false starts
Failure – Hardware
        – Basic Software
        – Interaction
Testing – Quality assurance
Terminal and line costs

CHECKLIST FOR PLANNING SOFTWARE SYSTEM PRODUCTION
prepared in August 1966 by
R. W. Bemer

1. Tooling

Is the first prototype or pilot of each hardware unit assigned (in sufficient quantity) to software production for a sufficient and continuing period of time?

Are these hardware units periodically updated and rotated to customers so that software production has up-to-date and complete equipment?

Is this hardware under the firm control of software production so as to be free of interference due to hardware test modification, confiscation for customers, etc.?

Is this hardware operated in a customer-like environment to reflect and anticipate customer needs before distribution to the field?

Is there sales representative service and field engineering service for the software systems equivalent to that for any other customer?

Is sufficient research undertaken in software production methods, such as construction languages and bootstrap methods?

Are the software production methods of other manufacturers studied if known, and sought out if unknown?

Is the manufacturer's most powerful computer used for controlled production, distribution and maintenance of software systems for all of his machine systems?

Is there a computerized system for software field reporting?

Is there a computerized system for software production control?

Is there a computerized system for automated software production?

Is there a computerized system for a customer roster, together with their hardware and software configurations?

Is this roster integral with the corresponding roster for manufacturing, projects and field engineering?

Does this roster contain the hardware field change level which could affect software or system performance?

Is there a software facility for file maintenance of source programs?

Is a general assembler provided which can assemble, using the tool machine, for any new machine?

Is there a tool for proving the identity of the general assembler to the specific assembler for the specific machine?

Are simulators provided for the tool machine which can simulate any new machine for which software is being constructed?

Are these simulators in a form suitable for any period of scarcity, such as early testing by customers?

Does the software production system have provision for

a) Updating the test library with additional quality assurance programs and suitable excerpts from the field reports.
b) Updating the roster.
c) Modifying itself.
d) Producing provisional systems for temporary programming usage and testing.
e) Producing modifiers to update customer's system and documentation for distribution.
f) Producing original manuals and updatings.
g) Producing the field report summary and statistics.
h) Producing records of all these processes for the manufacturer.
i) Acting as well or better than a human supervisor in the control of production (i.e., not accept software systems modifications submitted by the programmer unless they meet certain standards)?

2. Training and Organization

Are programmers given formal training in production methods and techniques?

Do the programmers provide training in system operation to field marketing and field engineering personnel so that they can pass such training on to customers?

Is there an excess of programming personnel to allow flexibility of redistribution, emergency and unbudgeted projects, meanwhile utilizing them in being trained, assisting in the field, and experimentation and research?

Are programmers periodically rotated to machine operation or to the field to obtain current hands-on experience?

Is a skills inventory maintained for the programming staff?

Is there a method to upgrade operators and other personnel to programming?

Are personnel operating the software production computers given the opportunity to review operating system design for proper man-machine characteristics?

Are basic manuals on software production available?

Is there an adequate library?

Is good usage made of the library by programmers?

Does an adequate percentage of programming personnel maintain membership in professional societies?

Is publication encouraged?

Is the software staff organized to participate in advanced projects (as opposed to the 85 percent of repetitive software production), particularly when hardware and software must be developed concurrently?

Does software production undergo continuous mechanization to minimize perturbations from management change?

Does the software organization provide comprehension courses for their management to ensure that its relative importance is properly reflected in their planning?

3. Design

Is the software planned for categorization by the relative amount of effort expended to produce, maintain and distribute it?

Are the criteria for this categorization published and distributed to field personnel and customers?

Are gross functional specifications for software provided by a joint effort of Product Planning and Field Marketing, with considerations and options for hardware tradeoffs?

Do these gross functional specifications include data on allowable configurations for both hardware and software, with suggested categories for quality and service?

Is there a formal procedure for planning basic software simultaneously with hardware, with an effective systems control for allocating tradeoffs?

Is there a formal review procedure for software specifications for
a) Marketing to ensure adequacy and efficacy of market coverage
b) Product Planning to ensure conformity to planning goals
c) Hardware Engineering to ensure accuracy and consistency
d) Internal computer operations to ensure user suitability and proper human engineering?

Is there a formal procedure to amend specifications as a result of such feedback, with provision for alternate methods when review schedules are not met?

Is there a mechanism for interchange (or at least crediting) of budgeted monies to facilitate maximum benefit from hardware-software tradeoffs?

Is the tradeoff principle extended to field maintainability, with a mechanism for interchange of budgeted monies?

Does Product Planning provide intelligence from competition and advanced development areas in the form of surveys and comparative evaluation materials, for due influence upon software design?

Is a substantial portion of the design staff familiar with current field operating methods, so as not to be insulated from changing requirements?

Is each software unit identified and numbered for direct correspondence to
a) Its corresponding quality assurance program?
b) Its actual source program instructions, listed?
c) Its actual source program instructions in entry form.
d) Its corresponding elements of user documentation.
e) Its corresponding elements of technical documentation.
f) The minimum hardware configuration required to run it.

Is each software unit equipped with a document detailing the following
a) Its purpose.
b) Its inputs and their forms.
c) Its outputs and their forms.
d) The processes applied to the inputs to yield the outputs.
e) The inventory of tools (other units, utility routines, usable store, executive controls) available to it.
f) The constraints of time and interaction with other software units.
g) Its operational design goals and characteristics.

h) The characteristics of its interfaces with other software units.

i) Its precision and accuracy, where relevant.

Are these questions complete before any flowcharting, programming or coding commences?

Are they matched against the other similar specifications to detect conflict, duplication or system imbalance?

Is there a periodically updated software design checklist available to all software designers?

Does it specifically include material on the following

a) International, national industry and company standards.
b) Design for offline vs. online operation.
c) Design for closed vs. open shop usage.
d) Flexibility for various customer job mixes.
e) Alternate software with different performance but same functional characteristics.
f) Diagnostics under the executive system.
g) Modeling for design decision (and simulation).
h) Initialization, bootstrap and restart procedures.
i) Optimizing human operating characteristics.
j) Special diagnostic aids for users.
k) Making the executive system forgiving and helpful in case of hardware faults.
l) Providing for special, nonstandard hardware.
m) Accounting and measuring procedures.
n) Modular construction.
o) Alternative modes of system operation, with a provision to indicate those selected.
p) User priorities, special accounting and custom software units supplied by the user.
q) Machine room operational procedures.

4. Scheduling and Costing

Do plant accounting procedures provide all necessary information on costs by project, rather than by cost center?

If not, does software production incorporate this in its own production control system?

Is the gathered data processed, not merely accumulated?

Is there a software production control system to fabricate to predicted schedules for predicted costs?

Are costs of previous system construction utilized in predicting new costs?

Are all sales commitments for software, and software delivery clauses in contracts, concurred in by software production for incorporation in the production control system?

Are there responsible software project managers who utilize the mechanized production control system to ensure that all elements are available on scheduled delivery dates?

Are there production documents for each phase of production of each software unit, representing a scheduling commitment upon the part of the unit manager?

Do these then yield gross schedules of *expected* completion which are published internally and incorporated in the production control system?

Are these *expected* schedules then modified by maximum slippage factors to produce schedules which can be incorporated into contracts without specific approval each time, particularly for non-delivery and non-performance penalty provisions?

Is it guaranteed that all contracts with schedules prior to these dates are subject to approval by software management?

Are all software commitments for items not in the price book, or variations of these, quoted at an additional cost to the customer, subject to the existence of adequate personnel and facilities for production?

If any software is furnished free as a sales concession, is there a signed acknowledgement attached to the final copy of the contract which states the distribution of cost against individual sales commission, regional sales or manufacturer's market penetration?

5. Production Control

Is the quantity of software to be produced of a manageable size by virtue of control of the number and character of hardware and software configurations which are permitted to be sold?

Given variation possible in store size, number and variety of peripherals, functional operations, etc., are all combinatorially possible hardware configurations generated by computer and submitted to

    a) Marketing — for reduction of variety with respect to saleability?

    b) Engineering — to ensure completeness of interface and interconnections?

    c) Software — to ensure software operability for each combination?

    d) Product Planning — for performance control (i.e., a salesman might claim that a low price system is saleable but it may not be of sufficient performance with only one tape unit as secondary store)?

Is this set systematically reduced to a reasonable size (i.e., no more combinations than number of machines planned to sell)?

Is this set then further reduced by matching with a software configurator?

Does this software configurator distinguish between software which is vital to operate the hardware and that which is optional for better system performance or added facility to the user?

Does general management then sign off that the deleted combinations are not to be sold (except with special permission, where software will be sold rather than furnished free)?

Does this information now form the basis for the price book?

Are the remaining (official) hardware/software configurations numbered so that a single number in the customer roster will indicate the exact hardware and software with which he is supplied?

Is software designed to minimize the automatic adjustment to variance in configuration?

Does software production have the right of concurrence for software announcements and publicity, with respect to accuracy and feasibility?

Given the possible combinations of hardware units the manufacturer is willing to supply, and the software units to be furnished free for each of these, is the customer told clearly that hardware or software outside of this group is supplied only at special cost?

Is such a policy enforced by a contract review board?

Does this review board also approve contractual commitments and penalties for software?

Is a request for any additional or special software accompanied by a dollar value which is either a) the amount the customer is willing to pay additionally or b) the amount by which salability is enhanced and which Marketing is willing to fund?

Are these categories open to query by salesman to determine the best performing hardware/software configuration to do the customer's job at minimum cost?

Does Marketing provide an assessment of marketing strategy which may influence the amount or nature of software provided, or rescheduling of production and delivery dates?

Is there a computerized system for manipulating the data on each software unit, such as

a) total size
b) maximum residency
c) set membership
d) the other units which may call it
e) the other units which it may call
f) the interfaces with these surrounding units, together with the entry and exit points

in order to determine

a) that the hardware configuration is not exceeded
b) that enough hardware exists to run the software
c) a mechanical diagram of the entire system for completeness and consistency for quality control, diagnostic and maintenance purposes?

Does the production control system recognize and allow for the relative invisibility of software?

Given a specific software unit of a minimum size feasible for individual control, do the responsible supervisors estimate total elapsed time and costs for man and machine hours as a function of their resources?

Is internal competitive bidding allowable for cost reduction?

Is the data for each stage (functional specifications, flowcharts, implicit quality test, coding, checkout in vacuo, checkout in processor, checkout in system, documentation, explicit quality test, release) of development of that software unit given by the supervisor on a signed document?

Are labor distribution reports developed from the timecards of programmers participating on each unit?

Does the individual programmer periodically give an estimate of the percentage of completion of each unit, for correlation to labor distribution and schedules, and perhaps PERT charts?

Are full records kept on original estimates, revised estimates and actual completion dates for

a) Recalibration of supervision
b) Improvement of future estimates
c) Deriving production standards
d) Possible rebalance of staff or redesign
e) Notification to marketing in case of slippage?

Are these viewed as official company records, so that detected falsifiers are subject to discharge?

Does effort expended on unapproved or bootleg projects put the controlling supervisor subject to discharge?

Is the production control keyed to a roster containing the list of official software units supplied without charge, keyed to the documentation units, and for each customer the

1) User's name, address and representative
2) Branch office name, address and representative
3) Contact pattern between user, branch and programming

4) Machine type, serial, installation date, on-rent date
5) Hardware configuration, operational dates of units
6) Channel assignments, other determinations of logical options
7) Field change orders affecting software and whether installed or not
8) Software options for:
   a. Required units
   b. Characteristics of their storage
   c. Characteristics of their usage
   d. Maximum store alloted for processing and usage
   e. Hardware restrictions affecting software operation, such as reserved elements or lockouts
   f. Delivery form of software unit (symbolic, relocatable, absolute, FORTRAN, etc.)
   g. Special software supplementing or replacing standard units, by whom supplied, data descriptions and linkage
9) Number of last system delivered. Updating pattern and requested frequency (6 month maximum interval for archivage limitation):
   a. Every system
   b. Every nth system
   c. Upon specific request
   d. First new system after elapsed time interval
   e. Only on change to specified software units
   f. Combination of these
10) Requirements for backup system on another machine
11) Special commitments by sales or programming personnel
12) List of customer's field reports by number?

6. Fabrication

Is software fabricated for utility in the international market?

Is there an active standards unit in the software production group policing compliance with national and international standards available?

Are there internal local standards for production consistency?

Does programmer terminology conform to the standard IFIP/ICC vocabulary?

Are sufficient personnel provided to participate in advanced standards-making work?

Is all system planning done with standard flowchart templates, where applicable?

Are logic equations an allowable alternative to flowcharting?

Are good records kept in any stage of development?

Are systems kept on tape or disc periodically copied on cards or tape for recovery?

Are there finite points in time during development and system updating when the system is reassembled to a clean form with updated listings?

Are hand coding sheets destroyed and each reassembly listing used as the legal representation?

Is periodic recoding recommended when a routine has lost a clean structural form?

Is the system oriented to reassemble with at least the ease of patching?

Are all system tools utilized as provided?

Is there periodic exchange of fabrication information and progress among the various programmer groups constructing an integrated system?

Are original programs and changes controlled so that they cannot be introduced without meeting certain minimum criteria (e.g., a minimum length of comments associating with the statement, or preventing entry or modification of a software unit unless the appropriate links and interfaces in both directions are given)?

Is adequate attention given to modularity in construction, but without over-emphasis which could destroy operating efficency?

Since it is cheaper to be prepared for a malfunction than not, are program units created in three forms for testing:

 a) As a self-contained unit, complete with synthetic input and output, created perhaps by a generator
 b) In a form suitable for usage within its own major program
 c) In a form suitable for use within the overall system?

Can the extra instructions required for (a) and (b) above be removed mechanically for the final stage?

Are statistics kept on the type of malfunction incurred, which may be:

 a) a hardware malfunction
 b) a malfunction in the programming system used
 c) an operating mistake
 d) data errors, such as unexpected type, outside of expected range, physical errors in preparation or reading, etc.
 e) programmer's mistake, such as a misunderstanding or disregard for the rules of syntax, grammar, construction, file layout, system configuration, flow process for solution, etc.?

Is considerable desk checking performed to

 a) Check conformity to rules, such as those for justification
 b) See that enough restart points exist for long programs
 c) Compare actual program logic for match with intended logic as given by a flowchart or equation
 d) Examine live input for peculiar characteristics which could cause erroneous branching, such as bad data, blank records, etc.
 e) Inspect the list of identifiers produced and assigned by the processor, looking for conflicts, insufficient definition, completeness and spelling
 f) Check permissible spellings of reserved words, allowable usage of spacing, hyphens and commas, and juxtaposition of illegal word or operation pairs?

Do the programmers plan for maximum machine utility per run in checkout by:

 a) Submitting multiple related runs
 b) Getting multiple service per run by modifying his program to read in correct conditions periodically to nullify any mistakes so the next section of program can also be checked
 c) Avoiding extensive store dumps
 d) Programming flow indicators which print to show the paths of decision in actual execution
 e) Providing a full range of controlled data input
 f) Designing testing on a "design of experiment basis" to achieve maximum progress for each run?

7. User Documentation

Is the user documentation given top priority and consideration for the sale and successful operation of the system?

Does the documentation conform to standard models?

Is the documentation uniform across product lines so that the user may expect to find similar information in corresponding places and form for every system?

Is user documentation consistent with itself and with national and international standards?

Do all flowcharting symbols and methods conform to international standards?

Does all terminology conform to the IFIP/ICC vocabulary?

Do software processors (Fortran, Cobol, Algol, etc.) conform to standard language specifications?

Are single manuals produced which are valid across machine lines (Fortran, File Structure, Labeling, etc.)?

Are variable software system characteristics excluded, but enclosed separately in machine line manuals with cross indexing?

Is there a formal, consistent document numbering system?

In consideration of the various audiences addressed (for the customers — purchasers, utilizers, programmers, operators, for the manufacturer — salesmen, customer technical assistants, basic software programmers, field engineers and maintenance programmers), are user documents looseleaf rather than bound?

Can pages have multiple set membership (i.e. present in several different manuals)?

Does the education staff provide other documents which are in effect road maps through these manuals to accelerate the learning process?

Is there a computerized system for writing, editing and boiler-plating this user documentation?

Are programmers forced to prepare documentation very early in the production cycle?

Are tentative manuals, with missing decisions identified, published in preference to having no manuals at all?

Is there a formal review procedure for manuals for

a) Marketing — to ensure adequacy and efficacy of market coverage

b) Product Planning — to ensure conformity to planning goals

c) Hardware Engineering — to ensure adequacy and consistency?

Is there a formal procedure to amend manuals as a result of such feedback, with provision for alternate methods when review schedules are not met?

Does hardware engineering provide complete operational specifications early in the software production cycle?

Are hardware manuals forbidden to exist separately for users, so that the system is described in terms of the software system?

When software is produced by a non-English speaking group, is a full set of English documentation provided?

Is this simultaneous with the non-English documentation, or at least within a 2 month lag?

Does the software allow only for writing programs in English, although the natural language of the user may be used for variables?

Is the software itself always written entirely in English?

Is the volume of manuals produced carefully controlled and charged to the field organization, so that these expensive documents will not be used for sales handouts?

Is the user documentation publishing a function of software production, including an art group?

Is there a computerized distribution system to control inventory and reorder points?

Is the decision for internal or external printing controlled by bids, or by delivery schedules in case of equivalent bids?

Is there a computerized system to ensure that user documentation is always correct and matches the current software system in the field?

Is responsibility for documentation allocated to individuals by software unit or groups of units, with a required sign-off on a checklist before distribution of changed software systems?

Is there a standard interior printing area to accommodate the difference between U.S. and ISO paper size?

8. Technical Documentation

Is the software system fully supported by correct flowcharts, descriptions of design algorithms, listings, performance specifications and structure descriptions for A.E's and Field Engineers?

Do listings carry a maximum of technical information in annotation?

Is such documentation susceptible to limitations on how much may be furnished users in proprietary cases?

Are there mechanical methods of producing technical documentation, such as flowcharters and structure decoders?

Is there a control mechanism to ensure that technical documentation is revised to correspond with actual program operation?

9. Quality Assurance

Is the quality assurance function recognized to be different from implicit and continuous quality control during fabrication, in that it is discrete, explicit following production, and ignores the sequence or nature of the fabrication steps or processes?

Is software quality assurance done by an independently reporting agency representing the interests of the eventual user?

Is the product tested to ensure that it is the most useful for the customer in addition to matching functional specifications?

Do software quality assurance test programs undergo the same production cycle and method (except Q/A) as the software they test?

Are they defined and constructed concurrently with the software?

Is at least one person engaged in software quality assurance for every ten engaged in its fabrication?

Whenever tests are specified as a part of national or international standards, are these utilized?

Are there tests for overall system performance as well as for components (i.e., road-testing, French — "rodage")?

Are software quality assurance tests a part of the general hardware acceptance test on the customer's machine before it leaves the factory?

Can software field release be held up if these tests are not passed?

Do the tests include a system logic exerciser?

Are tests provided to ensure matching of computational results with those of other equipment?

Is there a growing test library for each software system, including

    a) a test for roster consistency and permissibility of hardware and software configurations requested

    b) a program acceptance filter

    c) specifically designed quality assurance tests for components

    d) accumulated field reports?

Is this test library applied upon issuance of each modification of the software system?

Is each customer's system tape tested on the software production machine for a sufficient period of time, where feasible?

Are Q/A personnel employed part time on maintenance of older systems, for efficiency and competence in judging?

10. Field Installation

After delivery and putting hardware in service, is the software similarly delivered in person and verified to be operable on the customer's machine at his site?

Are a selected subset of the customer's programs, which previously ran upon his machine at the factory test line, then run in order to have him sign an acceptance form for rental payment or purchase price?

Does the field installation programmer remain at the site until programs execute correctly?

Is there a follow-up plan to ensure that systems do not stay off rental?

Is this service performed by Field Engineering personnel?

11. Distribution and Updating

Is there a centralized library and distribution operation?

Is it responsible for maintaining records on users and their equipment insofar as it is necessary to distribute
  a) software systems (cards, tapes, etc.)
  b) manuals and other documentation
  c) supporting material such as coding forms, code cards, CAD interchange forms, housing devices for supplies, flowchart templates, listing binders and training aids, both filmed and programmed
  d) lists of various software materials available to sales and support personnel, with order prices
  e) lists and abstracts of basic software and interchange programs available for distribution, grouped by category of software maintenance, by machine, by industry and by application —with schedules of availability
  f) updated and corrected materials as produced
  g) actual user programs for interchange?

Does this group maintain the standard software library, including systems from other software components?

Are updatings distributed in loose-leaf form, and remaining stock updated simultaneously?

Are all updates adequately supported by cover letters containing instructions and notification of obsolescence, with periodic summaries of available material on each system?

Does the library group utilize a computer for this service, for mailing lists, customer interest and software profiles, controlling and monitoring distribution?

Is a customer able to incorporate his own software units and special requirements without interference or malfunction as each system update is made?

Is the customer's software system modified to become the new system rather than replace his entire system?

12. Field Reporting and Maintenance

Is there an official, supported system for field reporting on
  a) Software malfunction
  b) Software mismatch to documentation
  c) Inferior software performance
  d) Requests for change to software design
  e) Nonconformity to standards?

Is this reporting procedure enforced by written instructions to
a) Software Production
b) Sales and A.E. personnel
c) Our customers?

Is turnaround service provided in the shortest time by means of high-speed communications systems?

Are field reports processed by formal procedures so the A.E. or customer can know the status at any time?

Are current lists of outstanding field reports furnished to A.E's so they may protect the customer intelligently against these dangers?

Do all field reports carry identification of software units used and actual level of field changes installed in hardware?

Is the customer supplied with manufacturer's recommended good practices in diagnostic methods, operations and use of processors?

Is the user clearly instructed that it is his responsibility to develop the simplest and smallest program which demonstrates the malfunction?

COMPLEXITY CONTROLLED BY HIERARCHICAL ORDERING OF FUNCTION AND VARIABILITY
by
Edsger W. Dijkstra

Reviewing recent experiences gained during the design and construction of a multiprogramming system I find myself torn between two apparently conflicting conclusions. Confining myself to the difficulties more or less mastered I feel that such a job is (or at least should be) rather easy; turning my attention to the remaining problems such a job strikes me as cruelly difficult. The difficulties that have been overcome reasonably well are related to the reliability and the producibility of the system, the unsolved problems are related to the sequencing of the decisions in the design process itself.

I shall mainly describe where we feel that we have been successful. This choice has not been motivated by reasons of advertisement for one's own achievements; it is more that a good knowledge of what — and what little! — we can do successfully, seems a safe starting point for further efforts, safer at least than starting with a long list of requirements without a careful analysis whether these requirements are compatible with each other.

Basic software such as an operating system is regarded as an integral part of the machine, in other words: it is its function to transform a (for its user or for its manager) less attractive machine (or class of machines) into a more attractive one. If this transformation is a trivial one, the problem is solved; if not, I see only one way out of it, viz. "Divide and Rule", i.e. effectuate the transformation of the given machine into the desired one in a modest number of steps, each of them (hopefully!) trivial. As far as the applicability of this dissection technique is concerned the construction of an operating system is not very much different from any other large programming effort.

The situation shows resemblance to the organization of a subroutine library in which each subroutine can be considered as being of a certain "height", given according to the following rule: a subroutine that does not call any other subroutine is of height 0, a subroutine calling one or more other subroutines is of height one higher than that of the highest height among the ones called by it. Such a rule divides a library into a hierarchical set of layers. The similarity is given by the consideration that loading the subroutines of layer 0 can be regarded as a transformation of the given machine into one that is more attractive for the formulation of the subroutines of layer 1.

Similarly the software of our multiprogramming system can be regarded as structured in layers. We conceive an ordered sequence of machines: A[0], a[1], ... A[n], where A[0] is the given hardware machine and where the software of layer i is defined in terms of machine A[i], into A[i+1]. The software of layer i is defined in terms of machine A [i], it is to be executed by machine A[i], the software of layer i uses machine A[i] to make machine A[i+1].

Compared with the library organization there are some marked differences. In the system the "Units of Dissection" are no longer restricted to subroutines, but this is a minor difference compared with the next one. Adding a subroutine of height 0 to the library is often regarded as an extension of the primitive repertoire which from then onwards is at the programmer's disposal. The fact that, when the subroutine is used, storage space and processor time have been traded for the new primitive can often be ignored, viz. as long as the store is large enough and the machine is fast enough. Consequently the new library subroutine is regarded as a pure extension. One of the main functions of an operating system, however, happens to be resource allocation, i.e. the software of layer i will use some of the resources of machine A[i] to provide resources for machine A[i+1]: in machine A[i+1] and higher these used resources of machine A[i] must be regarded as *no longer there!* The explicit introduction (and functional description!) of the intermediate machines A[1] through A[n-1] has been more than mere word-play: it has safeguarded us against much confusion as is usually generated by a set of tacit assumptions. Phrasing the structure of our total task as the design of an ordered sequence of machines provided us with a useful framework in marking the successive stages of design and production of the system.

But a framework is not very useful unless one has at least a guiding principle as how to fill it. Given a hardware machine A[0] and the broad characteristics of the final machine A[n] (the value of "n" as yet being undecided) the decisions we had to take fell into two different classes:
1) we had to dissect the total task of the system into a number of sub-tasks
2) we had to decide how the software taking care of those various sub-tasks should be layered. It is only then that the intermediate machines (and the ordinal number "n" of the final machine) are defined.

Roughly speaking the decisions of the first class (the dissection) have been taken on account of an analysis of the total task of transforming A[0] into A[n], while the decisions of the second class (the ordering) have been much more hardware bound.

The total task of creating machine A[n] has been regarded as the machine A[0] and in the dissection process this total abstraction has been split up in a number of independent abstractions. Specific properties of A[0], the reality from which we wanted to implement, were:
1) the presence of a single central processor (we wanted to provide for multiprogramming)
2) the presence of a two level store, i.e. core and drum (we wanted to offer each user some sort of homogeneous store)
3) the actual number, speed and identity (not the type) of the physically available pieces of I/O equipment (readers, punches, plotters, printers, etc.)

The subsequent ordering in layers has been guided by convenience and was therefore, as said, more hardware bound. It was recognized that the provision of virtual processors for each user program could conveniently be used to provide also one virtual processor for each of the sequential processes to be performed in relatively close synchronism with each of the (mutually asynchronous) pieces of I/O equipment. The software describing these processes was thereby placed in layers above the one in which the abstraction from our single processor had to be implemented.

The abstraction from the given two level store implied automatic transports between these two levels. A careful analysis of, on the one hand, the way in which the drum channel signalled completion of a transfer and, on the other hand, the resulting actions to be taken on account of such a completion signal, revealed the need for a separate sequential process — and therefore the existence of a virtual processor — to be performed in synchronism with the drum channel activity. It was only then that we had arguments to place the software abstracting from the single processor below the software abstracting from the two level store. In actual fact they came in layer 0 and 1 respectively. To place the software abstracting from the two level store in layer 1 was decided when it was discovered that the remaining software could make good use of the quasi homogeneous store, etc. It was in this stage of the design that the intermediate machines $A[1]$, $A[2]$, . . . got defined (in this order).

At face value our approach has much to recommend itself. For instance, a fair amount of modularity is catered for as far as changes in the configuration are concerned. The software of layer 0 takes care of processor allocation; if our configuration would be extended with a second central processor in the same core memory then only the software of layer 0 would need adaptation. If our backing store were extended with a second drum only the software of layer 1, taking care of storage allocation, would need adaptation, etc.

But this modularity (although I am willing to stress it for selling purposes) is only a consequence of the dissection and is rather independent of the chosen hierarchical ordering in the various layers, and whether I can sell this, remains to be seen. The ordering has been motivated by "convenience". . . .

The point is that what is put in layer 0 penetrates the whole of the design on top of it and the decision what to put there has far reaching consequences. Prior to the design of this multiprogramming system I had designed, together with C.S. Scholten, a set of sequencing primitives for the mutual synchronization of a number of independent processors and I knew in the mean time a systematic way to use these primitives for the regulation of the harmonious co-operation between a number of sequential machines (virtual or not). These primitives have been implemented at layer 0 and are an essential asset of the intermediate machine $A[1]$. I have still the feeling that the decision to put processor allocation in layer 0 has been a lucky one: among other things it has reduced the number of states to be considered when an interrupt arrives to such a small number that we could try them all and that I am convinced that in this respect the system is without lurking bugs. Fine, but how am I to judge the influence of my bias due to the fact that I happened to know by experience that machine $A[1]$, with these primitives included, was a logically sound foundation?

THOUGHTS ON THE SEQUENCE OF WRITING SOFTWARE
by Stanley Gill

In other papers presented at this conference, Dijkstra stresses the layer structure of software, and Randell refers to the alternative possibilities of contructing the layers from the bottom up (i.e. starting with the primitives) or from the top down (i.e. starting with the target system). Clearly the top-down approach is appropriate when the target system is already closely defined but the hardware or low-level language is initially in doubt. Conversely the bottom-up approach is appropriate when the hardware is given but the target system is only defined in a general way.

The obvious danger in either approach is that certain features will be propagated through the layers and will finally cause trouble by proving undesirable and difficult to remove, when they should have been eliminated in the middle layers. Thus in bottom-up programming, peculiarities of the hardware tend to be reflected in the higher levels (as for example in some high-level languages) when they would be better out of the way, while top-down programming may leave the programmer at the lower levels struggling to implement some feature inherent in the target system, which should have been dealt with higher up. The success of either approach depends upon the designer's ability to anticipate such problems, and to generate and to recognize solutions that avoid them.

In practice neither approach is ever adopted completely; design proceeds from both top and bottom, to meet somewhere in between, though the height of the meeting point varies with circumstances.

Each program module constitutes a definition, in terms of the primitives available in that layer, of a facility that constitutes a primitive (or primitives) of the layer above. It is thus a "downward-facing" definition. Associated with it is an "upward-facing" definition, which is referred to when the facility provided by the module is used in a higher layer. Downward-facing definitions are formal, and they are of course the means by which the system is implemented physically. Upward-facing definitions are used by the designer, and are usually informal.

In bottom-up programming the upward-facing definitions, though informal, are complete (or intended to be). Thus for example when a routine has been written in a defined language, the function performed by the routine should be unambiguously defined. In top-down programming this need not be so. In choosing the primitives one layer further down, out of which to construct the facilities required in a given layer, one has only to define them sufficiently closely to determine their role in this construction; the details may be left undefined. A classic example of this is the first step in breaking down a problem, as taught to all student programmers: drawing a flow chart. The blocks in the flow chart are by no means fully defined; their functions are only indicated sufficiently clearly to enable them to be put together correctly. As the lower layers are designed, they gradually complete the definitions of the top layers, and hence the outward functions of the whole system.

Thus in top-down programming one is often working with incompletely defined components. This demands more care and discipline; for example one must ensure that, in completing a definition, one does not introduce side effects that were not foreseen in the upper layers where the definition has been applied, and which could be harmful.

Top-down programming does however have an advantage in that it allows the designer to see which operations are called for frequently in the upper layers, and should therefore be given special treatment below. In bottom-up programming one must try to guess which primitives will prove most useful higher up. This is not easy; almost every programming language is littered with features that are hardly ever used.

In practice, a large software project is rarely a matter of implementing one single target system in terms of one given primitive system. The target is often modified in the course of the project, and the software may later be extended to meet several other targets also. It may be required to implement the whole system again on different hardware. The expectation of such later developments may influence the choice of programming method. Thus, for example, if later implementation on other hardware is likely to be needed, it is unwise to use the bottom-up approach except from a layer at which one can provide useful common facilities in terms of any of the hardware alternatives. Similarly if (as is often the case) later variations of the target system are likely, it is less attractive to use top-down programming except from a layer at which one can define a useful set of primitives applicable to all the target systems.

Thus although, with single primitive and target systems, one would nearly always program up from the bottom and down from the top to meet in the middle, in practice the picture is often more complicated. Multiple targets could result in an inversion of this arrangement in the upper layers, and multiple hardware could have the same effect in the lower layers. Thus for example a common strategy in such situations is to define a programming language at some intermediate level, intended for a range of target problems or for several different hardware systems. Having defined the language, one then proceeds to program both upwards and downwards from it.

It is in constructing such an intermediate system, before it has been formally related to either the lower or higher levels, that the greatest demands are made on a programmer's intuition. Programming is practically never a deductive process, but the depth of induction required can vary greatly according to the situation. The least demanding situation is that in which there is a single primitive system available, and a single clearly defined target system to be implemented, with only a small conceptual gap (i.e. number of software layers) between them. In the early days of programming such situations were common; now they only occur as small components of bigger tasks.

Within the last fifteen years the range of targets spanned by single software projects has increased greatly, and on the whole successfully. The range of hardware has also increased, but to a lesser extent, with greater difficulty and less success. One of the most fruitful areas for improving software productivity lies in devising an effective universal primitive system (such as Iliffe's "Basic Language").

THE TESTING OF COMPUTER SOFTWARE
by
A.I. Llewelyn and R.F. Wickens

Contents

1. Introduction

Computer software has changed rapidly from being merely an adjunct to the hardware to becoming an extremely important part of an installation and one that profoundly affects the overall performance. It is now widely accepted that computer hardware should be given some form of acceptance test by the customer and such tests have formed part of the United Kingdom government's computer contracts for about eight years. However, the weak area of most installations is now that of software.

Users complain that the software they received was badly designed and produced, was not delivered on time and when finally delivered, contained serious errors and restrictions and was also inefficient. Unfortunately, these criticisms are often only too true although, happily, it is unusual for all the criticisms to apply simultaneously. The consequences of inadequate software can be disastrous, both in financial terms as a result of delays and wasted effort in getting a system operational and also in terms of the morale of an installation's staff.

It is my opinion that software should now be subjected to a testing discipline just like any other product. The user should be provided with a specification of the software he is to receive and be able to have confidence that the software he gets will perform in accordance with this specification. By specification is meant a document that describes the product's operation and performance in some detail. Certainly, this specification should be more detailed than the typical user manuals provided today. To obtain the user's confidence, the software will have to be rigorously tested for conformity with the specification. This testing has two aspects: that carried out by the producer of the software to satisfy himself that it is fit for release to his customers and that carried out on behalf of the customer in order to give him sufficient confidence in the software to justify his paying for it. This paper is primarily concerned with the second aspect of testing. However, both aspects are very closely related and, of course, if the in house testing of the supplier is adequately carried out over a long enough period of time to gain customer confidence, the second aspect becomes largely unnecessary. It is certainly true that what might be described as the acceptance testing of software must not become a substitute for proper in house quality assurance.

2. The aims and problems of acceptance testing software

The aim of any testing scheme is to ensure that the customer gets substantially the software that he ordered and it must provide the customer with convincing evidence that this is so. However, any attempt to test software comes up against several basic problems.

One of the main problems is that of specifying unambiguously the facilities and performance to be provided by an item of software. This must be done in such a way as to allow the manufacturer to introduce improvements as time goes by and yet be capable of being written into a contract. A problem closely associated with this is that of defining the acceptance criteria to be used. These must be capable of unambiguous application and leave the supplier in no doubt as to the performance required.

Software can only function through the action of the hardware; fundamentally, only the combined effects of the software and hardware can influence events outside the computer, software alone is useless. Any testing method can only test the validity of the whole software/hardware edifice. Further, any testing procedure must take account of the fact that software is often capable of operating in several different environments representing the many possible configurations and patterns of system usage.

A problem under failure conditions is to determine what has failed; is it the software, the hardware, or a subtle combination of both? As systems become more complex, this latter condition is more likely. Modern software is called upon to interact in real time with its environment. The external stimuli can occur almost at random. Any attempt to test exhaustively such a system is going to be very difficult. It is, perhaps, fair to say that it is going to be as intellectually challenging to test the complex software systems of the future as it will be to design them initially.

3. The requirements of a software testing procedure

A test procedure should fulfill the following requirements:—

(a) Enable a user to check that he gets the product that he ordered. Any discrepancies should be detected and clearly defined so that meaningful discussions can take place between the user and the supplier.

(b) Be reasonably easy to apply and provide an effective measure of the acceptability of the software.

(c) Provide an incentive for the suppliers to improve their own Quality Assurance procedures for software.

(d) Check the "efficiency" of the software.

(e) Must be applicable from the first deliveries of a system onwards. Before a machine is ordered, a customer should have carried out a detailed appraisal of the competing systems. The tests carried out prior to final acceptance are to confirm that the information on which the chosen system was selected and finally ordered were correct. Thus, the software testing procedure may be regarded as the culmination of this appraisal. However, the depth of any such appraisal will depend upon the circumstances under which a system was selected and the organization doing the selection; thus, any test procedure should not rely upon any previous appraisal for its success.

4. Present software testing procedures

Most customers accept the software without any form of test; indeed, their contracts with the suppliers would often not allow them to do so even if they wished to. Those attempts that are made are usually limited to providing demonstrations of the more important features and the user writing special programmes that he believes will test areas important to him.

The United Kingdom government's standard computer contract allows for demonstrations of items of software to be called for during the acceptance trials. However, because of the limited time available, it is realized that these demonstrations do not represent a thorough test of the software: merely a check on the availability and a very limited test of certain critical items. When these demonstrations are based on a prior knowledge of the state of the software they can be arranged to highlight its failings and thus allow some action to be taken under the contract but without such knowledge these demonstrations are of little value. The United Kingdom government's Computer Advisory Service will, in general, have appraised the software of a computer before it is bought for use in the government service and will subsequently keep it under review. It is this fact that enables the present procedure to work reasonably well with the currently available software. However, it would be unrealistic to suppose that such a procedure will provide the user much protection against faults in the very complex systems that are likely to become available in the next few years.

The greatest benefits are obtained from a testing procedure in the early life of a new range of computers. Once a usable version of the required software is available, the basic needs of the user are satisfied. If subsequent issues are in error, it is inconvenient but not disastrous. However, this does not mean that testing standards can be relaxed for new issues of current packages, although it may make it less urgent. Seemingly, quite minor changes may have a profound effect upon the operation of a package. It is certainly necessary to check that a new issue of a package is compatible with its predecessor. It must not be expected that a test procedure will guarantee error-free software but it should tell the user what is the state of the software he is being offered so that he may decide whether it is capable of doing his work effectively.

5. Possible test strategies

There are, fundamentally, two different methods of determining whether a product meets its specification. One can analyse the product in great detail and from this determine if it is in accordance with its specification, or one can measure its performance experimentally and see if the results are in accord with the specification; the number and sophistication of the experiments can be varied to provide the degree of confidence required of the results.

Our current software appraisals are biased towards the analytic approach but the limited time and effort available and the often limited access to detailed information prevent the appraisal doing away with the need for an experimental approach to software testing.

6. A proposed test procedure

The proposed test procedure attempts to remove, as far as possible, software testing from the hardware acceptance trials. The aim of the procedure is to test software as soon as it becomes available and merely to check that each installation has a good copy of the required items in its library. It is intended for use by large organizations rather than by individual small users.

It is proposed that software should be rigorously tested outside the acceptance trials. It requires that items of software should be given "type" approval on a number of prescribed configurations as soon as possible after company release. During an acceptance trial, it should merely be proved that a correct copy of the software exists at the installation for that particular configuration.

Various levels of type approval would be required but only the more important packages need be subjected to all levels of the testing envisaged. The suggested levels of approval are:—

(a) Documentation. This would check that the user manuals are available, are in accordance with the specifications issued by the supplier, that they are of an acceptable standard of presentation and literacy and are self-consistent. Basically, the question that should be answered is "is it likely that the potential user will be able to use the documentation to write effective programs for his installation?" It would also be necessary to check that an acceptable up-dating system is provided so that a user can be sure that he has up-to-date manuals. The greater part of the work involved in this level of approval could be done as part of the normal appraisal of software carried out before a machine is ordered.

(b) Availability. This would check that an item of software had been released and was in general conformity with the documentation. This would not be a rigorous check but merely a check of a package's existence in a working form on a number of prescribed configurations. This check should be carried out as soon as possible after the contractor makes the software available. These tests would be very similar to the current demonstrations of software during acceptance trials.

(c) Detailed verification of facilities. This stage would consist of testing the specified facilities of each package in detail and checking the package's interaction with others with which it can be associated. Such tests should include the running of special test programs to check on facilities, plus "soak" or random tests using a wide variety of typical user type programs from a wide variety of sources.

(d) Performance assessment. This test would check on the performance of a package. It would determine the "efficiency" of a package in terms of its core store requirements, peripheral requirements and running times under various conditions.

Approval at each level would be given as soon as those carrying out the tests had established, with an acceptable degree of confidence, that a package would provide satisfactory service in field use. We cannot call for perfection; merely a reasonably high probability that the "average" user will find the package usable. In practice it may be necessary to provide partial approval to a package, for example approved for use on machines over a certain size only.

7. Application of the proposed procedure

It is envisaged that each "level" of testing should be carried out in the following manner:—

(i) Documentation check. This would be carried out very largely during the normal appraisal of the software before the machine was ordered, or at least as soon as the documentation became available. The work would take about three man-months for a major package. Every effort should be made to complete this work at least three months before a package's proposed release date. This phase of the work would be done by attempting to use the documentation to write test programs for use in subsequent phases of the testing procedure. However, as the manuals are often produced in parallel with the package itself, it is to be expected that the programs produced will have to be amended in the light of subsequent amendments to these manuals.

(ii) Availability check. This should be carried out as soon as possible after the release of a package. Only a few test programs would be required and these would be written during the documentation check. The final debugging and running of these programs would form the availability check. It should be possible in most cases to accept the supplier's own validation procedures for this check if, after investigation by those responsible for operating the "type" approval scheme, it is found to be effective. It would probably still be necessary to carry out random checks to ensure that the company's standards are being maintained. This phase should be concluded within a month of a package's release. The effort required is likely to be less than one man-month per major package tested.

(iii) Detailed check. This level of approval is the most onerous part of the test procedure. To be of real value to the user, this check should be completed as soon as possible after the release of a package, certainly within three months unless there is no requirement by the user for the package in the near future. For such packages for which there is no immediate requirement, evidence of extensive satisfactory use by other customers could be accepted in lieu of a detailed check. Such a procedure might also be adopted for the lesser used packages that are unlikely to be vital to the functioning of the approval organization.

The detailed testing will be made up of two types of work: the testing of packages limited to one manufacturer, or even one machine, such as operating systems, and testing those items that tend to be machine independent, such as high level languages. The effort required for machine dependent items is likely to be large and to be a continuing load for the "approving" body. However, the work involved on the standard languages, such as Cobol, Algol and Fortran, can very largely be done "once and for all" with only minor adaptations having to be made to suit each new system.

The effort required is likely to be about nine man-months to test an operating system and about three man-months to design and write test programs for the first test of the implementation of a well known language such as Fortran and about one man-month for each subsequent test of that language.

(iv) Performance check. Some idea of the performance of package will be gained during the "availability" and "detailed" checks but it is desirable to have separate tests aimed at measuring performance or "efficiency". These performance tests should be conducted three to six months after the release of a package. It might be easier to measure performance comparatively rather than absolutely, in that an absolute test of, say, a compiler's efficiency would be very difficult and time-consuming to carry out but for a comparative test, a variety of benchmark programs might suffice. However, for machine dependent packages, such as operating systems, absolute measurements will have to be made.

The likely effort required would be:—

(a) For computers using pre-written benchmark programs, about one man-month per language.

(b) For operating systems, up to six man-months per system.

8. Criteria of acceptance

The supplier would have to have a criterion to aim at for each level of the approval procedure and it is here that the greatest difficulty arises. Software is a highly versatile product whose performance depends very much on the precise use made of it and thus useful generalized measures of software performance are not easily found. The value of a piece of software is still very much a matter of opinion but the testing procedure is aimed at finding facts and highlighting failures so that reasonable discussion should be possible between the parties.

Approval at Level 1 could initially be given as soon as the appropriate set of manuals become available for each package and had been used to write a few simple programs. Criticisms would be fed back to the supplier but it is not realistic to expect manuals to be re-cast at the "approving" authority's request, although a long-term influence might be expected. Of course, it could be expected that errors would be corrected as soon as possible. Approval at Level 1 might be interpreted as indicating that usable manuals are generally available to customers.

Approval of Level 2 could be given as soon as demonstrations of a package had been witnessed by the approving body. The demonstration programs would, of course, have to be acceptable to the approving body. If the supplier's own validation procedures were acceptable, then documentary evidence of their completion might be acceptable instead of a demonstration.

Approval at Level 3 would be given when all the facilities offered or called for in the contract were shown to be working. However, we cannot expect perfection and it might be necessary to give partial approval in some cases. An alternative might be to divide the facilities into "required" and "desired" and call for 100 per cent implementation of the required facilities and, say, 70 per cent of the "desired" ones, together with, say, three months' grace to complete the implementation.

The requirements for approval at Level 4 can often be well defined, for example, "shall occupy not more than 8,000 words of core store", "shall compile at 1,000 statements per minutes for a program of 200 statements", etc.

9. Effort and cost estimates for the approval scheme

The total cost of implementing the previously described Type Approval scheme can be expected to vary greatly from system to system. The following figures are for testing a typical currently available operating system in accordance with the above proposals.

Software Item	Effort in Man-months				Machine time in hours			
	Level 1	2	3	4	Level 1	2	3	4
Languages								
Algol	2	1	2	1	0	1	2	1
Cobol	2	1	2	1	0	1	2	1
Fortran	2	1	2	1	0	1	2	1
R.P.G.	2	1	1	1	0	1	2	1
Assembly code	3	1	2	1	0	1	3	1
Operating system								
Supervision	3	1	3	2	0	1	3	1
File Control packages	3	1	2	2	0	1	3	1
Peripheral handling routines	3	1	2	1	0	1	3	1
Program testing aids	3	1	2	1	0	1	3	1

Application packages

Sort routines	2	1	1	1		0	1	1	1
Miscellaneous	3	2	3	1		0	1	1	1
Totals:	28	12	22	13		0	11	25	11

Thus, the total effort required is 75 man-months, together with the use of 47 hours of machine time. The total cost of the exercise would therefore be approximately £25,000 spread over a period of a year. This expenditure is not entirely over and above existing expenditure because, in effect, Levels 1 and 2 of the proposed procedure are already carried out by the present procedure. Thus, the new expenditure required is about £13,000, i.e. a doubling of current expenditure.

10. Consequences of approval

For the procedure to be effective, there must be some financial consequences of the software not obtaining approval. A possible approach is to attach 10 per cent of the purchase price or rental to each level of approval. This would allow up to 40 per cent of the price to be retained under late delivery conditions. It would also be necessary to require at least a minimum set of software being available before any money was paid. A possible approach would be for the contract to list the required items of software and against each item give the minimum level of approval required for acceptance of the installation. It will also be necessary to have associated with the contract the specifications of the required software. These would detail the facilities and performance of the software. However, this will require a change of attitude on the part of computer manufacturers who are often very reluctant to provide any detailed performance information until after the software in question is working. This attitude requires the customer to purchase his software almost as an "act of faith" in the supplier and is surely not something that can be allowed to continue.

11. Conclusions and discussion

This paper has attempted to present a possible method by which large organizations, such as the United Kingdom government, might test the software supplied by computer manufacturers to its installations. Its main aim may be described as an attempt to ensure that new computer installations can rapidly take on the work for which they were purchased by ensuring that installations have the best available information on which to plan their work. It is a procedure aimed at elucidating the facts about software; what works and what does not and how well does it work? The cost of doing this sort of exercise is not trivial but with the number of computer systems involved, the cost per installation is quite small and if the procedure can speed up the take-on of work by allowing the confident use of proved software, rather than the hesitant use of the unknown, it will prove worthwhile. Hopefully, such a procedure would encourage the computer manufacturers to improve their own quality assurance procedures, perhaps even to the point where use of testing of software becomes unnecessary.

PERFORMANCE MONITORING AND SYSTEMS EVALUATION
by
Tad B. Pinkerton

I. Performance Monitoring

There are many specific motives for evaluating the performance of a large-scale computing system. Today's systems are more complicated and more expensive than their predecessors; hence their operation is more difficult to comprehend and more costly to misjudge. At the same time, a utility-grade service of increasingly high quality is being demanded. These circumstances require the availability of performance data for use in

   (a) system design
   (b) system acquisition
   (c) changes in configuration
   (d) software production
   (e) system checkout
   (f) normal operation
   (g) and advanced research.

Raw data obtained from a computing system usually consist of descriptions of instantaneous events: the time at which each such event occurs together with information peculiar to its nature. The data reduction process under which such data become meaningful is often complicated, requiring considerable cross-referencing and consolidation of individual event descriptions. For example, the question of system behavior is bound up with the consideration of system load. Hence operational information must be combined with workload data in order to interpret the former. And at a more basic level, an analysis program must "invert" the operation of a job scheduler in order to extract resource allocation data from scheduling event descriptions. Many useful items are found in counts or averages produced by tabulating data over intervals of time.

At least four different techniques have been successfully used for the collection of system performance data:

(1) Hardware Measurement. Special purpose devices such as TS/SPAR for the IBM System 360 Model 67 and the UCLA "snuper computer" have been built to "plug in" to a machine and directly monitor signals in interesting places. The principal advantage of this procedure is that the measurement is non-interesting: no distortion of the data occurs as a result of its collection, which can take place during normal system operation. The extremely high resolution obtained with this technique is occasionally useful, but it is frequently a disadvantage in that problems are created with the storage and reduction of vast quantities of data. A more serious problem with hardware measurement is that the required engineering expertise and cost of special-purpose hardware place it out of the reach of most installations.

(2) Hardware Simulation. It is not at all uncommon to simulate one machine with a software package on another, or on the machine itself. A current example is the System 360 simulator at Princeton University. A simulation package provides data at a resolution nearly as high as that obtained by hardware measurement, under program control and in program-oriented terms. In addition, it is readily modifiable to produce information of different kinds. Unfortunately, the simulated system must run at such a small fraction of the rate of the actual system that it can only be run for short periods of time, and hence not under normal operating conditions. Most timing data is at least suspect, for it is difficult for the simulator to maintain comparative operating speeds of simulated components, to say nothing of unsimulated peripherals.

(3) Software Sampling. Data can be obtained from a system in normal operation by adding instructions to the system itself. Sampling, e.g. by periodically interrupting pro-

cesses to record their status, is usually not hard to implement and provides good control over the data collection overhead. The primary disadvantages of this technique are that certain kinds of information may be difficult or impossible to obtain, and considerable attention must be given to questions of sample size and validity.

(4) Continuous Software Monitoring. Provided that care is taken to control the overhead and that hardware-level resolution is not required, the most desirable data collection procedure allows continuous monitoring of events under program control. Such a facility can be turned on and off during normal operation, easily changed to adjust the quantity and kinds of data, and it provides a complete description of the monitored phenomena in a given period. The author's experience in implementing this kind of facility in the Michigan Terminal System (MTS) has shown that it can be done with surprisingly good resolution and low overhead, to produce invaluable data for the purposes mentioned above.

The following general observations may be useful in the implementation of a data collection facility (DCF);

    a. A DCF should be included in the design of a system, for part of it will be embedded in the supervisor at a low level, and careful planning is necessary to ensure a clean implementation.

    b. A DCF is very useful for the development of the system itself, and therefore should be produced early in that development.

    c. For reasons of both effectiveness and generality, as much of the analysis of collected data as possible should be deferred for independent processing.

    d. Both the collection and analysis phases of operation require a variety of data selection modes, e.g. by type of datum, by task, by recording time. Good selection capability reduces both the collection overhead and data reduction time.

II. Systems Evaluation

Once measures have been taken to provide accurate operating system data, it becomes reasonable to consider the problem of evaluating system performance. The performance criteria one uses clearly depend on one's motives for evaluation. Within a single installation, one usually focusses on criteria of *utilization* of both hardware and software components, and on standards of the *quality* of service provided. Discussions of both these factors require a basis for characterizing the *workload* under which given levels of utilization and response have been obtained. Indices chosen to describe these three operational factors are biased by the types of performance data available and the way in which they are obtained.

Because distinct installations rely on different performance data and emphasize different criteria for evaluation, it is difficult to compare their performance. Thus there is an additional need to define standards for the descriptions of workload, utilization and response so that performance in different environments can be meaningfully compared. It would be particularly useful to provide such standards for general purpose multi-access systems (where the need is greatest!) in such a way that they also apply to simpler multi-programming and single-thread systems as special cases.

TOWARDS A METHODOLOGY OF COMPUTING SYSTEM DESIGN
by
B. Randell

Introduction

Three independent, but related, projects concerned with the methodology of computing system design have recently been reported. The work described by Dijkstra [1] concerns the design of a multiprogramming system for the X8 computer, at the Technological University, Eindhoven. Parnas and Darringer [2] have described their work on a language SODAS and demonstrated its use in the design of a fairly complex hardware system. Finally F. Zurcher and the present author [3] have given a short discussion of "iterative multilevel modelling", the methodology being investigated to aid the design of an experimental multi-processing system [4] at the T.J. Watson Research Center. The purpose of the present note is to compare and contrast these three projects very briefly, and to attempt an identification of major problems still to be faced in achieving an effective methodology of computer system design.

Structuring the Design Process

The author's belief is that the most important aspect of all three projects is the stress they put on achieving a structuring of the design process, and on making the system being designed reflect this structure.

Computing systems are undeniably extremely complex. They are notoriously difficult to design successfully, and when complete are difficult to understand or to modify. A system can be thought of as being the embodiment of a set of solutions to a set of distinct although related problems. All three projects lay stress on a careful consideration of the order in which the various problems should be tackled, and of the consequences of each design decision, both on those decisions which have already been taken, and on those problem areas which remain to be addressed. Most important however, they make the system that they are designing contain explicit traces of the design process — in other words, the system is structured to demonstrate the way in which it was designed, and the designers' views as to how the various problem areas are related to each other.

The papers by Dijkstra and by Zurcher and Randell both use the term "level of abstraction". Their systems are constructed as a sequence of levels of abstraction, each consisting of a set of co-operating sequential processes [5]. In general, the primitives used to construct the programs which define processes on one level are provided by the processes of the immediately lower level. Each level therefore is in essence a set of solutions, specified directly in terms of appropriate quantities, to a set of problem areas which the designers have chosen to regard as being closely related. Less related problem areas are dealt with on other levels. For example, the lowest of Dijkstra's levels is one which contains solutions to problems caused by timing constraints, and the fact that there is only a single processor in his computing system. The levels above this can ignore these problems, and assume, for example, the existence of a multiplicity of processors. By such means Dijkstra and his colleagues have retained control of the complexity of their system to such a degree that they could convince themselves, a priori, as to its logical correctness.

The Ordering of Design Decisions

There is probably no single "correct" order in which to take a series of design decisions, though some orderings can usually be agreed to be better than others. Almost invariably some early decisions, thought at the time to have been clearly correct, will turn out to have been premature. The design structuring described above is an attempt to mitigate the effects of such occurrences.

There are two rather distinct approaches to the problem of deciding in what order to make design decisions. The "top-down" approach involves starting at the outside limits of the proposed system, and gradually working down, at each stage attempting to define what a given component should do, before getting involved in decisions as to how the component should provide this function. Conversely the "bottom-up" approach proceeds by a gradually increasing complexity of combinations of building-blocks. The top-down approach is for the designer who has faith in his ability to estimate the feasibility of constructing a component to match a set of specifications. The opposite approach is for the designer who prefers to estimate the utility of the component that he has decided he can construct.

Clearly the blind application of just one of these approaches would be quite foolish. This is shown all too frequently in the case of designers who perhaps without realizing it are using an extreme "bottom-up" approach, and are surprised when their collection of individually optimized components result in a far from optimum system. The "top-down" philosophy can be viewed mainly as an attempt to redress the balance. In fact a designer claiming to follow the top-down approach, and specifying what a particular component is to do before he designs the component, can hardly avoid using his previous experience and intuition as to what is feasible.

Of the three projects under discussion, those by Parnas and Darringer, and by Zurcher and Randell lay most stress on the top-down approach. Zurcher and Randell in fact state that their aim is to defer decisions as to whether a given component be constructed out of software or of hardware until a late stage in the design process, when cost/performance analyses can be made. In contrast, Dijkstra is concerned with the design of a multiprogramming system to run on an existing hardware system, so has at least presented the results of his design effort as if produced by a bottom-up approach.

The Place of Simulation in the Design Process

Since the computer profession insists on building systems which are more complicated than it can analyze mathematically, many designers have made extensive use of simulation. Probably the most successful uses have been for investigation of isolated problem areas such as storage interference or I/O buffering, and for detailed modelling of completed designs (see for example Nielsen [6]). Two of the three projects under discussion, namely SODAS and the Iterative Multi-level Modelling technique, involve the use of simulation. However in these projects simulation is regarded not as an adjunct to, but rather as an integral part of, the entire design effort.

In many design efforts it is difficult to identify exactly what is in the design at any given stage. Usually the partially completed design will consist of inaccurate and out-of-date documentation, unwritten "understandings" between groups of designers, and in late stages of the design, partially constructed components (hardware or software). The intent of the above two projects is to keep the design so formal that at each stage in the design process it is capable of objective evaluation — being machine-executable is a very practical means of achieving this goal. The machine-executable partial design is, since it can obviously not be doing the complete job required of the system, therefore just a "simulation" of the complete system. As design work progresses this simulation will gradually evolve into the real system.

With this view of simulation as part of the design process, there is no room for arguments that the design has not been simulated faithfully, that the simulation results are hopelessly pessimistic and in any case only apply to last month's design, etc. The simulation *is* the design.

Future Problems

It would be easy to talk about the problems directly connected with providing an effective tool for use by a large group of designers in simulating their system as the design progresses. However it is fairly clear that we have barely started to tackle the problem of finding an effective methodological approach to computing system design.

We are solely in need of techniques for representing our partial designs so that at each stage the spectrum of possible future design decisions is made clearer, and the consequences of a particular choice can be more easily evaluated. (For example, in programming the choice as to whether to make multiple copies of a given set of information, or to maintain just a single set and access it from different places by varying levels of indirection, is often very arbitrary). Similarly, if we could find some way of guiding designers as to what might be a good order in which to take decisions, this might have a considerable effect on the overall quality of our system designs.

Acknowledgements

The author's initial work in this area was carried out jointly with Frank Zurcher, with much valuable advice and criticism from Carl Kuehner, Meir Lehman and Hans Schlaeppi. The viewpoints, both on existing approaches to methodologies of system design and on future problems, expressed herein have greatly benefited from extensive discussions with Edsger Dijkstra at the Technological University, Eindhoven.

References

1. Dijkstra, E.W., The Structure of the "T.H.E." Multiprogramming System. Comm. ACM 11, 5 (1968) pp. 341-346.
2. Parnas, D.L., and Darringer, J.A., SODAS and a Methodology for System Design. AFIPS Conference Proceedings Vol. 31, 1967 Fall Joint Computer Conference. Thompson Books, Washington D.C. (1967) pp. 449-474.
3. Zurcher, F.W. and Randell, B., Iterative Multilevel Modelling, A Methodology for Computer System Design. IFIP Congress 68, Edinburgh, August 5-10, 1968.
4. Lehman, M., A Survey of Problems and Preliminary Results Concerning Parallel Processing and Parallel Processors. Proc. IEEE 54, 12 (1966) pp. 1889-1901.
5. Dijkstra, E.W., Cooperating Sequential Processes. Technological University, Eindhoven (September 1965).
6. Nielsen, N.R., The Analysis of General Purpose Computer Time-Sharing Systems. Doctoral Dissertation, Stanford University, California, (December 1966).

DOCUMENTATION STANDARDS
excerpted from
DOCUMENTATION FOR SERVICE AND USERS
by
Franz Selig

Documentation standards are set in many individual centers using forms easy to fill out which typically contain the following entries:

TITLE PAGE
  a. Project name and number
  b. Computer models on which it can be run
  c. Program language(s)
  d. Client department and number
  e. Client contact
  f. Frequency of program use (e.g. annual, monthly, continual)
  g. Program user(s) (i.e. individual, department, general)
  h. Date issued
  i. Brief abstract
  j. Issued by: (Programmer's name)

MODEL DESCRIPTION
  a. Problem statement
    1. Complete description with history
    2. Purpose and value
    3. Urgency
    4. Area of intended use
  b. Technical writeups and diagrams
  c. Basic formulae (with definitions of symbols and terminology)
  d. Restrictions concerning physical limitations and bounds
  e. List of references

USER'S GUIDE
  a. Description of how to use the program
    1. How to submit a job
    2. Where the program resides
    3. Sample job card
  b. Input cards description
    1. Sample deck layout of JCL cards and indication of where to insert data
    2. Data input
      i) Order
      ii) Layout
      iii) Sample input forms (filled in with data)
  c. Output
    1. Description of information
    2. Sample output from case data given in 2) iii
  d. Estimation of computer run times
  e. Table of error messages and recommended courses of action
  f. Complete list of options, with a brief description of how the programming affects these variations
  g. A list of related programs:
    1. Is there communication of data between this program and others under separate cover? If so, describe in detail.
    2. Are there other programs which could complement this program? What are the basic differences?
  h. Possible Extensions

PROGRAMMER'S GUIDE
  a. Overall logic flow diagram, including interaction of data sets
  b. If overlay, show the tree structure
  c. The map listing from the sample case shown in the User's Guide

d. List of definitions of all variables in common
e. Description of flow sheet of routines (for main routine and each subroutine)
f. Description of data sets
h. Off-line devices (plotter, etc.)
   1. Description
   2. Sample diagrams

OPERATOR'S GUIDE
  a. Job flow on computer
    Schematic drawing identifying all data sets and devices
  b. Input
    Exact layout of input streams, with detail of JCL (data cards, tape files, disc files)
  c. Operation
   1. Normal — instructions and description (with sample console sheet)
   2. Abnormal — list possible troubles, with recommended courses of action
  d. Output instructions
    E.g., tapes to be listed or plotted, no. of copies

SOURCE DECKS
  a. All source decks would begin with comment cards, identifying:
   1. Project name and number
   2. Client dept. name and number
   3. Programmer's name
   4. Completion date
  b. Additional comment cards throughout program to:
   1. Define nomenclature
   2. Identify areas of calculation
  c. Each source deck should have the project no. in columns 73 to 76
  d. All Fortran source decks would have sequence numbers in columns 77 to 80 (e.g. 0010, 0020, 0030 — to allow for additions). Cobol would have sequence numbers in columns 01 to 06.

APPENDICES

A1. PARTICIPANTS

Chairman: Prof. Dr. F. L. Bauer,
Mathematisches Institut
der Technischen Hochschule,
D-8 München 2,
Arcisstrasse 21,
Germany

Co-Chairmen:

Dr. H. J. Helms,
Director,
Northern Europe University
Computing Center,
Technical University of Denmark,
DK-2800 Lyngby, Denmark

Professor L. Bolliet,
Laboratoire de Calcul,
Université de Grenoble
Boite Postale 7,
F-38 Saint-Martin-D'Hères
France

Group Leaders
Design

Professor A.J. Perlis, (Chairman), Department of Computer Science, Carnegie-Mellon
University, Pittsburgh, Pennsylvania 15213, USA.
Dr. M. Paul, Leibniz-Rechenzentrum, D-8 München 2, Richard Wagnerstr. 18, Germany.
Mr. B. Randell, IBM Corporation, Thomas J. Watson Research Center, P.O. Box 218,
Yorktown Heights, New York 10598, USA.

Production

Dr. P. Naur (Chairman), A/S Regnecentralen, Falkoneralle 1, 2000 Copenhagen F, Denmark
Dr. H.R. Wiehle, AEG-TELEFUNKEN, D-775 Konstanz, Postfach 154, Germany.
Professor J. N. Buxton, University of Warwick, Coventry CV4 7AL, Warwick, England.

Service

Prof. Dr. K. Samelson (Chairman), Mathematisches Institut der Technischen Hochschule,
D-8 München 2, Arcisstrasse 21, Germany.
Professor B. Galler, The University of Michigan Computing Center, North University
Building, Ann Arbor, Michigan, USA.
Dr. D. Gries, Department of Computer Science, Stanford University, Stanford, California
94305, USA.

Mr. A. d'Agapeyeff, Computer Analysts and Programmers Ltd., CAP House, 14/15 Great
James Street, London, W.C.1., England.

Mr. J.D. Babcock, Allen-Babcock Computing Inc., 866 U.N. Plaza, Suite 554, New York, New York 10017, USA.

Professor R.S. Barton, Consultant in System Design, P.O. Box 303, Avalon, California 90704, USA.

Mr. R. Bemer, GE Information Systems Group, 13430 Black Canyon Highway, C-85, Phoenix Arizona 85029, USA.

Prof. Dr. J. Berghuis, N.V. Philips' Computer Industrie, Postbus 245, Apeldoorn, The Netherlands.

Mr. P. Cress, Computing Center, University of Waterloo, Waterloo, Ontario, Canada.

Professor L. Dadda, Politecnico, Piazza L. Da Vinci, I-20133, Milano, Italy.

Dr. E.E. David, Jr., Bell Telephone Laboratories Inc., Murray Hill, New Jersey 07971, USA.

Prof. Dr. E.W. Dijkstra, Department of Mathematics, Technological University, Postbox 513, Eindhoven, The Netherlands.

Dr. H. Donner, Siemens Aktiengesellschaft, ZL Lab Gruppe Programmierungsverfahren, D-8 München 25, Hofmannstrasse 51, Germany

Mr. A. Endres, IBM Laboratory, Programming Center, D-703, Böblingen, P.O.B. 210, Germany.

Mr. C.P. Enlart, European Program Library IBM, IBM — France, 23, Allé Mailasson, F-29 Boulogne Billancourt, France.

Professor P. Ercoli, Istituto Nazionale per le Applicazioni del Calcolo, Piazzale delle Scienze 7, I-00185 Rome, Italy.

Mr. A.G. Fraser, The University Mathematical Laboratory, Corn Exchange Street, Cambridge, England.

Mr. F. Genuys, IBM — France, 116 Avenue de Neuilly, F-92 Neuilly, France.

Professor S. Gill, Centre for Computing and Automation, Imperial College, Royal School of Mines Building, Prince Consort Road, London, S.W.7., England.

Mr. H.R. Gillette, Control Data Corporation, 3145 Porter Drive, Palo Alto, California 94304, USA.

Mr. A.E. Glennie, Building E.2., Atomic Weapons Research Establishment, Aldermaston, Berks., England.

Dr. G. Goos, Mathematisches Institut der Technischen Hochschule, D-8 München 2, Arcisstrasse 21, Germany.

Professor R.M. Graham, Project MAC, M.I.T., 545 Technology Square, Cambridge, Massachusetts 02139, USA.

Mr. R.C. Hastings, IBM Corporation, 540 East Main Street, Rochester, New York 14604, USA.

Mr. J.A. Harr, Bell Telephone Laboratories Inc., Naperville, Ill. 60540, USA.

Professor J.N.P. Hume, Department of Computer Science, University of Toronto, Toronto, Ontario, Canada.

Mr. H.Á. Kinslow, Computer Systems Consultant, 14 Donnelly Drive, Ridgefield, Connecticut 06877, USA.

Mr. P.M. Kjeldaas, Kjeller Computer Installation, P.O. Box 70, N-2007 Kjeller, Norway.

Mr. H. Köhler, AEG-TELEFUNKEN, D-775 Konstanz, Büchlestrasse 1-5, Germany.

Mr. K. Kolence, Boole and Babbage Inc., 1121 San Antonio Road, Palo Alto, California 94303, USA.

Dr. G. Letellier, Départment Techniques Nouvelles, Division Informatique, SEMA, 35 boulevard Brune, Paris 14e, France.

Mr. A.I. Llewelyn, Ministry of Technology, Abell House, John Islip Street, London, S.W.1., England.

Dr. R.M. McClure, Computer Science Center, Institute of Technology, Southern Methodist University, Dallas, Texas 75222, USA.

Dr. M.D. McIlroy, Bell Telephone Laboratories Inc., Murray Hill, New Jersey 07971, USA.

Mr. J. Nash, IBM UK Laboratories, Hursley Park, Winchester, Hants., England.

Mr. A. Opler, IBM Corporation, Thomas J. Watson Research Center, P.O. Box 218, Yorktown Heights, New York 10698, USA

Dr. T.B. Pinkerton, Department of Computer Science, 8 Buccleuch Place, Edinburgh 8, Scotland.

Prof. Dr. W.L. van der Poel, Technische Hogeschool, Julianalaan 132, Delft, The Netherlands.

Mr. G.D. Pratten, Department of Computer Science, 8, Buccleuch Place, Edinburgh 8 Scotland.

Mr. T.M.H. Reenskaug, Central Institute for Industrial Research, Forskningsvn. 1, Blindern – Oslo 3, Norway.

Mr. D.T. Ross, Electronic Systems Laboratory, M.I.T., Room 402A, 545 Technology Square, Cambridge, Massachusetts 02139, USA.

Mr. F. Sallé, C.I.I., Rue Jeans Jaurès, F-78 Clayes-sous-Bois, France.

Dr. F. Selig, Mobil Research and Development Corporation, Field Research Laboratory, P.O. Box 900, Dallas, Texas 75221, USA.

Mr. J.W. Smith, Scientific Data Systems, Station A-102, 555 South Aviation Blvd., El Segundo, California 90245, USA.

Mr. R.F. Wickens, Ministry of Technology, Computer Advisory Service, Technical Support Unit, 207 Old Street, London E.C.1., England.

Dr. P.L. Wodon, M.B.L.E., Research Laboratory, 2, avenue van Becelaere, Brussels 17, Belgium.

Scientific Secretaries

Prof. L.K. Flanigan, Department of Computer and Communication Sciences, The University of Michigan Computing Center, North University Building, Ann Arbor, Michigan, USA.

Mr. I. Hugo, International Computers and Ltd., 93/99 Upper Richmond Rd, London, S.W.15., England.

Observers

Dr. H. Haller, Deutsche Forschungsgemeinschaft, D-532 Bad Godesberg, Kennedy – Allee 40, Germany.

Mr. P.H. Kenney, OSCAD, SHAPE, B-7010, Belgium.

Dr. E.G. Kovach, Director, Office of General Scientific Affairs, International Scientific and Technological Affairs, Department of State, Washington D.C., 20520, USA.

Captain B. Pavlidis, R.H.N., HGNS, D.M.E.O. 14, Pentagon, Athens, Greece.

Major Gr. Tsiftsis, HGNS, D.M.E.O. 14, Pentagon, Athens, Greece.

A2. CONFERENCE SCHEDULE

MONDAY 7th OCTOBER

9.00 to 9.30	Introductory remarks by Professor F.L. Bauer, Conference Chairman
9.30 to 10.00	Keynote speech by Professor A.J. Perlis
10.20 to 12.30	Design of software, plenary session
14.00 to 15.00	Planning meetings of the three working groups
15.00 to 16.30 and 16.50 to 19.00	Production of software, plenary session

TUESDAY 8th OCTOBER
  9.00 to 10.00   Lecture on "Software Components" by Dr. M.D. McIlroy
  10.20 to 13.00   Service of software, plenary session
  14.30 to 16.30   Parallel meetings of the working groups
     and
  17.00 to 18.30
  19.00 to 00.00   Discussion on software pricing

WEDNESDAY 9th OCTOBER
  9.00 to 11.00   Design of software, plenary session
  11.25   Excursion for the rest of the day to Munich

THURSDAY 10th OCTOBER
  9.00 to 10.30   Production of software, plenary session
     and
  10.50 to 13.00
  14.30 to 17.00   Service of software, plenary session
  17.30 to 19.00   Discussion on "Techniques for Software Component Mechanisation"
  21.00 to 22.30   Discussion on "Gaps between Intentions and Performance in Software" and "Software Engineering Education"

FRIDAY 11th OCTOBER
  9.00 to 11.00   Parallel meetings of the working groups
  16.00 to 18.30   Summary plenary session

A3. ORIGINAL LIST OF TOPICS THAT WERE TO BE DISCUSSED

Working Group D — Design

D1. *General Guidelines*
  D1.1 Design as controlled by external function.
       The environments (user, equipment, etc.) guide the design.
       Example: User languages and storage requirement guide the design.

  D1.2 Design as controlled by internal function.
       The functions (parsers, 1/0 routines, file systems, symbol tables) guide the design.
       Example: Sharing of functions among sub-systems which appear different to the user.

D2. *General Techniques*
  D2.1 Deductive or inductive method of design.
       Increasing specialization of goal versus
       increasing complexity of combinations of building-blocks.

  D2.2 The search for modularity and establishment of general interfaces.

  D2.3 Complexity controlled by hierarchical ordering of function and variability.

  D2.4 Design controlled by increasing specialization of description.
       The use of simulation to monitor the design process.

D3. *Proscriptions*
   D3.1 Intrinsic features I: Completeness, efficiency, modularity, communicability. With respect to the goals performs and communicates well the complete set of functions using a minimum of units.

   D3.2 Intrinsic features II: self-monitoring and improvement of performance. Every system represent a compromise under insufficient knowledᵤe of load. Use should lead to improvement of performance.

   D3.3 Designing incremental systems. Reaching a target system from a given system. Adjoining and merging separately designed systems to form a new one.

   D3.4 The issue of balance I: Balancing the cost versus the merit of control, security, training, and convenience.

   D3.5 The issue of balance II: The virtue of limited goals to attain excellent performance.

D4. *Relevant Design Problems*
   D4.1 The influence of data structures on system design.

   D4.2 Allocation of fixed resources among competing processes. Application to time sharing.

   D4.3 Co-operation of processes among shared resources. Time sharing.

D5. *Documentation*
   D5.1 General properties of design documentation: Levels, precision and function (how and what). Incremental documentation.

   D5.2 The role of high level language in system design:

   D5.2.1 The use of PL/1 to describe Multics.

   D5.2.2 The use of an Algol-like language (PL/360) to describe a machine dependent assembly language.

Working Group P - PRODUCTION

P1. *The Organization for Producing Software*
   P1.1 Number and quality of people used;

   P1.2 Structure of large groups of programmers;

   P1.3 Control and measurement of a programmer's output and possibility of its improvement;

   P1.4 Project of product oriented organization;

   P1.5 Internal communication within a large group of programmers.

P2. *Production Techniques for Producing Software*
     P2.1 Schedules of work;

     P2.2 Standards for programming, testing and documentation;

     P2.3 Compatibility;

     P2.4 Use of simulators, high level languages, etc.;

     P2.5 Redesign of package specification during software production.

P3. *Monitoring the Production Process*
     P3.1 Reporting techniques and control of schedules;

     P3.2 Comparison of current costs, current estimated completion date, current
           estimated technical quality of the final product compared with specification
           requirements.

P4. *The Final Product and its Evaluation*
     P4.1 Evaluating performance and final quality control of software;

     P4.2 Evaluating adequacy of documentation for the user, for maintenance and
           modification.

Working Group S - SERVICE

S1. *Distribution of Software*
     S1.1 Characterization of distribution media;

     S1.2 Levels of language in which distributed software is represented;

     S1.3 Acceptance criteria for distributed software validation;

     S1.4 Documentation;

     S1.5 Adaption to configuration;

     S1.6 Parameter identification for adaption.

S2. *Maintenance and Extension of Software*
     S2.1 Detection of errors: responsibility, diagnostic techniques.

     S2.2 Error reporting: responsibility, direction of report.

     S2.3 Method of response to error reports.

     S2.4 Distribution of corrections.

S3. *Instruction of Users*
     S3.1 Manuals for different classes of users such as:
           a) computing centers
           b) large scale permanent users
           c) incidental users.

S3.2 Techniques of instruction (including automatic techniques).

S4. *Documentation for Service and Users*
S4.1 Levels of documentation such as:
a) maintenance
b) instruction;

S4.2 Criteria for documentation requirements;

S4.3 Techniques for document production.

S5. *Performance Monitoring and Systems Evaluation*
S5.1 Criteria and measures of performance;

S5.2 Methods of measuring
a) by hardware or by software
b) by sampling or continuous
c) micro or macro.

S6. *Feedback into Design and Production*
S6.1 Mechanisms for feedback (such as users groups);

S6.2 Responsibility;

S6.3 Description of feedback channels and recipients;

S6.4 Consideration of efficiency of feedback;

S6.5 Marketing considerations.

S7. *Modifications of Existing Software*
S7.1 Reasons for modifications;

S7.2 Improvement of performance;

S7.3 Problem modification leading to:
a) generalization of software
b) adaption of software, influence of cost estimates and marketing considerations.

S7.4 Responsibility for execution of modified product.

S8. *Variations of Software Available to the User*
S8.1 Criteria for determination of:
a) degree of variations needed by the user
tolerated by the user for variation in time, across group of users.
b) techniques for producing variations (incl. automatic).
c) communications service covering variations.

S9. *Reprogramming*
S9.1 Problem techniques (incl. automatic).

S9.2 Responsibilities.

S9.3 Alternatives.

S9.4 Cost estimates, etc.

A4. ADDRESSES OF WELCOME

Welcome address
by Dr. Otto Schedl,
Minister of Industry and Transport for Bavaria

Software engineering has become one of the most important and comprehensive aspects of the technology of Information Processing, or informatics. Developments in this area play a key role in the overall progress of technology and economy in our countries.

With a host of possible applications and many immediate necessities for its use in science and industry successful software engineering is today one of the basic conditions for competitive computer production. In Germany this aspect of computer science will be one of the main activities of the special research group Informatics which has been established at the Technische Hochschule München, following a recommendation by the German Science Council. This group at the Technische Hochschule München collaborates with the University of München and is supported by the Leibniz-Rechenzentrum of the Bavarian Academy of Sciences.

The international Conference on Software Engineering in Garmisch is, therefore, an event which is hoped to stimulate the work on computer science in Munich, and the conference may very well, as the first of its kind, become a milestone in an increasing collaboration between scientists engaged in software engineering, since the explosive development in data processing techniques in all areas of modern society throughout the world constitutes a challenge to international collaboration.

It is a particular pleasure to me, as Minister of Industry and Transport for Bavaria, to welcome the participants to this international conference. The Science Committee of NATO has found with Garmisch not only a meeting place which is preferred in Germany for its scenery but it has also chosen a German state where the development of data processing techniques has always been followed with interest and given all the support possible within the available economic framework.

Allow me to take a certain pride in the fact that by 1952 computer science had already found a home in Bavaria at the Technische Hochschule München. It is hoped that the Leibniz-Rechenzentrum of the Bavarian Academy of Sciences, when its construction is completed, will form the hub from which advances in data processing techniques will radiate to science and technology.

I wish the conference every possible success in its work and hope that all participants will have an enjoyable stay in Werdenfels country.

7th October, 1968

Translation of telegram from Mr. Gerhard Stoltenberg,
Minister for Scientific Research of the Federal Republic of Germany,
7th October, 1968

To Prof. Dr. F.L. Bauer, Chairman of the NATO Conference on Software Engineering.

Dear Professor Bauer,

The productivity in science, industry and public administration is to an ever increasing extent determined by the progress in data processing.

I am therefore particularly pleased that a working conference of such a high scientific level, devoted to problems in software engineering, is being held in the Federal Republic of Germany.

I wish you and all participants every success with the conference.

With best regards — Gerhard Stoltenberg, Bundesminister fuer Wissenschaftliche Forschung.

PART II

Report on a Conference Sponsored by the

NATO SCIENCE COMMITTEE

Rome, Italy, October 27-31, 1969

Chairman: Professor P. Ercoli

Co-chairman: Professor F. L. Bauer

Editors: J. N. Buxton and B. Randell

PREFACE

A working conference on software engineering techniques, sponsored by the NATO Science Committee, was held from the 27th to 31st October 1969, near Rome, Italy. The conference was intended as a direct sequel to the NATO conference on software engineering held at Garmisch, Germany, from 7th to 11th October 1968. About sixty people from eleven countries attended the meeting. A list of participants is provided in Appendix 1.

This report summarizes the discussions held at the conference and includes a selection from the more than 50 working papers prepared by the conference participants. The report has been prepared in much the same manner as was used for the report of the Garmisch conference, and which is described in the preface to that report.

Material from the working papers and from transcribed and edited discussions has been combined under specific headings into sections 1 to 6 of this report. Lengthy working papers that have been selected for the report are reproduced in section 7.

Two sessions at the conference, on the subject of the NATO Science Committee proposals for an International Institute for Software Engineering, which were in the main non-technical, have not been covered in this report.

The similarities of the structure of this report to that of its predecessor are to a certain extent superficial, owing to the fact that the Rome conference turned out to be rather different in form from the Garmisch conference. The reasons for this, and the effect that they have had on the report are discussed in the introduction. The opinions expressed in the introduction are entirely the responsibility of the editors. In the rest of the report the editors have endeavoured to restrict their role to that of selection and classification of material.

As with the Garmisch report, readers should keep in mind the fact that all those present at the meeting expressed their views as individuals and in no sense as representatives of the organizations with which they are affiliated.

The actual work on the report was a joint undertaking by several people. The large amounts of typing and other office chores were done by Miss Margaret Chamberlin and Miss Ann Laybourn. During the conference notes were taken by Rod Ellis and Ian Hugo, who also operated the tape recorders, and by John Buxton and Brian Randell. The reviewing and sorting of material for the report, and the final write-up were done by John Buxton and Brian Randell assisted by Rod Ellis and Ian Hugo. The final version of the report was prepared by The Kynoch Press, using their computer typesetting system (see Cox, N. S. M. and Heath, W. A.: 'The integration of the publishing process with computer manipulated data'. Paper presented to the Seminar on Automated Publishing Systems, 7-13th September 1969, University of Newcastle upon Tyne, Computer Typesetting Research Project), the preliminary text processing being done using the Newcastle File Handling System (see the paper by Cox and Dews in: Cox, N. S. M. and Grose, M. W. (editors): 'Organization and handling of bibliographic records by computer', 1967, Newcastle upon Tyne, Oriel Press Ltd.). Keypunching of the text and the composition control codes was done by Ron White of The Kynoch Press as part of a study undertaken with the support of the National Graphical Association. The computer time was generously provided by Professor E. S. Page, Director of the Computing Laboratory of the University of Newcastle upon Tyne. During the conference photocopying equipment was provided by the Dupleco Company.

One quotation from the discussion during the closing section of the conference seems appropriate to end this preface.

Randell: Writing this sort of report is like building a big software system. When you've done one you think you know all the answers and when you start another you realize you don't even know all the questions.

John Buxton
Brian Randell

INTRODUCTION

The Rome conference on software engineering techniques was intended as a direct sequel to the conference on software engineering held in Garmisch, Germany, 7th to 11th October 1968. The Rome conference took on a form rather different from that of the conference in Garmisch and hence the resemblance between this report and its predecessor is somewhat superficial. The role played by the editors has changed and this change deserves explanation.

The Garmisch conference was notable for the range of interests and experience represented amongst its participants. In fact the complete spectrum, from the inhabitants of ivory-towered academe to people who were right on the firing-line, being involved in the direction of really large-scale software projects, was well covered. The vast majority of these participants found commonality in a widespread belief as to the extent and seriousness of the problems facing the area of human endeavour which has, perhaps somewhat prematurely, been called "software engineering". This enabled a very productive series of discussions, in both plenary and informal parallel sessions, to take place. During these the goal was to identify, classify, and discuss the problems, both technical and managerial, which face the various different classes of software projects, up to and including the type of projects which can only be measured in man-millenia. Also, the fact that the goal of the conference was to produce a report was always kept in mind. As a result, at the end of the conference, the editors (Peter Naur and Brian Randell), had a comparatively clear idea of what the conference participants hoped for from the report and a detailed initial draft of the structure that the report should have. The role of the editors could therefore be largely restricted to that of selecting and classifying statements made by participants in working papers or at the conference.

The intent of the organizers of the Rome conference was that it should be devoted to a more detailed study of technical problems, rather than including also the managerial problems which figured so largely at Garmisch. However, once again, a deliberate and successful attempt was made to attract an equally wide range of participants. The resulting conference bore little resemblence to its predecessor. The sense of urgency in the face of common problems was not so apparent as at Garmisch. Instead, a lack of communication between different sections of the participants became, in the editors' opinions at least, a dominant feature. Eventually the seriousness of this communication gap, and the realization that it was but a reflection of the situation in the real world, caused the gap itself to become a major topic of discussion. Just as the realization of the full magnitude of the software crisis was the main outcome of the meeting at Garmisch, it seems to the editors that the realization of the significance and extent of the communication gap is the most important outcome of the Rome conference.

In view of these happenings, it is hardly surprising that the editors received no clear brief from the conference as to the structure and content of the report. It seemed to us that the most useful discussions centered around specific problem areas in need of solution rather than specific techniques in search of problem areas. We have therefore structured the report accordingly.

The problem areas into which we have classified the material are clearly neither all of the same importance, nor at similar states of development, nor even completely independent of each other. Rather, they constitute, in our opinion, a convenient classification of the discussions and the working material submitted.

Some of the material presented either in working papers or in discussion related directly to areas of the subject that were extensively discussed at Garmisch, such as various managerial and organizational problems. In general this material has not been included unless, in our view, it has substantially extended or thrown new light upon these areas. Furthermore much working material concerned subjects which were not discussed at the conference. In the absence of the guidance which such discussions would have given us, we chose in general not to include such material in this report. The material submitted by the editors themselves was in fact rejected on these grounds.

1 THEORY AND PRACTICE

Most of the material in this section is collected from a discussion which was held on the last day of the conference after many people had expressed the need for the conference to talk about, rather than just suffer from, the effects of the communication gap.

Strachey: I want to talk about the relationship between theory and practice. This has been, to my mind, one of the unspoken underlying themes of this meeting and has not been properly ventilated. I have heard with great interest the descriptions of the very large program management schemes, and the programs that have been written using these; and also I heard a view expressed last night that the people who were doing this felt that they were invited here like a lot of monkeys to be looked at by the theoreticians. I have also heard people from the more theoretical side who felt that they were equally isolated; they were here but not being allowed to say anything. We have seen a document by Aron and Needham essentially about "Can computing science be of any assistance to software engineering, or what can software engineering get out of computing science?" *(see section 7.11 — Eds.)* One can also ask the question the other way round: "What can computing science get out of software engineering?"

This sort of debating point is not helpful. The truth of the matter is that we tend to look with doubt and suspicion at the other side; whichever side of that particular barrier we are. On one side we say "Well, there's nothing we can get out of computing science: look at all this rubbish they are talking". Or we stand on the other side and look at the very large programs and we say "Goodness me; what rotten techniques they use and look: they all fail!"

One of the most interesting things that has been shown at this conference is that these projects don't all fail. It has been shown that some of them have been quite astonishingly successful. I think we ought to remember somebody or other's law, which amounts to the fact that 95 per cent of everything is rubbish. You shouldn't judge the contributions of computing science to software engineering on the 95 per cent of computing science which is rubbish. You shouldn't judge software engineering, from the high altitude of pure theory, on the 95 per cent of software engineering which is also rubbish. Let's try and look at the good things from the other side and see if we can't in fact make a little bridge. Let's see what the real difficulties are and whether we can do something to assist.

It seems to me that one of the difficulties about computing science at the moment is that it can't demonstrate any of the things that it has in mind; it can't demonstrate to the software engineering people on a sufficiently large scale that what it is doing is of interest or importance to them. Take a very simple example with which I think almost everybody in the small scale and more abstract way of thinking about programming would agree; that to use recursive methods is undoubtedly an assistance. No self respecting programmer would dream of programming in a language without recursion. A very large-scale complicated problem (and by large-scale, in this case, I mean something that one person can do) is greatly aided by the use of recursive methods; I think there is no question whatsoever that this is true and it has been amply demonstrated by all sorts of individual programming efforts. Now so far as I know recursive programming is not used in general in any large-scale software system, with a few exceptions such as the Burroughs people. In fact the statement seems to be completely true about all really large systems. They use methods which do not allow them to use recursion; I think the real reason for this is that they haven't thought seriously of doing it. They've been told to do it and they brush it away apparently because it hasn't got the right sort of software support or because their machine doesn't do it easily or because they don't know about it. How can we convince people who are dealing with hundreds of programmers and millions of instructions that something as radical as changing the basic core of the way in which they program is a good thing to do?

Clearly you can't expect anybody to change a very large project completely in a direction like that merely because you say it's a good idea. This is obviously nonsense. On the other hand it's equally impractical to ask a university department or even a technical institution to mount a demonstration project of 500 man years; they haven't got the money and they wouldn't know how to manage it anyhow. They have no managerial capabilities. Incidentally, we all know that many of the operating systems and specialist compilers and things that are written in universities appear to be written with very little effort and in very little time compared with some of the commercial ones. It is very important to realize that the result is still an amateur affair; it is not documented, it is not maintained, it is not maintainable and when the man who wrote it goes away, it collapses. There is a very great deal of difference between the amateur work which is done in the university and the professional work which is done by people who have very large-scale things to do and have commercial responsibilities.

We need something in the way of a proving ground, halfway between the very large projects which must rely on things that the managers already know how to use, and the more advanced techniques which we're quite sure are all right on a small scale but which we still have to develop on a somewhat larger scale. We need as it were a pilot plant and until we can do something like this we shall not be able to introduce into software engineering the speed of development change which is necessary for it to keep up with the extremely rapidly developing theoretical advances in the subject. I don't know how this ought to be done; a development pilot plant is an expensive operation and cannot be done by universities alone. It could be done, I think, by a co-operative effort between the manufacturers, who have the financial resources and the interest in very large systems, and the research institutions. It does require a pilot plant which has to construct a really fairly sizeable thing; a one man exercise redoing a job in a quarter of the time or tenth of the time or whatever is not good enough. You must build a reasonably sized system where management problems will arise and can be demonstrated to be soluble and where new techniques can be used by managers. You must have at least part of the real difficulty of the big problems.

The thing that saddens me about the present situation is that there's not much sign that the large engineering set-ups have yet been able to change their basic techniques. They can change the peripheral stuff, the editing and the documentation and things like this, but so far they haven't changed the central core of what they are doing: that is to say, the actual programming techniques. Right in the middle it is still, as somebody said the other day, classical programming and classical mistakes. FORTRAN was a very good language when it started but that was a long time ago; it's at least half the lifetime of this subject ago, and that is a long time. If in any other kind of engineering you used techniques that were half the life time of the subject old, you would be very much out of date.

Now I want to preach to people on the other side. It seems to me that the academics have been disgracefully arrogant in neglecting and denying the existence of large problems. For years and years they refused to admit that commercial data processing was a subject which had any intellectual interest at all. It was expressed in horrible language: COBOL is, as most people would agree, a horrible language; it leads to dreadful things like saying DIVIDE CAKE INTO 3 which means you get "three over the cake" and not "the cake over three". In fact commercial data processing had and still has very interesting problems about data structuring, which it had to deal with and started dealing with long before the academic side of programming would have anything to do with it. None of the early academic programming languages have data structures. The reason is that the academics just could not be bothered to look at this large, important area.

I think the same thing is true about very large, complicated programs; it seems to be quite clear that the large software engineering exercises introduce new and important ideas which we must acknowledge. For instance, how are we going to organize programs intellectually, which are so large that they can't be comprehended by one man? This is a very important problem. It's clear to me, or at least I think it's clear to me, that the only hope of doing this is by arranging these very large programs in hierarchical ways. It's extremely important that we should begin on the theoretical task of trying to understand how to mould messy, difficult and inconvenient objects into hierarchical structures. Another principle that comes from study of large engineering projects is that a great deal of the effort must be spent in dealing with malfunctions of some sort: program malfunctions, machine malfunctions or operator malfunctions.

These are things that are awkward to get into an elegant mathematical framework. Nevertheless we must somehow or other form a conceptual framework in which we can talk about these things in a clean and comprehensible way. I think we've got a lot to learn here; I don't know how to do it, I'm just beginning to think about it and I think it's very exciting.

Aron: Part of the gap that has been mentioned here between computer science and software engineering is the recognition that many software engineering projects start and proceed without the planned utilization of scientific methods. The fact is that if we look back we can see that many things were done wrong, but they were done wrong by people who thought they were doing the right thing.

Ross: What does a manager look for in a technique before he adopts it?

Aron: If he is engaged in an operational rather than an experimental project, he will insist that the technique is thoroughly tested; it must be shown to be reliable and shown to have performance parameters that are suitable. He acts on his own experience. He will adopt what you tell him only to the extent that you can demonstrate it to him.

Needham: How big does a project have to be to be a useful pilot project? It clearly can't be 500 men for five years; that's not a pilot project, it's a project. It clearly isn't a matter of one man for one year, because this is precisely what we say isn't good enough. Can we say what kind or size of pilot project, which would be done according to the best principles that computer scientists could devise, would look in some way acceptable to people who are in the really large-scale business, and would stand a chance of being imitated or developed? If we had some answer we might be able to go away and do such a pilot project.

Feldman: MULTICS!

Ulrich: What is the difference between a pilot project, and an actual project?

Galler: One important difference is that there be no predetermined time limit specified by marketing people.

> *During the discussion a rather different analysis of the situation was proposed by Sharp.*

Sharp: I think that we have something in addition to software engineering: something that we have talked about in small ways but which should be brought out into the open and have attention focused on it. This is the subject of software architecture. Architecture is different from engineering.

As an example of what I mean, take a look at OS/360. Parts of OS/360 are extremely well coded. Parts of OS, if you go into it in detail, have used all the techniques and all the ideas which we have agreed are good programming practice. The reason that OS is an amorphous lump of program is that it had no architect. Its design was delegated to a series of groups of engineers, each of whom had to invent their own architecture. And when these lumps were nailed together they did not produce a smooth and beautiful piece of software.

I believe that a lot of what we construe as being theory and practice is in fact architecture and engineering; you can have theoretical or practical architects: you can have theoretical or practical engineers. I don't believe for instance that the majority of what Dijkstra does is theory—I believe that in time we will probably refer to the "Dijkstra School of Architecture".

What happens is that specifications of software are regarded as functional specifications. We only talk about what it is we want the program to do. It is my belief that anybody who is responsible for the implementation of a piece of software must specify more than this. He must specify the design, the form; and within that framework programmers or engineers must create something. No engineer or programmer, no programming tools, are going to help us, or help the software business, to make up for a lousy design. Control, management, education and all the other goodies that we have talked about are important; but the implementation people must understand what the architect had in mind.

Probably a lot of people have experience of seeing good software, an individual piece of software which is good. And if you examine why it is good, you will probably find that the designer, who may or may not have been the implementer as well, fully understood what he wanted to do and he created the shape. Some of the people who can create shape can't implement and the reverse is equally true. The trouble is that in industry, particularly in the large manufacturing empires, little or no regard is being paid to architecture.

> *An alternative to the "pilot project" proposal was put forward by David.*

David: It has been suggested that demonstration systems or systems experiments are a good approach to solving the problems of large systems. But in many instances, I think, just the sheer size and cost of a demonstration and the difficulty of measurement and of generalization of the results prevents a convincing demonstration; it certainly prevents the conduct of a properly controlled experiment in many cases.

Another possibility for aiding technology transfer lies in studying in detail actual ongoing production efforts. I think a great deal of information on the influence of new methods on production can be gained by a bona fide analysis of project performance. A combination of that kind of hard information with selected experiments and demonstrations might be much more effective than either alone.

There is a great deal of uncertainty about the influence of new production techniques on cost, manpower and time, etc. This uncertainty, I think, rests on a profound lack of evidence and hard data about real cases. Techniques which are said to be the same succeed in some cases and they fail in others. That's no surprise to anybody but the crucial factors which actually contribute to the success or failure have not been successfully identified. They certainly have not been established quantitatively, even approximately. It is clear too, that many factors are involved in success and failure: many more than the discussions at various meetings or post-mortem papers after the end of a project would seem to imply.

Dijkstra: I would like to comment on the distinction that has been made between practical and theoretical people. I must stress that I feel this distinction to be obsolete, worn out, inadequate and fruitless. It is just no good, if you want to do anything reasonable, to think that you can work with such simple notions. Its inadequacy, amongst other things, is shown by the fact that I absolutely refuse to regard myself as either impractical or not theoretical.

David expressed the idea that "We can make case studies in industry, and then you can study the results. You can do these analyses." A probable effect of the distinction is that if such a study is made, the output of it can be regarded as theory and therefore ignored. What is actually happening, I am afraid, is that we all tell each other and ourselves that software engineering techniques should be improved considerably, because there is a crisis. But there are a few boundary conditions which apparently have to be satisfied. I will list them for you:
1 We may not change our thinking habits.
2 We may not change our programming tools.
3 We may not change our hardware.
4 We may not change our tasks.
5 We may not change the organizational set-up in which the work has to be done.
Now under these five immutable boundary conditions, we have to try to improve matters. This is utterly ridiculous. Thank you. *(Applause)*

Randell: There is a well known English saying, which is relevant to this discussion about pilot projects. The saying is as follows: "There's none so blind as them that won't see". A pilot project will never be convincing to somebody who doesn't want to be convinced. A problem out in the real world will never be a problem to a theoretician who doesn't want to look at it. Blindness goes both ways. If you have people who are completely stuck in their own ways, whether these are ways of running large projects without regard for possible new techniques, or whether these are ways of concentrating all research into areas of ever smaller relevance or importance, almost no technique that I know of is going to get these two types of people to communicate. A pilot project will just be something stuck in between them. It will be a Panmunjon with no way to it, from either side. You have to have good will. You have to have means for people to find out that what the others talk is occasionally sense. This conference may occasionally have done a little bit of that. I wish it had done a lot more. It has indicated what a terrible gulf we so stupidly have made for ourselves.

2 SOFTWARE SPECIFICATION

The various problems concerned with obtaining a specification of a system, which would serve as the foundation of the subsequent system implementation, were debated at length. Much of the discussion arose in response to the following short working paper.

Seegmüller: (from "Definition of systems")
"The following is a brief description of possible steps in which the definition of a system and the specification of an implementation of it might be achieved.

By a 'system' we understand a mechanism that is able to execute all of the functions given by its external interface.

1 Irrespective of hardware considerations, write in an informal way a list of all of the desired external functions and objects.
2 Put down performance limits for these functions.
3 Make a first guess whether there is a 'support system' (hardware or software system) which is likely to be capable of meeting the requirements listed under 1 and 2. If the answer is no, then redesign under 1 and/or 2 or build a new support system.
4 Describe in an informal way an abstract machine (representing the system) which accepts invocations of all functions listed under 1 and can handle representations of the objects listed under 1. If the result is unsatisfactory, then go to 1.
5 Formalize the description of the abstract machine (e.g. by means of the Vienna definition method), remove possible contradictions and minimize the complexity of the abstract machine during this step. If the result is unsatisfactory, then go to 4.
6 Use a software specification language (SSL) in order to define a first breakdown of the implementation of the abstract machine into program modules. Put down performance and size limits on these modules.
7 Use the resulting SSL statements in order to simulate the behaviour of these modules under the assumption of certain workload and support system characteristics. If the result is unsatisfactory, then redesign under 6 and repeat 7.
8 Refine the breakdown into modules.
9 Simulate the behaviour. If satisfactory, then go to 11.
10 Change the refinement. Go to 9.
11 If the level of detail is unsatisfactory, then go to 8.
12 Take the last refinement as implementation specification."

Engeli: I think that this outline works well for small systems, where it is essentially unnecessary, but does not work, other than in exceptional cases, for large systems.

Oestreicher: No matter how precisely you try to specify a system, once you have built it you find it isn't exactly what is wanted. In real life, an outline like Seegmüller's must contain at all stages the possibility of returning to step 1.

Scalzi: My experience is with OS/360, and I agree with the criticisms of Seegmüller's implication that one must obtain a fully defined specification before starting implementation. We have been building a growing system since 1966. By definition our design requirements are open-ended and our goal is to maintain a compatible interface to the user over a period of years.

The discussion was in fact quite lengthy and tended in part to duplicate what had been said at Garmisch. However, several extended comments, describing experience of large system projects were made and are reported in section 5. There was much interesting discussion on the requirements of languages that could be used for specifying and/or implementing systems; this is reported below.

2.1 Software specification languages

The first discussion concerned the question of whether there need be a difference between languages used for specifying and for implementing software.

Seegmüller: I assume that a software specification language must be different from one that is suitable for implementation. I think that the Vienna Method is a most promising technique for formally specifying what the external behaviour is to be. It has been used so far for giving a formal definition of several programming languages, but there are now some attempts under way to apply it to operating systems.

Lowry: I think a major reason for a divergence between languages for these two purposes is the lack of sufficiently powerful optimization techniques.

Lucas: There is an important difference between a fully executable specification of a system and what we have done at Vienna. For example, the state of our abstract PL/1 machine has to be indeterminate where PL/1 does not specify a meaning to an action, or specifies only constraints. The axiomatic part of our scheme is an important part, and it is just not executable in any traditional sense.

Feldman: (from "Towards automatic programming")
"The first problem one faces when trying to automate the writing of programs is this: how is one to say what is required without writing some kind of program? Workers in Artificial Intelligence have long faced this problem of *process description* and *state descriptions.* A state description for the function *square root* (Z) might be:
The X such that $X \times X = Z$
A process description for the same function might be an ALGOL program to carry out Newton's method for the solution.

The state description above is much simpler than any process description, though this is not always the case. It is easier to describe how to take the derivative of a polynomial than to specify a set of properties that a derivative must have. Similarly, the syntax of a programming language is given more clearly by a grammar than by a set of conditions for well-formedness."

A different viewpoint was expressed by Falkoff, who thought that there was basically room for two languages: one being English or some other natural language and the other being a formal programming language. A paper by Falkoff on this subject, using examples from APL, is reproduced in section 7.5.

Perlis: In the past several years I have had periodic contacts with the APL people and I find that they are very much like both ardent catholics and communists in that, when they get to certain topics, all discussions must be in their framework, otherwise no contact can be made. I wish to expose this as a virtue and not as a vice. There are several reasons why a COBOL compiler can be written in six months using APL as a specification language, as described by Ian Sharp. There is of course the fact that the APL primitives are very rich. However, there is something deeper than that, which is very important for software engineering. The APL people see all programming activities in terms of APL. When you talk about a table, they think in terms of APL algorithms for accessing and maintaining a table. Life is greatly simplified for them by virtue of the fact that all programming questions are recast into the framework of a language that they can carry around in their skulls. I have also observed this in the past with LISP programmers and it has been very important for them.

Falkoff: What Perlis was saying is in part that, since we have finite skulls, we have to have reasonably concise representations of processes.

A related subject, which was never discussed at length but which was briefly referred to many times during the conference, concerned the interrelationships between program and data.

Schwartz: In my experience on large systems, we have pictured the systems as a flow of data. On these projects we have people whose sole job is to develop and to change and re-do table specifications. Wherever possible we try to have programming languages which divorce the data definition from the actual procedures. That happened to be the philosophy behind JOVIAL, which has been used for some number of these systems. Experimenting with the data flow specification forces an understanding as to what is going on in a system.

Randell: I am reluctant to draw a definite line between the concepts of program and data. One of the nice things about SIMULA is that the concept of process definition in some sense includes, as special cases, procedure and data structure definitions.

Further discussion related to this topic, but primarily concerning questions of program portability, is given in section 4.1.4. A working paper by Hopkins which is concerned with the central part played by data flow and table structures in determining system performance is given in full in section 7.7.

2.2 Software implementation languages

Not surprisingly, there was a certain amount of discussion on programming languages at the conference.

Wirth: It might be thought quite remarkable what proportion of the submitted working material was on the subject of programming language development, although the conference is on software engineering. But in fact languages form our thinking habits and, are our daily tools, and I think it is fair to say that many of the problems plaguing the world of software are more or less directly attributable to the rather poor present state of language development.

One of the major points of discussion was the relationship between efficiency and naturalness of expression permitted by a programming language.

Wirth: The main objection to languages which are as distant from the actual computer hardware as the Galler and Perlis proposals, or APL, is that they are usually not very efficient. At the other end of the spectrum there are languages which reflect properties of the machine, so that you can get very efficient programs. I have produced languages belonging to each end of the spectrum. In the distant past I produced EULER, which proved to be an interesting academic exercise, and more recently, PL/360, which is nowadays quite widely used. Now if we are to talk about software engineering, we should talk about languages which have relevance to the reality of practical system development. A good engineering approach is to find a compromise which is as close to the machine as possible, while remaining machine independent.

Dijkstra: I would like to make a comment on Niklaus Wirth's story. I would like to point out that he starts from a tacit assumption which I wouldn't like to let pass unchallenged. His tacit assumption is that elegance or convenience on the one hand, and efficiency on the other hand, cannot go hand in hand . . . I just don't believe it, and I would like to point out that from the point of view of Niklaus Wirth, his assumption is just a belief. If I have any interest in computing science at all it is based on my firm belief that very often the most attractive solution is the most efficient one.

Feldman: (from "Towards automatic programming")
"The search for more natural programming languages need not necessarily lead to less machine efficiency. The level of description found natural by people is often a natural one for code economization; the inclusion of extraneous detail proves a hardship to both man and machine."

Lampson: It seems to me that it is somewhat confusing to talk about PL/360 as a high level language. PL/360 is an assembler and that's worth bearing in mind. Many of the issues which arise in trying to decide whether some language which is not an assembler, such as MOL/940, is desirable or not, simply don't arise in connection with PL/360.

Falkoff: I would like to suggest a slight change in point of view, namely: that efficiency goes down as machines become more and more user independent. There is apparently a gap between the way people would like to think, and the way machines do things. To call this gap machine independence and put the onus on the user strikes me as looking at it backwards.

A fairly extensive discussion of the pros and cons of various languages which were designed for writing systems is given by Lang, in a paper which is given in full in section 7.8. At the conference he made the following plea.

Lang: It is an unfortunate fact that so many many systems are still written in assembly language. The perfect machine independent system writing language that we would like to have does not exist yet. On the other hand it is well within our present capability to design a simple machine dependent system writing language for any machine, and to write an efficient compiler for it. We should make use of this capability. Further, a few machine independent system writing languages do exist, which deserve more use.

Buxton: I wish to respond to Charles Lang's plea for people to use simple programming languages more widely. This is a field which interests me because I have been gently growing one of these languages in my own backyard for the last four or five years, and by and large it's no better and no worse than any other such language, but it doesn't come into wide use other than with programmers in my own department. I think there is a quite subtle and rather fundamental reason for this. If you publish this sort of simple systems programming language, a system programmer will not use it because it is simple. He looks at it and says "This is so simple that I can design one of these myself this afternoon, so I'll dash one off and write a compiler in a week or two, rather than bother with somebody else's". It turns out that language design even of apparently trivial looking languages is a formidably difficult intellectual task—to do it right is very hard indeed. And unless he happens to be genuinely expert in language design he will end up with having produced a mess; a tiny mess, but nevertheless a mess. This psychological phenomenon prevents the use of other people's, sanitarily designed, systems programming languages.

3   SOFTWARE QUALITY

The subject of software production and quality was covered in a broad sense at Garmisch. The purpose of this meeting was to concentrate in particular on the technical problems of software; having got a specification, the next problem is to produce a product which is in some sense of high quality. We have separated this section into two main areas; correctness of the product in performing the specified task (3.1) and its performance efficiency (3.2). The magnitude of the problem is indicated by the following quotations.

Hopkins: We face a fantastic problem in big systems. For instance, in OS/360 we have about 1000 errors each release and this number seems reasonably constant. Now why do we have these errors? Does this number relate in some way with the real number of errors in the system? It has been suggested that error reports come in at a rate connected with the system update release cycle; initially people don't report errors because of too many problems and towards the end of a release nobody reports errors as the new release will present a whole new problem. It is also suggested that the number of errors is directly linked to the number of field systems engineers. What sort of errors are made on large systems? What is the error rate in various modules? For instance, is it much higher in supervisor modules? Who makes the errors, new programmers or experienced ones? How long do errors stay in the system? These are very difficult, unanswered problems.

There is also another theory: IBM have a large stock of new facilities back in Poughkeepsie waiting to be added to OS. Whenever the bug rate falls below 1000 per release, which seems to be about the user toleration level, they put in a few more facilities which has the effect of keeping the bug rate constant.

Schorr: It is not quite right that the rate is constant; it seems in fact to be slowly increasing!

3.1   Correctness

Section 3.1 is further subdivided into 3.1.1 on Formal Correctness (or, how to prevent bugs from ever arising) and 3.1.2 on Debugging Techniques (or, how to catch them when you have got them!)

3.1.1   Formal Correctness

Wirth: (from "The programming language PASCAL and its design criteria") "I believe that the art of computer programming is based on a relatively small number of fundamental concepts. It became clear during the development of PASCAL that most of these concepts are already present in mathematics in some form, usually surrounded by a terminology different from the one used by programmers. It is necessary to demonstrate this duality in the expression of concepts and to make the mathematician's knowledge of handling structures available to programmers. This knowledge will be particularly useful for the development of techniques for program verification, i.e. for proving the correctness of programs.

In fact, the idea of program verification has influenced the design of PASCAL considerably. Several commonly used features of other languages have been deliberately omitted from PASCAL, because they appear to be too sophisticated for presently known methods of proof. It became clear that those features which are least tractable to proof techniques are exactly the ones which are most difficult to define rigorously and which in practice present the most dangerous sources of programming error."

Feldman: (from "Towards automatic programming")
"This question, correctness of programs, has been studied for some time and a number of significant results are being produced. One technique is to attach predicates to various parts of the program, the last one of which describes the desired result. Although there is no adequate survey of this material as yet, London has produced a comprehensive bibliography." (London R. L. 'Bibliography on proving the correctness of computer programs', Tech. Rep. No. 64, Computer Science Dept., University of Wisconsin, June 1969.)

Hoare: One can construct convincing proofs quite readily of the ultimate futility of exhaustive testing of a program and even of testing by sampling. So how can one proceed? The role of testing, in theory, is to establish the base propositions of an inductive proof. You should convince yourself, or other people, as firmly as possible that if the program works a certain number of times on specified data, then it will always work on any data. This can be done by an inductive approach to the proof. Testing of the base cases could sometimes be automated. At present, this is mainly theory; note that the tests have to be designed at the same time as the program and the associated proof is a vital part of the documentation. This area of theoretical work seems to show a possibility of practical results, though proving correctness is a laborious and expensive process. Perhaps it is not a luxury for certain crucial areas of a program.

Perlis: Much of program complexity is spurious and a number of test cases properly studied will exhaust the testing problem. The problem is to isolate the right test cases, not to prove the algorithm, for that follows after the choice of the proper test cases.

Dijkstra: Testing shows the presence, not the absence of bugs.

Lucas gave a brief summary of the Vienna method (see P. Lucas and K. Walk: "On the formal description of PL/1". Annual Review in Automatic Programming, Vol. 6). He gave an example of an application of the Vienna method, which revealed an error in the mechanism for dynamic storage allocation of AUTOMATIC variables in the F-level PL/1 compiler (see P. Lucas: "Two constructive realizations of the block concept and their equivalence". TR 25.085; also W. Henahpl: "A proof of correctness of the reference mechanism to automatic variables in the F-Compiler". LN 25.3.048; both of which are available from the IBM Vienna Laboratory).

Lucas: The error was not found by the compiler writers; it was not found by product test and it would not easily have been found by any random tests. I am quite convinced that making this proof was cheaper than the discussions I have heard among highly-paid people on whether or not this allocation mechanism would cover the general case.

Galler: I think this relates to a common mathematical experience; when you cannot prove a theorem very often the sticking-point is the source of the counter-example.

Llewellyn: How often in practice do these obscure errors turn up?

Lucas: Nobody knows how often these cases turn up; that is just the point. A compiler writer is not a prophet of all computer users. Secondly, even if only one user meets the error it causes him a real problem and it causes a full system update mechanism to go into action. Even for only one such case, it is cheaper to make the proof than mend the bug.

Galler: Engineers use the "worst case" approach to testing. Has this been done in software?

Lucas: I can't see any possibility of specifying worst cases in this kind of field.

Reynolds: The difficulty with obscure bugs is that the probability of their appearance increases with time and with wider use.

Dijkstra described some basic features of his work over the past several years on the problem of making programming an order of magnitude easier and more effective. This is described in full in his working paper in section 7.4.

Perlis: Do you think the methods you have developed can be taught to those programmers who have always coded first and justified last?

Dijkstra: No one survives early education without some scars. In my experience, the intellectually degrading influence of some educational processes is a serious bar to clear thinking. It is a requirement for my applicants that they have no knowledge of FORTRAN. I am not being facetious.

Falkoff: How do you describe a set of computations precisely and completely without using a program in some language?

Dijkstra: The most basic aspects are, on the one hand, what a routine does for you and, on the other hand, how it works. My point is that on no level of abstraction are both of these aspects simultaneously of relevance if the routine is not recursive. These aspects can therefore be clearly separated.

Bauer: I agree entirely with Dijkstra; some current languages are doing considerable harm in the educational process; one can't help mentioning PL/1 here.

Randell: And ALGOL 68.

Bemer: I agree with Dijkstra on the value of elegance and simplicity in one's thought processes and in programming. I agree also on the difficulty of retraining people out of old habits and I wonder what percentage of the total programming population he would like to retrain?

Dijkstra: One hundred and ten per cent!

Lang: You describe some intellectual tools which you say have increased your own programming efficiency about five times. Have you been able to transmit these to your colleagues with a similar effect?

Dijkstra: Yes.

3.1.2 Debugging

This important topic occurred many times in discussion during the week. The working paper by Teitelman (given in section 7.14) is particularly relevant and much discussion centred round the work; in particular, on the relative advantages of on-line versus off-line debugging and on the distinction between debugging within individual modules and testing the total status of large systems. The latter distinction was expressed by Aron.

Aron: We are discussing two different things. One is debugging: the term we use for an individual finding errors in his own work within the design he created. The other is testing: the term applies to identifying and resolving problems that arise in the system as a whole rather than in individual components. Testing is done by groups, as an individual programmer lacks the total knowledge needed to test large sections of the system. The emphasis on testing should never be on individual modules and as long as system testing is confused with debugging we can expect test plans to be incomplete.

The paper by Needham given in section 7.10 is also relevant to the subject. Comment which, in the editors' opinion, relates specifically to that area defined by Aron as "testing" will be found in section 5.

3.1.2.1 On classical techniques

Brown: There are two classical techniques: the snapshot during execution and the core dump after the program has died.

Hopkins: Programmers call their errors "bugs" to preserve their sanity; that number of "mistakes" would not be psychologically acceptable!

I think that the higher level the language used in programming the better. This was clearly understood by Shakespeare who was against assembly language coding:

"Bloody instructions which being learned, return to plague the inventor" (Macbeth).

Programming languages should have structure. The user must be helped to write in a proper style which will improve the standard of the resulting program. Machines don't have side effects; neither should languages.

Dijkstra: I would like to applaud Hopkins' remarks!

Oestreicher: One has to remember the need to test exhaustively all conditions which might arise; things which seem locally impossible may well happen due to global effects. Testing for impossible errors is a fact of life.

Lampson: There is sufficient know-how available by now to make it possible to design a machine that would make the writing of reliable programs easier. Does anyone know of a manufacturer seriously doing this?

Mention was made of work by John Iliffe and of Burroughs equipment. An entirely different, but equally 'classical', technique was described by Burkinshaw.

Burkinshaw: Get some intelligent ignoramus to read through your documentation and try the system; he will find many "holes" where essential information has been omitted. Unfortunately intelligent people don't stay ignorant too long, so ignorance becomes a rather precious resource. Suitable late entrants to the project are sometimes useful here.

3.1.2.2 On on-line and off-line debugging techniques

Wirth: I would like to discuss the trend towards conversationality in our tools. There has been, since the advance of timesharing and on-line consoles, a very hectic trend towards development of systems which allow the interactive development of programs. Now this is certainly nice in a way, but it has its dangers, and I am particularly wary of them because this conversational usage has not only gained acceptance among software engineers but also in universities where students are trained in programming. My worry is that the facility of quick response leads to sloppy working habits and, since the students are going to be our future software engineers, this might be rather detrimental to the field as a whole.

Perlis: I hold the opposite belief: that conversational techniques aid and abet systems programming and improve the programmer. Better use can be made of the support software used in systems work with full interactive contact; and system programmers require to be on-line.

By its very nature, programming is done by development. Languages like ALGOL don't allow this; the program modules have each to be written in one fell swoop. People don't think like that; conversational systems permit programmers to work from the top down and to compute even with incomplete specifications.

Galler: Electric toothbrushes provide an interesting analogy. Like conversational systems they were regarded with great suspicion when new. However, it turns out that people using them have less dental caries just because the electric toothbrush is a better tool.

Teitelman: I agree with Perlis. My own experience with conversational systems is that rather than leading to sloppier use, if anything they promote a more efficient, systematic approach to debugging and testing. The fast response encourages users to checkout their programs thoroughly, e.g. run the program again after making a fix to see if the symptoms really go away. On the other hand, when system response is slow due to overloading, users get frustrated and try to second-guess their programs and *then* they get sloppy.

Ross: If you are worried about sloppiness on-line, make your users pay real money; this helps!

Needham: In dealing with systems of such complexity that the man fixing a bug doesn't understand too much of the system, you must avoid making it too easy. If it is too easy to walk up to a console and put in a fix you run the risk that it will be locally right but globally wrong.

3.1.2.3 On automatic analysis methods

Lowry: I will start with a strong statement of opinion. I think that ANY significant advance in the programming art is sure to involve very extensive automated analyses of programs.
— If you want better debugging of programs, then the computer must analyze the programs and find the bugs.
— If you want efficient code then the computer must analyze programs and restructure them from a simple flexible form to a highly stressed efficient form.
— If you want briefer, more natural programming languages then the computer must analyze the programs to provide accurate contextual interpretations of the new forms or expressions.
— If you want better documentation then the computer must analyze the programs to produce abstract representations of the programs from a variety of points of view.
— If you want programs which adapt easily to changing environments then the computer must analyze the programs to perform the adaptations — perhaps working from separate environmental descriptions — so that old code may be more effectively reused.
— If you want to decompile (or decouple) code to a less committed form then the computer must analyze the code very thoroughly (or psychoanalyze it as Perlis suggests).
— If you want more informal conversational computing then the computer must analyze the code to insert implicit constructs and recognize and query irregularities.
   Now I know that some of you are currently developing or applying techniques for analyzing program structure — but I think it is mostly nibbling at the periphery. To those others who are trying to make a significant contribution to the programming art in a way that does not involve extensive automated analyses of programs, I would suggest that you perhaps climb a tree — or seek some other solitude — and consider whether you have a chance.
   Doing thorough analyses of programs is a big job. I don't think you can just diddle at it. It requires that you use a programming language which is susceptible to analysis. I think other programming languages will head either for the junk pile or to the repair shop for an overhaul, or they will not be effective tools for the production of large programs.
   The main point I wish to make is that the analyses required to obtain the benefits I described are closely related and the more of these benefits we attempt to obtain in a single context, the more effectively all of them can be accomplished.

Perlis: What properties of language are important in the context of the need for thorough automatic analysis of programs? It seems to me that some languages may not be susceptible to analysis; can you give some examples?

Lowry: Assembler languages are very intractable. APL and PL/1 have some difficulties in flow analysis but these can be cured fairly easily. FORTRAN is easier to analyse.

Teitelman: However clever the analysis program is it doesn't know what the user really wants. One needs a snapshot of the right words and the only way to do this is by on-line debugging with the programmer present.

3.2 Performance measurement and improvement

The subject of software performance was covered in some detail at Garmisch and so relatively little material was presented at this conference. Papers were presented on a summary of system evaluation tools (by Gotlieb and McEwan) and on 1108 hardware instrumentation (by MacGowan). These are given in sections 7.6 and 7.9 respectively; for editorial reasons, the latter is given in part only.

Bayer: On a large dual processor system we studied recently we used hardware monitors for two purposes. One was to see what the hardware was doing and as a result we could reconfigure the hardware quite extensively. This gave us better performance and we could send much of the hardware back to the manufacturers. An additional benefit we found later was that the application programmers could make good use of the detailed hardware traces. They found it easy to correlate the traces with different parts of their programs; they then redesigned their programs and improved performance quite considerably.

Schorr: An interesting thing to try is using measurements on existing systems to extrapolate to new systems. This turns out to be very difficult. One problem is that programmers adapt readily to the machinery available and it is hard to tell whether you are measuring the characteristics of the hardware or of the user's adaptability.

Teitelman: Timesharing systems need to provide aids to measurement for user programs. Obvious things are access to a real time clock and a computation time clock so the user can hand tune his program. Our system has several facilities like this which are widely used.

Ross: Firstly, every computer should have a finely divided clock which is accessible to programs. Secondly, in the early days one had audio signals and store displays with which humans could recognize patterns in many ways and derive a great deal of valuable run time information. We still need such tools. Thirdly, is it possible to categorize in a handbook the useful things one needs to measure?

Galler: The ACM SIGOPS group is working on this problem.

Aron: One purpose of measurement is to tune up a program you expect to run often enough to warrant the expense of tuning. The second purpose is to evaluate a changing configuration. This is much harder to do; a designer faces a complex topological problem in trying to estimate the effectiveness of a range of configurations which he is considering. It is difficult at present to see what measurements would most assist.

Needham: Systematic techniques for measurement are only appropriate in some cases, such as when a system is doing a fixed job. It doesn't help in the changing behaviour patterns of the average big job shop.

Gotlieb: I disagree; I think that even in a university shop these user patterns have more consistency than you might think. This is exactly why we want measurement: to resolve such differences of opinion!

Galler: We have taken many statistics recently and find our users' behaviour surprisingly consistent. The statistics are shown to the users and are very helpful in enabling them to get more out of the system. Whatever is useful to the systems programmer should be made available, in general, to the user who needs similar tools.

Randell: Unless your multi-access system is large it is debatable whether there is enough statistical averaging for the measurements to be useful. There is a different problem: is an individual user to be allowed to improve his own utilization to the direct detriment of others? Preferably not! Avoiding this situation should be a design aim and until it is achieved maybe he is better off without the tools which would allow the problem to break out.

Ercoli: Computers and software are service systems of much complexity. Average measurements are difficult but the analytical tools are both inadequate for the study of this kind of system and often not familiar to software engineers.

Sharp: Scheduling multiprogramming systems is one of the least understood areas in the subject; with machines like ILLIAC IV coming along the situation will get worse. This alone seems to me to justify measurement; without some statistical evidence one cannot design. How, for instance, do IBM do it?

Schorr: Statistics are usually so biased by local conditions that in practice they are seldom of much real use.

4 SOFTWARE FLEXIBILITY

The material under this heading has been classified under two somewhat arbitrary subheadings: Portability and Adaptability.

Adaptability is concerned with enabling a given system to grow and change, as discussed for example by Warshall. A related problem is that of moving an existing large system without taking it out of service, as discussed by Hopkins. Portability is the more restricted problem area of moving a specific system from one environment to another.

4.1 Portability

4.1.1 Definitions of the problem area

Perlis: Portability is the property of a system which permits it to be mapped from one environment to a different environment; adaptability concerns the alteration of a system to fit the needs of a user without necessarily changing it from one machine to another.

On the definition of the terms "system" and "environment" I should like to make the following comment. There is a layering, like an onion, that cascades from out to in. The interface between any two layers is always characterized by a language and indeed if one does not have a language one does not have an interface. A system is constructed on an inner environment and prescribes an outer environment for the user.

Dijkstra: A very tiny both linguistic and educational remark concerning terminology we use. Please don't use the term "onion shaped," and I'll tell you exactly why. Because you're talking about something that is essentially a linear layer. When I was at MIT I heard people talking about protection rings and it turned out that as soon as you started talking about it they had to jump to the blackboard and make rings using a two dimensional representation for an essentially one dimensional hierarchy. If you now introduce the term "onion" you'll appeal to a three dimensional picture of essentially a one dimensional structure and it might clutter up your thinking, because there might be another dimension to be added to it. So please, no onion.

4.1.2 Description of techniques

Perlis: Technically we are concerned with the investigation and production of support on new machines sufficient to accept systems transported from old machines. Systems need support and should be adjustable and tunable if the new support turns out to be not too good.

The examples presented to illustrate portable systems were discussed under these headings, classified by the type of support to be provided in the new environment.

166

4.1.2.1 High level language support

> This assumes a common high level language between the old and new
> machines. See the working paper by W. S. Brown on the ALTRAN system
> in section 7.3.

Reynolds: A language can be unsuitable in two ways; if it is not sufficiently
concise then that can be overcome by macros but if it does not effectively
allow you to write the program or represent the data at all then macros will
not get you out of trouble.

Brown: Macros are used to overcome the inability to express target machine
characteristics in a FORTRAN program. Limitations with regard to data
representation are got round by using primitives.

Perlis: The representation of any kind of data as integers in an array can
be done if you have enough primitives around.

4.1.2.2 Bootstrap from the old system

> Ross described the AED system developed by the MIT Computer Aided
> Design Project over the last several years. We summarize the presentation
> here.

Ross: AED-0 is based on ALGOL 60 with data structures and other
extensions. Its compiler is mainly written in itself (95 per cent) and was
designed with portability as one of the aims. Portability can never be both
complete and efficient and it is therefore best to tune up critical modules
after the move to get an efficient result. This tuning can to some extent be
automated. The transfer is carried out by a complex bootstrapping approach
including a stage of "half-bootstrapping" in which code for the new machine
is generated on the old one.

Strachey: Martin Richards' BCPL was transferred from MIT to the KDF9 at
Oxford as two decks of cards and some scruffy notes. It was got running in
about a week. The entire compiler is in BCPL and is designed to be
machine independent. The support system, including I/O is in assembly
code. The code generator was rewritten in ALGOL to provide an initial
means of generating code.

4.1.3 Summary of techniques

Feldman: When one goes from one machine to another there'll be a large
set of environmental specifications: the size of a word and the kinds of
direct access, peripheral and tape storage and various other things of this
sort. This caused Stan Brown, for example, a reasonable amount of difficulty
in parameterizing his system in such a way that all the pertinent
parameters could be incorporated. Another thing is the transportability of
data. Now, of course, with a small piece of data that isn't a large problem. If,
however, there are large elaborate data files that are segmented in such a
way as to be compatible with certain strategies because of certain direct
access devices and one goes to another system in which the devices are
entirely different and one has to entirely restructure the files, then that is a
very large problem. The data itself must be entirely restructured.
  Two other points. Firstly, once a program has been moved it becomes part

of the support for the other programs to be moved. Secondly, not only does a portable system have to have its support specified but it is very important that the program that is about to be moved is written in such a way that it can tolerate less than perfect support. If one expects a certain exact support in order to move a program, one is going to be hard pressed. The program itself should be modifiable to make up for imperfections in the support of the target system. Furthermore, this flexibility will always be important in the second process, which is getting a system to run well. Assuming that one has got it running somehow, you can always get it to run much better by making changes in the way it goes about its business. So this flexibility in the way the program itself is written is necessary in order to move it in case the support is not perfect. This is what happened with the BCPL example; there was an ALGOL compiler on the target machine and BCPL was written in a sufficiently transparent way for the code generating rules to be written in ALGOL and put on the machine quickly. The text that was implemented was not identical to the text that was sent.

4.1.4 On portability of data

Bemer: (from "Straightening out programming languages")
"John Haanstra has said that compatibility is not a goal, but rather a property which enables the goal of data and program portability to be achieved. I have my own lemma that 'if the data is not transferable, the program cannot be transferable'. It is quite evident now that the separate divisions of COBOL facilitate program portability. However, we can and must do more for COBOL along this line and, more importantly, carry it to the other programming languages, both procedure and problem oriented. Let us concentrate on the distinction that information can be obtained only when one knows the conventions of data representation. This brings to mind a curious sequence of events, actually, a cycle. The name CODASYL (the coinage of which was my small contribution) incorporates 'data'. When we started the standardizing bodies, we got a little fancier and said 'Computers and Information Processing'. With the marriage to communication and data bases, the plain facts are that we will process *data* and, *incidentally,* some information. Computer based systems can move data around from place to place, put it away, find it again on the basis of its packaging, and (as in the case of cryptography, for example) perform transformation upon the data, *all of those absolutely independent of the information content.'* Data is our raw material. Software and hardware are only tools for manipulation. In some way the higher level languages, in the vacuum of not knowing enough about data structure, have achieved a disproportionate importance and a warped direction; one direction per language, in fact. Indeed, if I have a process to perform *upon* data, I may choose one of several information procedure languages. Conversely, more than one user of the same data should be allowed to operate upon that data by various information procedure languages."

4.1.5 On design for portability

Perlis: In a system such as Brown's, the assembler and linking loader are as important as the FORTRAN compiler. I suggest some principles to characterize the design of portable systems:
  1 Every output can be an input. (Closure)
  2 There is a set of properties that one can define to characterize a "block", and the coupling between blocks.

3 Then blocks may be gathered together so as to produce a new collection more intensely coupled than the originals.

4 This gathering process is subject to ever finer decomposition, i.e., it may operate within blocks, and interruption in the sense that it is a sequential process with memory—prior gatherings may be utilized in subsequent gatherings.

5 Naturally all gatherings may be named (identified).

6 Furthermore there is a set of properties called parameterization rules, which permit weak coupling ("coupling at a distance").

Then the problem is:

1 How to characterize blocks.

2 How to characterize permitted coupling.

3 How to characterize degrees of coupling, including parameterization rules.

4 How to characterize the sequential machine (control, operations and memory) which accomplishes the "gathering" task.

A new component, scheduling and resource allocation, is introduced when segmenting and parallel execution is possible. This is the new dimension introduced within operating systems.

One final point is that it is well worth looking at the work on "Generalized Programming" by Holt and Turanski.

Dijkstra: (from "Structured Programming")
"Any large program will exist during its lifetime in a multitude of different versions, so that in composing a large program we are not so much concerned with a single program, but with a whole family of related programs, containing alternative programs for the same job and/or similar programs for similar jobs. A program therefore should be conceived and understood as a member of a family; it should be so structured out of components that various members of this family, sharing components, do not only share the correctness demonstration of the shared components but also of the shared substructure."

4.1.6 On writing portable software

Lampson: What can we do to help the man writing portable software not to make mistakes?

Ross: Educate him. *(Laughter)* There is no other way. We should note that a simple system can indeed be transferred in a few days but bootstrapping a complex system cannot be made simple.

Lampson: The major problem is avoiding doing things that are machine dependent; for example, on word length. It does not seem unreasonable to hope that in the future one might have languages that will discourage one from writing this sort of thing and compilers that will detect when you have done it.

Brown: We have two tools of great value in writing portable software. One is a compiler which enforces the use of our subset of FORTRAN. The other is the mere existence of the macro facilities, which encourage the writing of clean code—by this I mean avoiding things like equivalence through mismatched COMMON statements.

Ross: A new word length is not a problem; utilizing new resources in a complex system is a major task.

Perlis: It seems to me that the first solution that one can see to this question of not making mistakes (premature bindings) is the recognition of a class of functions where only one function existed before. For example: a system programmer develops a system for a computer with one register, the accumulator, and wishes to map the system on to something like the PDP10 or the IBM S/360 where there are multiple registers, without losing efficiency. Clearly he should have designed the system so that the number of registers utilized was a variable; so that the number of registers of a particular machine may be a parameter when the system is mapped on to the machine. Now if he doesn't allow for the possibility that a single-register machine is a special case of n-register machines then portability is going to require a major rewrite of the system. How you anticipate possible machine designs, the logical design of machine systems, nobody I think can really say. So I think that you're always going to have to backtrack when transporting a system, but in backtracking the way to do it is to recognize that, in situations in which you have (say) two data points instead of one, the value "two" is still only a special case. Some of the things are obvious, such as machine core size, because we know that all machines don't have the same number of machine words. The number of registers is now obvious. I guess people are now saying that parallelism is obvious but take a machine like the ILLIAC IV where you have an arbitrary number of accumulators all of which work in parallel. In this case we're not talking just about (small) parallelism in data transfers. How could someone building a system in, say 1960, anticipate that the ILLIAC IVs might be setting the tone for a whole new line of machines in the 1970s? So I think that there's probably going to be a limited time range when we won't be making silly mistakes that make portability difficult. Beyond that limited time range we'll find we've made some disastrous mistakes.

Strachey: I want to come back to this business of how can we help people to make systems, write systems, in such a way that they can be transportable. It's not entirely a question of not putting in features that we haven't thought of—not putting in the right number of registers or something like that. I think one of the chief difficulties is that the general standard of programming is extremely low. Now this is a thing which I know Dijkstra's been talking about and this is actually what Doug Ross was saying. I think that I would like to suggest again, that the general standards of programming and the way in which people are taught to program is abominable. They are over and over again taught to make puns; to do shifts instead of multiplying when they mean multiplying; to multiply when they mean shifts; to confuse bit patterns and numbers and generally to say one thing when they actually mean something quite different. Now this is the standard way of writing a program and they take great pleasure in doing so—"isn't it wonderful? It saves a quarter of a microsecond somewhere every other month" Now I think we will not get a proper standard of programming, we will not make it possible to have a subject of software engineering until we can have some proper professional standards about how to write programs; and this has to be done by teaching people right at the beginning how to write programs properly. I don't know that we know how to do this yet but I think we should make a very serious effort to do so and I think one of the things we ought to do perhaps at this conference is to make a great point about trying to improve the standards of programming in general. I'm sure that one of the first things to do about this is to say what you mean and not to say something quite different.

Perlis: I think it is inevitable that people program, and will continue to program, poorly. Training will not substantially improve matters. Using subsets of language doesn't help because people always step outside the subset. We have to learn to live with it.

4.1.7 On effectiveness of portability in practice

Brown: A sufficiently radical change of hardware, e.g. the move to highly parallel multiprocessing, may render the algorithms themselves obsolete so that even if portability is achieved, the new hardware may be used hopelessly inefficiently.

Feldman: If you are using a system very hard and pushing it to its limits, you cannot expect that system to be portable.

Poole: It seems to me that inefficient software on a machine is better than none at all.

Feldman: (from "Towards automatic programming")
"The idea of extending a language through macro expansion is appealing and is certainly useful for minor syntactic changes. The problem is that to add a significantly new construct to a language with reasonable efficiency, one must change the compiler in nontrivial ways. The solution is to write compilers so that they may be altered without undue pain. Several translator writing systems make this possible. Alternatively one could write a clean compiler in a base language and extend the compiler when needed. Our understanding of compiler writing is reaching the point where it should be possible to design extensible compilers. This is a topic that deserves considerably more attention."

In connection with this topic, see the paper by Schorr, reproduced in section 7.12.

4.1.8 On transfer of know-how

Ross: We have never yet set foot in a user's premises to help put the AED system in. Furthermore, users are able to write systems they can bootstrap to new machines with little help from us. But knowing how to achieve a full bootstrap of the AED system itself is quite another thing. We can't tell people how to do that yet.

Brown: We hope to solve this problem by putting in a lot of effort on documentation and system support software.

Buxton: I want to make one or two slightly cynical remarks on the subject of portability.
   Since I've recently left the ivory towers of industry and returned to the sordid commercial life of running a university department, I feel a little cynical as a result. My impression is that we've been treated to an estimable and very interesting review of good, solid, working, successful techniques for transporting software around the place. On looking back, it occurs to me that some of these techniques really have been around for years—I can recall, no doubt most of us can, early bootstrapping between machines being done in the late 'fifties. An interesting question, which occurs to me then is to wonder: why isn't portable software with us? So I ask myself the

following questions. Firstly: who wants it? The answer is the users. Secondly: who has to produce it? The answer is the system designers—it seems very sensible to say that if you really want portable software you must design your software system with that aim in view from the ground upwards. Now, why is this not done? The answer here is, I suggest, that the system designers by and large reside in the manufacturers who actually produce the vast majority of software used by the average user. This software is not portable because the manufacturers do not regard it as in their best interests to have portable software. This is why we haven't got any. The portable software we have is, in the main, produced by users who are also systems designers, working in mainly academic environments. The only places where it tends to go into general commercial use is in fact in the bureau business. The business of a manufacturer is to get his clients and then to keep them and this he does by a process known as "Free competition in the open market". This is implemented by taking the clients he's managed to get and then totally insulating them from all other possible external influences. This is done by a process known as education. If this process is successful then with any luck his clients will see only his future range of machines. Portable software would be a disaster because they might be able to take useful application programs elsewhere. What a manufacturer might conceivably want is software that is portable on to his new range of machines, when he's thought of it, and only on to that new range, not any other machines.

4.2 Adaptability

One of the major contributions on the subject of adaptability was given in a talk by Warshall, who made reference to a report entitled "The Representation of Algorithms", available from Applied Data Research, 450 Seventh Avenue, New York, N.Y. 10001, U.S.A.

Warshall: When discussing portability we saw three examples that I regard as sensitive and competent applications of a conventional technology for moving programs. I would like to talk about the philosophical picture of portability that underlies that conventional technology. I claim that technology rests very critically upon the fact that the targets between which portability is occurring are very similar in structure.

In any of these systems or in any system which facilitates transport, what is being transported is, ultimately, descriptions by people of computational processes. People describe problems in some kind of language. It is a characteristic of languages which describe computational processes that they are a mixture of two things. First of all they implicitly define the mapping which you are trying to perform by executing the process. Second of all they define a certain intended allocation of resource to accomplish that mapping. If you are dealing with two more or less similar machines as targets for translation of your language, the trick throughout the conventional technology is to attempt to strip out of the linguistic form exactly those representational commitments which have to do with the differences between the two machines. If, for example, one machine has an instruction which does floating-point multiply and another machine does not, you raise the language level and you do not permit the language you write in to dispose in detail of this level of resource. The language speaks about "floating-multiply" and the translation is different in the two systems; in one case it is to a unitary operation and in the other to some kind of subroutine call.

To every part of the expression of the mathematical process in the "higher level language", there corresponds a structure downstairs in each of the targets. It is true of the conventional technology that the two programs in the two targets always look very similar to each other for that reason. They both reflect the structure of the program description in the higher language, and by higher level here, I do not mean more closely connected with the problem: I mean containing fewer details of resource commitment.

What happens when the target machines or the target environments become very dissimilar? Then two programs to express an identical mathematical function, for instance, on the two targets would look quite different from each other. For example, if you imagine an information retrieval system on a machine which has a couple of tapes for secondary storage, then the program will look like an enormous contortion to avoid dead rewind time. Now a program to perform the same function on a machine with random access storage would be written in an entirely different way. In effect, when the target machines for your translation become more and more dissimilar and you have to strip out more and more representational commitments from the linguistic form, you always end up in the same trap. The linguistic form you are working with when you get through is so far away from either of the targets, in that you have made no representational decisions worth talking about, that the software's problem of mapping down is epic in its proportions. For example, you might write all programs as though you had infinite memory and then let some automatic device worry entirely about storage strategy and resource strategy. That's certainly a harder job for the software than the job it has now.

The only way that we know out of this trap is to take the two dissimilar equipments and make them look similar. That is to say, we introduce a layer of software on top of either of the machines or both of them and regard these simplified machines, defined by the interposing software, as the real machines we are mapping to. They are more similar, the maps become more plausible, but of course you have introduced some degree of inefficiency; inevitably, because you are now regarding as atomic units things that are really combinations of atomic units, and solutions that involve breaking them up are no longer available to you. I claim we are already in the situation of dealing with targets that are in fact so dissimilar that a conventional approach to transport forces us to choose between an absurdly difficult compiling problem on the one hand and impossible inefficiency on the other. I think that is the reason why the conventional approach has shown no fruit at all when dealing with, for example the use of secondary storage as a resource.

I would like to say next that I am not claiming that you will ever reach a situation where the two target machines are so dissimilar there exists no language "high enough" to permit mapping down to both of them. I am merely asserting that if that language ends up looking like a Gödel numbering system for programs, I am not sure it is a useful logical construct for us, or even for mathematicians. Incidentally I would like also to say that it is not clear that such a "higher level language", if the target machines are sufficiently dissimilar, has very much to do with a suitable language for human beings to write in. "Higher level" here really means "less committed representationally" and has nothing to do with closeness to natural expression of problems. This is a confusion of issues which I think is found throughout our literature.

Having said that there are intrinsic limitations in conventional methodology, one might ask whether there is any alternative. I claim there is an alternative, although I certainly can't prove it is the right one, and I would like to give you an example of what I mean. This example comes from what may superficially seem a strange place: code optimization. Imagine that you are attempting to compile a program in, say FORTRAN, for a machine that does not look like the abstraction: the FORTRAN machine, and that in fact looks seriously dissimilar to that machine in a very crucial way. In particular the target of the compilation might be a machine that is not a sequential synchronized processor. Clearly, your program for the FORTRAN machine contains representational commitments about sequence and synchrony which are just plain wrong for the target. A group of people, friends of mine, have been working for some time on this problem. This group found that conventional techniques simply would not work. By conventional techniques I mean starting with the FORTRAN program as the highest level language dealt with and essentially compiling down in successive stages, each of which was more representationally committed than the previous stage. They found that the fruitful way to look at the problem was as an instance of the portability problem, i.e. to envisage it as an effort to transport from the FORTRAN machine to an asynchronous processor. What they did in effect was not to map down but to map up, i.e. perform a process which they themselves call "decompilation". Having isolated the most crucial representational commitment that was getting in their way, namely the commitment having to do with sequential synchronous processing, they developed automatic techniques for methodically transforming a program in the FORTRAN language to something at a "higher level". This does not mean something closer to the problem or closer to a human being's understanding of the problem, but merely something with fewer representational commitments. They convert the FORTRAN program into what might be regarded as an asynchronous automaton which happens still to have some structural features that came from the initial organization of the FORTRAN program. This expression in the form of an asynchronous process has the additional virtue of being deformable; that is to say, by formal techniques it is possible to alter a process with a different degree of asynchrony. In essence, instead of finding a language that a man can write in and that is "high enough" and then mapping down in all possible directions, they started with something in which a man could write that was not high enough, they mapped up, then across and then back down again.

I would submit that given our notable lack of progress in applying a current technology to situations in which the targets are seriously dissimilar and given the kind of remarks I made earlier about why you might expect this to be so, it might be an extremely worthwhile thing to break out of the mental trap of assuming that the highest level language in the system has something to do with a problem oriented language. We should consider the use of software as a device for eliminating representational commitments; maybe trying that strategy for a while will help us in solving this very difficult portability problem where the targets are systems that are quite dissimilar from each other.

Bayer: I don't quite understand what you mean by decompilation. Does this involve more than relaxing the strict ordering sequence of instructions?

Warshall: The representational commitments that derive from the model of the FORTRAN processor as a sequential synchronized device go much deeper than simply the problem of the ordering of instructions. In particular, one of the most crucial things to disintegrate in the source program is the concept of "variable name". The name "A" for example in a program is the name of a class of values no two of which are interesting at the same time; that's why they can share storage and why they can share a name. If you want to explode the process, that is to say take advantage of increasing degrees of asynchrony, it is necessary to explode the variable name to a set of other things, and how many other things is a very subtle function of how the program is constructed.

Perhaps it would be more informative if I gave you an idea of what kinds of deformation occurred. This group performed amongst other things the following:

1 Elimination of common sub expressions on a global basis, not on a flow block basis.

2 Loop flattening; by loop flattening I mean the following. Imagine that a loop has three computations in a row. In the i'th iteration it first computes A[i], then using A[i] computes B[i], then using B[i] computes C[i]. The optimizers do tricks like, for example, changing the initialization to make it more extensive so that, instead of starting out with A[0], B[0] and C[0], you start out with A[2], B[1] and C[0] and then the three lines of computation can march along in parallel.

3 Decision postponement; it is sometimes more economical not to decide which of two things to do but to do both of them at the same time before deciding which result to use.

4 Arbitrary degrees of internal buffering to interface parts of the process; for example, if you have a bunch of decisions, you have iterative decision making in one place while the results are being developed somewhere else. These two things can get arbitrarily out of phase with each other.

5 Most important of all, full pipelining at all levels. This means that if, for example, you have a machine which is operating on inputs and producing outputs, it is not necessary for the machine to wait until an output is produced before the next input starts being processed. Pipelining is used here in the same sense in which it is used in hardware in systems like the CDC 7600.

We conceive of a program as something that can, with the proper equipment, be solving more than one problem at a time and we have to provide the machinery for getting the right answer associated with the right question as we get through. Now, it is clear that this kind of explosion of a process is a good deal more extensive than the partial ordering of FORTRAN statements.

Schorr: The process of going up to a higher representation, then across and down again sounds like a nontrivial job. I wonder whether, in the case of FORTRAN for example, the cost might not in some sense be lowered by perhaps providing a "sift" from one FORTRAN to another followed by a correction process?

Warshall: One possible realization of this approach that we have considered is the idea of what we call the "FORTRAN laundry", based on our knowledge of the way in which two different manufacturers' compilers work. We take FORTRAN written for one machine and translate it to FORTRAN written for the other machine.

The more important and crucial thing to get across, however, is that I think there are three essentially different techniques that I am talking about. One—the conventional—is to have the language in which the programmer writes be the highest language, i.e. the least representationally committed language, in the system, and to restrict the software to mapping down. The second is to decompile, i.e. to eliminate some class of representational commitments, and deform, which is not the same as compiling down. You go across and then down. The third is to go all the way up to something so decommitted that you can sensibly compile down from it towards either target.

The remarks I made at the beginning suggest that we have reached the limits of the first technique and that perhaps the second will prove more fruitful than the third; it is the second that we are in fact involved with. The decompilation process is certainly extremely laborious, complicated and space consuming and unless you are really concerned with optimization I would not recommend using it. However, I think the application of this technology to other situations like, for example, the allocation of secondary storage, could have very fruitful results.

Bayer: Adaptability means the modifying of programs to relate them to specific users. This is of particular interest to those with large application programs. Aron pointed out the difficulty of getting a good initial specification and the need for continual changes at late stages in the design process in ways which are neither predictable nor even reasonable.

Where you are concerned with a large program and a large data base, the data structure must be included in the system design consideration, otherwise you are lost before you start. The logic of the data structure is tied into the logic of the program. Two extreme methods of including the data structure in the system design are:

1 Attach a full description of the data structure to the data base.

2 Represent the structure of the data entirely in the program logic. Neither extreme is particularly successful. What do we do about this problem?

See also "On portability of data" in section 4.1.4.

Lampson: (from "On Reliable and Extendable Operating Systems")
"If a system is to evolve to meet changing requirements, and if it is to be flexible enough to permit modularization without serious loss of efficiency, it must have a basic structure that allows extensions not only from a basic system but also from some complex configuration that has been reached by several prior stages of evolution. In other words, the extension process must not exhaust the facilities required for further extensions. The system must be completely *open-ended,* so that additional machinery can be attached at any point.

Secondly, the relations between a module and its environment must be freely redefinable. This means that any module, provided its references to the outside world are documented, can be run inside an *envelope* which intercepts all of these references and reinterprets them at will. In order to ensure that external references are documented, it must be normal and indeed compulsory practice to specify each module's environment precisely and independently of the module's internal structure.

Thirdly, it must be possible to introduce several layers of re-interpretation around a module *economically* without forcing all of its external references to suffer reinterpretation by each layer. In other words, a capability for extension by exception is required. Furthermore, the system's basic mechanisms for naming and for calls must permit a number of higher level modules to utilize other modules, rather than forcing each new module to create and maintain its own inventory of objects.

To summarize, a usefully extendable system must be open-ended, must allow each module to be isolated in an envelope and must encourage economical reuse of existing constructs. Such a system has some chance of providing a satisfactory toolkit for others to use."

Finally, we include this description of the way in which a system was transferred, while continuing to provide service.

Hopkins: I would like to comment on how to improve a given system to make it portable from a real, live, and successful example. My example is the American Airlines' SABRE system which in 1965 was handling about 2200 inputs a minute on a modified 7090. Their projection from the growth of the airline business was that by 1970 it would be handling 3000 inputs a minute. I don't think many of us have on-line real time systems that have to perform that way; this is a real example of software engineering. The problem was that the 7090 was completely saturated in 1965 and the system consisted of over 300,000 assembly language instructions. In its favour, the system was highly modular and had such things as standard communications areas, standard names, all the programs used copy facilities from libraries and it had supervisor system linkages which were all standardized. Now consider what the problem really was—they couldn't just pull the plug out of that system some day and stop selling tickets—airlines get very excited if they can't sell tickets for a week or more. The system itself had reliability problems which occur in any system where you've got 300,000 instructions. It was a growing system, in that the business changed and so the program had to change; this all meant that the system went down 3 or 4 times a day. They introduced new errors into the system 2 or 3 times a week; sometimes they did not flush them out for a month or more and they learnt to live with this.

Now imagine trying to take this system off a 7090 and get it on to a 360/65; this was a sort of nightmare and the solution was interesting. First of all, they attacked the problem in one very practical way. If you have a really bad problem, you spend all you can on hardware. They bought a system hookup consisting basically of a pair of 7090s, which have communication lines going into them, inputting into a pair of 360/65s. I believe they have twelve 2314 disc units, and they have a whole raft of other secondary storage units.

The short term solution was to simply take the 360 and put a small control program in it and let it watch the 7090s' I/O request queues and do all the drum I/O and the LCS transfers on the 360 large capacity core storage. This gave them about a 20 per cent improvement on the old 7090 system and they were able to get over the next Christmas rush. The long term solution was to bring up OS/360 on the 65 and write a control program on top of this which essentially duplicated the same functions as the 7090 control program. Then what they did was to gradually transfer modules over from the 7090 to the 65.

They were extremely upset about having written 300,000 lines of assembly language code the first time around and they were determined to write in a higher level language the second time. There was no suitable language which was available, which could interface with their systems so they wrote a new compiler, which was called SABRE PL/1, for a PL/1 dialect with low level features. It provides, and this is very important, a mechanism for having non-standard interfaces. In this kind of environment it is very difficult to persuade programmers who are designing the control program and the systems services not to design non-standard interfaces. If you have the prospect of 3,000 inputs a minute and your system has always been just one step ahead of the sheriff, you are not going to tell people that a microsecond isn't important; too many times they have had to rewrite code to save a microsecond or two. However, they are willing to live with a very few assembly language modules because they recognize the fact that most of the work is concentrated in a very few modules. The higher level language is machine independent in the sense that it knows nothing about the internal registers of the machine; however, it does know how to write non-standard calls to systems services and it is machine dependent in the sense that it knows that a byte has 8 bits on a 360. The performance is very good with no global optimization. This is because, as has been pointed out elsewhere, system programs really don't have very many loops and it doesn't pay very much to move things out of loops because the loops just aren't particularly important.

I venture to guess that one of the most important things in gaining acceptance of the product was the fact that it produced an assembly language type listing which showed after each statement exactly how much code was generated. As a sales gimmick, people could see that the compiler was producing clever code in certain instances and this pleased the assembly language programming types. It also proved to be a tool which enabled people to see when code being generated was disastrous; they could see it and make adjustments.

I think, in conclusion, that I'd like to point out that while I treat this as an eminently satisfactory exercise, I shudder to think what will happen if American Airlines have to go to a machine with a different word size or a radically different type of systems services. The machine dependence of the SABRE PL/1 language is rather high in those areas. If you've got this constant fight against time, you're going to have to constantly improve the system. I guess I'd like to conclude also with the fact that at this time I believe approximately half, closer to three quarters, of the system has been recoded in PL/1 and is now functioning on the 360. They are approaching the time when they will be the only people in the world who have a 64k word 7090 as a front end machine for a 360/65.

5 LARGE SYSTEMS

In this section we have attempted to collect together material that is specifically related to the problems of designing very large systems. By way of introduction, the following comment by Schwartz has been excerpted from the quotation given in full in section 5.1.1.

Schwartz: I must admit that I have frequently asked myself whether these systems require many people because they are large, or whether they are large because they have many people.

5.1 Case Histories

Several rather extensive reports were given at the conference summarizing experiences gained in the design of large systems. These reports and the ensuing discussion are the subject of this section.

5.1.1 A survey

This section is a transcription of a talk by Schwartz, who also provided a working paper "Analyzing Large Scale System Development", reproduced in section 7.13.

Schwartz: In the early 1950's, a small closely-knit group of skilled programmers working with 256 words of immediate access storage and relatively limited file storage and peripherals, produced a computerized aircraft surveillance system which included a limited set of radar inputs and tracked a few aircraft simultaneously.

Based on this successful effort, this small, closely-knit group, in co-operation with the U.S. Air Force, decided to produce a somewhat more complete system. This system would consist of a set of duplex computers covering the entire United States with communication between adjacent sectors, new radar equipment which would permit finer tracking, a number of additional functions, a wide variety of alphanumeric and vector displays and automatic backup between the various sectors as well as within the duplex computers.

The capacity of the system was to be considerably larger than the prototype development, and the computer was to have 8K words of core storage.

Any illusions that the original group had about retaining their past pleasant, intimate, technically exciting working relationship was soon shattered. Within a year approximately 1,000 people were involved with the development of the SAGE System. People were recruited and trained from a variety of walks of life. Street-car conductors, undertakers (with at least one year of training in calculus), school teachers, curtain cleaners and others were hastily assembled, trained in programming for some number of weeks and assigned parts in a very complex organization.

The core storage of the computer was expanded to 64K words. The originally hoped for capacities of the system were cut considerably. The system was first delivered over a year late at considerably more cost than was originally expected and not too long before people began to realize the threat of the manned bomber was beginning to decrease considerably as long range missiles began to become a reality.

So began the era of the large scale system engineering efforts.

Not too long after this actually reasonably successful start, another rather major effort was begun for an important military function. Those responsible for this one hired and transferred approximately six hundred people within a very short time. After this first step (hiring) was completed, the next problem was to determine what this system was to do. This took, to some people's chagrin, several years. Man's ingenuity being what it is, however, a large number of these people were not wasted. They were put to work on the support (utility) system which would assist the operational programmers when they got around to writing these programs. The support system for SAGE had approximately 1,000,000 instructions and was actually very good, considering the time at which it was built, but it was decided to improve upon the support system in many ways. It didn't make it: about two years later, the support system was not quite ready to handle the operational programs, which were finally being coded.

In 1961, a small group of highly skilled programmers produced, at MIT, one of the first general purpose time sharing systems, called CTSS. This system evolved into one of the better known and highly successful time sharing systems. Based on this experience, in 1964 ideas began to be formulated for a considerably advanced system called MULTICS. This was an ambitious effort, encompassing a number of new concepts, new hardware, and considerably more system programmers than were required for CTSS. I think it would be fair to state that this system has not proceeded with the same feeling of pleasantness nor satisfaction that accompanied CTSS.

These are a few of many experiences in large-scale system development which have taken place over the past 15 years. Very few of these have brought unanimous cheers from producers and customers because they were on time, met the original specification, stayed within original hardware and remained on budget.

We have heard today a number of reasons as well as solutions for problems in the production of these systems. From many of these experiences, we have learned of techniques and guidelines necessary to approach these massive software undertakings.

Pervading all discussions are several key words, one of these words is *control*. Control is needed by managers, so that they don't begin a task before the initial specification is clear. Programmers must be controlled, so that they don't invent beyond the requirements which are assigned to them. Control must be exercised over the testing of the system, so that tests for all levels of the system, including the smallest components, have adequate test specifications prior to their production. These tests must then be executed and verified. Control must be exercised over new versions of systems, to make sure that they are at least as good as the previous version, before they are unleashed on the world. Documentation must be controlled but must constantly keep pace with the system development.

Another word is *flexibility*. Managers must be willing to adapt as situations arise requiring changes in scope or technique. The basic system must, through such means as data description divorced from procedures, centralized data maintenance, and data-independent programming languages, be flexible enough to permit change and evolution without reprogramming. People must be flexible enough to tolerate rather drastic changes in direction.

The third word is *people*. A wide variety of levels of skills in people are required in this kind of effort. People differ enormously in capability and working styles. This presents considerable management problems. Better measurement techniques would be very valuable. Some subset of the people must be able to communicate outside of their own sphere, which might be software, documentation, testing, engineering, or administration.

Lastly, there is the word *management.* To handle large numbers of people, organized in a fairly complex structure, keeping them motivated while under quite stringent control, to understand the mass of details concerned with the production process, to make decisions based on too few or too many inputs of a sometimes highly emotional body of people, to be able to face superiors or customers with occasionally drastic recommendations for change in scope; all of these require the large scale system manager to be skilled, flexible, tolerant, informed, extremely tactful and, unfortunately, rare.

I must admit that I have frequently asked myself whether these systems require many people because they are large, or whether they are large because they have many people. There is little question that they could be done with fewer people than have sometimes been employed, given better initial planning, better key people and a more intelligent starting phase. But it is also true that these systems require many parallel activities outside the development of the central operating program; unrealistic goals and schedules are specified, communication problems exist at many levels. All of these factors and others beside conspire to create much larger organizations than seem theoretically necessary. Thus, although experience speaks against massive efforts, it also indicates they will continue into the future.

5.1.2 Apollo Programming Support

This section was transcribed from a talk by Aron which covered, at greater length, information that he gave in a working paper entitled "General Remarks on Apollo Programming Support".

Aron: I'd like to discuss the Apollo project, primarily for the purpose of giving a feeling of scale on a particular task which, through its visible results, can be seen to have been a successful project. The Apollo 11 mission, which actually landed men on the moon, was evidently successful because you all saw it. Within that project, which was an immense hardware/software/organizational activity, there was a large software system. In fact there were several large software systems. I'll talk about the ground support of the space mission and primarily about the portion of that which was conducted at Houston, Texas. There were other portions conducted by a number of different manufacturers at Cape Kennedy, at the Manned Space Flight Center, at the Jet Propulsion Laboratories, and at a number of tracking stations round the world; and of course in the space ship itself, where you had computational capability and direct communication with the ground. The significance of the many locations is that you have a much more difficult interface co-ordination problem because you have geographically separate activities that must work in synchronization and must trade information in real time during the mission.

As a first step in giving you a feeling for scale, the Houston, Texas operation by itself ranged over a period of years from 300 individuals to about 600 individuals, and at the largest point there were in the region of 300 programmers. The remaining people were in support or in administration associated with the job. This group started their experience in space activities about 1959 on a project called Vanguard, a Navy satellite project that put a very small satellite in earth orbit. This was then taken over and merged into the American space agency's (NASA's) program, called

Mercury, which put men into space, followed by Gemini, which went into the two man space mission, followed by Apollo, which had as its objective the landing on the moon. The initial project required a portion of a 704 to track and maintain trajectory and orbit information on the Vanguard satellite. The system, which was used on Apollo 11, ran on one IBM S/360 model 75, but the support system requires a total of six for its development, so in Houston there are six model 75's. In addition there was a model 50 for program support. All these machines were associated directly with the ground support programming, which excludes communications and activities associated with data reduction and planning; these are done on other NASA computers.

I mentioned the 10 year history primarily to indicate that there has been an opportunity here for the programming and NASA staff to get to know each other. Many of the people who worked on the original Mercury project are currently working on the Apollo project. They have developed an understanding of each other as individuals and this rapport between individuals is in our opinion a very significant factor in arriving at agreed upon specifications from which one can proceed to build a programming system. I should point out that we have other projects which lack this rapport, either because of personnel turnover in the military or because people don't like each other, and it is quite evident you cannot have an effective software engineering activity when you lack rapport.

It is obvious that Apollo was a real time system. What may not be obvious is that the system consists of a very large number of inputs and outputs, each of which is potentially unique and each of which changes for the next mission. There are many, many telemetry messages brought in from the space vehicle and from the tracking stations. The system supports a very large slide projection capability which can superimpose static displays over dynamic displays, all of these under program control. There is a very large number of displays which are monitored by the NASA monitors, usually assisted by one of the programming staff. These output displays are tailored to the individual who is going to sit there. Part of the design philosophy is to have the actual designer and engineer be responsible during the mission for supervising what he designs. That means that almost always your outputs are tailored to the personal interests of the man who is going to sit in front of the display console. It should be further pointed out that, at the time that programming started, it was not always possible to determine what the display unit would be in terms of hardware, so that in general the display systems required a symbolic generator. All display output programs were written in a standard form and a special program was written to convert the displays from the standard form to the proper device format.

The programming techniques were primarily assembly language and FORTRAN. However, it was necessary to build a special operating system called RTOS which initially was intended to look like OS/360 with real time appendages for device control. Because of schedule difficulties there was a divergence early in the development of RTOS so that, in fact, it is different from OS and is incompatible with it, but it has many of the same functions.

Five of the six model 75's are close to one another. They all have large capacity storage and are interconnected through storage and through input/output devices. NASA's safety requirement is that a single mission be supported by a portion of one machine, leaving room for peak load, but backed up by other machines. If the primary machine that is running the mission fails, the job is switched to a secondary machine. The reason for the six machines is to support the mission, which may last several weeks, to support program development and to support simulations of future missions.

During mission simulation and during real missions, these machines are connected to a very large display and control room as well as to the input/output devices. The result of this is that during checkout of the real time programs, it is essential to dedicate some portion of this complex. That leads to each individual programmer using, on the average, 10 or 11 hours of computer time on a model 75 every month. This interested us because it is quite a high amount, but it turns out that it is not much higher than that for our other real time systems. We run an average of seven to eight hours a month on data-based systems. The systems run in batch mode for debugging. In some of our locations we use remote entry; at the moment in Houston we still use couriers. The programmers get one or two shots a day, but they know what to expect and in most cases they find that they can adjust their work to fit this type of schedule.

Let me turn to the question of the use of modelling techniques to help program development. Modelling has been used extensively in the Apollo support system project. A group of programmers was convinced that you should have a model of the real time system and they went about producing it. They came up with some things that were sufficiently convincing for NASA to permit them to build a model to run alongside the system itself.

They started on a 7094. They are now working on a S/360. Their model consists of a simulation of the hardware, the real time software, and the application programs. The model can be operated at various levels of detail; it can treat the mission programs as black boxes, simply looking at the inputs and outputs, or the program itself can be substituted to see how it actually works. Because this model is developed in parallel and runs constantly it is useful for such things as determining when you are going to run out of memory capacity or CPU speed. It has been used as a guideline in changing the hardware configurations. In addition it has been used for evaluating programming proposals and trying to determine which one looks most promising and should go to the head of the priority list.

Now it is always difficult to validate such a system and people tend to lack confidence in it until it is validated. This involves measuring the modelled system. In order to measure the operation of an actual system, a program called the Statistics Gathering System was built, which runs in cohabitation with the real time operating systems. It records information on a great number of different software operations. The information that we got out showed that for certain missions simulation was within 5 to 10 per cent of the actual run, which was enough to convince anyone. So NASA has continued to depend upon the simulation and has supported a group of some 25 people over the years just for this purpose. I indicate the size of the group because it indicates that not everybody is going to be able to support the kind of simulation that has been successful at Houston.

Finally, a comment on the question of schedule control procedures. Control consisted of, among other things: defining small modules, assigning decision making responsibility for modules to individuals who would commit to solve the problem, reviewing progress weekly, maintaining a detailed specification and change document, measuring and/or predicting system performance, monitoring financial progress, and requiring advanced reservation of computer test time. At one time NASA required that we develop a PERT chart. They have since withdrawn that as a requirement. In its place, a development and test plan is maintained and reviewed weekly by the IBM and NASA counterparts. It was useful, however, in the design stage when it provided a tool to identify things that had to be done and to show their interrelationships and the activities they depended upon and those that depended on them.

Ross: Your statistics on amount of debugging time and number of programmers indicate that each debugging run takes an average of 15 minutes. Is this right?

Aron: This is an average. In fact some runs will last for many hours or a day or more, when one is involved in testing the overall system rather than debugging modules. Considerable attention is being paid to finding ways to reduce this figure.

Lang: What are the proportions of machine language to FORTRAN programs in the system? How was it decided which language to use for a given program?

Schorr: I understand that basically the orbit calculations, etc. are in FORTRAN. The modifications to OS/360 to produce RTOS were in machine language and that was basically the division. At the time I saw the project, there were 40 to 50 programmers working on RTOS, and approximately 250 programmers working on the application modules, and these people were writing almost completely in FORTRAN. About forty per cent of the total code was in FORTRAN.

Brown: I would like to know how many supervisory personnel are involved, how many levels of supervision there are, how many of these levels consist of people who are part time supervisors and part time programmers and how many levels consist of people who are able to read programs and do read the programs for which they are responsible?

Aron: This particular organization is heavy in programming background. It is a well known situation for an engineer to be managing programmers and not understand their product. Houston has been fortunate in having been built up for the purpose of programming. The typical organization starts with a first-line manager who will have six to ten people working for him. In general the first-line manager does not write portions of the program but he is responsible for the quality of the program. He always is capable of reading it and understanding it, and he may pick certain difficult parts of it to do himself. Above the first-line manager is a second-line manager. He will divide his time primarily between giving direction to the managers below him and coordinating the requirements with the user and his own boss. He is probably competent to read the code but he spends practically no time reviewing actual programs. I would assume that he gets involved only when there is a problem in testing and it is necessary to revise the design in some way. There are then two levels above that. The head of the project is a fourth-line manager; he is primarily an administrator, although he has a programming background.

Thompson: Could you comment on the division of responsibility between NASA and IBM, and on the problems associated with acceptance by NASA of the finished product?

Aron: The vendor in this case had total responsibility for the ground support programming package, meaning that NASA did not tell us how to do the programming and they did not look over our shoulders. On the other hand, as I explained before, it was impossible for us to make a step forward without understanding the user requirements, so there had to be close co-ordination between the user and the IBM personnel. In general every group had a contact in NASA.

We did not do the mathematical analysis for the most part. NASA itself defined the problem, determined how the problem could be solved and gave it to us to program and verify. This is quite common in our business; we have to have people who are very broad in their ability to understand applications, but they are not often asked to generate the initial solution to a scientific problem.

On acceptance: any mission required from one to two months of actual real time simulation. The simulation during the latter period involved the actual NASA people who had to run the system. To ensure that the inputs were realistic they were recorded from actual instrumentation and fed in on tape or, at certain stages, they would be transported to the remote sites and fed in from the tracking station to simulate the actual communication links. At the end of this period of simulation, if you were ready to run the mission, you had acceptance. In addition, a formal acceptance of system components took place when test reports were approved.

Haller: What kind of specifications did you get from NASA?

Aron: That's hard to say. It is primarily a specification written out in English, with formulae, describing a procedure. It is not a programming specification in any sense. The problem has changed over the years; therefore they continually give us new inputs. The original problem was to put a single vehicle into an earth orbit. A succeeding problem was to put more than one vehicle into orbit and to find a way to transfer from one orbit to another in order to perform a rendezvous in lunar orbit, plus the control of a lunar landing. You will perhaps have noticed from television that the ground support center was always in communication. Part of the specification requires that this system be foolproof and as a consequence there are a tremendous number of safety features built in so that, if something unexpected happens, there are people sitting on the ground who will make decisions so as to correct the situation. The ability to support decision making on the ground is built into the program or at least into the program documentation.

Schorr: The human aspect of that is, I think, very important. There is no attempt to do it all by program reliability alone. For example, during one of the missions they found an error involving a module not releasing core store when it should. It just kept on claiming more and more core, and this was not noticed in the simulations. As a result, when the system was running, after a few days it got more and more sluggish. It was working, but non-essential functions were being dropped, because of lack of core space. Over a period of eight to ten hours a second system was brought up, by hand transfer of inputs to the system, very laboriously, and then a cut-over was made to this system.

Bugs are taken out up to the last day. Very often expedient decisions are made right before a mission to avoid using particular modules.

Falkoff: How do you construct the modules in such a manner that you can at the last moment leave some out and still have the system operate?

Aron: The easiest part of the system is the algorithm for solving the Newtonian equations. Where you really run into difficulty is in the human interface and in trying to understand what should be put out on the

displays and what should be put out on the radio links. This leads to a very
early recognition that you must modularize things in such a way that if you
had a telemetry experiment that you couldn't test you'd have to delete it.
You couldn't allow it to interfere with the more formal, mathematical parts.
A second consideration was that the schedule is much more important than
the experiments, so that the management priority was to sacrifice
experiments in the mission in order to satisfy a particular schedule for
launching a vehicle. The modularity simply follows good rules of interface
definition. The real time operating system was completely independent of
the "problem modules". That meant that these modules could be extracted
from the total system without too much trouble. Each named problem
module could be worked on independently of other modules and it could be
installed or extracted from the library master program, which could then be
reloaded in the system. In addition, through the displays, you have the
power to select which modules should actually be used.

Randell: It would seem to me that one of the main reasons for the
undoubted success of the Apollo programming support system is its
environment. It is part of a much larger effort, the total Apollo project,
involving many other technological problems that had to be solved, and
which could only be tackled a few at a time. Hence the support system has
been done over many times; each time there has been a considerable
change but it hasn't been a revolution. What worry me are systems which
don't benefit from such a constraining environment, where software is the
only technology that would be involved in a huge leap forward.

5.1.3 The electronic switching system

*The Bell Telephone Laboratories system, subject of a paper by Ulrich
reproduced in full in section 7.15, caused some discussion. The overall
reliability of the system to date was summarized as follows.*

Ulrich: We had an initial objective of downtime for the system of no more
than two hours every 40 years, remembering that downtime is only caused
by situations in which both processors are down or where there is such
massive memory mutilation that we can't handle calls. Actually, we didn't
adequately anticipate the second when we made our downtime objective. We
thought primarily of how often we could reasonably afford to risk having
both processors fail simultaneously, and we felt that perhaps once in 40
years was a reasonable objective. I might add that we've had in the order of
50 years of experience, accumulative over all our central offices, and we
have not had an instance of this particular kind of trouble yet; so that
prediction may not have been too far out of line. In terms of our overall
achievement, however, instead of having two hours downtime in 40 years, in
this 50 years of experience we've had a total of about 60 hours of downtime.
Again, that's not bad; 60 hours in 50 years is about one hour per year, which
is a fairly high degree of uptime for any computer system. This is the
overall statistic since our first installation. More recently of course we've
been quite a bit better. Our more recent statistics indicate 15 hours
downtime per 40 years for large offices and perhaps five hours per 40 years
in smaller offices.

One of our big problems was to make sure that we would not get into a
situation where we had massive memory mutilation, otherwise known as a
crash, which would prevent us from setting up telephone calls, without our

recognize the situation. So we had to build facilities to make it possible to have a reliable scheme for recognizing that on an overall basis the program was cycling properly. The particular algorithm we used was to check the time required to go through all tasks, and if this time exceeded a certain specified amount, we became worried and we started performing progressively more serious initializations. I might add that our final step of initialization is to tear down all telephone connections, clear the memory, and start from scratch. This was not too favourably received by the Chairman of the Board of our corporation. When he first heard about this fact (after it had happened, of course) he is reputed to have remarked, "What idiot could have designed a system which deliberately tears down telephone calls?" He was not an experienced software man so he didn't appreciate the subtle beauties of initialization as a means of getting out of trouble.

The main types of programming error that caused crashes were the following:

1 We use pointers quite extensively and we interpret them literally without checking for range, primarily because of their extensive use and because of our need to conserve time on our main program legs. If a pointer is falsely overwritten, you quickly get into a situation where you start propagating trash throughout the memory and this can get you into trouble.

2 Another situation which has occurred in a number of cases is the unchaining of a lengthy list of pointers. This unchaining might occur because of almost simultaneous events which, when tested in the laboratory, did not show up. But when the random situation in the field turned up, the almost simultaneous event in effect violated what turned out to be a guard interval and caused problems.

3 One thing which happened a number of times and was a little embarrassing is that we falsely switched in a store which turned out to be faulty and which was perhaps being tested with a test pattern. You can imagine what happens when you interpret a chequer board pattern as the data concerning all the telephone calls in the system!

Hoare: I derived much encouragement from Ulrich's description of two of the most common kinds of programming bug, because it throws some credit on the people who organized a NATO Summer School in Grenoble a few years ago. I gave a paper on techniques for ensuring by some form of absolute, rather than run time, check that pointers are being used correctly. Edsger Dijkstra gave a paper on techniques for ensuring that unusual sequencings of events didn't cause unpleasant results. If there is a conflict at this conference between the theorists and the practical men, I hope this example will help to resolve it.

The problems of maintaining compatibility also came up.

Ulrich: Dijkstra's remark about puritans falling in love with the source of their misery also applies, I think, to telephone central office designers. One of the important sources of our misery is that we have to live and communicate with a very extensive existing telephone plant that is quite old and that was never designed to work with a modern system.
This is a classic example of having to be downward compatible for an indefinite period. For example, the teelephone instrument is really an improved version of an instrument designed for the Strowger system, which was the first automatic telephone central office, invented in 1889, and which is still highly competitive in the small office range.

Schorr: Ulrich's point about the necessity for the central office to be designed to be downward compatible with all the existing telephone company equipment is all too relevant to software engineering in general. We are getting into an era in software production where we will have to be very careful about how we design our interfaces so that we are downward compatible. Going from second generation to third generation it was simple to do some emulation. Maybe now the operating system interfaces and so on will be another piece of baggage we'll have to carry along as we go further and further.

5.1.4 The "Super-programmer project"

One further case history was given, this being of an experiment in which a single extremely expert programmer attempted to produce a system which was, though small by some peoples' standards, of considerable size. The report was given by Aron during discussion of the scheme proposed by Seegmüller (see section 2) for the design and implementation of a system.

Aron: I would like to describe an experiment we performed in which a single programmer, Dr. Harlan Mills, undertook to reproduce a project that had been started in a typical "army of ants" fashion and was still under way. He hoped to do in six man months what was regarded as being essentially a 30 man year project.

His approach was essentially similar to Seegmüller's scheme; his language was PL/1 and he used it from the top down. He started out using PL/1 as a pidgin English; he simply wrote out his abstract ideas in an English form which was closer to PL/1 than it was to conversational English and, as he proceeded into more detail, he generated the remaining parts of the PL/1 statement. The essentials to his procedure were (1) develop the programming system structure and (2) develop the data files and the intercommunication system within the program. He found that, having done that, it became fairly straightforward to fill in the algorithms within each program module. Now, we tried to study this project in order to determine whether it was a success or failure but we ran into difficulties; namely, that he didn't finish it in a single effort. There were interruptions, other projects along the way, so that it wasn't clear exactly what the results were. But it was clear that it didn't take six man months to do the job; it took more like six man years, which still wasn't bad since it was substantially better than the other group. On the other hand, during the period of the experiment, the other group's objectives changed substantially because the customer changed what he wanted.

The program was called the "definitive orbit determination system" and its purpose was to build a history of orbit programs and orbit observations for space agency and air force satellites. It was to be an interactive system whereby scientists could come up to a computer, request the assembly of information from old satellite activities and study it to determine such things as the geodetic shape of the earth, distances from the earth to the moon, etc. The system itself was, I would guess, around 50,000 instructions and the file was rather large. The structure of the information in the files was diverse because it was picked up from miscellaneous jobs, none of which had been performed with the intent of storing the results in this file.

Dr. Mills had the role of chief programmer and his function was to do everything regarding generation of the program down to the final code and testing of the code. In order to assist him, however, he trained his secretary to be his interface with the computer. Naturally, he found that he had to develop a small programming support system in order to enable her to communicate with the computer, the way a secretary would, rather than the way a programmer would. And he had a little help to get that programming system built. The second thing he found was that in order to write a program in PL/1 he had to spread out, like, 36 manuals on his desk. In order to get around this, first of all he requested us to assign him (part time) an expert PL/1 programmer, a programmer who was expert on the internal details of OS/360 and a few other consultants. Finally he acquired what we call a programmer-technician, a trainee programmer without a degree, whose job was primarily clerical support. He found that, in order to simplify the languages that he used (PL/1, JCL and linkage editor), he had to rewrite the manuals for JCL and linkage editor. This turned out to be fairly worthwhile because it was then easy to turn the description of these procedures mechanically into a set of control cards that his secretary could conveniently use.

The estimate of the man-power required increased from his original estimate. A second point that was far more significant was that, because the job he was doing was running parallel to an existing job, we chose not to give him a direct interface with the customer. We didn't want to confuse the customer about how many different IBM groups were supporting him, so we took one of the systems analysts from the contract project and made him the simulated interface with Dr. Mills. This turned out to be a mistake, in my opinion, because it shielded Dr. Mills from all of the actual problems of customer relations.

We have a second project of this type now, dealing with an information bank for a New York City newspaper and here we do have direct contact with the customer. Progress is substantially slower, and it is obvious that Seegmüller's first point is an extremely difficult one to reach since we are dealing, at least in the case of application systems, with users who don't really know what they want; moreover, they don't realize what they want until they're into the project itself.

Now let me turn to the question of why we don't use this technique in our many other projects. First of all a chief programmer such as Dr. Mills is a very unusual **individual.** We started out referring to him as a super-programmer; the term may not be accurate but it is descriptive because among the other 2,000 programmers there are not more than a few of equivalent capability. The capabilities required are extremely good programming knowledge, extremely good application knowledge and a desire to work very hard on this type of problem. It was necessary in the orbit determination system to understand sufficient mathematics to develop the orbit equations and so forth, as well as understand programming. In addition it was necessary to understand a subject that is dominant in many of our application systems, namely, the problems of interface with displays and with analog input such as radars and data acquisition devices. Now, in our remaining projects, because we cannot depend upon the existence of a super-programmer in any given project and, because we must transfer our people around in order to apply the right number of resources at the right time to a contract, we have found that it is important to build our systems without dependence upon any particularly strong individual. So we set up a management and control organization that makes the best out of the resources that are normally available. If we find that, within a project, we do have a great strength then we find that the individual concerned naturally introduces more advanced ideas. But we find that it is impractical to plan our project with the confidence that we'll find such an individual in the beginning. Our current goal is to fit the best implementation approach to each new project.

5.2 The sources of problems in large systems

One of the subjects that was discussed at length was the extent to which there are technical as opposed to managerial problems in the design of large systems. (Debate on managerial problems per se, has not in general been reported on; though working material which, in the editors' opinion, significantly supplements the material given in the Garmish Report has been included in section 7, i.e. the paper by Aron.)

Aron: We made a study of about a dozen projects, though not in a very formal manner. However, our results were convincing enough to us to set up a course on programming systems management.

The nature of the study was "Why do our projects succeed or fail?" We took as "successful" a project that met its requirements on schedule within the budgeted dollars and satisfied the customer. On this basis, out of 10 or 12 projects that we examined, we had one success and a whole lot of failures.

We analyzed the reasons for failure, as given to us by the project managers, and by people who had performed previous evaluations of the projects. They gave various reasons behind the failure of the projects, virtually all of which were essentially management failures. We ran into problems because we didn't know how to manage what we had, not because we lacked the techniques themselves.

Buxton: There are serious management problems of course—but are all the problems managerial in nature? I get the strong impression, from Aron for instance, that his view is that it is completely and totally a management problem and that his establishment is entirely satisfied with classical assembly language and FORTRAN programming techniques, which were well developed many years ago. Have you no need ever for, say, recursive programming techniques, for example?

McGowan: The problem is managerial in the sense that is is a managerial responsibility to learn new techniques and develop new tools to solve our problems. However, the Exec 8 system generation routine is essentially an example of a technical, rather than a managerial, solution. We have problems with multiprocessor interlocking and scheduling, and with storage allocation, for example.

Scalzi: One of the reasons that OS/360 is such a big management problem is that there are technical problems to be solved. We should not need to use anywhere near the same number of people again if we re-do OS/360. One of the major problems is testing the system; particularly since different components are produced in widely separated areas. Many of our problems arise from our inadequate means of specifying software.

Aron: I was not trying to claim that all problems are managerial in nature; rather that management decisions are required to take advantage of any technology that is available.

Perlis: Take, for example, OS/360 and its Job Control Language. I have yet to hear a good word about JCL. What kind of managerial structure is it that doesn't filter a new proposal against existing knowhow so that, for example, JCL would have the right properties of a language? It is failures like that which are technical faiiures on the part of managers, and which are largely responsible for major difficulties in the system. I think that, by and large, the managers wouldn't know a good technique if it hit them in the face.

Hoare: Basically all problems are technical. If you know what you want to do and you have the necessary technical background, there is no point in making a great management problem out of it. Obviously a certain amount of resource control and personnel work have to go on but that's all. On the other hand you might have a task which is difficult in that you don't know what you have to do, and that even if you did you wouldn't know how to do it. Since this is a very difficult task you can start out with the hypothesis that it will take a great number of people. Following down this slippery slope of reasoning, as soon as you have a very large number of people you have a very large management problem. But it all originated out of the fact that you didn't know what you were doing, or how to do it. Perhaps because we don't have large teams in Europe we tend either not to understand or perhaps to understand too well what the Parkinsonian slope is in this case; and we feel more inclined to cry that the Emperor has no clothes.

A subject that was discussed at much less length than its importance would seem to merit was the real meaning and significance of the concept "module".

Falkoff: On what basis, according to what discipline, have these people who built large systems decided what is a module?

Buxton: 4096 bytes!

Aron: For example: to take a very empirical look at the question Falkoff asked, a programming module can be defined in a very large system by looking at what a designer hands over to a programmer to implement. In general, we found that he hands over a programming module which ends up as about 400 to 1,000 machine language instructions when it is finally built. That was the smallest unit of the system. The size depended upon the degree of detail that was considered important by the designer, and it varied from one man to another. It also varied according to what he thought the capability of the implementing programmer would be.

Ulrich: For some of our programs this was a relatively straightforward process. A module was the response to a particular telephone event. For example, one of our modules is the response to the recognition that a customer has picked up his phone and wants to get a receiver into which he can dial. This was a reasonable algorithm for a portion of our program. However, it did not help us at all so far as setting up the large body of common programs.

5.3 Support software for large systems

During the conference a brief presentation was given by H. M. Brown of a system being used inside IBM to assist in the development of large-scale programming systems. The slides that he used during the presentation are reproduced as Figures 1 to 11.

Brown: CLEAR, standing for "Controlled Library Environment and Resources" is a programming development support system designed to help

IBM development programmers manufacture large systems. It aims to assist the administration and the accomplishment of the program development cycle. The second slide (Figure 2) gives more detail as to the adminstrative support provided.

The third slide (Figure 3) indicates some of the facilities provided for programmers. The preprocessor interface, for example, allows the programmer to use simple verbs, rather than complicated and lengthy JCL programs, for such jobs as modifying a piece of source code, followed by re-assembling it, and possibly testing it. The What Used/Where Used mechanism will scan a module and tell you the macros, LPSW instructions, supervisor calls, etc. that it uses. The so called "Delta Concept" allows you to avoid changing the actual source text but instead make your changes in a "Delta" data set, which is an increment to the source text. Therefore anything which was previously released is (hopefully) unchanged and will still be there with the next release of the system.

This so far has just been the CLEAR system, a batch processing system, which is several years old by now. The CASTER system (Computer Assisted System for Total Effort Reduction) is much newer, and is an extension of CLEAR: the two together being known as CLEAR-CASTER. This system provides on-line access to the information which the CLEAR system maintains, using both typewriter and simple graphic display terminals. It also provides a communications centre for passing messages between people.

The "Node Structure" referred to on slide 6 (Figure 6) is the means by which a filing system can be defined in a hierarchical structure, probably closely akin to the development group's organizational structure. Modules are attached at nodes. Conversational processing covers such things as syntax checking. You can also use conversational mode in connection with standards checking and flowcharting.

The whole of the data base for your programming system is contained in structural form in the filing system, as an interlinked set of nodes. The

SLIDE 1

Major Objectives—CLEAR System

I. Administration of Program Development Cycle

II. Assistance in Accomplishing Program Development Cycle

* **Specification**

* **Flowchart**

* **Development**

* **Document**

* **Integrate**

* **Release**

* **Maintain**

Figure 1

SLIDE 2

I. Administration

* Programming Parts Warehouse

* Flexible, Efficient.File Maintenance

* Common Inter-Center Environment

* Disaster Recovery Capability

* Maintenance of Statistics

* Authorization Scheme

* Minimum Hardware Requirements

* Time Accounting

* Management Report Network

Figure 2

SLIDE 3

II. Development

* Preprocessor Interface

* Central Library Facility

* Powerful—Efficient File Maintenance

* Positive Level Control

* What Used/Where Used Mechanism

* Delta Concept

* Unique Sequencing Scheme

* Powerful—Flexible Data Extraction

* Statistical Data Maintenance

* Authorization Scheme

* Support for any OS/360 Program

* Convenient Data Recovery Facility

* All Features of OS/360 Available

Figure 3

possible classes of node are given in slide 7 (Figure 7). For example: a node can contain a source code module, documentation to be used by technical writers, standards to be adhered to in writing code, specifications, etc. The second column indicates the types of data set available: source code, delta, object code, listing of an assembly or compilation, information data set, etc. (The information data set contains statistics concerning, for example, changes made to modules.)

The next slide (Figure 8) indicates the facilities provided for programmers by the system. When a programmer creates a module he copies into the beginning of it a set of module specifications which existed as a skeleton data set in his library. Keywords have to be answered according to prompting information. Eventually this will be joined by the source code and flowcharting information that he produces. Facilities for syntax analysis of individual program statements are provided. A keyword data set can be given at a major node of a library to hold a set of standards for the source code in that library. For example: labels might have to start with a certain sequence of letters, program jumps relative to the current values of the instruction counter should be of limited size, etc. A command could be used to check that the source code adhered to these standards. Conversational debugging, which should be available in six months, is designed to help in the early development of a module rather than during later stages of system development, since object code is executed interpretively. The phrase "Library for Integration" relates to facilities for integrating source code modules developed in various different programming centres around the world into a single system.

SLIDE 4

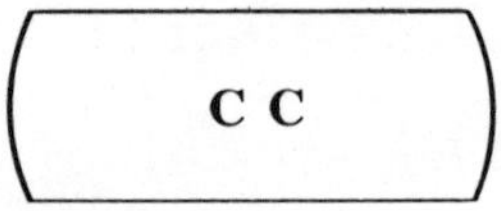

C C

**Computer Assisted
System for Total
Effort Reduction**

Figure 4

SLIDE 5

CASTER

An Extension to Clear

A Development Tool

An Integral File System

An On-Line Keyboard—Graphic Terminal System

A Communication Center

Figure 5

On slide 9 (Figure 9), a Defined (keyword) Dataset is in effect a questionnaire which is copied to a node and then filled in, e.g. module specifications. Answers could be machine checked. Designers can update module specifications and send messages alerting people to the changes. Similar facilities, concerning control information, are directly available to management personnel.

SLIDE 6

CASTER Functions

Node Structure

Terminal Data Entry and Manipulation

Conversational Processing

Remote Job Entry and Reply

Figure 6

SLIDE 7

File System

Node	Class	Type
	Module	SRC
	Macro	DEL
	Plan	OBJ
	Preface	LST
	Specification	IDS
	Message	KWD
	Documentation	TXT
	Control Info	Module Class—
	Form	Module Specs
	Standards	FL/1
		Source Code

Library . Comp. Module . Class . Type . Gen

Node Name

Figure 7

Finally slide 11 (Figure 11) indicates that technical writers can also have access to information concerning, for example, module specifications and flowchart statements associated with pieces of source code, and can use a text formatting processor (currently TEXT/360) to help format documentation, written at the terminal.

Oestreicher: It would appear that the CLEAR-CASTER system could be very valuable to users, and could reduce the machine time they use in developing large programs; is it available to them?

Brown: It is an internal tool, and to my knowledge there is no current intention to release it. A system like CLEAR-CASTER requires extra machine time, which has to be balanced against the benefits that might accrue in the long run to a complete development project. We haven't proved yet, one way or the other, whether it will significantly reduce the time taken to complete a project.

Scalzi: OS/360 is developed in a decentralized manner, using groups in 15 to 20 different placess all around the world. Our major problems have been not knowing all the interactions which exist between components, and not

SLIDE 8

Support for Development/Implementation

Programmers:

Correlation Among Module Specifications, Flowchart, and Source Code

Syntax Analysis

Standards and Convention Checking

Conversational Debugging

Library for Integration

Figure 8

SLIDE 9

Support for Designer/Planner/Architect

Defined Datasets Attached to Major Nodes For All Types of Information

Maintain Continuity of Design Information Throughout Development

Figure 9

having a structure which would enable us to define an interface formally
and then police its use. (For example, we have found that tables that we laid
out in 1966 are no longer adequate and we want to change them but are not
completely sure in all cases who uses them.) We are trying to get tools that
will help with these problems.

We use the CLEAR system. We have a central library in Poughkeepsie
where everything is collected. Everyone sends programs into the central
library for each release. When we come up with a mechanism for interface
control and monitoring we will do it in this one central location. One of our
practical problems with CLEAR is turnround time. We are therefore very
interested in CLEAR-CASTER, which is essentially "on-line CLEAR".

Aron: We find that our projects often develop a CLEAR-like library control
system which keeps track of what is going on. We have an experimental
timesharing system which is used for building system programs. The
concept here is a little bit different to the CLEAR-CASTER concept in that
our system is intended for use from the beginning of a project to the end,
and it is intended to be an interactive program development tool in addition
to being a library control tool. Its major weakness at the present time is
that you can't extract yourself from it in order to go into a batch operation.

SLIDE 10

    Support for Management

    Easy Access of All Control Information

    Reporting

    Automatic Message Transmission

Figure 10

SLIDE 11

    Writers

    Entry of Data

    Entry of Control for Formatting Processor

    Immediate Access of All Source Material

    Text 360 Processor

Figure 11

Kanner: (from "Software engineering tools")
"If the premise is accepted that computer manufacturers' establishments
have the most to gain from the introduction of software engineering tools, it
is pertinent to ask how this introduction might be accomplished. Some
enlightenment might be gained by observing the initial experiences of a
project manager trying to develop such tools, this work being done in a
small research department of a not so small computer manufacturer.

The project, which started out with the title System Programming Tools,
was a direct response to pressures from immediate management that might
be paraphrased: 'Make some tools for those guys out there,' and quickly
discovered that those guys out there really did not want any tools other
than possibly those of their own construction. In fact, the existence of about
five small, possibly bootleg, implementation language projects was
discovered within two software production divisions of the company. The
project manager came to the conclusion that:
1 He should positively not produce any type of small tool that was
   already in production elsewhere, and should probably not devote much
   effort anyway to individual tools.
2 He should direct his efforts to producing an integrated collection of
   tools operating as a single system in the sense of, though not
   necessarily as ambitious as, CLEAR.
3 In any event, he should devote considerable time to studying the
   problems of software production with the purpose of identifying the
   areas for which possible tools might provide the greatest assistance.

About this time, the name of the project was changed to Software
Engineering Tools, and the bandwagon had a passenger!

The obvious theme of these remarks is that there has as yet been
regrettably little experience with the employment of tools in software
production. There are gross uncertainties as to their cost, effectiveness and
reliability. In parallel with research on tools and techniques as such, a much
more mundane sort of research should be prosecuted: the systematic
experimental application of software engineering tools to real or contrived
software projects for the purpose of evaluation and improvement thereof."

6 SOFTWARE ENGINEERING EDUCATION

A session at the conference was devoted to discussion of this topic. In an opening speech Perlis proposed three questions:
1 Is there a real distinction between software engineering and computer science?
2 Given that the answer is yes, is there a need for education in software engineering as a separate discipline?
3 What form should university courses in software engineering take?

The discussion that followed ranged widely over these and other topics, including the question whether computer science is well enough established to be taught to undergraduates and whether it has any discernible basic principles.

The majority of the discussion is reproduced, subject to the customary amount of editing, in the following section. (A quotation from Strachey given in section 4.1.6 is also relevant to this subject).

Perlis: The first question to which we might address ourselves is: Is there a difference between software engineering and computer science? I suspect there is a big difference between them and so do some other people. Doug Ross, for example, has devoted a great deal of effort in his own bailliwick and has been driven out of the temple (by the money changers) still firmly believing there is something called software engineering. What he practices, be it software engineering or not, is certainly quite different from computer science.

If there is a subject called software engineering, I think we ought to ask ourselves if we need an output from our educational system different from that which we are now producing. I would argue that, in the United States at least, we are not producing software engineers; indeed our general organized Ph.D. programs are going to make it difficult for us to produce software engineers and the situation is likely to become worse as time goes on. So, if there is a distinction between computer science and software engineering and a need for people trained in the latter, then half the universities had better start doing something about it.

In computer science, at least in the United States, we do have a large number of quite good Ph.D. programs—good in the sense that they are rapidly accelerating towards ossification, which establishes in a reasonable way their legitimacy. I think that all of us who are in universities at least have a pretty good understanding of the nature of a computer science doctorate program: a healthy dose of logic, automata and computing theory, a diminishing dose of numerical analysis, one or two courses in advanced programming of one sort or another, some artificial intelligence, and some of this and some of that. Then one does thesis topics in any of the areas that are covered by Computing Reviews.

Evidently computer science is able to generate its own problems, understood and appreciated by only its own people. There doesn't seem to be any shortage of Ph.D. thesis topics in the Ph.D. area; there doesn't seem to be any shortage of positions for people educated in such programs in other Ph.D. programs in computer science, so everything is really quite healthy in the academic sense.

But is there something else: a different point of view, a different emphasis that we find in computer science programs both in industry and in the universities?

Bauer: We have had a committee in Germany working on a curriculum. We have called the subject "Informatik". The course will include both theoretical work and workshops in programming. We expect our students will have the choice of becoming either computer scientists or software engineers.

Feldman: I occasionally do a certain amount of work in industry and find out some surprising things in this way. For example: practical people do not read the literature, even though sometimes there are real solutions to their problems to be found there. The people who have been through an educational program in computer science seem more effective in this sort of respect.

We are trying to face up to this problem at Stanford by setting up a degree course in applied computer science, aimed at producing effective people for industry. Now suppose we give this a first degree, can people really choose between theory and practice as a career? I think not; I think it is very hard for people with a natural tendency in one direction to move in the other.

Perlis: I agree with Feldman that one does not become a theoretical person by studying mathematics or a practical one by ignoring it. That's not really an issue. The real issue is: what are the important problems and how much effort do we sink into them? The way Ph.D. programs are organized in computer science it is inconceivable for a professor and for his students to sink, for example, five to seven years on a long term project. In almost no department of computer science was it required that every student take a course in operations research and management science and yet I claim that to be a fundamental course in software engineering; as fundamental as automata theory and more fundamental than any mathematics course I can think of.

Galler: I don't think it's unheard of for a professor to work with his students for several years on a project. Some of our students have been around for seven years working on system projects; some of them get so involved they never finish.

I would like to describe a course which we've given twice now, and which I think is a software engineering course. We have taken either two or three professors as a team with 20-25 students and given them a project. The first was a mathematical graphics system, the second was a BASIC system. We've given them the complete job of designing, stating the specifications, dividing up into groups of two or three each, implementing, describing their work to each of the other groups, designing interfaces, documenting and making the thing work. In each case the product was something that was almost useable; in one semester you can't necessarily complete something of that scale. This kind of experience goes beyond writing a small class project type compiler and gives a kind of software engineering experience. I think it can be done, and I think maybe one should begin to recommend that for a curriculum.

Ross: This is the same as teaching electrical engineering by building a crystal set, then a one-tube receiver and then something else. That was indeed the way it started but not the way it is now. It isn't the proper way to set about teaching an engineering subject.

Falkoff: I think that software engineering is too restrictive a name for the curriculum; it must include some hardware work. Also, I always thought that engineering had to do with economics questions; it seems quite essential that a discipline which has to do with problems of complex use of resources should contain some operations research and related courses.

Needham: I have a cautionary tale which supports in many ways what Perlis said at the beginning. A few years ago our graduate students took part in a large project; they did things that fitted in with other people and they worked all hours and they wrote a lot of programs in an imaginative way, but with very strict discipline on the interfaces. Academically it was not a sucess. It didn't lead to prompt or very excellent theses, but on the other hand the people produced were perhaps the best contribution to the software industry we could have made.

Aron: The field of software engineering is mainly concerned with people writing programs for money. The expense on education is an overhead which is normally minimized to a standard level; programmers understand how to apply one high level language or maybe a macro-assembler to a real problem. The deeper concepts may never reach them.

McClure: Universities have a considerable problem with which I sympathize and yet I condemn them. I have watched this at close range. Let me see if I might illuminate the problem to see where some of the solutions might possibly lie. I think it's at the heart of whether there is a dichotomy between software engineering and computer science. I believe that the computer science departments are turning out a reasonably high grade of individual, you might call them computer scientists, most of whom go into stocking the faculties of other computer science departments. This has been true of a number of other disciplines as well—the medical schools have had the situation. In fact some medical schools specialize in turning out faculties for other medical schools. I think that part of the problem lies in the fact that there are really two classes of universities, at least in the United States. We might describe them as those that are in and those that are out. Having been associated with one that would have to consider itself out I can speak with some authority. It seems that the ones that are in are determined to maintain their in-status. Those that are out desperately want to get in, which they feel they can best do by emulating those that are in rather than charting for themselves an independent course of action which would suit their local purpose.

Most of the ones which are spread around the United States are community and industry supported, and industry urgently needs their output. The intent of these graduates is to go into and man the works of all these places as they do in electrical engineering and other disciplines. Now in fact, however, external support of universities hinges to a large extent upon their relative reputation. The industries don't make independent judgements for themselves as to the quality of the product but look at the universities' relative ranking among other academic institutions. These, of course, are judged by other academics.

Let me say why I think this leads into a difficulty. Graduates with bachelors degrees in engineering traditionally are equipped with a bag of tricks that they're willing to perform for their employer. Their employer knows that, if a man has a bachelors degree in engineering, he is capable of doing certain things. A masters degree means that he is capable of doing more tricks, and a doctorate in engineering means that he is capable of yet additional tricks. Now on the other hand, Ph.D's are supposed to be capable of extending the state of the art, as contrasted with doctors of engineering who are merely capable of performing high class tricks. At the present time most people feel that they cannot succeed academically without getting Ph.D's. In fact graduates themselves only want Ph.D's because doctors of engineering are looked down upon—when in fact industry most desperately requires doctors of engineering because it has shops that it must man. It wants people not capable of extending the frontiers in science in some abstract theoretical sense but people who are knowledgeable about what really goes on.

We have said that teaching OS/360 is in a sense bad, because OS/360 is a bad system. On the other hand, medical schools reliably teach pathology— disease structures. The only way one can learn to recognize mistakes is by studying things that are wrong. That means that you must study listings and study documents much as a medical student spends many hours poring through a microscope. This is very painful and unfortunately it's not glamorous but it's at the heart of what I call software engineering. Until universities get around to believing that in fact there is a requirement for people who really understand how things happen we'll not make any progress in an engineering discipline. We may make a great deal of progress in computer science, but we'll not make any progress in software engineering.

Teitelman: I agree with McClure's remarks on the relative status of the Ph.D. and doctor of engineering. Speaking from personal experience, when I had to choose what program to follow in school, one of the factors that influenced me was the knowledge that the Ph.D. meant something in terms of status and freedom that might perhaps outweigh the merits of an engineering program.

Ercoli: Those who have to be trained to use computers in accountancy don't need to study automata theory or some theoretical substitute for it. We need to train these people: it is far more urgent than training more scientists or engineers to use computers.

Oestreicher: I think that one thing which is happening in universities is that they are becoming more down to earth. I have often heard of compilers and even operating systems coming out of universities which, if they hadn't been done by so few people, might have been thought to be large software projects.

The only contribution we can make in industry is to expose young people to the problems they meet in industry, without discouraging them too much. They need to be allowed to make their own mistakes in order to learn; they need to be exposed to customers and so on. Quite often they respond by doing things you thought to be impossible!

Dijkstra: A Dutch definition of a university professor is someone who casts false pearls before real swine!

Otherwise my position differs greatly from that which Perlis describes. I am engaged in teaching, at graduate level, in producing one variety of "mathematical engineers". The most powerful test that I know of for an applicant to be one of my students is that they have an absolute mastery of their native tongue: you just need to listen to them.

I find it difficult to find worthwhile research subjects and think it wrong to teach material which I know will be obsolete in a few years. What finally remains isn't so much. You have to teach a grasp of method, a sense of quality and style. Sometimes you are successful. This cannot be all of computer science or software engineering. It may well be that it is a rather small subject but it may take very good people to work in it.

A neglected part of software engineering is the area of hardware design. If a software engineer cannot specify hardware design, who can?

Strachey: Computing science has been under some attack on the grounds that it isn't software engineering. I propose to attack it on different grounds. I think we should seriously ask ourselves the question: is computing science?

Recently I did a small survey as to whether computing is suitable as an undergraduate subject in an English university. I did this by grading all the topics I could think of under the headings of relevance and state of development. The premise is that it is clearly wrong to teach undergraduates the state of the art; one should teach them things which will still be valid in 20 years time: the fundamental concepts and underlying principles. Anything else is dishonest.

The gradings for relevance ran from "clearly relevant and essential" to "part of another subject" (like numerical analysis) and those for state of development from "well developed with theorems, laws and text books" to "a fruitful field for research". Note, incidentally, the importance of text books. They are designed to be taught from; they are quite different from treatises and even further from research papers. Now, it turned out that all those subjects which score highly for relevance score very low on state of development and vice versa.

Until we have a sufficient body of topics which are important, relevant and well developed we cannot call the subject a "science". I am quite convinced that in fact computing will become a very important science. But at the moment we are in a very primitive state of development; we don't know the basic principles yet and we must learn them first. If universities spend their time teaching the state of the art, they will not discover these principles and that, surely, is what academics should be doing.

I do not for a moment underestimate the importance of the state of the art in engineering. Clearly it is essential and furthermore from engineering practice we must get our experience and material from which we develop theory. But, before teaching students we must get our basic principles right.

Woodger: I wonder what a basic principle in computer science would look like if I saw one. Seriously, in what terms might it be expressed? It's no good using unexplained terms like "language" or "compiler"; we have very few clear terms in which to express any fundamental principle of computer science. Would any professor here tell me a single basic principle?

Perlis: Some principles: every interesting program has at least one variable, one branch and one loop. An interesting program is one whose number of execution steps is not linearly proportional to the length of the text.

Strachey: And at least one bug!

Perlis: No, I don't accept that that is a principle.

Woodger: Well, the concept of "variable" is far from trivial, at the least.

Falkoff: I'm not a university professor but I would like to say something about basic principles. Last summer we assembled a group of school mathematics teachers and set out collecting material to give them a basis for working with APL in teaching high school mathematics. We found there were only a few essential notions that the pupils needed in order to use a programmable machine. These were:

1 The notion of assignment, which I think covers the idea of a variable.
2 The notion of a conditional expression or branch.
3 The notion of function definition.

I propose that these three ideas are central to computing and will remain so.

Gotlieb: One basic principle with regard to programs is that execution time and store utilization are interchangeable. In a good program, you can improve one only at the expense of the other.

The problem of lack of text books was discussed by Lampson.

Lampson: In my experience of trying to teach this subject in university, one of the most annoying aspects is that there is nothing to teach it from. You sit down to teach a course, any course, and you have to start from scratch. You have to think for yourself about what to do, and the amount of time it takes to do a quarter-way decent job is more time than you can afford to spend on preparing one course. It seems to me that the situation could be improved. There are several areas in which very substantial contributions could be made by a small group of people, working for two or three months, trying to produce a document which would describe, in some sense, some essence of the state of the art. I suggest three areas in which this could profitably be done

1 What programming is all about.
2 The basic technology for writing compilers (not just for describing programming languages).
3 The basic principles for writing operating systems.

The right group of three or four people, working for two or three months, could produce a document of perhaps 150 to 200 pages that would really serve as a standard for the field, in that it would provide a base from which one could teach, and in many cases a base from which one could talk and think. This would eliminate a great deal of our terminological difficulties and a great deal of the re-thinking that one has to do when one embarks on a new project.

The attempt should be to tell what is known, not to break new ground and not to produce a complete or finished work in any sense; that would be disastrous. Neither do we need to produce anything like Knuth's books, for which I have the greatest admiration, but which can only be viewed as an encyclopaedia. I feel very confident that this could be done.

Schorr: I could provide facilities for such an enterprise.

7 WORKING PAPERS

7.1 List of working papers

Aron, J. D. Estimating resources for large programming systems

Aron, J. D. General remarks on Apollo programming support

Bauer, F. L. and Goos, G. Requirements for programming languages for basic software

Bayer, R. Towards computer-aided production of large application programs

Bemer, R. W. Straightening out programming languages

Bemer, R. W. A note on software specifications

Bemer, R. W. A note on implementation correctness

Bemer, R. W. A plea for consideration of computing as it will be, not was

Brown, W. S. Software portability

Burkinshaw, P. How to avoid some pitfalls in software project management

Buxton, J. N. A note on sharing software

Clingen, C. T. Program naming problems in a shared tree-structured hierarchy

David, E. E. Adoption of new tools and methods in creating large systems

Dijkstra, E. W. Structured programming

Donner, H. Systems for multiple or changing environments; properties required for software portability

Ebbinghaus, K. Organization and human factors

Falkoff, A. D. Criteria for a system design language

Feldman, J. A. Towards automatic programming

Galler, B. A. Construction of generators to produce programs for specific applications

Galler, B. A. and Perlis, A. J. Criteria for the design of a language

Gotlieb, C. C. and MacEwen, G. H. System evaluation tools

Hoare, C. A. R. An axiomatisation of the data definition features of PASCAL

Hoare, C. A. R. The problems of software development

Hofmann, F. Computer-aided software production for process control

Hopkins, M. E. Computer aided software design

Italiani, M. On progress control of a software project

Kanner, H. Software engineering tools

Kanner, H. Tools

Kjeldaas, P. M. Facilitating efficiency and generality by using run time information in compilation

Lampson, B. W. On reliable and extendable operating systems

Lang, C. A. Languages for writing system programs

Lemma, A. and Rossi, E. The production cost of the software for little programming systems

Lowry, E. S. Proposed language extensions to aid coding and analysis of large programs

MacGowan, Jr., J. M. UNIVAC 1108 instrumentation

Needham, R. M. Software engineering techniques and operating system design and production

Needham, R. M. and Aron, J. D. Software engineering and computer science

Oestreicher, M. D. Operating systems

Poole, P. C. and Waite, W. M. Machine independent software

Randell, B.   Interacting sequential processes
Reenskaug, T.   Some notes on portable application software
Reynolds, J. C.   A set-theoretic approach to the concept of type
Ross, D. T.   Reproduction of slides for bootstrapping of the AED system
Schorr, H.   Compiler writing techniques and problems
Schwartz, J. I.   Report on literature search on management
Schwartz, J. I.   Analysing large scale system development
Seegmüller, G.   Definition of systems
Sharp, I. P.   Systems design for a changing environment
Teitelman, W.   Toward a programming laboratory
Thompson, K. L.   Software quality control at Michigan State University
Tixier, V.   O/S writing systems
Ulrich, W.   Design of high reliability continuous operation systems
van der Poel, W. L.   A simple macro compiler for educational purposes in
    LISP
Warshall, S.   Software portability and representational form (abstract)
Wiehle, H. R.   Means of communication in operating system 1/TR440
Wirth, N.   The programming language PASCAL and its design criteria
Woodger, M. and Duncan, F. G.   An overdue comment on ALGOL 60

7.2 Estimating resources for large programming systems

by

J. D. Aron

Abstract
This paper presents a Quantitative Method of estimating manpower
resources for large programming jobs which represents a simple,
feasible guideline. The method combines program structural data with
historical data on the productivity of programming groups. This data is
then adjusted to cover non-programming resource requirements. This is
not a precise method and, in fact, it is not as good as an estimate based
on sound experience. But it is offered as an aid to estimators working
in unfamiliar areas and as a verification of estimates obtained by other
methods.

Introduction
It is very common for the cost and schedule of large programming systems
to exceed initial estimates. This is most often due to changes in the
functional specifications but, even where the specification is fixed, it is
difficult to estimate software resource requirements accurately. Not only
does the main resource — manpower — vary widely in productivity and quality
but the secondary resources, such as machine time and publications support,
are frequently unavailable at the appropriate times. Most important, every
large system is an aggregate of so many elements — program modules,
organizational interactions, logistics, etc. — that no manager can precisely
determine the amount of work to be done. On the other hand, managers of
some large jobs, such as the Mercury-Gemini-Apollo mission support
systems, have learned how to meet rigid schedules successfully. By
examining the methods used in successful areas, it is possible to draft
guidelines for use on new projects.

This approach has been taken by IBM's Federal Systems Division (FSD). It draws on FSD experience in many large jobs since 1959 as well as on other relevant background. The result is a set of guidelines that, while subject to error, are useful for arriving at a *quantitative estimate* of manpower resources. The method is taught in the FSD Programming Project Management Course, where it has been recommended as an aid to estimating projected work (during proposal or early design stages) and as a cross check on estimates of work in progress. Among the more than four hundred managers who have taken the course were many experienced managers who corroborated the quantitative guidelines and few who contradicted them.

Large systems defined
For the purpose of this paper, a large programming system is a "structured aggregate of elements that satisfies a set of functional and performance specifications" and that requires
- more than 25 programmers
- more than 30,000 deliverable instructions
- more than six months' development time
- more than one level of management.

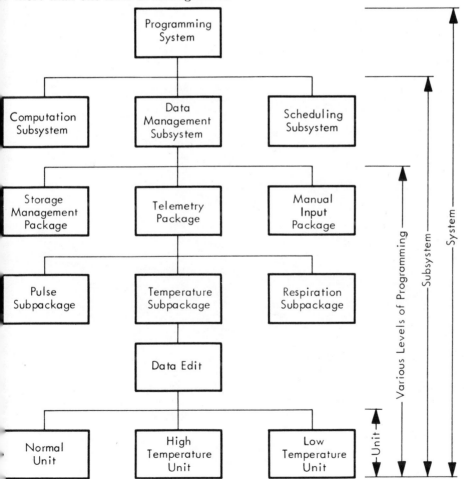

Figure 1. Organization of system components

These arbitrary parameters describe a system which has enough elements interacting within it to create a management problem. Such systems are large enough to absorb the imprecision of a quantitative estimating system. For example, if there are 25 programmers it is possible to ignore their individual differences and use an average productivity parameter in a quantitative formula. The very size that creates large system problems is turned to advantage.

A system contains subsystems which are further divided into smaller hierarchical structures until the smallest programming element is reached (Figure 1). The smallest element is referred to as a "unit" in later sections.

System design consists of defining the component and their interactions; the definition is a "specification." Detailed design consists of defining the subsequent lower levels of the structures until each unit is described in terms of its function and performance. Detailed design of a single unit is done by the implementing programmer; therefore, the unit can be viewed as the smallest element of interest to the system architect. This last point is significant because, although different designers work to different levels of detail, *each designer is rather consistent in deciding when to stop designing and hand the work over to the programmer.*

System development life cycle
The system is built according to a life cycle, as shown in Figure 2.* The life

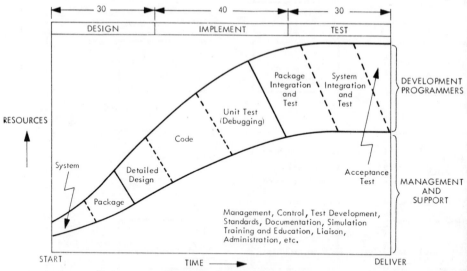

Figure 2. System life cycle

cycle shows the activities that must take place in system development and the level of manpower required to do the job. The chart is truncated at both ends, omitting concept formulation at the beginning and maintenance and improvement at the end. The slope of the boundaries in the upper half of the chart represents the fact that activities overlap; some programming may

---

*This chart and much of the background material is adapted from Mr. A. M. Pietrasanta's work at IBM on programming system development. The System Development Corporation's (SDC) Programming Management Project, under Mr. V. LaBolle and others, and the FSD Programming Project Management Course and Guide, prepared by Mr. P. W. Metzger, were also referenced.

start before all packages have been designed or some test and integration may begin before the last unit is debugged.

Certain gross features of the life cycle are important when using a quantitative estimating guideline because the result of the estimate applies only to certain parts of the chart. The total estimate is an extrapolation based on the following simple ratios:

1 The ideal project is planned so that about 30 per cent of the elapsed time is used for design, 40 per cent for implementation and 30 per cent for test. (Maintenance, which is omitted from consideration here, continues throughout the life of the program.)
2 The management and support resources are 40 to 50 per cent of the total resources.
3 System design resources are negligible compared to total resources. (This point is made simply because the quantitative method does not consider system design resource requirements explicitly since they can be ignored for practical purposes.)
4 The duration of the project is determined by the manager to meet a delivery commitment or to allow orderly recruiting. (The formulae produce estimates of man-months. It is up to the manager to spread them according to a schedule.)
5 The life cycle chart includes all the manpower resources needed to do a specific job. It includes management and clerical support assigned full-time to the job but does not include headquarters management or other manpower that may have an occasional responsibility in the project. Neither does it include overhead activities, such as machine operations, publications, etc., which are used as a service.

Methods of estimating
Before describing a quantitative guideline, it is necessary to re-emphasize that a "guideline" is just that. It cannot be more than an aid to decision-making. As Mr. Pietrasanta said in his paper "Resource Analysis of Computer Program System Development,"

"The problem of resource estimating of computer program system development is fundamentally qualitative rather than quantitative. We don't understand what has to be estimated well enough to make accurate estimates. Quantitative analyses of resources will augment our qualitative understanding of program system development, but such analyses will never substitute for this understanding."

This is why, when methods of estimating are ranked, the list is headed by the *Experience Method*. Experience on a large programming system can be carried forward to similar systems. An ability to anticipate resource requirements and a cautionary attitude toward contingencies are part of one's experience. As long as a manager does not try to apply his experience to a larger or substantially different job, he can do no better than to base his estimates on experience. The remaining methods are substantially less reliable, including the Quantitative Method described later. In order of desirability, the methods are: Experience, Quantitative, Constraint, Units of Work.

Experience method
This approach takes advantage of experience on a similar job. In order to use the method, the new job must be clearly specified, at least down to the package level. This permits the estimator to compare the new system to one or more completed systems. At this point, the estimator can assume that like tasks take like resources. He can obtain the base data from his own

experience or from that of other people as long as he knows he is
comparing genuinely similar projects. If the two projects are alike in size
and content, minor differences in algorithms or utility routines can be
allowed for by adding a contingency factor to the total estimate: the
contingency factor should be less than 25 per cent. As in any method, it is
wise to lay out the design in detail to permit the men who must implement
the job to make their own estimates on their portion of the job. Their
estimates will also be based on experience and should be more precise than
the total estimate. In other words, two similar orbital mission systems of
150,000 instructions each may be within 25 per cent of one another in effort.
Two telemetry data processing programs of 1000 instructions each may
appear in these systems. A specialist in telemetry data processing should be
able to estimate his tasks to within 10 per cent.

The major problem in the method is that it does not work on systems
larger than the base used for comparison. System complexity grows as the
square of the number of system elements; therefore, experience with a small
system cannot account for all the things that will have to be done in a large
system. Neither will the Experience Method apply to systems of totally
different content. The Quantitative Method is applicable in such cases.

Quantitative method
The Quantitative Method to be described in this paper is based on
programmer productivity in terms of the number of deliverable instructions
produced per unit of time by an average programmer. The deliverable
instructions include the source statements and data descriptions written by
the programmer in a macro-assembly language. The method is not precise;
it is necessary to adjust the answer by large amounts (see Factors affecting
the estimate). The estimator should never allow himself to treat the answers
as anything other than approximate representations of system size or
manpower requirements.

Constraint Method
This method is equivalent to taking an educated guess. Based on schedule,
dollar, or manpower constraints, the manager simply agrees to do the job
within the constraints. His decision is unrelated to the design complexity of
the system. The merit of this approach is that it is often possible and, in
some cases, beneficial for the user and the developer to reach mutual
agreement on the constraints. Once agreed, they can proceed to define a set
of specifications which can be achieved within the estimate. In cases in
which either party does not understand the consequences of constraint
estimating on product specifications there is great risk of overrun.

Referring again to Mr. Pietrasanta, he points out that a given set of
specifications will require a certain number of man-months to produce.
These man-months can be spread over a short or a long period of time. If
the man-months are not available, though, the specifications will have to be
reduced in scope or the job will not get done. The Experience Method and
the Quantitative Method assume that specifications are fixed and that the
man-months are estimated to satisfy the specification. The Constraint
Method, if properly used, holds the man-months fixed and varies the
specification to fit.

Units of work method
The history of small programming efforts, particularly in administrative and
business data processing, shows far better estimating performance than
large systems. This seems to be due to the use of a special case of the

Constraint Method, which is called "Units of Work" for lack of a more descriptive name. In this method each programming task is defined in such a way that it takes one programmer 4 to 8 weeks. Each task is designed, implemented and tested independently of all other tasks. This approach eliminates the interactions that cause trouble in large systems but *programs written this way cannot be linked to form a large system*. The purpose of mentioning the Units of Work Method here is to highlight its limitations and to suggest a better method to estimators with large systems to build.

Factors affecting the estimate
An estimate prepared by any method is based partly on fact and partly on assumption. It also contains errors due to imprecise inputs. Managers are advised to make sure that every estimate they prepare or review contains enough information. As a minimum they must know how the estimate was prepared and what the input data was. In addition they need the assumptions and the contingencies used by the estimator. With this data the managers can evaluate the estimate and make knowledgeable judgments. If they decide to reduce the estimate, they know how far they can go in trading cost for risk. They also know where they can reduce risk by changing an assumption, for instance: substituting a more experienced programmer for a weak one. The result of their evaluation will be a commitment to perform the job for a given price. (Whereas an estimate may contain a contingency factor, a commitment does not.) Since managers depend for their success on the successful performance of their people, good managers invariably use the assumptions and contingency data to improve the project. The employee must have enough confidence in his manager to believe this, or else he will hide a little "fat" in the estimate and not admit it.

The variables in estimating are so large they cannot be ignored. The SDC Programming Management Project spent several years analyzing a large amount of historical data to identify the factors that affect programming cost the most. Starting with 104 variables in the programming process, they obtained statistical data showing 11 to be significant enough to use in estimating indices. Although the Quantitative Method does not use the indices, it does recognize that the variables can affect the estimate and it permits major adjustment of results. The key variables fall into three groups:
1 Uniqueness
2 Development environment
3 Job type and difficulty.

Uniqueness is concerned with the familiarity of the development team with the hardware, software and subject matter of the project. If they are unfamiliar with any of these because they lack experience or because the item is new in the field, the cost of the project will increase by an unknown amount. Development environment involves customer/programmer capability, working relationships and organization. Development environment also involves geographic dispersion and working facility quality. Weak people, poor communications channels due to organization or dispersion, unpleasant facilities, etc., increase cost by reducing productivity. These two groups of variables must be evaluated by the manager and reduced to a single factor, which he uses to modify the estimate. The adjustment in the Quantitative Method can range from about −25 per cent if all the factors are favourable to +100 per cent if all are unfavourable. The adjustment is chosen subjectively, based on a judgment of how much the factors differ from the norm for the estimator's organization.

Job type and difficulty deal with the number of system interactions due to program and data base elements and the relative difficulty of various types of programs. These variables are accounted for in the quantitative formula.

Quantitative estimating procedure
The quantitative estimating procedure starts with a design. The degree of detail in the design depends on how much time is available. At proposal time the system design may be completed only through the package level. After the job has entered the design phase, re-estimates can be based on lower levels of detail. At any stage, some structural detail is required for the size of the system to be determined. At least one package in the system should be laid out to the unit level. The package selected for this purpose should be the one considered the most difficult by the estimator. The detailed design of this computation accomplishes two things: it ensures that there are no mathematical or logical problems in the package that cannot be handled and it gives a measure of system size. It is important that, since a large system involves many man-years of effort, it is worth the trouble of a good design at the start.

After the first step of system design, the process proceeds to:
- Estimate number of deliverable instructions
- Estimate difficulty of programs and duration of project
- Determine man-months for programming
- Adjust for higher-level language
- Extrapolate man-months for the project
- Adjust result
- Schedule effort.

This procedure is repeated at a frequency of the order of once a month to obtain increasingly better estimates as the project develops.

Estimating number of instructions
The key to estimating system size is found in the design. Since the system is an aggregate of elements, its size can be determined by counting the number of elements and multiplying the result by the average element size.

Deliverable instructions=number of units×average unit size

The number of units is estimated from the design by carrying at least one package design down to the unit level. This shows how many units are required for that particular package. The number of units in other packages or programs can be estimated by:
- Experience with similar packages
- Sketching the design for the package
- Using the same number obtained for the base package.

The number of units in the system is simply the sum of the units in the packages.

The average unit size depends on the operating habits of the designers. Typically, units written in assembly language contain 400 to 1000 instructions. The average length is becoming smaller as modular programming is emphasized. Units written in high level language are about one-fourth the size but generate deliverable programs of comparable size. Although this is a wide range, any individual manager, designer, or architect tends to normalize his design so that the resulting units fall within a narrow range. By examining his habits he can determine the average unit size that he assigns to his people. The average is perfectly adequate for the purposes of the quantitative estimate.

Estimate difficulty

Some programs take more time to program than others. Three levels of difficulty: easy, medium and difficult, are used to improve the estimate. The three levels result from many factors in the job, but they are conveniently characterized by the number of interactions found in various program classes.

1 Easy—very few interactions with other system elements. The class includes most problem programs or "application" programs. Any program the main function of which is to solve a mathematical or logical problem is probably in this class. Easy programs generally interact only with I/O programs, data management programs and monitor programs.

2 Medium—some interactions with other system elements. In this category are most utilities, language compilers, schedulers, I/O packages and data management packages. These programs interact with hardware functions, with problem programs, with monitors and with others in this class. They are further complicated by being generalized enough to handle multiple situations: e.g., I/O from many different I/O devices or management of data files with variable numbers of indices.

3 Difficult—many interactions with other system elements. All monitors and operating systems fall in this class because they interact with everything. Special-purpose programs such as a conversational message processor may be in this class if they modify the master operating system.

As a project proceeds, the implementers learn their job better. The "learning curve" is the rate of improvement. The productivity data in Figure 3 shows that the rate of improvement for easy and medium programs is good, but difficult programs are still hard to produce after many months of experience.*

In the Quantitative Method the degree of difficulty determines the productivity values to be used. Figure 3 shows the levels of difficulty (rows), numbered 1, 2, and 3. One way to estimate difficulty is to pick a value from 1 to 3 representative of the overall character of the system. If the result is a decimal fraction, interpolate between rows of the table. The second way to estimate difficulty is to break the instruction count into three parts, estimating the number of easy units, medium units, and difficult units separately. Then calculate the man-months for each batch and total the results.

Determine man-months

Using Figure 3, it is a simple matter to select a productivity rate and divide

---

*The data in this table summarizes historical data from IBM projects involving system programs—1410, 7040, 7030, System/360 OS/PCP—and application systems— Mercury, SABRE, banking and brokerage, FAA. It has not been formally validated, but it has been informally checked against other IBM and some non-IBM estimates. It is interesting to note that the contents of the table seem as good in 1969 as they were in 1960. It is not clear why this is so. There are several speculations to explain the apparent lack of any increase in productivity in the industry:

  The capacity of the computer to give improved debugging service limits the programmers' output.

  Untrained programmers enter the field at such a rate that the average ability to use programming knowhow is equivalent to about one year's experience.

  Programmers fail to learn better methods.

And, the thought that I favour:

  Programs are getting more difficult at the same rate that programmer skills improve. This implies that as computers become more powerful we use them to tackle harder problems.

it into the system size to obtain the resource requirement for writing programs.

$$\text{Man-months} = \frac{\text{Deliverable instructions}}{\text{Instructions per man-month}}$$

The *selection of a row* in the table was described as a function of job difficulty and job type. The *selection of a column* depends on the proposed length of the project. There are two reasons for multiple columns:
1 The numbers are more convenient to use because they are more appropriately scaled to system size.
2 The columns are adjusted to include learning.

Example
At this point, a number has been generated representing a portion of the system resource requirement. Suppose the system of interest has seven major packages. One of these is concerned with data management, which contains three main programming activities. One of these is telemetry, which is unique to the development group so it is selected for detailed design. In developing the detailed design a set of subpackages is laid out, each of which is broken into its basic units. There are a total of 50 units. Lacking other data, the number of units in the system could be taken as $7 \times 3 \times 50 = 1050$. More likely the other packages are better known and specific unit counts can be generated for each. The total unit count this way is, say, 800. Suppose now that a poll is taken of the key men who will design and assign units to programmers. Each man reviews his previous results and explains how large his unit assignments turn out to be on the average.

The average for all responses is 500 assembly instructions and associated data descriptions. Further, assume that one package (150 units) is judged to

Difficulty / Duration	6-12 Months	12-24 Months	More Than 24 Months	
Row 1 Easy	20	500	10,000	Very Few Interaction
Row 2 Medium	10	250	5,000	Some Interaction
Row 3 Difficult	5	125	1,500	Many Interaction
Units	Instructions per Man-Day	Instructions per Man-Month	Instructions per Man-Year	

Figure 3. Productivity table

be difficult, two (200 units) to be medium, and four (450 units) easy. One year is planned for system development. The procedure will produce an estimate as follows:

Deliverable instructions	$=800\times500=400,000$
Difficult	$=150\times500=75,000$
Medium	$=200\times500=100,000$
Easy	$=450\times500=225,000$

Using column 2, an answer in man-months will be obtained.

$$\text{Man-months} = \frac{225,000}{500} + \frac{100,000}{250} + \frac{75,000}{125}$$
$$=1450 \text{ man months}=120 \text{ man-years.}$$

Adjust for higher-level language

Up to this point, only assembly language source statements have been considered. Productivity using higher-level languages such as FORTRAN, COBOL and PL/1 is highly variable. An experimental factor of 2:1 improvement over assembly language is suggested. Thus if the estimator counted deliverable instructions generated from source statements he could divide the man-months obtained from the table by 2 to adjust for the advantages of the higher-level language. If he entered the table with the number of high-level source statements and data descriptions, he could multiply the resulting man-months by 2. This allows for 4 deliverable instructions to be generated, on the average, by each high-level statement.

Extrapolation

Figure 4 illustrates the activities in the life cycle that are estimated from the table of Figure 3. System design, system test and management and support are not included. They must be brought in by extrapolation, as follows:

1 System design can be ignored—it is less than one per cent of an effort the size of the above example.

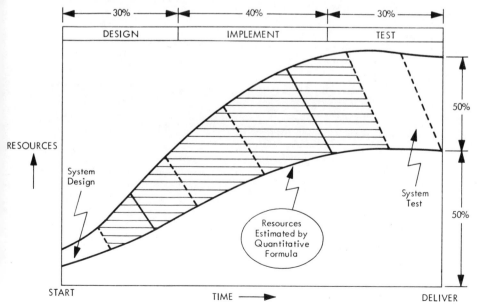

Figure 4. Scope of quantitative estimate

2 System test represents about half the test time or 15 per cent of the schedule. But since the number of people on hand at that time is very high system test actually uses closer to 20 per cent of the resources, not counting management and support.
3 Management and support utilize approximately half of the system resources.
4 The extrapolation is done by the following formula:

$$\text{System man-months} = 2 \left(\frac{\text{man-months}}{0.8} \right)$$
$$= 2.5 \times \text{man-months}$$

In the example of a 400,000 instruction system the total resource estimate would be 3625 man-months or over 300 man years.*

Adjust results
The productivity table assumes the use of average programmers organized in a normal pyramidal hierarchy. That means that there is a range in experience from many junior people to fewer senior people. The formulas also assume average uniqueness and development environment. *No adjustment of the result is necessary unless the project deviates in an obvious way from the norm.* Such an obvious deviation would be the assignment of all junior people with no experienced technical people to lead them. Another would be the requirement to use the first machine of a new line—one that has never been used before in an operational environment. The amount of adjustment appropriate is entirely subjective, since it represents the manager's confidence that he can overcome the effects of deviation.

Scheduling
The development of an actual performance schedule and budget will not be discussed in this paper except to point out that the estimate projects only resource needs. Plans, schedules, budgets, reviews, etc., are needed to get the job going in a controlled way. The form of the schedule and budget varies from organization to organization, so no format guidelines are uniformly acceptable. A couple of general points are useful:
1 Schedule documents should include activity networks (PERT charts) and bar charts.
  (a) Activity networks are essential in design because they are the best tool for showing system interactions.
  (b) Bar charts are good at all times because they show who is assigned to each task and when significant events (checkpoints and milestones) occur.
  As shown in Figure 5, management attention is directed to interactions during design and test. It shifts to the components themselves during implementation. The activity network is most valuable, then, during design and test but it is a burden during implementation. If it is not properly maintained it should be dropped in implementation for economy and the bar chart should be retained.
2 The schedule of manpower follows the life cycle. Other activities that must be scheduled include machine time and other job shop services such

---

* The method can be used for much smaller systems, although it is not advisable for jobs under 10 men or under six months' duration. These cases are not big enough to cancel out the inherent errors of the quantitative method.

as publications. These activities tend to fall in the last one-half to one-third of the life cycle.

(a) Machine time can be estimated in gross terms by knowing how many machine-hours each man in the organization uses each month. (A survey report by Mr. Ralph Arthur and this author showed that in FSD 7 to 8 hours debugging time per man per month was predictable from the history of several dozen projects.)

   The gross estimate can be spread by allowing 2 to 3 hours during implementation building to about 20 hours in test, but averaging 8 hours per man per month over the last 50 to 70 per cent of the project.

(b) Other service activities are best estimated by the specialists in those areas. This means that their inputs must be requested during the estimate process.

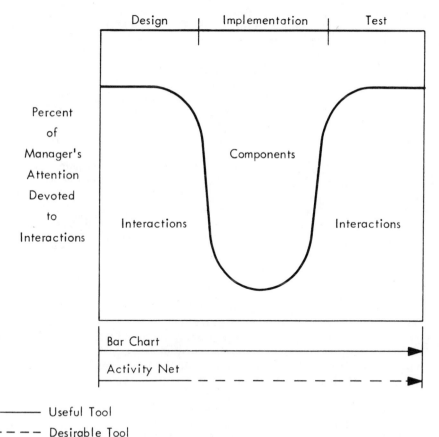

Figure 5. Manager's attention curve

Conclusion

The Quantitative Method of estimating manpower resources for large programming jobs is presented as a simple, feasible guideline. It is not being presented as a precise method and, in fact, it is not as good as an estimate based on sound experience. But it is offered as an aid to estimators working in unfamiliar areas and as a verification of estimates obtained by other methods.

7.3 Software portability

by

W. S. Brown

Abstract
A program or programming system is called *portable* if the effort
required to move it into a new environment is much less than the
effort that would be required to reprogram it for the new environment.
This paper consists of a general discussion of software portability,
followed by a description of the portability plan for ALTRAN-F, a
special purpose programming language now being implemented.

1 Introduction

A program or programming system is called *portable* if the effort required
to move it into a new environment is much less than the effort that would
be required to reprogram it for the new environment.

Most software is not portable. The resulting situation is becoming an
increasingly serious obstacle to progress in computer science. Many
programmers spend much of their time doing work that has been done
better elsewhere before. More often than not, programs described in journals
are unavailable to the readers. Every project must be implemented from the
ground up and, when a computer is replaced, many running programs are
effectively lost.

Problem oriented languages were originally expected to provide a cure for
this situation but they have succeeded only to a very limited extent. In
Section 2 of this paper we examine the reasons for this. In Section 3 we
classify software according to difficulty of achieving portability, and in
Section 4 we describe the portability plan for ALTRAN-F (see *Reference* 1),
a special purpose programming language now being implemented.

2 Problem oriented languages

A problem oriented language is a language which allows the programmer
to describe a procedure in terms of the problem rather than the machine. It
was originally hoped that programs written in a problem oriented language
could be moved from one machine to another, simply by recompiling them,
but experience has made us aware of several serious pitfalls:

1 Problem oriented languages come in many dialects. In fact each compiler
  defines a somewhat different source language from every other. A
  program that runs well on one machine is very likely to collapse on
  another. Furthermore, because of inadequate documentation, it is often
  difficult to learn what the differences are.

2 There may be no existing language which is well suited to the task at
  hand. For example, one may need to handle numbers, character strings,
  lists, structures and input/output. Most languages tend to specialize in one
  or two of these. FORTRAN and ALGOL are excellent for numerical
  computing, while SNOBOL is especially designed for the manipulation of
  character strings. LISP specializes in lists and COBOL is excellent for
  structures and for input/output. PL/1 and ALGOL 68 do all of these things
  but both are ponderous; furthermore PL/1 is supported only by IBM and
  ALGOL 68 has not yet been implemented at all. Dialects often incorporate
  extensions to overcome some of the deficiencies, but a program using the
  extra facilities cannot easily be moved.

3 Only a few languages are widely available.
4 The use of a problem oriented language may entail an unacceptable loss of efficiency. If a compiler is to produce efficient object programs then the language must permit the programmer to express his intentions clearly. If he is forced into circumlocutions, the compiler may compile efficient code for what he said, but it can hardly be expected to compile efficient code for what he meant. A compiler can go to tremendous extremes of program analysis and searching for special cases in order to optimize its object code, but if so the compiler itself will be bulky and slow.
5 A problem oriented language cannot readily provide portability if any significant part of the problem at hand is machine dependent.

3 Classes of software

We define four classes of software in increasing order of the difficulty of achieving portability.

Small procedures

A small procedure performs a conceptually simple computation on (or transformation of) arguments provided by its invoker. Input/output can usually be avoided, and there is a good chance of an adequate language being available.

Large subsystems

A large subsystem provides for the solution of a multitude of problems, each of which can be described without reference to the computer. Facilities for input/output must be provided and there may be no available language which permits natural expression of all parts of the subsystem.

Compilers

A compiler presents all of the difficulties of a large subsystem and also includes a module, the code generator, which is inherently machine dependent. In spite of the obvious difficulties there is hope and even some evidence that portable compilers can be produced. If so, both the necessity and the harmful consequences of having many dialects of each language may be eliminated.

Operating systems

An operating system must not only deal directly with the machine, as a compiler does, but it must also satisfy service requests which are explicitly stated in terms of the machine. The hope for portability rests on the observation that most service requests are not so stated and that large parts of typical operating systems involve ordinary processing of numbers, strings, lists, arrays and structures.

4 Portability plan for ALTRAN-F

ALTRAN is a FORTRAN-like language incorporating certain symbolic algebraic data types and operations on data of these types. A new version called ALTRAN-F is now under construction, and is intended to be portable.

The overall structure of the system is illustrated in Figure 1. The translator translates ALTRAN source into FORTRAN source, which can then be compiled by a FORTRAN compiler.* The resulting object deck consists

---

*Because of this reliance on FORTRAN, the translator is not a compiler in the sense of class 3 above; hence the entire ALTRAN system fits into class 2.

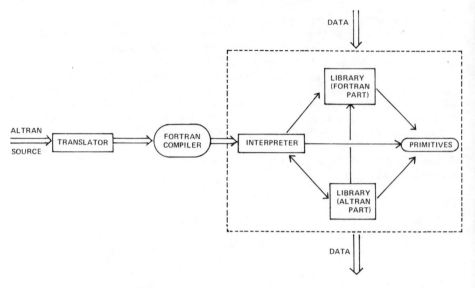

Figure 1. Overall structure of the system

primarily of an encoding of the source program into a highly compact intermediate form. Identifiers are replaced by code numbers and their names and attributes are stored in a symbol table. The intermediate text and the symbol table are represented as integer arrays, and are decoded by the interpreter. Algebraic operations are performed by library routines— some written in FORTRAN and others in ALTRAN. A few machine language primitives, written separately for each installation, are also required.

The implementation language is a carefully defined subset of FORTRAN IV. A program unit is composed of (up to) seven parts in a prescribed order. Some statement types have been excluded, while others have been restricted. This language is supported by the standard FORTRAN compilers on the IBM 360, GE 625/635, CDC 6400/6600 and UNIVAC 1108 computers. To escape from its limitations, both macros and primitive subroutines are used. Macros permit extensions of the implementation language, while primitives allow for the efficient coding of critical operations.

A macro processor called M⁶ (see *Reference* 2) is included as a part of the ALTRAN system. This processor is written in the FORTRAN IV subset discussed above. The ALTRAN translator and interpreter and the FORTRAN part of the ALTRAN library are written in a machine independent macro extension of this subset. When these modules are processed by M⁶, the output is pure FORTRAN (in the subset), but is no longer machine independent. Certain macro definitions must, of course, be supplied separately for each installation.

The primary use of macros is to permit the introduction of machine and implementation parameters into the language. For example the number of characters per machine word is represented as a macro, to be used in FORMAT statements, DATA statements and the manipulation of character strings. The relative sizes of different data types are important for the proper use of EQUIVALENCE and COMMON. Implementation parameters such as the size of the work space, the length of an identifier and the unit numbers for various data streams are also represented as macros. Similarly macros permit the use of nonstandard types such as INTEGER*2 on the 360. Finally, macros permit the easy insertion and deletion of optional debugging

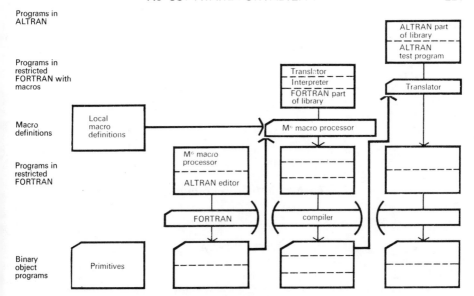

Figure 2. Installation steps

statements, and the macro calls that separate decks on the system tape can be used to generate control cards.

Primitives are used for the most elementary operations on strings, integers, reals and packed exponent sets. They are also used for the association of procedure names with entry addresses.

The complete system consists of a system tape and some associated documentation. Manuals will be provided to describe the definition, implementation and use of the language. Another manual will discuss the procedures for installing, improving and maintaining the system.

The system tape consists of six logical files. The first contains the ALTRAN character set and the second contains an editor to be used for incorporating system updates. The third file contains the macro processor, M^6, in source language and the fourth contains some basic macro definitions. Finally, the last two files contain the FORTRAN and ALTRAN parts of the system, respectively.

To install the system (see Figure 2), a recipient must first write some basic macros and some primitives, and transliterate the system tape into his local character set. Next he compiles the macro processor using his local FORTRAN compiler. Then he compiles the translator, the interpreter, and the FORTRAN part of the library, using the macro processor followed by the FORTRAN compiler. Then he compiles the ALTRAN part of the library, using the ALTRAN translator and the FORTRAN compiler. Finally he compiles and runs an ALTRAN test program to be sure that everything is in working order.

Once the system is operational, it can be improved by replacing critical procedures with more efficient machine language versions. These replacements can be made at leisure and in an order determined by local experience. However, the documentation indicates procedures that are known to be critical.

Improvements will be distributed occasionally in the form of an update letter. The changes can be keypunched from the update letter and incorporated with the aid of the editor. The editing technique has been designed in such a way that unrelated local modifications need not interfere with this process.

References

1. **Brown, W. S.** *The ALTRAN language for symbolic algebra,* unpublished, January 1969, pp. 84.
2. **Hall, A. D.** *The M^6 macro processor,* (unpublished), March 1969, pp. 16, 1 appendix. M^6 was designed by M. D. McIlroy, using ideas from many sources. The FORTRAN implementation is a translation by A. D. Hall of an original written in MAD by R. Morris.

7.4 Structured programming

by

E. W. Dijkstra

Introduction
This working document reports on experience and insights gained in programming experiments performed by the author in the last year. The leading question was if it was conceivable to increase our programming ability by an order of magnitude and what techniques (mental, organizational or mechanical) could be applied in the process of program composition to produce this increase. The programming experiments were undertaken to shed light upon these questions.

Program size
My real concern is with intrinsically large programs. By "intrinsically large" I mean programs that are large due to the complexity of their task, in contrast to programs that have exploded (by inadequacy of the equipment, unhappy decisions, poor understanding of the problem, etc.). The fact that, for practical reasons, my experiments had thus far to be carried out with rather small programs did present a serious difficulty; I have tried to overcome this by treating problems of size explicitly and by trying to find their consequences as much as possible by analysis, inspection and reflection rather than by (as yet too expensive) experiments.

In doing so I found a number of subgoals that, apparently, we have to learn to achieve (if we don't already know how to do that).

If a large program is a composition of N "program components", the confidence level of the individual components must be exceptionally high if N is very large. If the individual components can be made with the probability "p" of being correct, the probability that the whole program functions properly will not exceed

$$P = P^N$$

for large N, p must be practically equal to one if P is to differ significantly from zero. Combining subsets into larger components from which then the whole program is composed, presents no remedy:

$$p^{N/2} * p^{N/2} \text{ still equals } p^N \quad !$$

As a consequence, the problem of program correctness (confidence level) was one of my primary concerns.

The effort—be it intellectual or experimental—needed to demonstrate the correctness of a program in a sufficiently convincing manner may (measured in some loose sense) not grow more rapidly than in proportion to the program length (measured in an equally loose sense). If, for instance, the labour involved in verifying the correct composition of a whole program out of N program components (each of them individually assumed to be correct) still grows exponentially with N, we had better admit defeat.

Any large program will exist during its life-time in a multitude of different versions, so that in composing a large program we are not so much concerned with a single program, but with a whole family of related programs, containing alternative programs for the same job and/or similar programs for similar jobs. A program therefore should be conceived and understood as a member of a family; it should be so structured out of components that various members of this family, sharing components, do not only share the correctness demonstration of the shared components but also of the shared substructure.

Program correctness

An assertion of program correctness is an assertion about the net effects of the computations that may be evoked by this program. Investigating how such assertions can be justified, I came to the following conclusions:

1 The number of different inputs, i.e. the number of different computations for which the assertions claim to hold is so fantastically high that demonstration of correctness by sampling is completely out of the question. *Program testing can be used to show the presence of bugs, but never to show their absence!* Therefore, proof of program correctness should depend only upon the program text.

2 A number of people have shown that program correctness can be proved. Highly formal correctness proofs have been given; also correctness proofs have been given for "normal programs", i.e. programs not written with a proof procedure in mind. As is to be expected (and nobody is to be blamed for that) the circulating examples are concerned with rather small programs and, unless measures are taken, the amount of labour involved in proving might well (will) explode with program size.

3 Therefore, I have not focused my attention on the question "how do we prove the correctness of a given program?" but on the questions "for what program structures can we give correctness proofs without undue labour, even if the programs get large?" and, as a sequel, "how do we make, for a given task, such a well-structured program?". My willingness to confine my attention to such "well-structured programs" (as a subset of the set of all possible programs) is based on my belief that we can find such a well-structured subset satisfying our programming needs, i.e. that for each programmable task this subset contains enough realistic programs.

4 This, what I call "constructive approach to the problem of program correctness", can be taken a step further. It is not restricted to general considerations as to what program structures are attractive from the point of view of provability; in a number of specific, very difficult programming tasks I have finally succeeded in constructing a program by analyzing how a proof could be given that a class of computations would satisfy certain requirements; from the requirements of the proof the program followed.

The relation between program and computation

Investigating how assertions about the possible computations (evolving in time) can be made on account of the static program text, I have concluded that adherence to rigid sequencing disciplines is essential, so as to allow step-wise abstraction from the possibly different routings. In particular: when programs for a sequential computer are expressed as a linear sequence of basic symbols of a programming language, sequencing should be controlled by alternative, conditional and repetitive clauses and procedure calls, rather than by statements transferring control to labelled points.

The need for step-wise abstraction from local sequencing is perhaps most convincingly shown by the following demonstration:

Let us consider a "stretched" program of the form

$$S_1; S_2; \ldots ; S_N \qquad (1)$$

and let us introduce the measuring convention that when the net effect of the execution of each individual statement S_i has been given, it takes N steps of reasoning to establish the correctness of program (1), i.e. to establish that the cumulative net effect of the N actions in succession satisfies the requirements imposed upon the computations evoked by program (1).

For a statement of the form

$$\textbf{if } B \textbf{ then } S_1 \textbf{ else } S_2 \qquad (2)$$

where, again, the net effect of the execution of the constituent statements S_1 and S_2 has been given; we introduce the measuring convention that it takes 2 steps of reasoning to establish the net effect of program (2), viz. one for the case B and one for the case not B.

Consider now a program of the form

$$\textbf{if } B_1 \textbf{ then } S_{11} \textbf{ else } S_{12};$$
$$\textbf{if } B_2 \textbf{ then } S_{21} \textbf{ else } S_{22};$$

$$.$$
$$.$$
$$.$$

$$\textbf{if } B_N \textbf{ then } S_{N1} \textbf{ else } S_{N2} \qquad (3)$$

According to the measuring convention it takes 2 steps per alternative statement to understand it, i.e. to establish that the net effect of

$$\textbf{if } B_i \textbf{ then } S_{i1} \textbf{ else } S_{i2}$$

is equivalent to that of the execution of an abstract statement S_i. Having N such alternative statements, it takes us 2N steps to reduce program (3) to one of the form of program (1); to understand the latter form of the program takes us another N steps, giving 3N steps in toto.

If we had refused to introduce the abstract statements S_i but had tried to understand program (3) directly in terms of executions of the statements S_{ij}, each such computation would be the cumulative effect of N such statement executions and would as such require N steps to understand it. Trying to understand the algorithm in terms of the S_{ij} implies that we have to distinguish between 2^N different routings through the program and this would lead to $N*2^N$ steps of reasoning!

I trust that the above calculation convincingly demonstrates the need for the introduction of the abstract statements S_i. An aspect of my constructive approach is not to reduce a given program (3) to an abstract program (1), but to start with the latter.

Abstract data structures

Understanding a program composed from a modest number of abstract statements again becomes an exploding task if the definition of the net effect of the constituent statements is sufficiently unwieldy. This can be overcome by the introduction of suitable abstract data structures. The situation is greatly analogous to the way in which we can understand an ALGOL program operating on integers without having to bother about the number representation of the implementation used. The only difference is that now the programmer must invent his own concepts (analogous to the "ready-made" integer) and his own operations upon them (analogous to the "ready-made" arithmetic operations).

In the refinement of an abstract program (i.e. composed from abstract statements operating on abstract data structures) we observe the phenomenon of "joint refinement". For abstract data structures of a given type a certain representation is chosen in terms of new (perhaps still rather abstract) data structures. The immediate consequence of this design decision is that the abstract statements operating upon the original abstract data structure have to be redefined in terms of algorithmic refinements operating upon the new data structures in terms of which it was decided to represent the original abstract data structure. Such a joint refinement of data structure and associated statements should be an isolated unit of the program text: it embodies the immediate consequences of an (independent) design decision and is as such the natural unit of interchange for program modification. It is an example of what I have grown into calling "a pearl".

Programs as necklaces strung from pearls
I have grown to regard a program as an ordered set of pearls, a "necklace". The top pearl describes the program in its most abstract form, in all lower pearls one or more concepts used above are explained (refined) in terms of concepts to be explained (refined) in pearls below it, while the bottom pearl eventually explains what still has to be explained in terms of a standard interface (=machine). The pearl seems to be a natural program module.

As each pearl embodies a specific design decision (or, as the case may be, a specific aspect of the original problem statement) it is the natural unit of interchange in program modification (or, as the case may be, program adaptation to a change in problem statement).

Pearls and necklace give a clear status to an "incomplete program", consisting of the top half of a necklace; it can be regarded as a complete program to be executed by a suitable machine (of which the bottom half of the necklace gives a feasible implementation). As such, the correctness of the upper half of the necklace can be established regardless of the choice of the bottom half.

Between two successive pearls we can make a "cut", which is a manual for a machine provided by the part of the necklace below the cut and used by the program represented by the part of the necklace above the cut. This manual serves as an interface between the two parts of the necklace. We feel this form of interface more helpful than regarding data representation as an interface between operations, in particular more helpful towards ensuring the combinatorial freedom required for program adaptation.

The combinatorial freedom just mentioned seems to be the only way in which we can make a program as part of a family or "in many (potential) versions" without the labour involved increasing proportional to the number of members of the family. The family becomes the set of those selections from a given collection of pearls that can be strung into a fitting necklace.

Concluding remarks
Pearls in a necklace have a strict logical order, say "from top to bottom". I would like to stress that this order may be radically different from the order (in time) in which they are designed.

Pearls have emerged as program modules when I tried to map upon each other as completely as possible, the numerous members of a class of related programs. The abstraction process involved in this mapping turns out (not, amazingly, as an afterthought!) to be the same as the one that can be used to reduce the amount of intellectual labour involved in correctness proofs. This is very encouraging.

As I said before, the programming experiments have been carried out with relatively small programs. Although, personally, I firmly believe that they show the way towards more reliable composition of really large programs, I should like to stress that as yet I have *no* experimental evidence for this. The experimental evidence gained so far shows an increasing ability to compose programs of the size I tried. Although I tried to do it, I feel that I have given but little recognition to the requirements of program development such as is needed when one wishes to employ a large crowd; I have no experience with the Chinese Army approach, nor am I convinced of its virtues.

7.5 Criteria for a system design language

by

A. D. Falkoff

A system is a collection of programs and a program is a formal statement of an algorithm or a process. This paper proposes that the appropriate design medium for systems is a formal programming language.

Since the programs that comprise a system may be implemented in various gradations of hardware and software, the proposal is not restricted to software, although it is the software design problem that is of interest at the moment. Indeed, the unifying effect of using a common medium and the flexibility it provides in the timing of implementation decisions are two of the major advantages to be expected.

In proposing the use of a programming language in system design it is not intended to outlaw the use of English or other natural languages, either in the formal documentation that should be part of a design effort, or in the casual communication that always occurs in an engineering operation. Rather, the use of the two types of languages should be complementary. The natural language can be used to convey broad ideas quickly, while the formal language can be used to make these ideas precise and ultimately to act as a guide in preparing natural language documentation, such as manuals.

The criteria that are proposed for the choice of a formal design language are:
1 It should be easy to learn its basic use.
2 Formulations in the language should be suggestive and thought provoking.
3 It should allow meaningful formal manipulation of both expressions and larger program segments.
4 It should lead to the development of aesthetic criteria for judging the quality of a design.
5 It should be convenient for documentation.
6 It should be uncommitted to any particular technology or problem area.
7 It should be applicable in a consistent way to systems of any foreseeable complexity.
8 It should be executable on a machine.

Each of these criteria will be briefly discussed below, with some examples in terms of APL (see *References* 1, 2 and 3).

1 Because of the continual problem of training new designers and the immediate perturbation when working designers start to use it, the basic use of a design language should be easy to learn. That is to say, the beginner should be able to produce correct and usable programs in a

relatively short time, while power and elegance in the use of the language come with practice.

This requirement suggests that the language should have a syntax and semantics built up from a small number of internally consistent rules. Syntactical restrictions and semantic surprises of the kind that have arisen when convenience of implementation was taken as a significant guide in language design must be avoided.

2 Apart from clerical tasks, good design requires thought. A language which is awkward to use or which suppresses all detail will, in the first instance, discourage experimentation with different formulations and, in the second instance, fail to suggest alternative lines of attack. This suggests that, while the design language should have a simple structure, it should at the same time have a rich set of primitive operations so that, even at fairly high levels of design, actions can be expressed succinctly in terms of primitive operations.

For example, Figure 1 gives two systems of skeletal programs for maintaining a table. The APPEND-DELETE system maintains LST by appending to it and contracting it, as required. The INSERT-ERASE system maintains TBL, conceived as a fixed length object, by keeping a dynamic record of the next available space. This record also serves in a complementary fashion to identify valid table entries for readout. The two systems were obviously easy to write and are not very hard to understand. Which would be better in a given environment, or would a combination of the two be best?

```
     ∇ STARTLST                          ∇ STARTTBL
[1]    LST←⍳0                      [1]     TBL←MAXLENGTHρI←1
     ∇                                   ∇


     ∇ APPEND N                          ∇ INSERT N
[1]    LST←LST,N                   [1]     TBL[1↑I]←N
     ∇                             [2]     →4 IF 1<ρI
                                   [3]     →0,I←I+1
                                   [4]     I←1↓I
                                         ∇


     ∇ DELETE N;J                        ∇ ERASE N;J
[1]    →0 IF(ρLST)<J←LSTⵑN         [1]     →0 IF(ρTBL)<J←TBLⵑN
[2]    LST←((J-1)↑LST),J↓LST       [2]     I←J,I
     ∇                                   ∇


     ∇ PRINT                             ∇ SHOW;J
[1]    LST                        [1]     J←⁻1↑I
     ∇                             [2]     (~(⍳J)∊I)/J↑TBL
                                         ∇
```

Figure 1. Two systems for maintaining a table

3 One aspect of formal manipulation is that it opens a way to finding proofs of equivalence among programs, an acknowledged problem in system design and implementation. A more immediately practical aspect of it, however, is one related to the second criterion. That is, formal manipulation provides a quasi-mechanical way to search for equivalent formulations that are in some sense better than others.

The exploitation of complete formal equivalence has been treated at length in a general context by Iverson (see *Reference* 4) and an instance of its use in hardware design has been shown by Falkoff (see *Reference* 5).

Substitution of nearly equivalent forms can bring to light, by their connotations, facets of problems that might otherwise be overlooked. Thus it is clear that the following formulations for the selection of an element from a vector are equivalent, over the range of possible indices of the element, and that they are mechanically derivable one from another:

$Q \leftarrow TBL[P]$ (indexing)

$R \leftarrow ((\iota \rho TBL) \in P)/TBL$ (compression by the characteristic vector of P over the set of indices of TBL)

$S \leftarrow {}^{-}1 \uparrow P \uparrow TBL$ (select the last of the first P elements of TBL)

$T \leftarrow {}^{-}1 \uparrow P \rho TBL$ (select the last of the P replications of the elements of TBL)

If P is outside the index range: Q is never specified and an error is reported; R will be an empty vector; S will be set to zero, the default action provided for on the exceeding of a vector bound; and T will be the element reached by end-around addressing. Stating the last case formally it can be seen that the circle is closed in two senses: ${}^{-}1 \uparrow P \rho TBL$ is completely equivalent to $TBL[(\rho TBL)|P]$ (in zero-origin). Which of the foregoing results is best in a given situation is, of course, a moot question but the formal manipulation makes it evident that a question exists.

To allow effective formal manipulation a language should have a syntax that is context-free, a semantics that is free of side-effects and a well chosen set of primitive operations. A graphic quality is helpful, if not essential, for the treatment of program segments larger than individual statements.

4 In engineering or architectural design, aesthetic criteria are the ultimate basis for design decisions that are not dictated by strictly technical considerations. Good designers are distinguished from others by their exercise of aesthetic judgment. A good design language should therefore promote the development of such criteria. This means that it should be possible both to comprehend the total structure of a system in some graphic fashion and to examine details, as required. If a language has this property designers will develop both conscious and intuitive bases for judging the symmetry, balance and general rightness for its purpose of a proposed design.

Consider the program in Figure 2, which is a description of the channel behaviour of System 360, taken from *Reference* 2. The area blocked out in a heavy line is the part of the program in which data transfer actually takes place between a peripheral device and the central memory. The other parts of the program perform control functions of one kind or another. On the face of it, is this a reasonable balance? The answer, at this time, is not known but a good design tool should provoke questions of this kind.

To provide such a facility, a formal language should clearly be amenable to graphic display. But more significantly, it should have a simple structure so that it does not burden the design with its own complexity. It should be sufficiently rich in primitive operations to permit reasonably complex substructures to be displayed directly, so that the heavy use of defined functions becomes a measure of what is actually being swept under the carpet, rather than an enforced way of life.

5 The need for convenience in documentation need not be laboured. Two things are meant by convenience in this context. One is that primary documents should come naturally out of the design process as is the case, for example, with mechanical parts drawings. The other is that it should not require massive equipment or microscopic records to document large systems.

The first purpose could be served by almost any programming language, if properly used, and its pursuit will lead naturally to consideration of work organization and administrative procedures. The second purpose is best served by a language that permits terse constructions both within statements and in the display of program sequences.

6 Because programming is a tool in so many fields, a formal design language will be enhanced in usefulness if it is not biased toward any particular field. The operation of a computing machine is only one instance of the application of programming; the design of the machine itself is another; and certain aspects of its manufacture are others. In particular, because of the hazy division between hardware and software, it is important that a system design language be not biased in favour of one or the other.

A bias toward a particular field is most often manifested by the incorporation in the language of specialized data objects (e.g. pointers), by the pre-assignment of functional significance to otherwise abstract structures (e.g. 1 0 1 taken as the number five rather than a vector of three elements) and by a preoccupation with the representations of numbers and characters. Since considerations of this nature can be conveniently handled by functions defined on abstract objects that are at home in any field, a design language can be free of such bias. But, as a corollary, a design language must have a strong function-definition capability. It should be possible to define easily functions on the primitive objects of the language and to use them without syntactic distinction from the primitive functions provided by the language.

7 In a general way, system complexity is characterized by the degree to which different programs in a system interact. Such interaction seems to take two basic forms: the exercise of control over one program by another, and the use of common variables by different programs.

For the exercise of control, the ability to use one program in another (which is inherent in the notion of a defined function) together with the ability of one program to alter explicitly the execution sequence of an otherwise independent program seems to be sufficient. The use of common variables requires only the conventions necessary to establish that they are common (or, conversely, that some variables are not). *Reference* 2 is an example of a complex system, with many interactions among programs, in which these devices were sufficient.

8 Like documentation, the need for machine testing of designs requires no argument. It need be noted only that a formal language capable of expressing the design of a system at different levels of detail can be used directly for simulating the system at any design stage. It is necessary only to substitute appropriate tables for functions that are not yet detailed. Machinability also provides the opportunity to have "live" catalogues on interactive systems, in which functional units can be displayed and executed for gaining understanding of their behaviour.

In conclusion it is worth noting a significant aspect of the use of a formal language in system design. Namely, any formal specification can be viewed either as a function which specifies certain transformations or as a set of instructions for executing these transformations. The choice of viewpoint is the prerogative and obligation of the user. It is, in fact, one of the

230

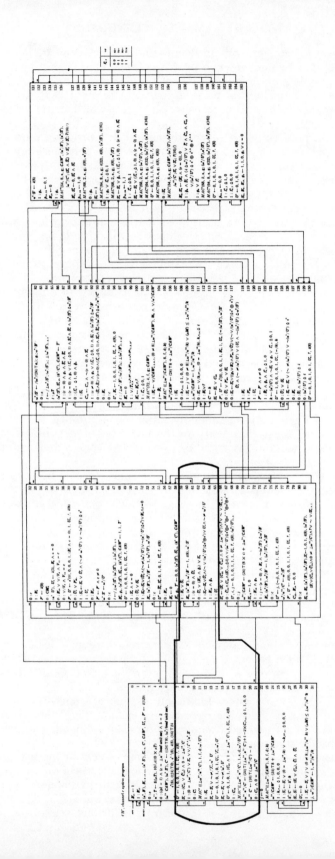

Figure 2. System/360 channel program (from *Reference 2*)

advantages of the use of formal specification in design that, even though the formulator may write a program with the intent that it be literally followed in some more detailed representation, it is nevertheless also a functional specification, and the perceptive designer will see it in this light and perhaps be able (because it is also well defined) to find an equivalent formulation that has greater economy or other engineering advantages.

References

1. **Iverson, K. E.** *A Programming Language,* Wiley, (New York), 1962.
2. **Falkoff, A. D., Iverson, K. E.** and **Sussenguth, E. H.** A formal description of system 360, *IBM Systems Journal,* **3,** No. 3, 1964.
3. **Falkoff, A. D.** and **Iverson, K. E.** *APL\360 User's Manual,* IBM Research (Yorktown Hts., New York), 1968.
4. **Iverson, K. E.** Formalism in programming languages, *CACM,* **7,** 1964, pp. 80-88.
5. **Falkoff, A. D.** Algorithms for parallel-search memories, *JACM,* **9,** 1962, pp. 488-511.

7.6 System evaluation tools

by

C. C. Gotlieb and G. H. MacEwen

Classification of tools

At the first NATO Conference on Software Engineering Pinkerton (see *Reference* 1) listed techniques for the collection of system performance data and discussed some of the uses of such data. Data collection, or monitoring, may be regarded as one of two basic tools useful for system design, the other being modelling. Each of these basic tools, modelling and monitoring, may be further subdivided into two types yielding four kinds of system evaluation tools, as follows:

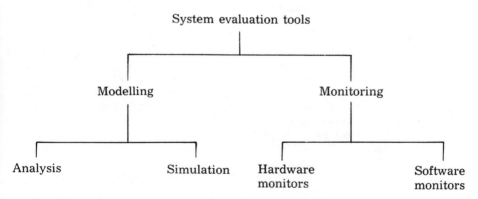

Applicability of tools and comparisons

Very broadly we have three phases of system design: conceptional, construction and operational. On studying or designing a system it is possible to bring more than one of the above tools into play. Each is particularly useful during different phases and the results can reinforce each other. In general modelling is most useful during the conceptional and construction phases, while monitoring is most useful in the construction and operational phases.

Figure 1 illustrates in simplified form the interaction between the tools and the system. Briefly:
- models predict performance and monitors measure it.
- models are useful in determining which quantities should be monitored.
- monitors can be used to determine which quantities should be designated as design parameters.

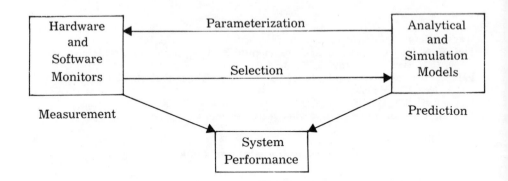

A more detailed comparison of the tools and their range of use is given in Table 1.

Some implementations
Analytical models have been used extensively to study the behaviour of computer systems where queueing plays an important role, e.g. in time sharing systems (see *References* 2 and 3) or in job shop scheduling (see *Reference* 4). They have also been successful in characterizing the behaviour of a particular hardware or software component, e.g. a disc memory (see *Reference* 5), or a system of addressing (see *Reference* 6).

General purpose simulators have been used for some time. At least two, GPSS (see *Reference* 7) and SIMSCRIPT (see *Reference* 8), have very wide currency and many of the computer system studies reported in the Second Conference on Applications of Simulation (see *Reference* 9) are based on them (see for example Frank (see *Reference* 10)). Another type of computer system simulation takes as input a description of the hardware corresponding to a configuration (peripheral devices, controllers and channels, memory banks, CPU) and also specifications of the operating system. When a proposed configuration and load are input, the activity is simulated and measures of how much system resources are needed to handle the load are produced. Examples of this type of simulator are S3 and CASE (see *References* 9a and 9b), a system available from the Computer Learning and Systems Corporation. A number of special purpose simulators are also described in the Conference Digest referenced above and elsewhere in the literature (see for example *Reference* 11).

Although some hardware monitors are described in the general literature (see for example Estrin *Reference* 12, and Schulman *Reference* 13), until recently most were developed by manufacturers in the process of their system design, or as an aid for analyzing a special configuration of some customer. Monitors of this type are now available commercially and as well there are software monitors developed by manufacturers or available commercially. Table 2 lists some monitors, hardware and software, currently available, with comments on the information they yield.

Table 1—Comparison of system evaluation tools

	Models		Monitors	
	Analytical	Simulation	Software	Hardware
Required input	Model of system under test		Functioning system	
	Knowledge of hardware and software Mathematical tools e.g. statistics, queueing theory, etc.	Simulation package or special simulator	Software monitor program	Hardware monitor device
Range of application	Design, construction		Construction, operations, optimization	
Results	Performance data		Utilization of resources	
	For a wide range of parameters	For specified sets of parameters	Software and hardware	Hardware
	Dependence of performance on parameters		Statistics gathered may be	
	Calculated	Displayed	in any form, e.g. counts, durations, mean values, histograms, etc.	special form, e.g. counts of events, total time duration of some condition or logical combination of conditions

Table 1—Comparison of system evaluation tools (*continued*)

	Models		Monitors	
	Analytical	Simulation	Software	Hardware
Validity of results	Very dependent on model		Very dependent on work load during testing e.g. job mix, load level, etc.	
	Accuracy need not have statistical dependence	Accuracy dependent on run time of simulation—results invalid if steady state not achieved		
Advantages	Performance can be determined over a wide continuous range of parameters. Time dependent or steady state models possible	Work load and configuration—can easily be varied—can concentrate on parts of system which are bottle necks	Can monitor hardware and software performance Work best when monitors are incorporated into system design	Can monitor any accessible hardware function. Does not alter system under test
Disadvantages	Mathematics soon become intractable for all but simple systems	May be difficult to model sufficient detail of system and maintain manageable size of program. Must be written and maintained for each release of each system	Alters system under test. Difficult to make changes and gather new data. Must write and maintain a monitor for each release of each system	Cannot directly measure software functions, e.g. queueing times must be calculated by supplementary analysis

Table 2—Some available monitors

Name	Type	Supplier	Comments
Configuration Utilization Efficiency Product (CUE)	Software Mon. (OS/360)	Boole and Babbage Inc.	Measures total times for certain conditions, e.g. CPU busy, channels busy. Cannot measure times for logical combinations of conditions. Gives count of SVC module loads. Gives count and Track addresses of disc seeks
MVTANAL	Software Mon. (OS/360/MVT)	IBM (for use by IBM only)	Gives count of usage of OS routines. Measures usage of I/O devices and distribution of queue length for each device. Measures hardware utilization, e.g. CPU, channel. Measures usage of system datasets
Problem Program Efficiency (PPE)	Software Mon. (OS/360)	Boole and Babbage Inc.	Used on applications and programs—identifies portions of programs with high usage, where I/O waits arise, etc.
System Utilization Monitor (SUM)	Hardware Mon.	Computer Synectics Inc.	Readings taken every millisecond and stored on tape. Data reduction program gives: (a) Total time that certain conditions or logical combination of conditions were active, e.g. CPU busy, channel busy and CPU waiting. (b) Counts for certain events, e.g. total number of disc seeks
Computer Performance Monitor (CPM)	Hardware Mon.	Allied Computer Technology Inc.	Similar to SUM
Basic Counter Unit (BCU)	Hardware Mon (System/360, 1800, 1130)	IBM (for use by IBM only)	Readings are taken manually or punched on cards. Output consists of the total time that certain conditions or logical combination of conditions were active

Some possible directions

The list of monitors and models given in the table and in the references is by no means a complete list of those generally available. And it is likely that there have been more of these types of tools developed by computer manufacturers for their own design, than have been described in the general literature. There would still seem to be some useful direction of exploration for these tools. Examples are:

- very little has been reported on the consistency of the results that might be found on using different tools on the same system.
- it would be useful to have specific guidelines for knowing when to use which tool.
- models or simulators should be developed so that they can accept as input descriptions of configurations that are not tied to the devices of a particular manufacturer. The components should have key parameters specified to the extent that will allow effective prediction of performance. For example there might be a memory hierarchy, where for each level of memory (high speed core, low speed core, drum, disc and tape) the access time, latency, memory size, etc. are specified. The tool should be able to yield information on how the storage transfers and memory overlays should take place. The information might be in the form of a general strategy but even failing this it would be useful to know how a particular program should be structured, or even how the memory blocks should be distributed on a particular disc. As seen above, such tools are useful enough generally to make them attractive possibilities for commercial development, but more needs to be done.
- more analysis is needed of devices that are coming to be used very heavily, for example: disc memories with multiple modules or with more than one channel, multiplexers as used in remote job entry systems, etc.

References

1. **Pinkerton, T. B.** Performance monitoring and systems evaluation. Software Engineering, NATO Scientific Affairs Division, Brussels 39, pp. 200-203.
2. **Coffman, E. G.** and **Kleinrock, L.** Feedback queueing models for time-shared systems, *JACM* **15**, No. 4, October 1968, pp. 549-576.
3. **Adiri, I.** and **Avi-Itzhak, B.** A time-sharing queue with a finite number of customers, *JACM,* **16**, No. 2, April 1969, pp. 315-323.
4. **Rolfson, C. B.** *Scheduling workflow in a computer system,* Ph.D. thesis, Dept. of Computer Science, University of Toronto, 1968.
5. **Abate, J., Dubner, H.** and **Weinberg, S. B.** Queueing analysis of the IBM 2314 disc storage facility, *JACM,* **15,** No. 4, October 1968, pp. 577-589.
6. **Peterson, W. W.** Addressing for random access storage, *IBM Journal of Research & Dev.* **1**, 1957, pp. 130-146.
7. **Herscovitch, H.** and **Schneider, T.** GPSS III—An expanded general purpose simulator, *IBM Systems Journal,* **4**, No. 3, 1965, pp. 174-183.
8. **Kiviat, P. J.** and **Villamueva, R.** *The SIMSCRIPT II programming language,* The RAND Corp. R-460-PR, 1968.
9. Digest of the second conference on applications of simulation sponsored by SHARE/ACM/IEEE/SCI, December 1968, New York.
9a. **Cohen, I. J.** S3, The system and software simulator, Digest of the second conference on applications of simulation sponsored by SHARE/ACM/IEEE/SCI, December 1968, New York, pp. 282-285.
9b. **Thompson, W. C.** The application of simulation in computer system design and optimization, Digest of the second conference on applications of simulation sponsored by SHARE/ACM/IEEE/SCI, December 1968, New York, pp. 286-290.
10. **Frank, A. L.** The use of simulation in the design of information systems, Digest of the second conference on applications of simulation sponsored by SHARE/ACM/IEEE/SCI, December 1968, New York, pp. 87-88.

11. **Katz, J. H.** System/360 simulator, *Comm. ACM,* **10,** No. 11, November 1967, pp. 694-702.
12. **Estrin, G.** *et al.* SNUPER computer—a computer instrumentation automaton, *Proceedings of the SJCC,* 1967, pp. 645-656.
13 **Schulman, F. D.** Hardware measurement device for IBM S/360 time-sharing operation, *Proceedings of the 22nd ACM Conference,* 1967, pp. 103-109.

7.7 Computer aided software design

by

M. E. Hopkins

Performance is one of the main concerns of those designing and developing any large programming system. The great paradox is that by common consent too much effort is expended to obtain performance and yet our great failures are often the result of an inefficient system.

Designers generally recognize that high performance is usually obtained through managing logistics in an optimal manner rather than by clever code. Logistics here is taken to mean the organization and flow of data which is in tables and files. A designer will employ various strategies in organizing data to realize an efficient flow. Where the task is well understood, the environment is reasonably stable, and the application is not subject to new developments, the designer can make early, judicious decisions about data organization. A typical example of this is our ability to write all but the most complex compilers with a small effort compared to that which was required several years ago when compilation was not as well understood. One wonders whether history will be repeated with operating systems. The experience of the last few years should certainly provide understanding but it seems questionable whether increased understanding alone will be enough to cope efficiently with the wide range of hardware configurations and job mixes which a general purpose operating system must handle.

In designing a general purpose operating system or any large application, the complexity of the task and requirements, which only become apparent late in development or during maintenance, tend to vitiate early design decisions made to improve performance. At this point the designers must be able to restructure the data to obtain their goals. In the absence of such capability several courses will be taken.

1 New tables will be specified by the designers which, they hope, will provide faster access than the few central tables of the initial design.
2 Multiple methods of access are created to improve information flow. This implies complex interconnection in the form of pointers, complex searching procedures, etc.
3 Implementors develop their own private information repositories which again provide economies not available in central tables under design control.

All of this is almost inevitable in a production situation but several iterations produce disastrous results. For example OS/360 has a manual of over 100 pages describing "the major control blocks and tables". A casual examination of components reveals that each module has many complex private tables which are not included among "the major control blocks and tables." For example the Job Scheduler Program Logic Manual describes about 20 private tables. It seems that most of this mass of information is duplicated or derivable from some other table and efficiency considerations which provided the rationale probably now no longer apply. It is, however, impossible to restructure the data because the design group has long since lost control to various implementation groups who have been building local performance improvements and perhaps inadvertently taken over the function of the central design team. In other words nobody understands the system well enough to make any major changes. In any case the programs have been written so that only trivial changes in tables can be made without bringing on a rewrite of all existing code.

In summary, given a long fluid design, implementation and maintenance schedule, there will inevitably be a series of decisions made to improve performance. Each such decision will be based on current understanding which inevitably includes the fact that a major modification of logistics is not possible. Thus there is a tendency to invent new data structures which increase the complexity and reduce the level of overall performance. As the logistics become more complex there is a concomitant loss of design control which results in a further increase in complexity and decrease in performance. The evidence of this process is a sort of stratification of levels of information, observable in any large system, which is like an archaeological record of many attempts to improve performance.

The above requires some qualification. The confusion, which is observable in so many large systems, is also due to a great deal of "fence building" by those designing and implementing components. Given a task to accomplish and little understanding of the entire system, there is a tendency to define an environment which insulates oneself from the design perturbations of the entire system. While the motives are somewhat different, the effect of such local design also reduces performance. It is also apparent that "performance" must be described rather more broadly to indicate how serious are the problems of many current programming systems. Reliability, serviceability, and graceful degradation are often cited as goals. Complexity, which destroys the throughput of many systems, also makes the above goals unattainable. There is just too much information for the necessary simplicity and stability.

Ultimately the way out of this must be a new methodology for writing large systems. This would include the following:

1 An algorithmic programming language, which is free of most considerations of efficiency.
2 A compiler and run time environment which permit the development and check out of a large system without reference to its performance.
3 The process of making a choice of options and specialization for a particular hardware configuration at a particular location, commonly called system generation, which might also be the opportunity to bind design decisions that relate to performance.

Developing a system with such tools would permit several iterations of design and implementation to develop the required functional capability and to ensure accuracy. The system would then be bound for performance. Super optimizing compilers would treat all the modules in an optimal manner. Tables, data structures, and access methods would be restructured through a terminal system which would provide for co-operative optimization by a designer and system simulator-optimizer program. This in turn requires statistics supplied by accounting routines which function while the system runs in unoptimized form.

The technical problem which must be solved centers on the problem of binding. Loose binding makes it easier to change decisions but often results in a loss of performance. (In some sense optimization may be viewed as the process of making binding decisions at the earliest possible time.) In our work at the T. J. Watson Research Center, the problem of binding storage has been one touchstone for discussing the performance problem. The conventional approach in FORTRAN, COBOL and assembly language is that while some or even most information about data is kept in symbolic format, there are some cases where structure is bound into the program at an early date. For example, PL/1 has CELL, FORTRAN programs have EQUIVALENCE statements which determine storage allocation in detail and COBOL programs treat a structure as an atom which can be manipulated as if it were an entity rather than a collection of entities. In these and other cases it is impossible to change data formats without changing, or at least examining, much of the source program.

An alternative approach is to treat data as objects in the manner of ALGOL 60. This is most attractive, especially if the historical situation of millions of lines of working code in other languages is ignored. Even ALGOL may not be ideal owing to its lack of data structures of greater complexity than an array. Unfortunately the languages which possess this attribute, such as LISP or McG, acquire it through list structure which seems to imply a high degree of interpretation or late binding which is very inefficient. The study of how to bind such functional languages at the earliest moment will yield very significant results, for it will then be possible to design and program in the same language. The basic techniques that will be employed in this situation are those developed for optimizing more conventional languages, such as FORTRAN, as well as new techniques for optimizing data formats and more global units, such as entire procedures. It is interesting to note that the emphasis will be different from that of FORTRAN optimizing. There will be less attention to operations that result in improvements in the 10 per cent range and more to those that yield orders of magnitude improvement. This is only possible in languages which have a very loose structure and are thus usually interpreted. It is just these languages that do not bind the data structure into the solution that are ideal for the designer.

Thus the optimizing compiler can be seen as the vehicle which permits software designers to work at a high enough level and still retain control of system design decisions. This should result in systems which are simpler, more reliable and perform better.

7.8 Languages for writing system programs

by

Charles A. Lang

I find it alarming that in spite of the enormous amount of research and development effort that has gone into programming languages by way of syntax definitions, theories of type, compilers, compiler-compilers and the like, the majority of system programs are still written in assembly language. Why is this? Is it desirable? If not, can anything be done to improve the situation? I shall not attempt to define "system program", but merely point out that I consider compilers, operating systems, program overlay schemes, storage allocation packages, on-line commands for a multi-access system and graphical input/output routines to be examples of system programs.

Why assembly language?
There are a number of reasons why assembly language is used.
1 Assembly language has no peers for producing efficient programs, that is,
   programs efficient in terms of compiled program size and speed of
   running. Efficiency does matter. People often pay lip service to it and
   then write extremely inefficient programs. High efficiency reduces
   operating costs and makes things possible that are impossible if the
   programs are inefficient. Two examples are fast console response to filing
   operations in a multi-access system and wringing the most out of a small
   (say 8K) machine. The skill and ingenuity of the programmer also have a
   great effect on efficiency, but this is just as true for high level languages
   as for assembly code.
2 Assembly language enables you to get as close to the machine as is
   possible. It does not prevent any operation that the machine is capable of
   executing from being programmed. This is certainly not true of high level
   languages. Further, the discipline of learning assembly language ensures
   that the programmer learns about the machine. High level languages
   screen the programmer from the machine. While this attribute is highly
   desirable in many applications, system programs can benefit from the
   programmer thoroughly understanding the actual machine and its
   capabilities.
3 Assembly language can be quickly compiled; this is a great convenience
   when developing programs, especially on-line with a single user or multi-
   access machine.
4 On-line debugging systems are an enormous aid to debugging at the
   assembly language level. Typical facilities are interrogation and setting of
   registers, searching for bit patterns and break points, free running and
   interpretive execution and so on. Correction of errors with high level
   languages normally involves editing the source document, re-compiling
   and re-loading.
5 Assembly language systems do not require the use of a run-time system
   to perform functions such as space allocation. This leaves the system
   programmer with maximum flexibility to organize his system program to
   suit the problem at hand.

Is the programming of system programs in assembly language desirable?
The answer is no, but unfortunately it is still the most suitable language on
many machines. Briefly, because they are well known, the very grave
disadvantages of assembly language are:
1 Apart from the few who delight in such intricacies, most people find
   assembly language programs harder to write, read, understand, debug and
   maintain than high level language programs.
2 It provides the poorest conceptual framework for the programmer to
   express the computing operations he wants performed.
3 It is completely machine dependent, thus requiring any machine language
   program to be completely rewritten when it is transferred to a different
   machine.

Can anything be done to improve the situation?
The answer to this question is yes. A completely machine independent
language particularly suited for writing system programs and which
compiles code of comparable efficiency to that of a good assembly code
programmer on every machine on which it is implemented, would be ideal.
This is impossible with the present state of the art, so what sort of a
language is it possible to produce now? I shall not define an actual language

but rather discuss what type of a language it should be. BCPL, MOL940, PL360 and SAL (see *References* 1, 2, 3 and 4 respectively) come a good way towards meeting the requirements, while EPL (see *Reference* 5) falls shorter. BCPL offers machine independence but falls short in other requirements discussed below compared to MOL940, PL360 and SAL.

Clarity

A programming language provides the conceptual framework within which a programmer must think about his problem, so influencing his method of solution. The language should enable the programmer to state clearly the computing operations he wants performed; further, the program must be clear to read both by himself and others. A high level language such as FORTRAN, ALGOL or AED meets these requirements better than assembly language, but these languages fail to meet the other requirements discussed below. The language itself must be easy to learn and have a short, well written programming manual with an index.

Efficiency

The language should be capable of being compiled efficiently to produce efficient code, say not more than 20 per cent longer or slower than the code produced by a good assembly language programmer. This is a great blow for machine independence. For if the language were to contain all the features desirable for system programs then it would not be possible to compile all the features efficiently on each machine because of the hardware differences (e.g. character operations implemented on one machine may be completely absent on another). Programmers could still write efficient programs for particular machines by using only those features of the language that they knew to compile efficiently on their machine. They would then, however, have the advantage of only a subset of the language. When programs were transferred from machine to machine the running efficiency would vary greatly.

Simple and flexible language design

The language should be simple, but not at the expense of its generality or practicability. Simplicity also aids efficient compilation to produce efficient code. The target should be a high power-to-complexity ratio; if the basic operations provided by the language are well chosen, then these provide the tools with which the programmer may fashion more complicated and specialized operations. Much can be achieved with a very general syntax, avoiding exceptions and special cases as far as possible. BCPL is a particularly good example of this. Further, as much as possible should be left out of the language rather than the reverse. Stacks are often used in system programs so stacking operations might be included. To provide all possible stacking operations (first-in first-out, pushing and popping different numbers of words, popping the top item, copying the top item, etc.) is too complicated; if only a subset is implemented it may not include the operations programmers want. Far better to omit them altogether, since the language should contain basic operations from which stacking operations may be readily implemented.

The language must not prevent the programming of anything that the hardware can execute. Languages offer two types of restrictions here. First, the language may not have a construction, perhaps for a particular type of shifting operation or character manipulation, that is implemented directly in the hardware. When these operations are required, either the programmer must program around them, which is inefficient, or in most languages he may call an assembly language subroutine. This too can be very inefficient when the number of orders executed to get into and out of a subroutine is comparable to or greater than the number in the subroutine itself. Secondly, the language may prevent certain operations that are highly useful. For example, the description of an "object" in memory may contain several items of data which it is convenient to store in a contiguous block. This data may be of mixed type, in which case FORTRAN would not permit them to be stored in a single array. The problem could be fudged around with an assembly language program but only very inefficiently and inconveniently. This is but one example of the restrictions that types impose. Types are a menace to the system programmer as they reduce the flexibility of a programming language enormously. They do enable the compiler (at some expense) to report on type mismatches. However, this is no staggering advantage since such faults are usually easy to find, especially if the programmer adopts some convention in his mnemonics to identify types which are conceptually different to him. Even using a language that has types, the programmer may still have to group under one type, say pointer, types that for him are different, such as tables, lists and character strings. Types also allow mixed mode expressions, which are marginally useful, and the repeated use of the same symbol to indicate different operations; for example, $+$, $-$, $*$, $/$ can be used for integer or real arithmetic. Without types different operators could be used, e.g. $+$, $-$, $*$, $/$ for integer arithmetic and £$+$, £$-$, £$*$, £$/$ for real arithmetic.

Machine dependence
Machine independent programming is to be applauded, but it must be recognized that there are times, even if very few, when machine dependent programming is desirable. For example, when very high efficiency is essential or intimate control is required over the machine, such as in the control of peripherals or loading of machine registers. Many operations in the language can be machine independent. Nested arithmetic and logical expressions, IF, FOR, WHILE, UNTIL, UNLESS statements, assignment statements and GO TO statements are examples. One way to provide machine dependence is to make assembly language statements valid statements of the language itself and able to refer to the same variables as in the high level statements. Special statements could be added to the language to make the frequently used assembly language statements somewhat easier to use, but this could also be achieved by the use of a macro generator. Advantages of the assembly language approach are that all possible assembly instructions are included, it is very easy to recognize the machine dependent parts on a print-out (important when transferring to a different machine), and it provides the most machine independent way of compiling a machine dependent language! If the compiler produces assembly language which is then passed through a standard assembler on a machine, then the compiler need only copy the assembly language statements while compiling the high level statements into assembly language. Conceivably a language could be designed with a machine independent part plus assembly language. A machine independent compiler could be written that would have to have its code generator changed when transferring from machine to machine (like any other compiler) but in addition would only have to be able to recognize the machine language statements of the particular machine so as to copy them, since they would require no further processing by the compiler. Users wanting to transfer programs from machine to machine could write solely in the machine independent part of the language, at the cost of efficiency, if they wished to minimize reprogramming.

It is highly convenient to be able to refer directly to machine registers in expressions as in SAL and PL360. This would give more, but not insurmountable, trouble when transferring the compiler, or a program from machine to machine.

No run-time system
The language must have no run-time system of any kind. That is, nothing should be loaded along with the program "behind the user's back", such as an input/output package, or run-time routines to operate stacks or dynamic use of working space. In this sense it is like a conventional assembly language. This requirement allows it to be used to write any type of system, leaving the programmer quite free to control everything loaded into the core along with his system program.

The consequence of a statement
The consequence of each statement should be clear to the programmer. Hidden mechanisms should not be brought into play without his knowledge. Apparently there are statements in EPL which look simple and inoffensive on paper (e.g. for character manipulation) which compile to lengthy code and run incredibly slowly. It is advantageous to have the language simple enough so that programmers may, if they wish, even be aware of the code that the statement compiles into.

Ability to run together programs written in different languages
Despite many attempts, no programming language has yet been devised which is suitable for all programming tasks. Apart from this, the more comprehensive a language becomes the more unwieldly the compiler and system that go along with it tend to become also. Different languages may be most suitable for different parts of a single system. FORTRAN is unsuitable for writing a graphics package but a FORTRAN user may want to use such a package written in another language. Programs must, therefore, run within some mixed language system where programs written in separate languages may be compiled separately but loaded and run together. Many such systems exist but often the methods used in inter-language communication, which are a function of the loading system as well as the languages, are limited to the FORTRAN requirement. This provides one way of calling procedures and passing arguments, plus communication via COMMON. As a result of these restrictions, some languages, notably ALGOL, are not included in a mixed language system. The same loader, however, is sometimes used to load into core the compiled code of these languages and of languages within such a mixed language system. A system language program must have the same freedom as an assembly language program to communicate with programs written in any language that may be loaded into core with it by the same loader. Desirable facilities are: COMMON, global variables (association by name rather than order as in COMMON), multiple entry points to separately compiled "hunks" of program and the ability to call procedures and pick up arguments from procedure calls, both written in any language within the mixed language system.

Input/output
Input/output operations are most easily provided by sub-routines.

Summary
In summary, the language should be simple enough to permit efficient compilation of efficient code. It must provide the programmer with a

comprehensive set of constructions to perform the most frequently required computing operations. This should be as machine independent as possible, chosen so that it can be compiled efficiently on the majority of machines. Any construction that, due to particular machine hardware, cannot be compiled efficiently should be brought to the programmer's attention in the documentation for that implementation. Further, the programmer should be able to include assembly language orders as a natural part of the language and be able to communicate with program statements in other languages. Based on existing experience, an estimate of the effort required to implement a system writing language on any machine is of the order of one first class man for one year (SAL took a man-year, PL360 rather less I believe).

References

1. **Richards, M.** BCPL: A tool for compiler writing and system programming, *Proc. SJCC*, AFIPS, 1969, p. 557.
2. **Hay, R.** and **Rulifson, J. N.** MOL940: Preliminary specification for an ALGOL like machine oriented language for the SDS940, *Interim Tech. Report* **2,** Project 5890, Stanford Research Institute, March 1968.
3. **Wirth, N.** PL/360 A programming language for the 360 computer, *JACM* **15,** No. 1. January 1968.
4. **Lang, C. A.** SAL—Systems assembly language, *Proc. SJCC,* AFIPS, 1969, p. 543.
5. **Corbato, F. J.** PL/1 as a tool for system programming, *Datamation* **15,** No. 5, May 1969.

7.9 UNIVAC 1108 instrumentation

by

J. M. MacGowan, Jr.

Introduction

For a number of years the 1108 project has been interested in the development of techniques to observe closely the operation of 1108 processing systems. Insufficient information is available on precisely how an 1108 is used. The frequency of instruction usage, the sequence of events in operation and the balance between input/output and processing are all areas of interest in examining current system performance. That the 1108 can provide correct answers is insufficient. We are vitally concerned with the manner in which it goes about developing these answers.

Simulation is an important tool in the implementation of complex systems. But the observation and measurement of system performance is equally valuable. Techniques of evaluation for finding system deficiencies are as important as the tools used to construct the system. The interaction of thousands of decisions in a product as complex as the 1108 operating system are extremely difficult to simulate accurately and simply. It is equally difficult to visualize the net result of operation of many small components, even though the logic of each component is well understood.

We are aware of many prior attempts by others to instrument their systems in order to gain a more thorough understanding of their operation.

Analog devices have been used to meter the use of various system components. The rough percentage of tape channel utilization would be an example of the output derived. Others, with special hardware devices, have recorded partial samples of the instruction execution sequence. One device wrote the data directly on to magnetic tape. The relative speed of the tape was so slow however that only a small fraction of the data points could be recorded.

A number of papers have appeared lately which use a real time clock interrupt to interrupt the instruction execution sequence frequently and log the point at which execution was occurring. Again, only a statistical sampling of what that machine is doing is possible. Particularly, software instrumentations contribute to system overhead in almost direct proportion to the quantity of data captured. Any significant interference with the process observed can distort this process so severely as to make the data captured unusable.

We have experimented with the insertion of counters in our Executive to record the frequency of key events. This recording is very limited and does not relate the time sequence in which the events occurred. To limit the overhead of the software instrumentation a minimum number of counting sequences can be inserted. You must predict the desired information, insert the counter by hand and go through an iterative process until the proper data has been recorded.

We once instrumented the routine which controls all data space allocation in the Executive in order to develop a better understanding of the requests and releases of buffer space. To protect the timing relationships within the system, one entire tape channel was dedicated to recording the output. While we were successful in recording the sequence of buffer requests and releases, the information gathered presented no relationship with the other components of the system. The tape channel was able to record only this one small set of events.

Instrumentation system description
The instrumentation approach described in this paper makes use of data collection hardware and software to monitor activity in one processor for presentation to another processor for recording. Neither the insertion of monitoring hardware nor the operation of the collection software in any way affect the operation of the monitored system. Therefore, data received is an exact record of system operation. An absolute requirement for the instrument was that there be no impact whatsoever on the system being observed. The operating system must be unaware that it is being watched.

The system consists of three basic parts:
1 A hardware monitor to gather data from a monitored processor and to present that data to an I/O channel of the recording processor. The data gathered consists of absolute addresses to which jumps are made, time base information, information on the state of the monitored processor, and loop summaries.
2 Data collection software used by the recording processor to gather data from the monitor, to temporarily store that data on drum, and to prepare tape output for data reduction.
3 Data reduction software to analyze the collected data.

Monitor logic
The monitor logic consists of five basic sections:
1 Logic to detect the execution of jump instructions within the monitored processor and to capture P-register values relating to those jumps.

2 Registers to provide a buffered data path from the monitored processor to the recording processor.
3 A free running time base with a 0.5 μsec period to provide time information relating to jump occurrences.
4 Jump loop detecting and counting logic.
5 Control logic to sequence data flow through the monitor.

Monitor hardware
The monitor device is built of a logic family compatible with the monitored processor and is mounted on a card rack inside the monitored processor. Power and clock are obtained from the monitored processor. Connection to the recording processor is via the input cable of a standard I/O interface. The figure shows the monitor installed in a partitioned multiprocessor system. This hardware is applicable to other processors using the same logic family after appropriate changes in the monitor logic, to detect jump executions and sampling of the P-register and processor state information, have been made.

Monitor operation
The monitor creates a data word each time a jump instruction is executed in the monitored processor and when certain time and jump loop conditions occur. At the time of jump execution the absolute value of the jump address is extracted from the processor and inserted into the first of a series of buffer registers in the monitor; the time and jump loop conditions are described below. The various fields of the data word are as follows:

S (bits 0-17): Contains an 18-bit absolute P-value of the address to which a jump is made, or a 9-bit value in bits 0-8 defining the number of times a single loop was executed, where a simple loop is defined to be two successive jumps to the same absolute P-value.

T (bits 18-26): A time value defining a relative time at which the data word was created. This time is derived from a free running time base in the monitor which is incremented by one every 0.5 μsec. A maximum time of 256 μsec can be defined by the T field.

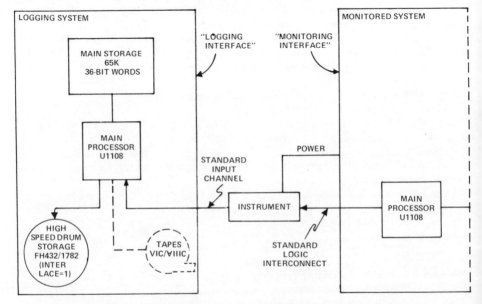

Figure 1. Instrumented system configuration, functional block diagram

F (bits 27-29): Bit 27 defines the content of the S field: Bit 27=0 defines S to be an 18-bit absolute P-value, bit 27=1 defines S to be a 9-bit loop count. A data word having bit 27=1 is defined as a loop *summary word*. Bit 28=1 defines a *timer overflow* condition, which marks a 256 μsec time interval. Bit 29=1 defines a *buffer overflow* which implies that the monitored processor and the monitor are generating data words at a rate faster than the recording processor can accept words; a data word with bit 29=1 represents invalid data.

M (bits 32-35): These represent the state of various bits of the processor state register (in the monitored processor) at the time of a jump execution.

Loop summarization

Since the data rate produced by jumps in "typical" coding is of the order of a·jump every 5 μsec, the monitor contains hardware to perform limited "on the fly" data reduction. This reduction is done by detection of simple loops (i.e., two successive equal P-values). Only two data words are sent to the recording processor to describe a loop. The first word defines the first loop jump; the second word defines the number of times through the loop and the time of the second loop jump. Therefore, the length of loop and the total time in a loop can be calculated.

Data collection

Collection of data words from the monitor is done on a system which is independent of the monitored system. This recording system may be a physically separate system or a portion of a partitioned multiprocessor system. It is necessary that the core storage and drums used are private to the recording processor so that the recording activity does not affect operation of the monitored system. Collected data is transferred to drum via two large core storage buffer areas in the recording processor. The length of monitoring period is a function of the number of drums available to the recording system. The collection software allows selection of recycling a drum area or transferring from drum to tape at the completion of filling a drum. The recycling mode permits maintaining a recent history prior to some stop point.

Data reduction

The purpose of the instrument discussed in the first part of this paper is to approach the problem of inefficiencies in a complex data processing system by concentrating on a narrow slice of the problem; namely, inefficiencies in the structure and utilization of software, and in particular, the Operating System. Owing to the nature of the data collected (i.e., this instrument captures a dynamic picture of a non-degraded Operating System), the information which is obtained on the monitored system through data reduction will provide a unique perspective on software performance. In particular, both statistical and graphical results will provide facts whereby software performance can be evaluated by not only *whether* certain specified functions are performed, but also how *efficiently* they are performed. The initial results of data reduction seem to indicate that a step in the right direction has been taken in the development of a capability for identifying and eliminating software inefficiencies.

As dictated by input, a structure is placed on the data in order to organize it into a form more amenable to analysis. This structure consists of matrices of data called sub-divisions, which are defined to be restricted time and/or P-ranges. Generally, only the P-ranges will be restricted and these will be coincidental with known logical sections (e.g., the resident elements of the Executive system). The usefulness of this structure will become apparent when discussing the statistical and graphic-associated printout.

Graphic results

The graphical output simply consists of a plot of P-vs. time-values over any portion of the P and time-ranges monitored. The user is able to obtain both gross and detailed graphs by varying the number of microseconds plotted per inch. The gross plot is adequate for the user familiar with the detail of various activities as these will leave a "signature" through the graphical pattern displayed on the chart. Those areas with which the user is not familiar can be expanded, i.e. a detailed graph with fewer than μsec per inch for the area of interest. Once the user is able to correlate a particular graphical pattern with an activity, there is no further need to examine that area in detail. Also, there is the capability of obtaining a detailed columnar print report which gives the time, the subdivision into which the jump occurred and the relative location of the jump within the subdivision. This print report is then used together with the graph and a listing of the monitored program in order to determine the activities performed. It has been found that graphical patterns are easily correlated with various activities, thus giving a strikingly clear picture of the sequence of events.

This dynamic picture of the monitored system is not only useful to programmers knowledgeable in the activities being monitored, but also has been found to be a valuable training aid for those unfamiliar with the operating system. Flowcharts, manuals, program listings, etc., are static aids which only tend to come alive when verbal descriptions of various activities can be visualized through the graph and by following the dynamic flow of the logic using the detailed print.

Also, it should be noted that this graph and its associated print can be a useful debugging tool. Should a particularly difficult bug exist in the system, then the recording of environmental data just prior to the detection of a system or program failure will provide a high speed trace capability since the instrument will capture an accurate record of the system destroying itself.

Statistical results

The data reduction program also provides the capability of obtaining statistical information on the subdivisions; this consists of such items as percentage of time spent in each subdivision, percentage of time spent in the Executive system mode, number of times the subdivision is entered, etc.

Once system inefficiencies have been removed using information gained from the graphical method described above, then the user may collect statistical summaries for various simple job mixes. Then, when more complex job mixes are introduced, the system can again be instrumented in order to determine what new time distributions have resulted from the more complex mix. It may be found, for example, that use of certain executive elements is highly correlated to the new mix causing them to be executed a disproportionately large percentage of the time, and this would show up in the statistical results of an experiment on the instrumented system. The user would then determine whether inefficiencies had been introduced with the new job mix and, if they had, whether the inefficiencies stem from the method of using the equipment, from software inefficiencies not previously detected or, perhaps, from an inherent system inability to handle the particular mix.

MacGowan's paper continued with a detailed example of this method keyed to samples of extensive graph-plotter output. This is not reproduced here (Eds.)

7.10 Software engineering techniques and operating system design and production

by

R. M. Needham

Operating system production perhaps presents rather a different challenge to the software engineer than do some other forms of the art. Two of the reasons for this are the liability of operating systems to contain unrepeatable faults and the fact that operating systems frequently have to be developed for computers which do not have a very large amount of support software in existence already. For reasons of this sort it is perhaps even more essential than elsewhere to proceed in an orderly and organized manner and to devote substantial amounts of effort to software of a diagnostic or other ancillary nature. This note mentions some points which have occurred to me on this topic, some of them being allusions to things that I feel should be provided or done and some of them mentioning difficulties and unexpected pitfalls.

It is quite essential to equip oneself with adequate mechanized means for handling the source text of one's system. If it is to be a system of any complexity, it will presumably be able to handle its own source text when complete. However it clearly cannot do so before it has been written. One is likely, therefore, to be involved either in using another computer for performing this file maintenance function or in writing a temporary system which will be thrown away when the main system is at a sufficiently advanced stage. However, there is a danger here. It is very awkward if the ways in which one handles the text in the earlier stages are grossly different from the ways in which one handles it later on. This can be extremely hard to avoid; if I am handling the text for a new system on an existing one, it is probably the case that the conventions for such operations on the new system will be different and there will have to be a possibly painful period of turnover and retraining at a nasty time in the middle of the operation. My feeling is that this problem has to be faced and circumvented as best one can.

It is commonplace to realize that earlier decisions in the designs of an operating system are of great importance, because they may very well determine the logical structure of much of what follows and the general shape of interfaces between different parts of the system. One therefore knows that it is necessary to get the early parts right, because if they are subsequently to be changed a very large amount of work may be involved. However, commitment to a particular structure can arise from a rather different source, which is not so obviously connected with the basic system. If one is to preserve sanity and to make any kind of regular progress, there is going to be a need for software aids to the diagnosis of faults in the system under construction. These take a considerable variety of forms; there are routines for permitting on-line inspection and changing of registers from, for example, the operator's console; there are programs that are interposed in the calling sequences of one routine to another to check that things are being done properly; and there are packages designed to facilitate the understanding of core-dumps. It may be worth elaborating on this last. If one is dealing with a flexible operating system for a large machine, it may easily be the case that a particular part of the core store may be used for a large variety of purposes, both system and private, at various times. If there is some obscure crash in the system it is not much good expecting to take an octal dump of ½ million bytes of core and leave one's programmers to thread their way around it. Most system problems leave the core in a fairly respectable state, and it is practicable and almost necessary to equip oneself with a package that knows about the data structure the system uses, knows the values of important parameters in it, and arranges to print out an interpreted map of the core-store when wanted. Now the point I am getting at is that a very considerable and thoroughly justified investment is frequently made in this kind of software, and it must not be overlooked that what may be comparatively minor changes to the structure of the system as a whole can lead to a radical upset in the diagnostic software. Since the function of this software is to be thrown away once it is finished with, one does not wish to become involved in rewriting more often than necessary.

Having alluded to a point about rewriting, it is perhaps not wholly out of place to add a comment on rewriting parts of the system itself. Inevitably this happens; sometimes because a piece of it was written incompetently, sometimes because the specification one expects of a piece has to be so radically revised as the result of experience that nothing short of a rewrite will do. It should be urged, however, that this sort of thing should not be planned for in advance. Experience strongly indicates that putting in pieces of temporary and ill-thought-out software, often written by junior and inexperienced people, in order to have something to plug a gap, is often disastrous. In our own experience whenever we have yielded to the temptation to do something deliberately temporary the results have been bad. Either it never gets replaced at all, or when it does get replaced all kinds of problems arise. A trivial example could be in the case of a routine for organising disc transfers. One may start with a version which does no optimization, and executes the requests in strict order of seniority. A later optimized version may perhaps deviate from strict order of seniority in order to achieve its optimization, and thus expose horrors when it is discovered that other pieces of the system rely on a piece of behaviour which no longer occurs. Notice that it is not in any direct sense a case of getting the interface wrong. The way in which one asked for a disc transfer to be done would be the same in each case, as would be the way one would be informed that it had been done.

Once one has a going system, it is almost certain to get used for holding useful information, even if we are talking about a machine which is dedicated to system development. This point applies with much greater force to special purpose operating systems which are designed to work on a single machine in a single place for a single purpose. It is essential in these circumstances, and very desirable in others, to be able to run one's system in some kind of testing mode in which it is insulated as far as possible from harming valuable information. It can, for example, have special disc areas reserved for the purpose and, when it is loaded, have diagnostic facilities in it that would be uneconomic in a running system. It is important that the switch between a testing version and a running version should be easy, straightforward and automatic, so as to minimize the occasions when something works under testing conditions and not under real ones. Allied to the problem of testing versions is the problem of fallback. It is bound to happen that while the system is being run with a particular version of the system operating in it something will happen that is clearly a bug. It must be possible to fall back to an earlier version with as little fuss and confusion as is achievable or there will be a temptation to rectify the existing version by patching the binary. One of the most important software engineering techniques for operating systems is a negative one: do not patch the binary. In order to achieve this kind of fallback it is necessary to plan at a very earlier stage what one's warm-start mechanism is going to be and to arrange, wherever humanly possible, that successive versions of the system are warm-start compatible. It is an obvious consequence of this that any changes that are made that affect, for example, the format of the data upon which warm-starts are based, have to be planned and executed with extreme care. If this has been done, it is then possible to arrange that, if a system crash occurs, in almost all cases the computer operators can cause diagnostic information to be recorded and fallback to an earlier version in a smooth manner taking, shall we say, less than two minutes without the intervention of any system programmers. The very possibility of doing this makes it much easier to introduce minor modifications.

Early in this note I talked about the necessity of having satisfactory ways for handling the source text of one's operating system. One of the important things about this is to recognize that, very commonly, the same text will be worked on by several people and to arrange one's handling system accordingly. No matter how much one thinks that one's system is divided into pieces, and each piece is only touched by its master, this is not the way things happen. The best technique is certainly one based on storing edits separately from the original document, only making a new version of the original document at fairly rare intervals. It is probably worth going so far as to arrange that whenever a new edit is inserted in the edit document the system automatically appends to it the date, time and name of person involved. If one's system is not capable of doing that automatically, then it should be.

Of these points some, perhaps all, are obvious. It has to be emphsized that they add up to a very considerable amount of planning work and coding work. This work should be done by one's best people, not one's worst people. It is accordingly expensive. It is however about as appropriate for the software engineer to try to by-pass it as it is for the civil engineer to try to avoid expensive heavy earth-moving equipment, relying instead upon armies of men with baskets.

7.11 Software engineering and computer science

by

R. M. Needham and J. D. Aron

Computer science aims at defining general principles underlying the design and application of software systems. It regards elegance and consistency highly, and tends to ignore small and awkward corners in its subject matter. Thus the computer scientist is tempted to analyze and treat that fraction of his problem that is amenable—rather in the same way that the differential equation expert treats the vanishing subset of equations that are analytically soluble.

The software engineer wants to make something which works; where working includes satisfying commitments of function, cost, delivery and robustness. Elegance and consistency come a bad second. It must be easy to change the system in ways that are not predictable or even reasonable—e.g. in response to management directives. At present theorists cannot keep up with this kind of thing, any more than they can with the sheer size and complexity of large software systems.

A theory must be independent of implementation. In practice large systems implementation is influenced by many factors: available personnel, management structure, and so on. If theoretical work cannot adapt to this it can at best do no more than give helpful hints, while at worst it is irrelevant or unpractical.

Much theoretical work appears to be invalid because it ignores parameters that exist in practice. Thus a system that depends on failure-free operation is unrealistic. In the sense that medical diagnosis is empirical rather than scientific—because the observable parameters are an insufficient subset of the operable parameters—so will computer science be empirical until better methods are available for describing the structure and behaviour of actual systems.

Theoretical work becomes impractical when it ascribes (mathematically) analytical behaviour to software—or at least to the software design, development and test processes. Present day software is the sum of individual activities operating in discrete and usually asynchronous time steps with a presumed common goal. The time steps depend on such factors as individual productivity, computer availability, predecessor activities, conflicting demands or resources, and quality of task specification. The common goal is "presumed" because semantics cause individuals to interpret the goal and its constituent tasks according to their own backgrounds. To contribute further to the random discrete behaviour of the implementation process (looked on as a system) is the necessary iterative nature of the goal itself.

Software engineering managers learn how to make decisions under conditions of uncertainty. Where possible, they reduce the uncertainty by applying theory or standards. In no case do they assume that a course of action will go perfectly and not require redirection. Theorists have not learned to cope with this randomly discrete set of events in an uncertain environment. Therefore, their impact on the engineers is minimal.

If theorists could demonstrate the application-independent value of their conclusions and could guarantee that they would work reliably on another job, engineers might overcome their conservative attitude toward new techniques and try them out. Unfortunately, an adequate demonstration requires two or more different large-scale implementations. This is usually beyond the scope of the theorists' interests or resources.

Pending major theoretical advances, software engineering should concentrate on the development of, and the exchange of experience about, practical tools such as:

    diagnostic aids
    protected testing facilities
    automatic or semi-automatic fallback
    aids to continuity during development,
    etc.

We believe that there is much to be gained by discussion and development in these areas.

7.12 Compiler writing techniques and problems

by

H. Schorr

It has been stated that Translator Writing Systems (TWS) represent the most serious attempt yet to automate software production. It might be better restated that TWS techniques have introduced formal or mathematical techniques into one phase of the compiling process; it is not clear that they have really addressed the engineering aspects of that phase. This paper will try to fit TWS into the context of other methods for writing compilers, examine some of the shortcomings of each method and point out some of the areas that need research; examples will be taken from some industrial compilers.

Categories of compiler engineering techniques

Ad hoc techniques
Compilers written in machine language can be said to represent the use of *ad hoc* techniques. However, the understanding of the compiling process has reached the stage where the structures of most compilers are as shown in Figure 1; the standard phases being: statement recognition, storage allocation, optimization, code generation and output editing.

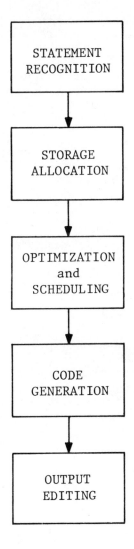

Figure 1. Phases of a compiler

Statement recognition: The first phase may consist of a prescan (to determine the statement type in FORTRAN, for example) and a parsing of the input string. A symbol table is developed during the parsing process along the way thereby reducing the size of the input string and determining the identifiers, constants, reserved words, etc. The output is usually in Polish form.

Storage allocation: This phase allocates storage for variables, arrays, structures, format lists, parameter lists, etc.

Optimization and scheduling: The basic machine independent optimizations most usually employed are the elimination of common sub expressions, removal of code from loops, reduction in strength (for example: conversion of array addressing to index register incrementation), etc. (see *Reference* 3). Scheduling refers to the machine dependent optimizations such as general and arithmetic register allocation and, in look-ahead type machines, the scheduling of machine operations to minimize the execution time of the statement or loop (see *Reference* 2). This phase is the one most commonly eliminated or combined within other phases.

Code generation: This phase generates relocatable machine code from the internal form using the dictionary. Also, many object code optimizations that essentially are locally applicable coding tricks are carried out here, for example: replacing a multiply by a power of two by a shift.

Output editing: This phase produces the actual decks and listing and may carry out the assembly of the code if this has not been done in the previous phase.

Comments: The IBM FORTRAN G and FORTRAN H compilers fit pretty well into the above categorization. The FORTRAN E compiler, which operates in only 15K bytes of core, has many more phases (12 plus 3 interludes) and is less coherently organized. The COBOL F compiler loosely fits the categorization for each COBOL language division but must also handle the interaction between the divisions.

Table driven techniques
Table driven techniques included in this broad category are all of the techniques reviewed by Feldman and Gries (see *Reference* 1). Broadly speaking, some formal description of the language to be compiled with perhaps the semantics of each production, usually in table form, serve as one input to the compiler. The compiler uses this input to parse the source statements. The main advantage of this approach is that the tables can be changed to those for another language; these tables are usually highly stylized and rewriting them requires much less work than the rewriting of an entire compiler. Such compilers therefore can be looked upon as the framework or *scaffolding* for the production of a processor for any particular language. Table driven compilers essentially use the tables in an interpretive way, i.e., scanning the source and matching it with productions in the tables. In industrial compilers these techniques have been employed mostly in the front end scan or parsing phases.

Compiler writing machine
This set of techniques consists of defining a set of macros or functions in which the compiler is to be written, instead of being written in instructions.

This presumably turns a general purpose computer into a computer which is better designed to write compilers for, i.e., a compiler writing machine. Included in the above are compiler writing computers whose machine language is one of the common higher level languages such as NELIAC, FORTRAN, etc. A compiler written in one of the latter languages is usually compiled so that the compiler writing oriented language is turned into true machine language. Various forms of this step are usually called bootstrapping. Examples include the NELIAC compilers and the IBM FORTRAN H compiler. In addition to the above a compiler writing language can be interpreted, two examples of this are the IBM FORTRAN G and FORTRAN D compilers. The interpretive method has the advantage of taking very little memory space and thus can be profitably employed when space is an important consideration or when an all in core compiler is desired. Some speed is lost but may be made up by not having the I/O delays while loading various phases. Transferability is enhanced because primarily only the interpreter (which is relatively small) has to be rewritten for a new machine.

Large primitives
Large primitives consisting of phases of an old compiler can be used to speed the production of a new compiler. That is, parts of an old compiler are borrowed, in toto, to make a new compiler. On an even richer primitive level an existing compiler can be re-interfaced with a new operating system. Within IBM both of these techniques have been employed and their use will probably increase as more and more types of compatibility are demanded by the users.

Another proposed method of reusing components is by having a well defined language (which may include symbol tables and pointers) for expressing the input to each of the well-defined phases of Figure 1. In this manner, for a given size compiler a new language can be added by changing only the syntax and probably storage allocation phases.

Problems in compiler design
The discussion on techniques of writing compilers has glossed over the difficult problems in writing a compiler. Some of the problems such as those encountered in the statement recognition phase have been subjected to considerable study and the application of mathematical or formal methods. It is this area that the bulk of the work of TWS is applicable, but unfortunately seems to account for between only 5 per cent and 10 per cent of the code; the original FORTRAN compiler using inefficient methods also did not exceed this bound. Other areas that might profitably be subjected to more formal study are optimization, error diagnostics, debugging, the non-regularity of languages, data structures,* code generation and register allocation. In addition to those features of compiler design that may be

---

*The effect of data structures on language processors can be dramatic. We quote from an unpublished memorandum by A. Opler. "The variability of permitted data types and data structures in a language has a dramatic effect on industrial compiler design and performance. FORTRAN I and II with only *two* data types and a simple data structure were fortuitous starting points in compiler development. As the complexity of data types and structures increase, the compiler complexity soars. The problems occur in (i) parsing and representing these data structures, (ii) generating and optimizing procedural code for their manipulation and (iii) more complex interaction with whatever part of the environment handles external data and backing storage. JOVIAL, COBOL and PL/1 are in a 'different ball-park' because of their data description capabilities."

amenable to more formal treatment there are many software engineering questions that arise for the compiler itself and the object code modules, i.e., at compile time and run time. These are mainly questions of resource allocation, interface with the operating system, maintenance and documentation and libraries.

Resource allocation
The compiler usually must be designed to utilize only a portion of the resources that are available in a system. A prime constraint is the amount of core in which the compiler itself must operate. This means that spill and overlay techniques must be developed. For example: IBM FORTRAN H while 403K bytes long executes out of 89K bytes; the overlay structure is shown in Figure 2. Choice of residence device and I/O techniques also radically affect performance. The I/O requirements for the FORTRAN H compiler aside from overlays are shown in Figure 3.

Within the compiler itself the choice of table structure and data representation radically affects the size of the compiler and the size of program that can be compiled. For example, in the IBM FORTRAN E compiler if the dictionary and the overflow table (which contains all dimension and subscript information) overlap (each one being built from one end of storage towards the middle) no new entries are made.

Operating system interface
Interfacing the compiler and the load modules produced by the compiler is a nontrivial task. Optimal use of the operating system and the translation of language features into standard operating system procedures is required. The IBM FORTRAN H compiler has an 18.6K byte main segment which is the system director; it initializes the compiler, loads compiler phases, allocates storage, processes I/O requests from the phases, generates initialization code and deletes and terminates compilation. Similar phases exist in the other IBM compilers.

Similar interfacing exists at run time and is handled by library subroutines. An example for the IBM FORTRAN H compiler is shown in Figure 4 for an I/O request.

Maintenance and documentation
Care must be given to the design of the compiler to permit debugging and maintenance. This includes the design of good interfaces which minimize the amount of information to be passed but not necessarily cost. Several compilers include tools for debugging the compiler itself. Documentation is necessary to aid in maintenance since the latter may often equal the cost of developing the compiler in the first place. The diagnostic system into which the compiler is embedded plays a crucial role in debugging object modules.

Subroutine libraries
The design of a subroutine library is usually required for a commercial compiler. The IBM FORTRAN H has the following object time library subprograms:

IHCFCOMH (object time I/O source statement processor)
IHCFIOSH (object time sequential access I/O data management interface).
IHCNAMEL (object time namelist routines).
IHCDIOSE (object time direct access I/O data management interface).
IHCIBERH (object time source statement error processor).
IHCFCVTH (object time conversion routine).

IHCTRCH (object time terminal error message and diagnostic traceback routine).

IHCFINTH (object time program interrupt processor).

IHCERRM (object time error message processor. The module monitors all execution time errors).

IHCADJST (object time boundary adjustment routine).

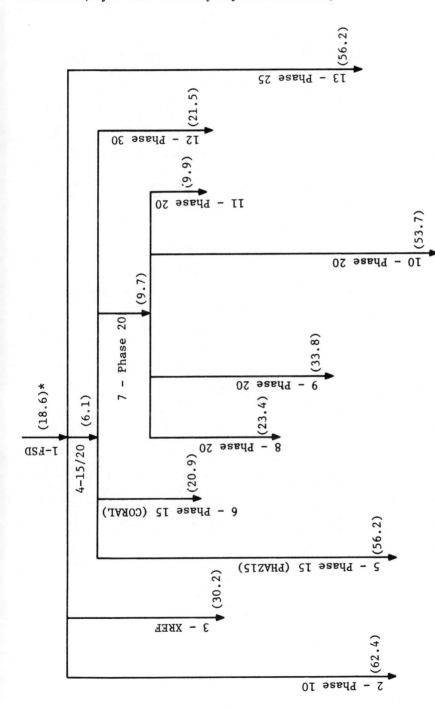

Figure 2. IBM FORTRAN H compiler. Overlay structure

* The number in parentheses times 1,000 equals the approximate segment length.

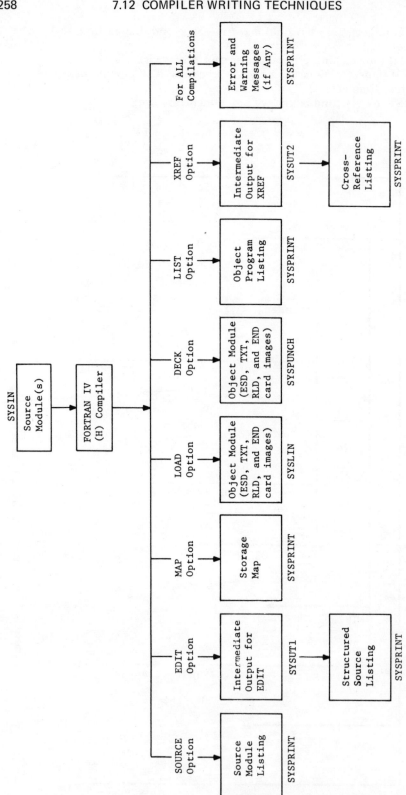

Figure 3. IBM FORTRAN H compiler. Input/output data flow

Most of these subroutines are also available in another version which provides an extended error message facility. In addition, a new function library both single and double precision, must be provided for a new machine.

Shortcomings of techniques

Ad hoc techniques
These techniques fail in their ability to accept language changes easily and in the lack of a set of consistent design principles. The cost and schedule delays result from this.

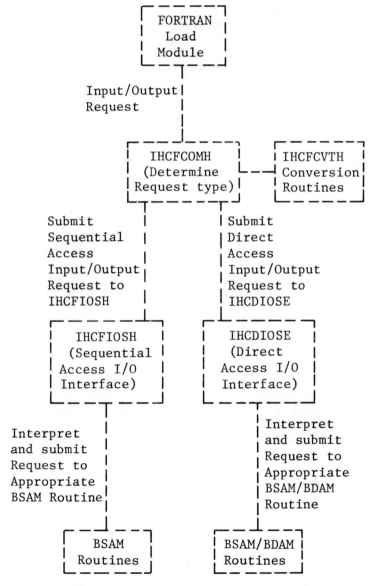

Figure 4. IBM FORTRAN H compiler. Object time library subroutines for input/output data management interfaces

Table driven techniques
Papers on these techniques, and many of the TWS compilers written neglect and do not clarify any of the engineering considerations; very little is said or done about the problems faced in the last four phases of the usual *ad hoc* compiler. A major difficulty usually encountered with these techniques is in producing good object code and error diagnostics. Compiler-compilers face the difficulty of interfacing with new operating systems when the compiler is produced for another machine. Space requirements may also often be larger than those of hand coded compilers.

Compiler writing machines
The interpretive techniques seem to run into difficulty in providing extensive optimization. Most higher level language compilers are bulky and the common languages are not particularly well suited (because of their data structures) for writing compilers.

Large primitives
Definition of good interface languages to each phase of a compiler may offer the best hope of cutting down the cost of compiler production. If a sound structure can be found then improvements can be continuously made to it and the programming debugged; transferability would be the next consideration.

Conclusions
Compiler designers usually have to meet very rigorous objectives: minimize space, high compilation speed, rapid implementation, low cost, low maintenance costs, good object code, good use of the operating system, good diagnostics and listings, etc. The problem of logistics or resource allocation dominates the design. The challenge is somehow to obtain an optimum and none of the present methods help the designer or guide him in achieving it. For example, more should be known about the design of compilers to operate in a very small memory. COBOL and PL/1 compilers need study. While many of the above problems are common to all of good programming, perhaps starting from the better understood structure of compilers would allow gaining further insight into their solution.

Much research remains to be done and very little of it has been started.

References

1. **Feldman, J.** and **Gries, D.** Translator writing systems. *Comm. ACM* **11**, February 1968, pp. 77-113.
2. **Allard, R. W., Wolf, K. A.,** and **Zemlin, R. A.** Some effects of the 6600 computer on language structures. *Comm. ACM* **7**, February 1964, pp. 112-119.
3. **Allen, F. E.** Program optimization. *Annual Review in Automatic Programming*, 1968.

7.13 Analyzing large-scale system development

by

Jules I. Schwartz

The era of large-scale programs began in the mid 1950's with the development of the SAGE system. Since that time, probably of the order of 100 such systems have been built. A significant percentage of these systems have been sponsored by military agencies but in recent years civilian installations have produced such efforts as airline reservations' systems, large-scale time-sharing executives and major business management systems. In Steel (see *Reference* 21), very large programs are defined as those that require "many times the available primary storage" for code and data and require "more than ten coders" for implementations. These two characteristics are true for all large-scale system efforts, although the number of people involved in most are considerably more than ten. Even in this case, however, the fact that ten "coders" are specified begins to demonstrate the complexities of such efforts. In addition to the team of coders some management personnel must be present; and designers, documenters, testers and other support personnel are required. The implementation of these systems is an expensive, difficult undertaking and the history of many of them has demonstrated that there is by no means a complete understanding of the methods and technology necessary to accomplish successfully the aims of these systems.

The stages necessary to implement such systems include definition, design at many levels, production, testing, operation and evaluation. These stages interact and are subject to a substantial number of feedback loops. The organization necessary to carry out such an effort is large and complex, and must contain people with a variety of skills. In analyzing the problems in producing such systems, one could look at any of these phases, and in fact the original intent of this paper was to discuss the subjects of testing and evaluating these systems.

Although recognised to be one of the major problems in data processing, the subject of testing and evaluation is probably one of the least discussed subjects in the literature. It is recognized that close to 50 per cent or more of the production of large systems is devoted to the period of testing. It has also been noted that little, if any, formalization of the process has been developed; and for a variety of reasons, much of the experience has not been described in writing. One reason for this is that some techniques are considered proprietary (although perhaps "embarrassing" is a more likely descriptive term). Also, much of what does exist is imprecise enough to defy formal description.

The author has been involved in the design and checkout of a number of large-scale programming systems. From these experiences, it seems as though one could state principles and procedures which others should follow in the checkout of large-scale systems. Unfortunately, this is not easy to do. The author has the distinct feeling that, to a large extent, his and other experiences were the result of system development done in a style rather like a random walk. Certain techniques are recognized to be of value for producing large-scale systems; some of these are referenced in the following. Other techniques are extremely difficult to define. They lack algorithmic interpretation and no methodology really exists.

One of the difficulties in synthesizing available information is that the subject "testing and evaluation" actually covers a wide range. First of all, there is the actual checkout of systems; this includes the checkout of the lowest level of programs through operational testing. During this period, one is trying to verify whether the system is performing in conformity with existing specifications. Then there is the subject of relative testing—that is, can a function be performed better given different hardware or different programming? Included in this area is the subject of bench-mark testing, on which there is a relatively large set of references (2, 3, 4, 6, 9, 11, 12, 13, 22, for example). These articles on bench marking define techniques that will verify or measure the relative throughput, turnround time or efficiency of one system versus another. The normal problem in large-scale system testing is quite different. In this case, one is given a particular configuration and a major mission to perform. Implementing such a system is normally a major task, and the ability to compare its results with another system is virtually absent.

A third area of evaluation has recently been receiving more attention. This includes the subject of measuring user interest and performance on a particular system. To a large extent the increasing interest in this subject has come about because of the rising interest in timesharing and interactive computing over the last few years. For some reason, prior to on-line or interactive computing, very little concern was given to the user and how he performs with or benefits from various aspects of the system with which he operates. However, with the influx of timesharing systems, a great number of questions have been asked concerning the value of these systems versus the more traditional techniques. Consequently, there have been a number of experiments run to compare the value of interactive and non-interactive computing (see *Reference* 18).

After some contemplation, it appeared that divorcing the testing from the remainder of the system development task would not be appropriate. New ideas devoted to this area alone are not worth a complete paper at this point, at least with the author's current set of ideas. The entire system development cycle is, or should be, thoroughly integrated. Testing should be a consideration through the entire development. The major problem is the total effort on these systems, of which testing is one part. Many ingredients contribute to the ultimate success or failure of a large-scale system. It seems then that a discussion of these factors would be of more value than a treatise on testing alone. Thus this discussion will proceed on the basis that overall system evolution is the major problem, with testing as one of the major factors.

Experiences with large-scale systems

Producing a large-scale system is a massive undertaking. Figures 1 and 2 show graphically the typical steps necessary in just the test process for these systems. These Figures (originally published elsewhere*) are discussed in Sackman (see *Reference* 17) in a chapter on the experimental method in man-machine systems. Sackman points out that, throughout the entire system development process, there has been little if any methodology developed. In the area of testing the people involved have had little experience in the use of experimental design and analysis and, consequently, few if any statistically valid attempts at testing large-scale systems are made.

Another description of the system development process is given by Hosier (see *Reference* 10). Figure 3 is from Hosier and graphically illustrates the complexity of a system development task. Hosier's article, although published in 1965, gives a thorough description of the system development process and difficulties. Among other things, Hosier discusses at some length the need for both stereotyped samples and random tests generated by statistically valid means. Hosier also makes some observations on the administrative problems involved in system development and testing. He points out that the ones who have the primary responsibility for accounting for the status of the schedule are the non-programmers, who have "little understanding and less sympathy" for problems in meeting schedules. Their probable attitude towards slippages may be reflected by threats and lectures, rather than by any attempt to see if the schedule, original program design, table design or other factor is at fault. Meanwhile, of course, programmers are in their own world, reluctant to "stop tinkering" (Hosier) with their product. Somebody must be able to distinguish the problems associated with the programmer, design, hardware or administrative factors.

There is a considerable body of reference material on techniques for programming and debugging. Whether the technique utilizes CRT, on-line typewriter, memory dump, trace or other device, numerous authors have been able to communicate ideas in this area (*References* 5 and 7 are two discussions). However, these tend to be largely in the area of individual program production. Rather little literature exists on the checkout of assemblages of components. Even in the area of individual checkout, many weaknesses are recognized. It appears that as the hardware and

---

*Willmorth, N. E. System Programming Management, TM-(L)-2222, System Development Corp., Santa Monica, Calif., 1965.

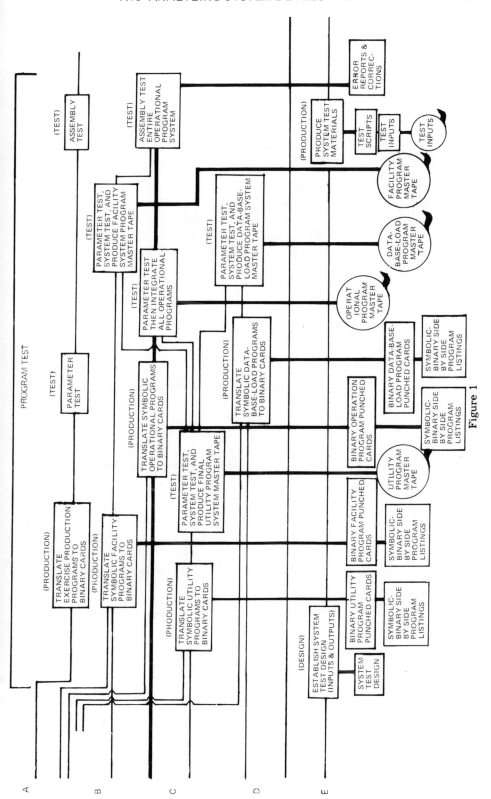

Figure 1

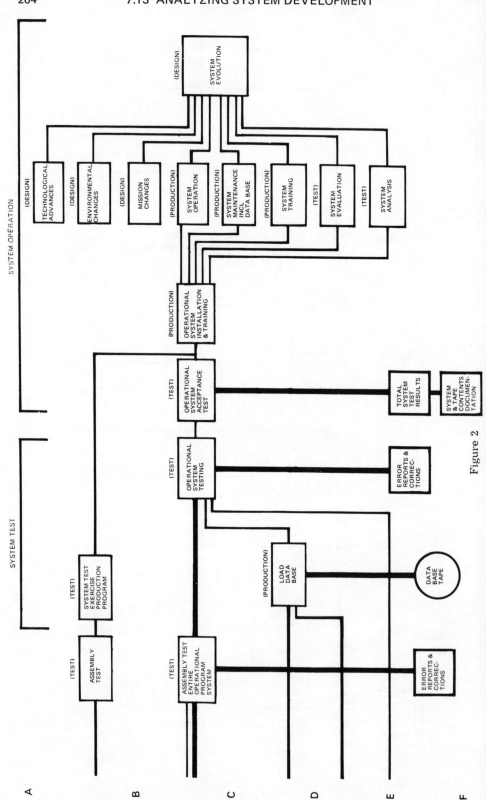

Figure 2

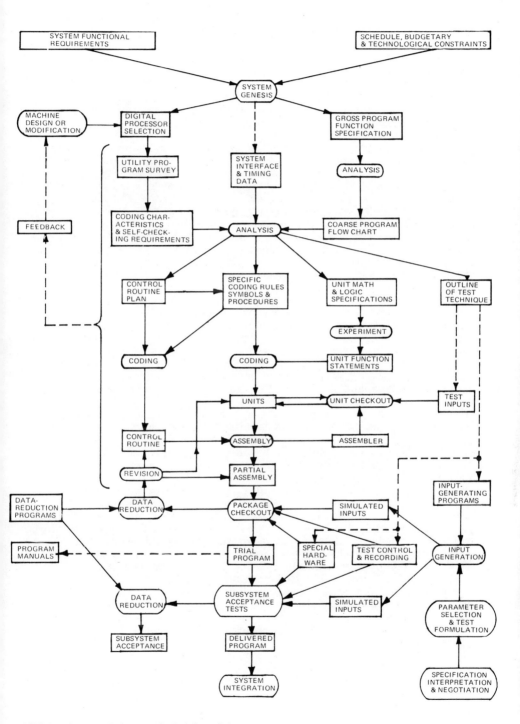

NOTE: Only Major Lines of Influence and Feedback Shown. Broken
      Lines Show Omission of Contributary Processes.

Figure 3

programming systems have improved, we have about stayed even. That is, it takes about as long to check out programs as in the past, although the programs are now much bigger and more complex. Another interesting and perhaps startling possibility is mentioned in a report by Sackman and Grant (see *Reference* 19). They describe an experiment comparing debugging in the interactive and off-line environments. They found that, in these tests, the difference between the two environments was approximately a factor of 2, while the noticeable difference in programmers who participated in the experiment seemed to range up to more than a factor of 20! This set of subjects was taken from what was presumed to be a fairly homogeneous, and skilled, organization.

Another experience was reported on informally which further illustrates the confounding nature of these systems. One of the managers of the SAGE program development effort was once asked to recount the experience with the development of that system. He described the history that led to this being one of the largest programming efforts of all time. The early effort was based on experience with a prototype system at MIT. Based on this effort, the SAGE program should have required a reasonable number of people and time. But it soon became apparent that the actual system required substantially—that is, orders of magnitude—more effort than the prototype. Documenters, testers, operational programmers, utility programmers, designers, table experts and interface specialists were needed. All of these required managers at a variety of levels. The managers required help of both administrative and technical nature. As schedules tended to slip, or difficulties were recognized, more people were hired. This, of course, required more management and communication. This cycle continued for several years until many hundreds of people were involved in the programming effort. The program, although considered by most people to be a landmark as well as one of the relatively few successes in large-scale system programming, was delivered later than originally planned and with somewhat less capability than that originally desired. When asked what he would do differently if he had to do a system like this again, the manager, after some period of reflection, said he would hire twelve good people to do the whole job. Outside of that, he could not think of much he would have done differently.

Another large-scale system was produced using much the same concept as SAGE: a massive effort mounted rapidly and requiring a high degree of organization and management talent. This system received considerable publicity when a high-ranking dignitary made the observation that the development of this system cost $35 an instruction. This amount was presumably high or else, unfortunately for the system's producers, this was the first time anybody ever labelled a system's cost in this way. It might be pointed out, however, that in this case probably several hundred man-years were spent on the system before the operational programs were begun. That is, it required considerable time to reach an understanding of what the system was supposed to do, after work on it was begun.

Although the field of large-scale system programming is barely fifteen years old, there are many stories like the preceding. Few systems have been complete successes in that they were on time, within the original budget estimates and contained all the expected capabilities on the originally planned equipment. The reasons for this are many but it is clear that one factor is paramount. This factor is people. Although the manager of the SAGE effort who stated that he would like to do the job with a dozen people was probably exaggerating, he was expressing a frustration felt by all managers engaged in these efforts.

The key element

A large-scale system effort requires a substantial number of people. Some of the things we know about these people are:

1 They don't know the complete operational problem.
2 They communicate badly.

3 Within a group of programmers, there may be an order of magnitude difference in capability.

4 Good programmers are creative. They are creative in situations that may not require creativity.

5 Non-programmers involved in these systems can't understand programmers. Put in a position of responsibility, however, this does not normally restrain them from hiring more.

6 It is extremely difficult to find out from people how a job is really progressing. Most programmers are optimistic by nature. Most managers are gullible. Our methods of prediction are incredibly bad.

7 The people involved in large-scale system testing are lacking in knowledge of methodology which enables them to state with confidence that a system is checked out.

8 No one person understands the whole system or its status.

The problems and some recommendations

One can conclude, then, that the large-scale system development process is complex, expensive and uncertain to a significant degree because large groups of people are utilized who are either not equipped to do their job or who may be doing the wrong job.

Normally, of course, one doesn't recognize the difficulties of a system's development until the testing phase. Consequently, the people involved in this area bear the wrath of those who, until that time, assumed things were going well. In fact, the situation might have deteriorated quite badly by the time it got to the testing stage. It seems clear, however, that many of the difficulties are recognizable and perhaps some effort can improve the situation.

In the preceding, some points were made concerning the people involved in producing these systems. Since people are the major resource and problem in the production of these large systems, a more detailed discussion of these points should be developed.

People don't understand the complete operational problem

In the early stages of the development of these systems, it is sometimes unclear that even the "customer" knows what he really wants. Of course, some subset of the customer group might have most of the information but the communication of these ideas is not easy. However, many venture into these systems quite unafraid, willing to figure it out after the work starts. Before allowing the build-up of the people and equipment necessary to implement the system, the customer and producer should be clear as to the mission to be performed. At least some subset of the producing organization should be operationally oriented. In addition, that difficult-to-find operationally oriented but computer knowledgeable person should be available. A measure of understanding is the ability to define tests for the system at this early stage. The test design should continue from the first analysis until the system completion. It has recently been argued by some that it will be impossible to test adequately the programming of a currently proposed major procurement. If true, this foresight can be of considerable value. In any case, no system should be produced without thorough comprehension of the operational problem and the technique for its testing.

During the past several years, the Air Force (and recently the Department of Defense) has adapted management concepts to the problem of computer program acquisition. These Air Force 375 Management Concepts as applied to software are based on the decision that a computer program can be defined as a Computer Program Contract End Item (CPCEI). Described in some detail in *References* 14, 15, 16, and 20, the procedures detailed in this system include the definition of specifications and review procedures which assist considerably in assuring that the operational requirements are defined before the system implementation begins. It also assures that test specifications are written concurrently with the system definitions.

People communicate badly
Communicators are needed. This includes people who can define the
required system documentation. Then management must see to it that the
documentation gets written. Frequently this is one of the chores left to
programmers, who are in the main notoriously reluctant as well as not very
skilled at writing. There are, however, individuals who understand
programming and like to write. These people must be isolated and assigned
the task of working with the operational and programming people to
produce a complete series of operational, utility and test program
specifications.

There is a great difference in programmers' capabilities
We have all recognized this to some degree. Perhaps, however, we have been
surprised by the quantitative aspects of this problem. Part of the difficulty is
the fact that programmers are different in what they do well and in their
styles of work, as well as in how well they perform. There are the extremely
fast coders who check out for a long period. There are also those who code
with great care and rarely go to the computer until the deadlines are near.
The latter cause particular strain on managers. There is some possibility of
measuring progress once the program is running. But in the long run it is
not clear that either style is better. This difference in programmers,
however, does make it much more difficult to schedule and to measure
progress in the early phases.
    The key is, of course, the manager. He must be able to recognize whether
progress is adequate at any time. If it is not he must take corrective action.
This may be the adjustment of priorities, the shifting of personnel or the
sometimes painful removal of a person. If a manager is willing to recognize
the fact that some programmers are bound to be considerably less capable
than others, and he constantly tries to filter out the less capable set, he is
much more likely to succeed than by adhering strictly to procedural
techniques.

Good programmers are creative
The art of programming requires creativity. The nature of code is such that
there is an almost unending set of possible improvements. There are
probably an infinite number of ways to program any problem. Few
programs exist that seem to satisfy all the possibilities that one might
imagine. All these factors further complicate the problem of system
production. The manager must constantly be on the alert for creation
beyond the bounds of discretion. Testing can be delayed considerably by
those who are changing the thing being tested. Decisions as to satisfactory
performance must be made and the line drawn, so that further
"improvements" are forbidden.
    This is a particularly sensitive area. One must limit imagination in some
sense, yet try to keep a technical environment that will encourage good
people to remain on the job. This is a somewhat perplexing problem in
large-scale system development anyway, since these are usually large team
efforts and individual contributions have to be made subservient to the total
job. There are various techniques for directing this kind of effort. One can
be called the "top-down" approach. Using this technique, the system is
designed and first level specifications are written at the top level. At each
succeeding level the specifications are reviewed and more detailed
specifications are written. The specifications eventually include descriptions
of programs that are to be written at the next level. These, in turn, might
generate the requirement for more routines at lower levels. In sum, then,
the programmer never writes the specification for the program he is coding,
and the person at a particular level knows rather little about the total
system or even the characteristics of other programs at the same level. In
the extreme, the person at a given level does not know who prepared the
specification he is using. This technique has the advantage of clearly
delimiting the requirements at any level and forcing relatively clear thought

processes throughout the production cycle. It presents co-ordination problems when difficulties that arose at some previous level are detected. One can assist this type of process by forcing the specifications at any level to include the description of validation tests at the next lower level, although these could be written by someone other than the specification writer.

Another common occurrence in large-scale system development is due partially to programmers' urge to create, partially to the usual start-up period before operational programs are ready for checkout, and perhaps somewhat to the recognized complexity of systems. For most new systems, it has been found that totally new and advanced support tools are needed. These utilities are, in themselves, quite sophisticated and usually a large step over the previous versions for other systems. They are the creative programmer's dream; but they are subject to the same developmental difficulties as the operational system. They are usually not ready by the time operational programs need checkout. They use the operational program for their own checkout. This has obvious implications for the operational program. It seems as though a somewhat less advanced utility system would be in order in most cases.

There are non-programmers involved in most aspects of the system development process
They may be experts in their respective fields but they don't necessarily understand the transformation of their ideas to the computing process. The non-programmer can state in operational terms the function to be performed. He can be particularly valuable in writing test criteria. He serves as an excellent liaison with the customer. He can give unbiased commentary on the human interface with the system. He has difficulty, however, in understanding the feasibility of a particular recommendation. Things which may appear to be of widely disparate difficulty to the programmer may appear to the non-programmer to be of equal difficulty, or even the inverse of the programmer's ranking.

Non-programming managers usually have the option of trusting the programmer in situations or of trying to inflict their judgment on the programming personnel. Either course without adequate understanding is dangerous. As noted before, programmers have various degrees of skill, so that complete faith in all of them is precarious. On the other hand, the non-programmer's judgment as to the proper course to take in a given case is not necessarily correct. The only realistic possibility lies with the programming manager. A programming manager who understands the situation and its potential and can communicate with the non-programming personnel is essential. He must represent the programming group. He must negotiate the possibilities and the course of action to be taken. He must then communicate decisions and courses of action to the programming group in their terms.

It is extremely difficult to judge the actual status of a system at any given time
A variety of documents have been written on the subject of planning and measuring progress of large-scale systems. Milestone schedules, PERT charts, progress reports and various other techniques are used. But a number of practical situations exist that make precise statements of progress and predictions very difficult.

First there is the relatively obscure nature of coded programs prior to checkout. To know whether the code that is being written accurately reflects the specifications requires detailed analysis, which is more than many managers can handle. One method of checking consists of extremely thorough production and review of various steps prior to coding. Successively detailed levels of specification, including flow diagrams, will create a situation where the coding is a relatively straightforward translation as opposed to an invention. These steps require careful analysis, considerable co-ordination and much time: probably much more time before checkout begins than a relatively brief planning period followed by coding. The total elapsed time through checkout may or may not be greater in either situation. To a large extent, the success or failure of either technique depends on the programmers involved. Some can, with relatively little preliminary effort, produce accurate code and know precisely how far along they are. Others are not so trustworthy. In any case, tracking the effort at this state requires an organization where the lowest-level manager has teams small enough to permit thorough inspection of the ongoing work.

During the checkout of sub-programs, it is somewhat easier to understand the status than during the coding period. This assumes, of course, that reasonably precise tests have been specified for this level. Verification of correct results is only one part of the testing at this phase, however. A well designed system should have time and space constraints included for all modules. This is obviously critical in systems that have operational constraints but can also produce catastrophic results if no measures are made at this time on systems that are not absolutely constrained. A number of these latter systems have "worked" but in what amounts to impractically slow times.

Most people are reluctant to admit defeat. This is reflected in their inability to recognize that some schedules may be slipping. Until the actual deadline is passed, there is always the "hope" that things will somehow come out all right even though they are temporarily not in line. Of all the system manager's difficulties, this is probably one of the worst. Schedules do slip, whether because of inaccurate prediction, poor programming or other phenomena. These slips, or impending slips, must be recognized and actions must be taken. A particular component's slip may not have a deleterious effect on the rest of the development. With good planning, this can be recognized and corrections can be made locally. But other slips or excessive capacity requirements can have serious ramifications affecting the entire system. These must be recognized and effective measures taken immediately. Reactions taken early are considerably more valuable than later steps taken in panic.

The Air Force 375 procedures make a significant attempt to define the milestones required for the measurement of progress. They do serve as excellent signposts of progress while a system is in production. Of course, these measures assist in the measurement of progress but do not offer alternate courses of action when required. They alert people that things have gone awry earlier than would have been possible without these procedures.

There is little methodology used in testing or system development
Characteristically, large systems deal with great masses of information. There is not enough time to verify "all cases" at every level. There has been a significant amount of study devoted to the problem of statistically valid sampling. However, little use of this field is made in the testing of large systems. The people involved in testing are usually the same ones who developed the programs, until the final stages of the system production. They are usually unconsciously biased, are anxious to get through with the job and are not well qualified in the field of testing. These personnel, although able to execute the tests, should not be the test designers. Personnel who understand the methodology and system reqirements should be assigned the job of writing test specifications and should verify the results of all tests. This testing organization should work with the implementation personnel only enough to understand the system structure sufficiently to prepare the test specifications. For this purpose, as well as for the rest of the system development, a total system implementation philosophy must evolve.

Figure 4 is a simplified description of a large-scale system. There are several approaches to the design and implementation of such a system. There is the "algorithmic" approach, where one is concerned with the

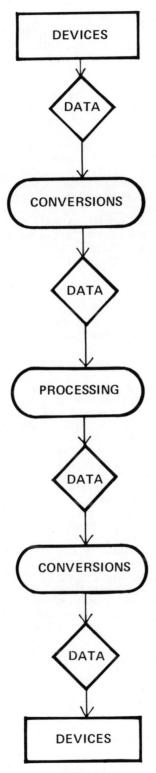

Figure 4

calculations, decisions, control mechanism, interrupt mechanisms and, probably directly, with the devices at either end of the system. The system is structured around these areas. The algorithms are designed and the data structures grow to fit the need of the algorithms. In a sense, the system is built from the inside outward.

Another approach is the building of the system around the data. In the "data" approach, one conceives of the system as a set of elements, tables and files in various states. The states vary from raw, probably well-defined structures associated with the devices at either end to completely designed problem oriented structures that are associated with the processing.

In actuality, of course, most systems are produced using both techniques to a certain degree. It is impossible to develop a system using either approach in its pure form. However, it is probably true that a large number of systems are produced with the emphasis on the "algorithmic" approach, whereas it seems more appropriate to emphasize the data in the development of a large system.

The reasons for the usual emphasis on function rather than content are probably largely due to the mathematical and scientific backgrounds of the majority of people involved. Most people tend to think in terms of the functions involved in a process and assume rather restricted characteristics of the data. This is also demonstrated by the limited nature of many programming languages, FORTRAN and ALGOL being excellent examples, where data definitions beyond arrays of real numbers have been lacking. Some languages, like JOVIAL, COBOL and PL/1 have had considerably more emphasis on the data approach to problem solving. (JOVIAL has frequently been called a language for Command and Control. Perhaps a better description would have been a language for System Programming.)

There are various reasons why the building of a system around its data at different stages is advantageous.

The description of the data provides an unambiguous statement of the system at each stage. By clearly defining the elements and their values, one must understand and convey the essentials of the process. In addition, one can create a reasonably efficient system by thoroughly analyzing the data-flow through the components, eliminating redundancies, excessive paths and missing paths. The data definitions serve as an excellent vehicle for specifying the operating components of the system. The definition of each operating component can consist primarily of its input and output data.

In defining the data, the system designer must understand the capacities required for the various stages of system operation. Allocations of space and positions for the data can be made independent of the algorithm involved in processing them. This prevents the construction of algorithms which work well only with data that may be incompatible with system requirements.

The system test tools can be built systematically around the data. A scheme for testing must be developed which lends itself to automation. It is desirable to have the technique apply to all levels of system checkout even when all the input and output devices haven't been installed. Also; it is imperative that a component, or subsystem, once checked out, can be guaranteed to work in the total system environment. These requirements can be met through a checkout scheme oriented around the system data description.

The data types for large-scale systems are quite varied and can be structurally organized in a variety of ways. For example, the data as input from devices or the formatted data needed for output devices may be relatively difficult to describe in higher-level program language terminology. Frequently, they are strings of information defined more in terms of what the hardware can produce as opposed to design for ease of programming and conversion. The data used by the central processing programs can be designed much more logically and within the scope of at least some programming languages. In either case, it is possible to define the information with the technique that permits the naming of the elements and the association of specific data types with each element. In some cases, the data is strictly numeric and in, perhaps, standard array form. In other cases, it is logical: where specific bit patterns mean certain states. In other cases, there's alphanumeric information. Some elements are frequently found to occupy more than one computer word and, for large-scale systems particularly, some elements occupy only parts of words. Some elements are simple in that they occur only once and others are repetitive.

The major part of the system should be the definition of the variety of element and file descriptions. Once this is done, specifications for programming and checkout of the system can be done in a fairly systematic manner. Specification for each component includes the list of elements that are input to it and the list of elements and files which it should output and the corresponding states for the output given certain inputs. The checkout of each component, then, can be done in terms of the input elements and the associated output. Likewise, subsystems or groups of components can work with element descriptions.

Since a large-scale system is actually composed of many sub-components and systems, it is important that the data used to verify individual pieces is consistent through all tests. One technique which was originally used in the development of the SAGE system still seems to hold the greatest potential in this area. The technique consists of defining for the entire system all data that will be used by more than one component. These data descriptions, including their types and structures and capacities, are entered into a single data definition table, which applies to the entire system. This table was called, in the SAGE system, the Communication Pool. The advantages of a centrally defined data set are several. First of all, it provides uniformity throughout the system during the checkout phase. Secondly, it permits the devising of checkout tools that are data oriented. Third, given that a compiler or assembler exists that is sensitive to the data description, it permits the programming of a system that requires minimal change when the data definitions are changed—a common problem in the development of large systems.

Given the existence of a centrally assembled data definition such as the Communication Pool, one can now devise a hierarchy of system checkout tools. First of all, there are relatively simple table simulation programs which permit the definition of the value for the elements required by each component. Thus, this component level simulation program can automatically produce environments for each component during check out. At succeedingly higher levels, simulation programs are permitted which again deal in terms of the element names and their natural values, as opposed to hand-input computer oriented values. For output of tests, similar kinds of format routines can be produced which take a given binary or computer form of the file structures and produce formatted output at the end of a run, using the central data definition as the source for formatting. Considerably more automation can be added to the system by table generation routines and routines that compare outputs of runs with pre-specified expected results. It is here, of course, that valid sampling techniques should be used.

No one knows the whole system

We frequently hear of successful implementations of complex systems by one or several people. These small-scale efforts are totally in the control of a small set of people. By virtue of this, all planning is integrated, reasonably optimum solutions can be conceived over the whole system and reaction to contingencies may be developed within the total system context. We are concerned here, however, with systems that require, or at least utilize, considerably more than several people. The program is large and probably fragmented into a number of quite distinct logical functions. The hardware complex is usually large and not standard. System specifications must evolve through interaction with non-programming personnel. Stringent demands on operating capabilities and capacities generally exist. Testing must proceed with extreme caution. Problems of adaptation to new environments and evolving situations must be accounted for throughout the system development. If only by virtue of the variety of personnel involved, the large-scale system development must use an organization considerably larger and more complex than the small efforts. One effect of this situation is the diffusion of information. Actions must be taken and problems diagnosed by people with either a very detailed knowledge of only one part or those who have a rather general "big picture" view of the situation. Those responsible for major decisions must weigh the not always completely accurate advice of many people.

From this plethora (or paucity) of facts such decisions as changing scope, modifying schedules, hiring or firing people or reconfiguring the hardware must be made. Managers must understand and have very trusted, competent subordinates.

Summary

In summary, large-scale system development is a "people" problem. There are procedures, techniques and systems which can assist in the development of a system, but they are aids only to the personnel involved in carrying out the implementation. The known techniques describe the documentation, provide a philosophy for production and serve as guide-lines for automating the technique of checkout at the various levels of system checkout. They do not solve some of the more intangible problems such as accurately measuring progress, developing precise testing methodology and making serious contingency decisions.

Considerably more research must be done in understanding capabilities of individual programmers. Even in relatively homogeneous groups there is a great spread in capability. People experienced in testing and experimentation should be applied to the problems of system testing. People should be assigned full time to the data analysis, design and change areas. Also, the support system should be built around the data at all levels. Studies should be made of the qualities of management personnel necessary to guide complex developments such as these to a successful conclusion. Choosing the lowest level manager is one of the most important decisions in such efforts. Analysis of the organization required to specify, produce and test such systems needs to be done in order to better specify the types, numbers and levels of the people needed in such efforts. Until all these things are adequately accomplished, large-scale system development will remain an art which is more dependent on luck, hard-to-define experience and tenacity, rather than on well-defined principles of production.

References

1. **Adams, W. I.** and **Federico, P. R.** Cadfiss test system computation and data flow integrated subsystem tests, Proceedings of the 19th National Conference, Association for Computing Machinery, Philadelphia, August 1964, pp. A2.3-2/A2.3-7.
2. **Arbuckle, R. A.** Computer analysis and thruput evaluation, *Computers and Automation,* January 1966, pp. 12-19.
3. **Buckley, Fletcher J.** Estimating the timing of workload on ADP systems: an evaluation of methods used, *Computers and Automation,* February 1969, pp. 40-42.
4. **Calingaert, Peter** System performance evaluation: survey and appraisal, *Communications of the ACM,* **10,** No. 1, January 1967, pp. 12-18.
5. **Chapin, Ned (Dr.)** Logical design to improve software debugging—a proposal, *Computers and Automation,* February 1966, pp. 22-24.
6. **Estrin, G., Hopkins, D., Coggan, B.,** and **Crocker, S. D.** SNUPER computer—a computer instrumentation automaton, *SJCC,* 1967, pp. 645-656.
7. **Halpern, Mark** Computer programming: the debugging epoch opens, *Computers and Automation,* November 1965, pp. 28-31.
8. **Hext, Jan B. (Dr.)** Recovery from error, *Computers and Automation,* April 1967, pp. 29-31.
9. **Hillegass, John R.** Standardized benchmark problems measure computer performance, *Computers and Automation,* January 1966, pp. 16-19.
10. **Hosier, W. A.** Pitfalls and safeguards in real-time digital systems with emphasis on programming, IRE Transactions on Engineering Management, **EM-8,** pp. 99-115.

11 **Joslin, E. O.** Application benchmarks: the key to meaningful computer evaluation, Proceedings of the ACM 20th National Conference (Session 2: Evaluation and Performance of Computers), 1965, pp. 27-37.

12. **Joslin, Edward O.** and **Aiken, John J.** The validity of basing computer selections on benchmark results, *Computers and Automation,* January 1966, pp. 22-23.

13. **Karush, Arnold D.** Benchmark analysis of time-sharing systems, System Development Corporation, Santa Monica, California, 31 March 1969.

14. **Liebowitz, Burt H.** The technical specification—key to management control of computer programming, in AFIPS Conference Proceedings, Thompson Book Co., Washington, D.C., 1967, Vol. 30, pp. 51-59.

15. **Piligian, M. S.** and **Pokorney, J. L.** Air Force concepts for the technical control and design verification of computer programs, in AFIPS Conference Proceedings, Thompson Book Co., Washington, D.C., 1967, Vol. 30, pp. 61-66.

16. **Ratynski, Milton V.** The Air Force computer program acquisition concept, in AFIPS Conference Proceedings, Thompson Book Co., Washington, D.C., 1967, Vol. 30, pp. 33-44.

17. **Sackman, H.** *Computers, system science and evolving society,* John Wiley & Sons, Inc., New York, 1967.

18. **Sackman, H.** Time-sharing versus batch-processing: the experimental evidence, Proceedings of the Spring Joint Computer Conference, 1968.

19. **Sackman, H.** and **Grant, E. E.** An exploratory investigation of programmer performance under on-line and off-line conditions, IEEE Transactions on Human Factors in Electronics, **HFE-8,** No. 1, March 1967.

20. **Searle, Lloyd V.** and **Neil, George** Configuration management of computer programs by the Air Force: principles and documentation, in AFIPS Conference Proceedings, Thompson Book Co., Washington, D.C., 1967, Vol. 30, pp. 45-49.

21. **Steel, T. B. (Jr.)** The development of very large programs, in Proceedings of IFIP Congress 65, Kalenich, Wayne A. (Ed.), Spartan Books, Inc., Washington, D.C., 1965, Vol. 1, pp. 231-35.

22. **Totaro, J. Burt** Real-time processing power: a standardized evaluation, *Computers and Automation,* April 1967, pp. 16-19.

7.14 Toward a programming laboratory

by

Warren Teitelman

Abstract

This paper discusses the feasibility and desirability of constructing a "programming laboratory" which would co-operate with the user in the development of his programs, freeing him to concentrate more fully on the conceptual difficulties of the problem he wishes to solve. Experience with similar systems in other fields indicates that such a system would significantly increase the programmer's productivity.

The PILOT system, implemented within the interactive BBN LISP system, is a step in the direction of a programming laboratory. PILOT operates as an interface between the user and his programs, monitoring both the requests of the user and the operation of his programs. For example, if PILOT detects an error during the execution of a program, it takes the appropriate corrective action based on previous instructions from the user. Similarly, the user can give directions to PILOT about the operation of his programs, even while they are running, and PILOT will perform the work required. In addition, the user can easily modify PILOT by instructing it about its own operation and thus develop his own language and conventions for interacting with PILOT.

Several examples are presented.

Introduction

The research described in this paper focuses on the programmer's environment. This term is meant to suggest not only the usual specifics of programming systems and languages but also such more elusive and subjective considerations as ease and level of interaction, "forgivefulness" of errors, human engineering, and system "initiative". (The anthropomorphism is deliberate.) In normal usage, the word environment refers to the aggregate of social and cultural conditions that influence the life of an individual. The programmer's environment influences, to a large extent determines, what sort of problems he can (and will want to) tackle, how far he can go and how fast. If the environment is "co-operative" and "helpful" then the programmer can be more ambitious and productive. If not, he will spend most of his time and energy "fighting" the system, which at times seems bent on frustrating his best efforts.

One immediate goal to strive for is an environment comparable to that found in the well designed laboratory of the physical sciences. Such a laboratory usually contains equipment for many applications as well as facilities for designing and building new apparatus, or adapting that already present. In a large (well-funded) installation, the researcher will also often have available assistants for performing the routine tasks. For example, a chemist might simply request an analysis of a sample, and not have to itemize each step in the process. This type of assistant and assistance frees the researcher for problems more worthy of his attention.

Computer based systems have been constructed that create this type of laboratory environment for certain well-defined areas, e.g., mathematics (see *References* 3, 5 and 6), design of electronic circuits (see *Reference* 7), and generalized graphical design (see *References* 4 and 8), such as for aircraft, automobiles and bridges.

These systems are organized to allow the computer to perform the routine work (where routine is a function of the sophistication of the system), while the user guides and directs the process at a relatively high level. For example, in the mathematical laboratory developed by William Martin (see *Reference* 5), the mathematician interacts with the computer by asking questions or making requests. The system employs graphical input and output (light-pen and display) to allow the mathematician to operate in an environment that closely resembles the pencil and paper with which he is already familiar. For output, the display utilizes subscripts and superscripts and observes the conventions concerning physical size, grouping, and placement of sub expressions which mathematicians have adopted to make it easier to read and comprehend mathematical formulae. For input, the mathematician can communicate directly with the computer via the light pen, either by writing new expressions, or by pointing to old ones or portions thereof.

In a typical case the user might be trying to find the solution of a differential equation. On the screen are displayed one or two equations, while the user has in his head the name of several other expressions or partial results already studied and filed away. The user decides to perform an action such as substituting a displayed equation, solving it for some variable, expanding some sub expression in a certain way or perhaps asking to see something else. He makes the request using a combination of light-pen and keyboard signals. These are encoded and transmitted to the system where the appropriate routines compute or retrieve the required new expressions and transmit them back to the display routines which then compile and display the desired new picture. In this way, the user can perform in a few minutes a long and involved analysis which, assuming he did not make any mistakes or lose track of what he was doing, might otherwise take him many hours.

This paper describes a step in the direction of such a laboratory for programming and programmers: the PILOT system. As with the mathematical laboratory, the goal is to allow the computer to perform the routine tasks while the user, in this case a programmer, is left free to concentrate on the more creative aspects of his problem, which is the writing and debugging of a program.

Most of the previous efforts aimed at improving the environment of the programmer have concentrated on providing and improving packages, such as editors, compilers, trace packages and display routines. While a good deal of effort has been devoted to such facilities in the design of PILOT, the basic innovation of the PILOT system is the emphasis placed on the problem of making changes in programs. The reason for this emphasis is that making changes in programs is the task that occupies most of a programmer's time and effort, from the early stages in the development of a program, when his work consists primarily of correcting syntactical and simple logical errors in individual subroutines, to the final stages when the programmer makes the type of logical and organizational changes that affect many different parts of his program.

The problem of making changes to the PILOT system itself is handled as a special case of the problem of making changes to programs in general. Since PILOT is designed to facilitate making changes in programs, its tools and techniques can be applied directly to itself in what is essentially a bootstrapping process. The user can thus easily introduce new tools and/or modify existing ones to suit his own methods and problems. In short, the user can tailor the performance of the system to suit himself. Furthermore, PILOT is designed with this in mind, so that it can co-operate with the user during this phase of the development.

The PILOT system

PILOT is implemented in the LISP programming language at Bolt, Beranek and Newman Inc., Cambridge, Massachusetts (see *Reference* 1). Although there is a PILOT subsystem in LISP, all of the features and tools described in this paper were incorporated directly into the BBN LISP system once their usefulness was established, and are now in general use by the entire community of LISP users. It is thus more meaningful to view PILOT as a conceptual system, a philosophy of design. It is this philosophy that we are trying to impart in the hope that it may prove useful in the design and construction of systems in other languages.*

Automatic error correcting

The initial stages in the implementation of a large program are usually devoted to the writing and debugging of independent component routines. Only after these have been checked out, at least superficially, can the programmer begin to assemble the program and check for inter-routine problems. However, before the programmer can even begin to debug a routine, he must first get it to run, i.e. eliminate those syntactical and/or simple logical errors that cause complaints from the language or system in which he is operating. Facilitating the correction of these lowest level errors

---

* LISP is especially suited for implementing a system such as PILOT because of the ease with which LISP programs can be treated as data by other programs. This capability is essential for creating tools which themselves will create and/or modify programs, an indispensable feature of a programming laboratory.

would improve the efficiency of debugging by allowing the programmer to proceed directly to higher level problems.

From the user's standpoint, clearly the best of all possible solutions would be for the system to correct these low level errors automatically and continue with the computation. This is not far-fetched: a surprisingly large percentage of the errors made by LISP users, e.g. misspellings and certain types of parenthesis errors, are of the type that could be corrected by another LISP programmer without any information about the purpose or application of the LISP program or expression in question.* If these corrections were performed automatically by a program that was called only after an error occurred in the execution of a LISP program, it would in no way detract from the performance of the LISP system with debugged programs. Thus the efficiency of the error correcting program would not be a critical factor in its usefulness.

A primitive program which corrected certain types of spelling errors was implemented in PILOT and users were encouraged to experiment with it and comment on its features. As a result of this experience, we discovered that in order to be acceptable to users:

1 The program must have a measure of how certain it is about the nature and correction of a mistake, and use this measure in determining the amount of interaction with the user.
2 The program must be able to distinguish between significant and trivial corrections, and to be more cautious, i.e., more interactive, about correcting the former.
3 The user must be able to specify to the program his degree of confidence in its ability to correct his mistakes, as reflected by the amount of interaction he desires.
4 The user must be able to interrupt and/or abort any attempted correction.
5 The user must be able to disable or overrule the entire correcting program whenever he wishes.

With these criteria in mind, a more sophisticated set of error correcting routines were implemented. These routines make up the DWIM package (Do-What-I-Mean). The following output is representative of the kind of corrections and flavour of interaction of DWIM. User input is preceded by an arrow (←).

```
←DEFINE (((FACT (LAMBDA (N)
(COND ((ZEROP N9 1) ((T (TIMS N (FACTT 8SUB1 N]
(FACT)
←PRETTYPRNT((FACCT]
=PRETTYPRINT
=FACT

(FACT
  (LAMBDA (N)
    (COND
      ((ZEROP N9 1)
        ((T (TIMS N (FACTT 8SUB1 N)))))))))
NIL
←FACT(3)
EDITING FACT . . .
N9 > > – – > N)
EDITING FACT . . .
(COND – – ((T – –))) > > – – > (COND – – (T – –))
TIMS=TIMES
```

---

*We conjecture that this is also true in other languages.

```
FACTT=FACT
EDITING FACT . . .
8SUB1 > > – – >  (SUB1
6
```

←PRETTYPRINT((FACT))

```
(FACT
  (LAMBDA (N)
    (COND
      ((ZEROP N)
        1)
      (T (TIMES N (FACT (SUB1 N)))))))
NIL
```

In this example, the user first defines a function FACT of one argument, N, whose value is to be N factorial. The function contains several errors: TIMES and FACT have been misspelled. The 9 in N9 was intended to be a right parenthesis but the teletype shift key was not depressed. Similarly, the 8 in 8SUB1 was intended to be a left parnthesis. Finally, there are two left parentheses in front of the T that begins the second clause in the conditional, instead of the required one.

After defining the function FACT, the user wishes to look at its definition using PRETTYPRINT, which he unfortunately misspells. Since there is no function PRETTYPRNT in the system, an UNDEFINED FUNCTION error occurs, and the DWIM program is called. DWIM invokes its spelling corrector, which searches for the best possible match in a list of functions frequently used (by *this* user). Finding one that is extremely close, DWIM proceeds on the assumption that PRETTYPRNT meant PRETTYPRINT, informs the user of this, and calls PRETTYPRINT.

At this point, PRETTYPRINT would normally print (FACCT NOT PRINTABLE) and exit, since FACCT has no definition. This is not a system error condition, but the DWIM facility is not restricted to just system error conditions. DWIM also modifies selected system functions, such as PRETTYPRINT and DEFINEQ, to make them co-operate more closely with the user: DEFINEQ is modified (by ADVISE, to be described later) to note any new functions defined by the user, and add them to the spelling list of user functions. Similarly, PRETTYPRINT is modified so that, when given a function with no definition, it calls the spelling corrector. Thus, PRETTYPRINT determines that the user wants to see the definition of the function FACT, not FACCT, and proceeds accordingly.

The user now calls his function FACT. During its execution, five errors are generated, and DWIM is called five times. At each point, the error is corrected, a comment made of the action taken, and the computation allowed to continue as if no error had occurred. Following the last correction, 6, the value of FACT(3), is printed. Finally, the user prints the new, now correct, definition of FACT.

In this particular example, the user was shown operating in a mode which gave the DWIM system the green light on all corrections. Had the user wished to interact more and approve or disapprove of the intended corrections at each stage, he could have operated in a different mode. Or, operating as shown above, he could have at any point aborted the correction, or signalled his desire to see the results of a correction after it was made, by typing a ? on the teletype.

We have found from our experience with DWIM that most users are quite willing to entrust the program with the correction of errors, although each different user may want to operate with a different "confidence factor", a parameter which indicates how sure DWIM must be before making a correction without approval. Above a certain user-established level, DWIM makes the correction and goes on. Below another level, DWIM types what it thinks is the problem, e.g., DOES PRTYPNT MEAN PRETTYPRINT ?, and waits for the user to respond. In the inbetween area, DWIM types what it is about to do, pauses for about a second, and if the user does not respond, goes ahead and does it. The important thing to note is that since an error has occurred, the user would have to intervene in any event, so any attempt at correction is appreciated, even if wrong, as long as the correction does not cause more trouble to correct than the original error. Since DWIM can recognize the difference between trivial corrections, such as misspellings, and serious corrections, such as those involving extensive editing, bad mistakes are usually avoided. When DWIM does make a mistake, the user merely aborts his computation and makes the correction he would have had to make anyway.

Error handling in general

Certain types of errors that occur in the BBN LISP system cannot be handled by the DWIM program, for example, NON-NUMERIC ARG, an error generated by the arithmetic functions; ARG NOT ARRAY, from the primitive array functions, etc. These are data type errors.* Another class of errors not handled by DWIM are the "panic" errors: BP FULL, a complaint from the compiler meaning it has run out of binary program space; NONXMEM, an attempt to reference nonexistent memory, usually caused by treating an array pointer as a piece of list structure; PDL OVFLW, meaning pushdown list overflow, which usually implies a looping program, etc. Both data type and panic errors are not *fixable,* but they are *helpable.*

In our system, whenever an error occurs, it causes a trap to a user-modifiable program. (It is through this program that DWIM works.) If DWIM has not been enabled, or if the user aborts an attempted DWIM correction, or if DWIM cannot fix the error that has occurred, the system goes into a *"break"* and allows the user to interact with the system while maintaining the context of the program in which the error occurred. This allows the user to intervene to try to rectify the problem or to salvage what he can of the computation. While in the break, the system accepts and evaluates inputs from the teletype. Since all of the power of the system is available to him, the user can examine variables, change their values, define and evaluate new functions and even edit functions he is currently in. If another error occurs in a computation requested while in the break, the system goes into a second, lower break, and so on. Thus it is rarely the case that the results of a lengthy computation are lost by the occurrence of an error near its end.

The following example illustrates this process (user input is preceded by ":" or "*"). The user is running a large, compiled system, one of whose subroutines is to peform the alphabetization of a list of names. The first indication of something wrong in the system is the error message ATTEMPT TO CLOBBER NIL, meaning the program is attempting to change the value of NIL (not allowed in our system). The system goes into a break (1), and the user determines where the error occurred by requesting a backtrace (2). He sees that he is inside the function ALPHA and interrogates the value of some of ALPHA's variables (3). He realizes that the problem arose when his alphabetization routine attempted to compare the last element in the list to the one following it, i.e. an end-check problem. Still in

---

*Sometimes these errors are in fact caused by misspellings, but it is impossible to tell in general.

the break, he proceeds to call the editor on the function ALPHA (4). DWIM corrects his spelling, and since ALPHA is compiled, the editor retrieves its defining symbolic expression from its property list, typing PROP (5) to call this to the user's attention. Consulting his listing, the user instructs the editor to find the expression beginning with COND that contains RETURN, (6) which he then examines (7). The expression he wants is the one before the COND, so he backs up (8), and makes the appropriate correction (9). He then recompiles ALPHA (10). *Notice he is still in the original break.*

```
ATTEMPT TO CLOBBER NIL
TEITELMAN

(RPLACA BROKEN)                               1
:WHERE?                                       2
RPLACA
ALPHA
ACCOUNTS2
ACCOUNTS1
ACCOUNTS


:X
(BOBROW OUILLIAN MURPHY BELL NIL)             3
:Y
(NIL)
:Z
TEITELMAN
:EDITF(ALHPA)                                 4
=ALPHA
PROP
EDIT                                          5
*(COND CONTAINING RETURN)
PP                                            6
  (COND                                       7
    (FLG (GO LP))
    (T (RETURN X)))
*BACK PP                                       8
  (NULL (SETQ Y (CDR Y)))
*(EMBED SETQ IN CDR)                          9
*PP
  (CDR (SETQ Y (CDR Y)))
*OK
(ALPHA)
:COMPILE(ALPHA)                              10
LISTING?
ST
(OUTPUT FILE)
NONE
(ALPHA COMPILING)
(ALPHA REDEFINED)
(ALPHA)


:ARGS
(U V)
:(SETQ U Y)                                   11
(NIL)
:EVAL                                         12
RPLACA EVALUATED
:X
(BOBROW OUILLIAN MURPHY BELL TEITELMAN)       13
:OK
RPLACA                                        14
```

Now the user wishes to continue the computation. He must therefore correct the immediate problem in the function RPLACA i.e. its first argument is NIL. He does this by changing (setting) the first argument, U, to Y (11). He then evaluates RPLACA (12), double checks it by looking at X, and releases the break by typing OK (14).

As illustrated above, when an error occurs a user invariably wants to look back and see what happened earlier in the computation to cause the error situation. In BBN LISP, *all* information regarding the state of the computation in progress is stored on the push-down list and is explicitly available to the user and to user programs. In fact, without this capability, DWIM could be used only to correct certain trivial errors. We believe that for any type of programming laboratory environment, it is absolutely essential that programs be able to examine the state of the world at any point in the computation. In terms of LISP, this implies being able to examine the sequence of functions that have been called and to look at variable bindings. Since the same variable may be bound a number of times in nested function calls, especially during a recursive computation, the program must be able to specify which binding of a variable it is referencing and be able to change a *particular* binding if necessary. For example, had X and Y been the names of RPLACA's arguments, the user should still be able to interrogate the value of X and Y in *ALPHA* while inside RPLACA. Finally, the user or program must be able to cause the computation to return back to a specified point, i.e. to a particular function on the push-down list, regardless of the number and type of intervening functions that have been called. All of these capabilities are present in our system.

User breaks
The capability of stopping a computation and maintaining its context while executing teletype inputs is also *directly* available to the user in a variety of forms as an aid in debugging (see *Reference* 2). In the simplest case, the user can request that selected functions be modified to cause breaks whenever they are called, or only when a certain condition is satisfied; for example (BREAK ALPHA (GREATERP (LENGTH X) 10)) will cause the alphabetization routine to break whenever it is given a list of length greater than 10. At this point the user can intervene and examine variables, edit functions, etc. exactly as in the case shown above when an error occurs and the system causes a break.

Another way of using the break feature is to specify that a function be "broken" only when it is called from some particular function. For example, the user would be reluctant to break on the function SETQ, since almost every function uses it and the system would forever be going into a break. However, he could (BREAK (SETQ IN ALPHA)), which would break only on those calls to SETQ from *within* ALPHA. In this case, the performance of SETQ is not affected or degraded when called from any other function.

The user can also request that breaks be inserted at specified points *inside* a function. The editor is then called (in this case the function must be an interpreted one, i.e. have an S-expression definition) to find the appropriate point and insert the break. For example, the user could (BREAKIN ALPHA (BEFORE (COND CONTAINING RETURN))), which would cause a break just before executing the indicated form.

Finally, the user can request a break at any *time* during a computation by simply depressing a special key on the teletype. The next time a function is called, usually within a few milliseconds, a break will occur and again the user can intervene and examine the state of the computation, etc. These capabilities are invaluable for localizing problems in complex programs, especially recursive ones, and are powerful tools for finding *where* to make changes that complement those described below that provide *how* to make changes.

Advising

PILOT was originally motivated by the difficulties encountered in using computers for solving very hard problems, particularly those in the area of artificial intelligence (see *Reference* 9). These problems can be characterized as being extremely difficult to think through in advance, that is, away from the computer. In some cases, the programmer cannot foresee the implications of certain decisions he must make in the design of the program. In others, he can compare several alternatives only by trying them out on the machine. Even after he gets his program debugged, he *continues to make alterations to see their effects.* Only by experimenting with his working program can he evaluate its performance or hope to extend its generality. Since he cannot accurately predict the effect of changes on the behaviour of the program because of its size and complexity, he must adopt the more pragmatic policy of "let's try it and see what happens." In short, he must be able to treat the computer as his laboratory.

Unfortunately, making changes in programs, especially large and complex programs, is often not a simple matter. Since they may require so much effort, many experimental changes are simply not implemented, with the result that programs soon become "frozen." For this reason, considerable attention and effort in the design and development of PILOT has been devoted to the problem of making changes. One of the results is the concept of *advising*.

The operation of advising consists of modifying the interface between individual functions in a program, as opposed to modifying the functions themselves, which is called *editing*. The advantage of advising is that it allows the user to treat sections of his own (or some-one else's) program as black boxes, and to make modifications to them without concern for their contents. Since each modification is itself a small program, and modifications can be inserted so as to operate either before or after the original function would be run, advising is a very general and powerful concept.

Advising is carried out in LISP by creating a *new* function definition in which the original function definition is embedded, and surrounded by the "pieces of advice." This procedure is completely general: the function being advised can be arbitrarily large or small, complex or simple, compiled or interpreted, a system function or one of the user's own.

The individual pieces of advice are each LISP expressions, and so they too are completely general. Thus a piece of advice may simply change the value of some variable or, at the other extreme, request a lengthy computation including perhaps calling the entire advised function recursively. Advice can also be given so as to bypass the entire advised function.

For example, the user could have repaired the problem in ALPHA shown earlier by giving the appropriate advice to RPLACA instead of editing ALPHA. Since RPLACA is called from many functions, the user would probably want to advise RPLACA IN ALPHA:

ADVISE((RPLACA IN ALPHA) (COND ((NULL U) (SETQ U Y))))

As with the corresponding break, this would modify only the call to RPLACA rom *within* ALPHA.

This operation demonstrates the advantage of advising. It allows the user to make on-line modifications quickly and simply. In addition to using it for correcting bugs, the user can perform modifications for the sake of experimentation, undo the modifications if he wishes, try out other configurations, etc., all without disruption to his high level, problem oriented train of thought. Such disruption usually follows when implementing changes requiring a lengthy sequence of operations.

Note that advising complements rather than competes with editing as a way of making changes. In the early stages of debugging, the user is primarily attending to local phenomena in his program and thus may find it natural to make changes by editing. In later stages, he considers his program more in terms of what each piece does, rather than how it does it, and here advising is the tool he wants to use for making changes.

Advising as a tool for modifying the system
Advising not only provides the user with a convenient tool for making changes in his own programs, but also with the means for experimenting with and tailoring the *system* to his own particular tastes. For example, suppose a user wished to modify PRETTYPRINT to print comments along the right hand side of the page, where a comment was to be indicated as an expression beginning with the atom *. Knowing that SUPERPRINT is the function that "does the work" of prettyprinting, he could

    ADVISE(SUPERPRINT (COND ((EQ (CAR E) (QUOTE *))
                 (RETURN (COMMENT E)))))

and then define the function COMMENT to do the appropriate formatting.*

Admittedly this particular piece of advising requires the user to have some detailed knowledge of the workings of PRETTYPRINT. However, the important point is that by using ADVISE, changes *can* be easily effected, even with system functions where changes were *not* anticipated.

Conversational input
PILOT can be viewed as an interface between the user and his programs. The following somewhat oversimplified diagram illustrates the user-PILOT-program configuration:

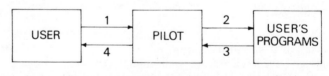

Figure 1

Most of the effort in PILOT is concentrated at interface 2 and 3. However, in order to be really effective, a programming laboratory should not only provide the means whereby changes can be effected immediately, but also *in a way that seems natural to the user*. Accordingly, we have been experimenting with an English-to-LISP translating program that operates at interface 1, and translates the users requests to PILOT into the appropriate LISP computation. For example, the user could have effected the advice on RPLACA IN ALPHA shown above by:
TELL (RPLACA IN ALPHA): IF ITS FIRST ARGUMENT IS NIL THEN SET IT TO Y.

---

*The comment feature is now a part of our system. However, it was initially introduced in precisely this way, in order to evaluate its usefulness. Advising thus provides system designers with a quick means for trying out new features.

The following dialogue gives the flavour of user-PILOT interactions obtained with this program. User input is preceded by ">".

```
PILOT(T)
PROCEED:
> TELL PROGRESS: IF THE CANNIBALS OUTNUMBER THE MISSIONARIES ON SIDE1,
    OR THE CANNIBALS OUTNUMBER THE MISSIONARIES ON SIDE2,
        THEN RETURN FALSE.
THE CANNIBALS OUTNUMBER THE MISSIONARIES ON SIDE1 ??
> THE X OUTNUMBER THE Y ON Z MEANS
    Y IS CONTAINED IN Z AND THE NUMBER OF X IN Z
        IS GREATER THAN THE NUMBER OF Y IN Z.
THE NUMBER OF X IN Z ??
> DEFINE NUMBER, X Y, AS PROG (N)
    SET N TO 0;
LP: IF Y IS EMPTY THEN RETURN N,
    IF X IS EQUAL TO THE FIRST MEMBER OF Y THEN
        INCREMENT N;
    SET Y TO THE REST OF Y;
    GO TO LP.
(NUMBER)
> THE NUMBER OF X IN Z MEANS NUMBER X Z.
I UNDERSTAND.
> CONTINUE

I UNDERSTAND.
> CONTINUE

PROGRESS
```

The user instructs PILOT to advise the function PROGRESS with the statement beginning "TELL PROGRESS:". PILOT recognizes this form of request, but does not understand the part about outnumbering. The user then attempts to explain this with the input beginning THE X OUTNUMBER THE Y. This statement will cause an addition to PILOT's already fairly extensive capability for converting English statements to LISP, so that PILOT will be able to understand expressions of this type encountered in the future. However, PILOT cannot interpret the phrase THE NUMBER OF X IN Z in this explanation and so interrogates the user at this lower level. At this point, the user defines a new function NUMBER and then explains the troublesome phrase in terms of this function. PILOT responds that it "understands." The user then instructs PILOT to continue with what it was doing, namely translating the explanation of OUTNUMBER. When this is completed, the user instructs PILOT to continue with the original request, which PILOT now successfully completes.

The current English-to-LISP translator contains a large assortment of useful, if *ad hoc*, transformational rules written in FLIP (see *Reference* 10), a string processing language embedded in the BBN LISP system. The set of FLIP rules can be easily expanded or modified. For example, the dialogue shown above resulted in rules for transforming expression of the form THE X OUTNUMBER THE Y ON Z and for THE NUMBER OF X IN Z being added to the translator.

In addition to the FLIP portion of the translating program, there is a post-processor which allows intermingling of LISP expressions with the English, as well as a sort of pidgin-LISP which looks like LISP with the parentheses removed. The translator also contains specialized information for dealing with quantifiers and and/or clauses. For example, the following expressions will be translated correctly into the equivalent LISP forms:
NO MEMBER OF X IS ATOMIC AND NOT NULL

THE FIRST ELEMENT OF X IS GREATER THAN THE SECOND AND
    NOT LESS THAN THE THIRD
THE FIRST ELEMENT OF SOME MEMBER OF X IS A NUMBER THAT IS
    GREATER THAN THE SECOND ELEMENT

The translator also "remembers" certain contextual information such as what
was the last operation requested, what function it referred to, etc. For
example:
>TELL FOO: IF ITS FIRST ARGUMENT IS ATOMIC THEN RETURN IT.
FOO
>WHAT IS ITS SECOND ARGUMENT?
Y
We are not asserting that English is a good or even desirable programming
language. However, if the user is thinking about his programs in English,
then providing him the facility for expressing requests in English will allow
him to concentrate more fully on the problem at hand.

Improving PILOT
"PILOT is the result of an evolutionary process extending over more than
two years. However, there is no reason to assume that this process has
terminated, nor that PILOT has reached some sort of ultimate state" (see
Reference 9). This statement was written in my Ph.D. thesis three years ago
and, in the elapsed time, many of the goals established for improvements
and additions to PILOT have been realized in our present system. But the
statement is still true, and the process still continues.
    One area of current interest is that of program-writing programs.
Programming languages are currently designed to allow the programmer to
express the operations he wants the computer to perform in a simple and
concise fashion. However, often the programmer may not *know* precisely
what operation he wants the computer to perform, although he may have a
clear idea of what he wants the program to accomplish. That is, he may be
able to describe its output, or the changes it should make in a data

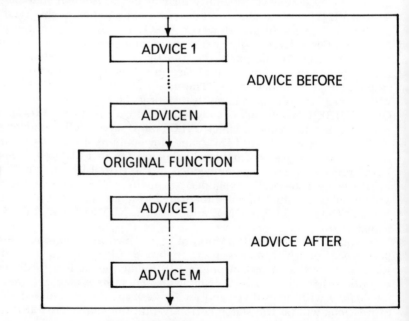

Figure 2

structure. This is not to say that the programmer could not construct the program. However, a system which could accept more goal-oriented descriptions of tasks and produce programs to accomplish them, even if only effective for simple, subroutine-level tasks, would further free its users for high-level operations. Such a system would require a fair degree of problem solving capability and should have a sufficiently rich store of information about programming and programs to enable it to determine similarities in tasks. It should be able to adapt previously written or constructed programs to a new task. In other words, we are trying to construct a system that can handle more of the routine aspects of programming in order to free the human to concern himself more with the creative aspects of the problem.

This is the basic philosophy of the PILOT system: let the computer do it. The significance of PILOT is that it demonstrates the feasibility and desirability of this approach. Even in its current form, PILOT clearly shows that it is possible to get computers to participate in, and co-operate with, research efforts in programming to a much greater extent than is now being done.

References

1. **Bobrow, D. G., Murphy, D. L.,** and **Teitelman, W.** *The BBN LISP System,* April 1969.
2. **Bobrow, D. G.** and **Teitelman, W.** *Debugging in an on-line interactive LISP,* November 1967. Bolt Beranek and Newman Inc.
3. **Engelman, C.** "MATHLAB 68" IFIP Congress 68, pp. B91-B95.
4. **Johnson, T. E.** "Sketchpad III: a computer program for drawing in three dimensions," *Proc. SJCC,* Spartan Press, Baltimore, Maryland. 1963.
5. **Martin, W. A.** *Symbolic Mathematical Laboratory,* Doctoral dissertation, MIT, Cambridge, Massachusetts, January 1967 (also Report TM-36, Project MAC, MIT).
6. **Maurer, W. D.** "Computer experiments in finite algebra," *Comm. ACM,* **9,** No. 8, August 1966, pp. 589-603.
7. **Reintjes, J. F.** and **Dertouzos, M. L.** "Computer-aided design of electronic circuits," presented at *WINCON Confer.,* Los Angeles, California, 2-5 February 1966.
8. **Sutherland, I. E.** "Sketchpad: a man-machine graphical communication system," *Proc. SJCC,* Spartan Press, Baltimore, Maryland. 1963.
9. **Teitelman, W.** *PILOT: a step toward man-computer symbiosis,* Doctoral dissertation, MIT, Cambridge, Massacusetts, June 1966 (also Report TR-32, Project MAC, MIT).
10. **Teitelman, W.** *Design and implementation of FLIP, a LISP format directed list processor,* BBN Report No. 1495, July 1967.

7.15 Design of high reliability continuous operation systems

by

W. Ulrich

Scope of problem

To serve telephone customers in switching systems being installed at a present rate of several hundred thousand lines per year and ultimately at a rate of several million lines per year. The electronic control for these systems must be fully operational in both software and hardware respects to be able to give any kind of service to its customers. Clearly, therefore, there

is a need for a very high degree of software as well as hardware
dependability.

Characteristics of ESS control program

Large
The program for the more complex ESS installations is in excess of 220,000
37-bit instructions. Probably half of these instructions are for maintenance
while the rest are for telephone operation control. A program of this size
was written by a large number of individuals with all the interface problems
resulting from such a procedure.

Read only and read/write memories
The program and certain categories of very rarely changed information are
stored on a read only (off-line write) memory. A more conventional
read/write memory is used for more frequently changed data and for
input/output data.

Common data base
Many programs access and alter certain types of common data, including
common scratch data, common switching network control data, and
constants of the office. Moreover, a single short segment of memory is
devoted to each call in progress and this segment is also accessed by many
different programs.

Pointers
For reasons of efficiency, a large number of pointers are used. One of the
biggest problems comes when a pointer is inadvertently overwritten with
completely different data. Such an action permits a rapid propagation of
invalid information through the read/write memory of the system and often
results in the complete denial of a telephone function.

Real time problems
The program operates on two levels—an input/output level, which must keep
up with the incoming customer signals, and a base level processing the work
that results from these signals. In general, the processing of a call requires a
large number of separate and separated program actions which must be
separated in real time because further action is required by the customer or
by the peripheral system before work can be continued. A call may take 14
seconds of elapsed time but require only about 35 milliseconds of active
processing time.

Scheduling algorithm
Requests for work to be performed are discovered by input/output programs
which place these requests in a hopper. Periodically these hoppers are
examined and, with the single exception of the service request hopper, all
hoppers are emptied completely whenever they are examined. As a means of
controlling the load, no more than a fixed number of service requests, i.e.
requests for new telephone connections, are handled each time the service
request hopper is examined. This is a very convenient way of avoiding
excessive overload and responds to such overload in a very good way, i.e. by
accepting only a limited amount of new business. Hoppers also provide
means for differentiating high priority work, such as effecting the transition
from a ringing to a talking connection, from low priority work, such as
disconnecting a call.

Need for real time efficiency
The system which was designed using 1960 technology components has a 5.5 microsecond memory cycle time. The requirements of the Bell System are such that it is important that the capacity of the system be at least 60,000 calls per busy hour and preferably considerably more. Therefore, there is a very strong need to keep down the average number of cycles required to process each call and there is a very high payoff for a programming scheme which minimizes this number of cycles.

Electronic memory map control of the switching network
When new paths are to be selected in the switching network, an image of the network in the read/write memory, containing the busy/idle status of all links, is examined in order to find a new path. Thus, new paths are selected on the basis of a memory image, not directly on the basis of the physical status of the network.

Signal processor
In larger offices, a separate signal processor controls I/O actions. This processor communicates with the central processor via its own memory which is accessible to the central processor. It generates the same types of hopper entries that are generated by the central processor in the interrupt level activity in smaller offices.

Types of data

Generic program
An identical program is placed in all offices of a particular class. (At present there are only five such classes.) The program is arranged so that the variations in features, size, types of inter-office trunk circuits, layout of memory, are handled through a different set of tables of office characteristics. The program itself is identical in its binary form.

Office characteristics
The tables of office characteristics define the parameters of the particular office and allow the generic program to work properly in the equipment and telephone feature environment of that office. Some of this data is used, for example, to initialize memory and to indicate where various blocks of memory begin and end. Most of this data remains intact until a major addition or major new feature offering (such as a block of memory or a frame of network equipment) is made to the office.

Customer and inter-office data
This data describes the numerical data of a customer, such as his telephone number and his location on the switching network, and gives details concerning the special services which he has been offered. Inter-office data includes an indication of which group of inter-office trunks is associated with any given office code, the method of signalling over these trunks, the identification of all the members of given trunk groups and the network location of all these trunks. All of this data is normally kept in the read only memory; however, small portions of it may be modified on a day-to-day basis and are periodically put into read only memory by an off-line process.

Supervisory and per call data
This data gives the busy/idle status of all customers and trunks and details of all connections that are in the talking state.

Transient data
This data includes data about calls that have not yet reached the talking state, e.g. calls in the middle of dialing, and usually requires frequent updating.

Signal processor data
This data, all of which is kept on a read/write store with appropriate back-up on the read only store, consists of instructions for the signal processor and data necessary to control I/O actions.

Scratch data
Scratch data is somewhat different in this environment since it is kept separate from the program and is frequently shared among many different programs.

Techniques for reliability

On-line checks for data consistency
Relatively little of this is done since such checks require the expenditure of a significant number of extra program cycles and therefore reduce the capacity of the system.

Audits
Most of memory is audited as a matter of routine to check for the consistency of most of the data. In particular, pointers and the memory status of all customer lines and inter-office trunks are audited. Call control segments are audited to make sure that, in case of trouble, the customers controlled by these segments can be released so that they can reoriginate their call. The network map is audited for consistency. Tables of constants, stored for efficiency in read/write store, are checked. Signal processor data and programs are audited.

Emergency audits
When it is apparent to the system that substantial memory mutilation has taken place, a number of audits are called in and call processing stops until these audits have been completed. These audits attempt wherever possible to retain calls that have already been set up and restore other customers at least to a state from which they may originate new calls and receive terminating calls.

Problems

Difficulty of discovering overload and mass memory mutilation
The indication most frequently used that mass memory mutilation has occurred is the failure to complete all required call processing work within a reasonable time. This is also the characteristic of heavy overload. We have found it difficult to distinguish between the two.

Escalation of emergency audits
When emergency audits are called, they are called in phases such that each audit takes progressively more drastic steps to remove the source of the memory mutilation. We have had problems in which the first phase of the emergency audit should have cleared up the problem but created further symptoms of overload or trouble such that subsequent phases were automatically initiated even though the cause of the memory mutilation had

already been cleared up. The final phase, which includes network initialization, is one we particularly try to avoid.

Recovery from emergency audit

The emergency audit leaves the system in a state resembling that of a crash overload since a number of customers have been disconnected and are trying to reoriginate and traffic has been blocked out during the audit. Originations can be admitted slowly but there is more difficulty in limiting the response to seizures from inter-office trunks that have calls destined for this office dialled by customers in another office.

Manual interference

The single biggest source of problems, as might be expected, has been improper actions by maintenance craftsmen that cause the system to perform emergency audits. Furthermore, it is difficult for the craftsman to get experience so that he can make a good judgment of whether or not to advance to a particular phase and how long he should wait for the system to try to straighten out the problem automatically.

Overloaded offices

There has been a strong temptation on the part of many telephone operating companies to apply more load to the office than it is capable of handling. Under these circumstances, because of the sensitivity of the system to overload, emergency audits are performed more frequently and recovery following an emergency audit takes longer.

Memory protection

No memory protection exists in the system and therefore the propagation of poor data arising from incorrect pointers cannot be readily controlled except where out-of-range addresses are generated.

Results

Unsatisfactory offices

A small number (in the order of 20 per cent) of the offices have had a significant number of emergency audits for some weeks after they were cut over to service. In some cases, as many as a dozen separate occasions occurred during the first month of service; however, all of these offices, including those in which too much load was applied, have performed well after an initial bad period of as much as one week and a subsequent period of one or two months that was less than satisfactory. In most cases the unsatisfactory offices presented some new characteristics of load that could not be adequately simulated in the laboratory. The unsatisfactory offices are primarily offices with signal processors that have a larger load and more complex interfaces than the offices with no signal processor and whose programs are newer and therefore less thoroughly shaken down.

Satisfactory offices

The large bulk of the offices installed have an emergency audit rate of about one or two per year after the first three or four months. It is hoped that this number will decrease with time but we must recognize that new features are constantly being added to the program so that the program is not necessarily monotonically approaching the perfectly debugged stage.

APPENDIX 1

Participants in NATO Conference
on Techniques in Software Engineering,
Rome, 27th to 31st October 1969

Chairman:
Professor P. ERCOLI,
Facolta di ingegneria,
Via Eudossiana 18,
I-OO184 Rome, Italy.

Co-Chairman:
Prof. Dr. F. L. BAUER,
Mathematisches Institut der
Technischen Hochschule,
D-8 München 2,
Arcisstrasse 21, Germany.

Mr. J. D. ARON,
IBM Corporation,
18100 Frederick Pike,
Gaithersburg, Maryland 20760,
USA.

Prof. R. S. BARTON,
Computer Science,
Merrill Engineering Building,
University of Utah,
Salt Lake City,
Utah, USA.

Dr. R. BAYER,
Boeing Scientific Research Laboratories,
P.O. Box 3981,
Seattle,
Washington 98124, USA.

Mr. R. W. BEMER,
General Electric Company,
Information Systems Group,
13430 Black Canyon Highway,
M-2, Phoenix,
Arizona 85029, USA.

Prof. L. BOLLIET,
IMAG,
CEDEX 53,
F-38 Grenoble, Gare, France.

Mr. P. BRINCH HANSEN,
A/S Regnecentralen,
Falkoneralle 1,
DK-2000 Copenhagen F,
Denmark.

Mr. H. M. BROWN,
IBM UK Laboratories,
Hursley,
Winchester, England.

Dr. W. S. BROWN,
Bell Telephone Laboratories, Inc.,
Murray Hill,
New Jersey 07974, USA.

Mr. P. BURKINSHAW,
ICL,
Brandon House,
Broadway,
Bracknell, Berks., England.

Prof. J. N. BUXTON,
School of Computer Science,
University of Warwick,
Coventry,
CV4 7AL, England.

Mr. A. CARACCIOLO DI FORINO,
IEI-CNR,
Via S. Maria 46,
I-56100 Pisa, Italy.

Mr. C. T. CLINGEN,
General Electric Company,
Cambridge Information Systems
Laboratory,
575 Technology Square,
Cambridge, Massachusetts 02139, USA.

Dr. E. E. DAVID, Jr.,
Bell Telephone Laboratories, Inc.,
Murray Hill,
New Jersey 07974, USA.

Prof. Dr. E. W. DIJKSTRA,
Department of Mathematics,
Technological University,
Postbox 513,
Eindhoven, The Netherlands.

Dr. H. DONNER,
Siemens AG, Dv T SP
D-8000 München 25,
Hofmannstrasse 51,
Germany.

Mr. JEAN-JACQUES DUBY,
Centre Scientifique,
IBM France,
47 rue de Villiers,
F-92 Neuilly, France.

Dr. K. EBBINGHAUS,
IBM Laboratories, Dept. 767,
D-703 Böblingen,
Schönaicher First 10,
Germany.

Dr. M. ENGELI,
FIDES Treuhand-Vereinigung,
Bleicherweg 33,
CH-8002 Zurich,
Switzerland.

Mr. A. D. FALKOFF,
IBM Scientific Center,
T. J. Watson Research Center,
P.O. Box 218,
Yorktown Heights,
New York 10598, USA.

Prof. J. A. FELDMAN,
Computer Science Department,
Stanford University,
Stanford,
California 94305, USA.

Prof. R. W. FLOYD,
Computer Science Department,
Stanford University,
Stanford,
California 94305, USA.

Prof. B. A. GALLER,
Computing Center,
1000 North University Building,
University of Michigan,
Ann Arbor,
Michigan 48104, USA.

Dr. G. GOOS,
Rechenzentrum,
Technische Hochschule,
D-8 München 2,
Arcisstrasse 21, Germany.

Prof. C. C. GOTLIEB,
Institute of Computer Science,
Sandford Fleming Building,
University of Toronto,
Toronto, Ontario, Canada.

Prof. J. W. GRAHAM,
University of Waterloo,
Department of Computer Science,
Waterloo, Ontario, Canada.

Dr. H. J. HELMS,
Northern Europe University
Computing Center,
Technical University of Denmark,
DK-2800 Lyngby, Denmark.

Prof. C. A. R. HOARE,
Department of Computer Science,
Queens University,
Belfast,
BT7 1NN, Northern Ireland.

Dr. F. HOFMANN,
Siemens AG, E54,
D-852 Erlangen,
Günther-Scharowsky-Strasse, Germany.

Mr. M. E. HOPKINS,
IBM Corporation,
T. J. Watson Research Center,
P.O. Box 218,
Yorktown Heights,
New York 10598, USA.

Mr. M. ITALIANI,
Syntax,
Via Camperio 3,
Milan, Italy.

Dr. H. KANNER,
Technology Development Department,
Control Data Corporation,
3145 Porter Drive,
Palo Alto, California 94304, USA.

Mr. P. M. KJELDAAS,
Kjeller Computer Installation,
P.O. Box 70,
N-2007 Kjeller, Norway.

Dr. K. LAGALLY,
Rechenzentrum,
Technische Hochschule,
D-8 München 2,
Arcisstrasse 21, Germany.

Dr. B. W. LAMPSON,
Department of Computer Science,
University of California,
Berkeley, California 94720, USA.

Mr. C. A. LANG,
University Mathematical Laboratory,
Corn Exchange Street,
Cambridge, England.

Dr. A. LEMMA,
Selenia s.p.a.,
Via Tiburtina Km. 12,400,
Rome, Italy.

Mr. A. I. LLEWELYN,
Director, Computer Aided Design
Centre Cambridge,
Ministry of Technology,
Dean Bradley House,
Horseferry Road,
London, S.W.1, England.

Mr. E. S. LOWRY,
IBM Corporation,
Systems Development Division,
Building 706, Department D76,
Poughkeepsie,
New York 12602, USA.

Dipl.ing. P. LUCAS,
IBM Laboratory,
Parkring 10,
Vienna 4, Austria.

Dr. R. M. McCLURE,
3741 Alta Vista Lane,
Dallas,
Texas 75229, USA.

Mr. J. M. MacGOWAN, Jr.,
UNIVAC Data Processing Division,
2276 Highcrest Drive,
Roseville, Minnesota 55113, USA.

Dr. R. M. NEEDHAM,
University Mathematical Laboratory,
Corn Exchange Street,
Cambridge, CB3 2SG,
England.

Mr. M. D. OESTREICHER,
Computer Analysts and
Programmers Ltd.,
CAP House,
14/15 Great James Street,
London, W.C.1, England.

Prof. A. J. PERLIS,
Department of Computer Science,
Carnegie Mellon University,
Pittsburgh, Pennsylvania 15217, USA.

Prof. B. RANDELL,
The Computing Laboratory,
University of Newcastle upon Tyne,
Claremont Tower,
Claremont Road,
Newcastle upon Tyne,
NE1 7RU, England.

Dr. J. C. REYNOLDS,
Applied Mathematics Division,
Argonne National Laboratory,
Argonne,
Illinois 60439, USA.

Mr. D. T. ROSS,
SofTech, Inc.,
391 Totten Pond Road,
Waltham,
Massuchusetts 02154, USA.

Mr. J. P. ROSSIENSKY,
Compagnie Internationale pour
l'Informatique,
Les Clayes/Bois 78,
France.

Mr. C. A. SCALZI,
IBM Corporation,
Building 705,
Poughkeepsie, New York, 12602, USA.

Dr. H. SCHORR,
IBM Corporation,
T. J. Watson Research Center,
P.O. Box 218,
Yorktown Heights,
New York 10598, USA.

Mr. J. I. SCHWARTZ,
c/o King Resources,
12011 San Vicente Blvd.,
Los Angeles,
California 90049, USA.

Dr. G. SEEGMÜLLER,
IBM Laboratories, Dept. 770,
D-703 Böblingen,
Schönaicher First 10,
Germany.

Mr. I. P. SHARP,
P.O. Box 71,
Toronto-Dominion Centre,
Toronto 111, Canada.

Mr. T. H. SIMPSON,
IBM Corporation,
11141 Georgia Avenue,
Wheaton, Maryland 20902, USA.

Mr. C. STRACHEY,
Oxford University Computing
Laboratory,
45 Banbury Road,
Oxford, England.

Dr. W. TEITELMAN,
Bolt, Beranek and Newman, Inc.,
50 Moulton Street,
Cambridge, Massachusetts,
USA.

Mr. K. L. THOMPSON,
Computer Laboratory,
Computer Center,
Michigan State University,
East Lansing,
Michigan 48823, USA.

Dr. W. ULRICH,
Bell Telephone Laboratories Inc.,
Room 2C-235,
Naperville,
Illinois 60540, USA.

Prof. dr. ir. W. L. VAN DER POEL,
Delft University of Technology,
Department of Mathematics,
132 Julianalaan,
Delft, The Netherlands.

Mr. S. WARSHALL,
Applied Data Research,
450 Seventh Avenue,
New York City,
New York 10001, USA.

Dr. H. R. WIEHLE,
c/o AEG/Telefunken,
D-775 Konstanz,
Postfach 154, Germany.

Dr. HANS-W. WIPPERMANN,
D-7500 Karlsruhe,
Rechenzentrum der Universität,
Englerstr. 2, Germany.

Prof. N. WIRTH,
Eidg. Technische Hochschule,
Fachgruppe Computer-Wissenschaften,
Leonhardstr. 33,
CH-8006 Zurich, Switzerland.

Mr. M. WOODGER,
Ministry of Technology,
National Physical Laboratory,
Division of Computer Science,
Teddington, Middlesex, England.

Scientific Secretaries:
Mr. R. ELLIS,
ICL,
30-31 Friar Street,
Reading,
RG1 1DX, England.

Mr. I. HUGO,
Infotech Ltd.,
Nicholson House,
High Street, Maidenhead,
Berkshire, England.

Observers:
Mr. P. H. KENNEY,
DACOS,
ADP Division,
SHAPE,
B-7010, Belgium.

Mr. L. CARIOU,
Chef du Service Etudes Informatiques,
Compagnie d'Etudes et de Realisations
de Cybernetique Industrielle,
22 rue de Charonne,
Paris 11e., France.

Dr. H. HALLER,
Deutsche Forschungsgemeinschaft,
D-53 Bonn-Bad Godesberg,
Kennedy-Allee 40, Germany.

Dr. H. VON ISSENDORFF,
Forschungsinst. f. Funk u. Mathematik,
Werthoven,
Königstrasse 2, Germany.

Dr. J. KONTOS,
Electronic Computers Division,
Greek Atomic Energy Commission,
NRC "Democritus",
Athens, Greece.

Col. A. MPATIS,
Operational Research Division,
Hellenic Armed Forces Command,
Athens, Greece.

Ten.Col. M. CARLA,
Istituto Geografico Militar Italiano,
Via Cesare Battisti 8,
Firenze, Italy.

Lt.Cdr. G. FALCIAI,
Maricensadoc Maristat,
Rome, Italy.

Dr. M. M. PACELLI,
Italsiel,
Via Abruzzi 3,
Rome, Italy.

Mr. G. M. PALERMO,
Italsiel,
Via Abruzzi 3,
Rome, Italy.

Dr. E. ROSSI,
Selemia,
Via Tiburtina Km. 12,4,
Rome, Italy.

Mr. T. DE HEER,
c/o Bewerking Waarnemings-
uitkomsten TNO,
Moningin Marialaan 21,
The Hague, The Netherlands.

Mr. W. LIMBURG,
Laboratory for Electronic
Development of the Armed Forces,
Haarlemmerstraatweg 7,
Oegstgeest, The Netherlands.

Dr. P. C. POOLE,
UKAEA Establishment,
Culham Laboratory,
Abingdon, Berks.,
England.

Secretaries:
Miss E. I. AUSTIN,
Scientific Affairs Division,
NATO,
Brussels 39, Belgium.

Miss M. CHAMBERLIN,
Room S 106,
St. Clements Building,
London School of Economics,
Houghton Street,
Aldwych, London, W.C.2, England.

Miss A. LAYBOURN,
The Computing Laboratory,
University of Newcastle upon Tyne,
Claremont Tower,
Claremont Road,
Newcastle upon Tyne,
NE1 7RU, England.

Scientific Affairs Division:
Prof. G. RANDERS,
Assistant Secretary General
for Scientific Affairs.

Dr. H. ARNTH-JENSEN,
Head of Operations.

Mr. F. M. BLAKE,
Consultant on Computer Science.

APPENDIX 2

Addresses of Welcome

Translation of the telegram from Senator G. Bo, Italian Minister for Coordination of Scientific and Technological Research.

To Prof. P. Ercoli, Chairman of Nato Conference on Techniques in Software Engineering.

Thank you for your kind invitation to the Conference on Techniques on Software Engineering to be held in Rome from 27 to 31 October. Please convey to the participants my most cordial welcome and good wishes. I am sure that the work of such outstanding personalities of the scientific world gathered together in Rome will lead to valuable results in this field which is of the greatest importance for scientific research and technological progress.

Bo, Minister of Scientific Research.

Translation of the telegram from Prof. L. Dadda, President of the Italian Computer Society (AICA).

To Prof. Ercoli, Chairman of Nato Conference on Techniques in Software Engineering.

On the occasion of the opening of the Conference on Techniques in Software Engineering may I ask you to extend a hearty welcome to all participants and wish them a pleasant stay and a stimulating exchange of ideas in this most important field of engineering.

Dadda, President of the Italian
Computer Society.

CONTRIBUTOR INDEX

SUBJECT INDEX